Survey of Personal Insurance and Financial Planning

Survey of Personal Insurance and Financial Planning

Edited by

Ann E. Myhr, CPCU, ARM, AU, AIM, ASLI

2nd Edition • 2nd Printing

The Institutes
720 Providence Road, Suite 100
Malvern, Pennsylvania 19355-3433

© 2017
American Institute For Chartered Property Casualty Underwriters

All rights reserved. This book or any part thereof may not be reproduced without the written permission of the copyright holder.

Unless otherwise apparent, examples used in The Institutes materials related to this course are based on hypothetical situations and are for educational purposes only. The characters, persons, products, services, and organizations described in these examples are fictional. Any similarity or resemblance to any other character, person, product, services, or organization is merely coincidental. The Institutes are not responsible for such coincidental or accidental resemblances.

This material may contain internet website links external to The Institutes. The Institutes neither approve nor endorse any information, products, or services to which any external websites refer. Nor do The Institutes control these websites' content or the procedures for website content development.

The Institutes specifically disclaim any implied warranties of merchantability or fitness for a particular purpose. No warranty may be created or extended by sales representatives or written sales materials.

The Institutes materials related to this course are provided with the understanding that The Institutes are not engaged in rendering legal, accounting, or other professional service. Nor are The Institutes explicitly or implicitly stating that any of the processes, procedures, or policies described in the materials are the only appropriate ones to use. The advice and strategies contained herein may not be suitable for every situation.

Information which is copyrighted by and proprietary to Insurance Services Office, Inc. ("ISO Material") is included in this publication. Use of the ISO Material is limited to ISO Participating Insurers and their Authorized Representatives. Use by ISO Participating Insurers is limited to use in those jurisdictions for which the insurer has an appropriate participation with ISO. Use of the ISO Material by Authorized Representatives is limited to use solely on behalf of one or more ISO Participating Insurers.

This publication includes forms which are provided for review purposes only. These forms may not be used, in whole or in part, by any company or individuals not licensed by Insurance Services Office, Inc. (ISO) for the applicable line of insurance and jurisdiction to which this form applies. It is a copyright infringement to include any part(s) of this form within independent company programs without the written permission of ISO.

2nd Edition • 2nd Printing • May 2018
ISBN 978-0-89463-981-4

Foreword

The Institutes are the trusted leader in delivering proven knowledge solutions that drive powerful business results for the risk management and property-casualty insurance industry. For more than 100 years, The Institutes have been meeting the industry's changing professional development needs with customer-driven products and services.

In conjunction with industry experts and members of the academic community, our Knowledge Resources Department develops our course and program content, including Institutes study materials. Practical and technical knowledge gained from Institutes courses enhances qualifications, improves performance, and contributes to professional growth—all of which drive results.

The Institutes' proven knowledge helps individuals and organizations achieve powerful results with a variety of flexible, customer-focused options:

Recognized Credentials—The Institutes offer an unmatched range of widely recognized and industry-respected specialty credentials. The Institutes' Chartered Property Casualty Underwriter (CPCU®) professional designation is designed to provide a broad understanding of the property-casualty insurance industry. Depending on professional needs, CPCU students may select either a commercial insurance focus or a personal risk management and insurance focus and may choose from a variety of electives.

In addition, The Institutes offer certificate or designation programs in a variety of disciplines, including these:

- Claims
- Commercial underwriting
- Fidelity and surety bonding
- General insurance
- Insurance accounting and finance
- Insurance information technology
- Insurance production and agency management
- Insurance regulation and compliance
- Management
- Marine insurance
- Personal insurance
- Premium auditing
- Quality insurance services
- Reinsurance
- Risk management
- Surplus lines

Ethics—Ethical behavior is crucial to preserving not only the trust on which insurance transactions are based, but also the public's trust in our industry as a whole. All Institutes designations now have an ethics requirement, which is delivered online and free of charge. The ethics requirement content is designed specifically for insurance practitioners and uses insurance-based case studies to outline an ethical framework. More information is available in the Programs section of our website, TheInstitutes.org.

Flexible Online Learning—The Institutes have an unmatched variety of technical insurance content covering topics from accounting to underwriting, which we now deliver through hundreds of online courses. These cost-effective self-study courses are a convenient way to fill gaps in technical knowledge in a matter of hours without ever leaving the office.

Continuing Education—A majority of The Institutes' courses are filed for CE credit in most states. We also deliver quality, affordable, online CE courses quickly and conveniently through CEU. Visit CEU.com to learn more. CEU is powered by The Institutes.

College Credits—Most Institutes courses carry college credit recommendations from the American Council on Education. A variety of courses also qualify for credits toward certain associate, bachelor's, and master's degrees at several prestigious colleges and universities. More information is available in the Student Services section of our website, TheInstitutes.org.

Custom Applications—The Institutes collaborate with corporate customers to use our trusted course content and flexible delivery options in developing customized solutions that help them achieve their unique organizational goals.

Insightful Analysis—Our Insurance Research Council (IRC) division conducts public policy research on important contemporary issues in property-casualty insurance and risk management. Visit www.Insurance-Research.org to learn more or purchase its most recent studies.

The Institutes look forward to serving the risk management and property-casualty insurance industry for another 100 years. We welcome comments from our students and course leaders; your feedback helps us continue to improve the quality of our study materials.

Peter L. Miller, CPCU
President and CEO
The Institutes

Preface

Survey of Personal Insurance and Financial Planning is the textbook for CPCU 553, part of The Institutes' Chartered Property-Casualty Underwriter (CPCU) designation program.

Survey of Personal Insurance and Financial Planning provides the learner with an understanding of the property and liability loss exposures faced by most individuals and families, as well as the types of insurance coverages that can be used to treat those exposures. Personal insurance professionals may be called upon to assist their clients in life insurance planning, retirement planning, and health and disability insurance planning. Therefore, *Survey of Personal Insurance and Financial Planning* includes a discussion of the public and private life and health insurance marketplaces and the product options available for individuals and families.

The Institutes are thankful to the individuals who contributed to the development of previous forms of the content, including manuscript reviewers and various advisory committee members. In particular, The Institutes would like to thank George E. Rejda, PhD, CLU, for his valuable insight. For this edition of Survey of Personal Insurance and Financial Planning, The Institutes would also like to thank Burton T. Beam Jr., CLU, ChFC, CPCU, CASL, for his assistance.

For more information about The Institutes' programs, please call our Customer Success Department at (800) 644-2101, email us at CustomerSuccess@TheInstitutes.org, or visit our website at TheInstitutes.org.

Ann Myhr

Contributors

The Institutes acknowledge with deep appreciation the contributions made to the content of this text by the following persons:

Pamela J. Brooks, MBA, CPCU, AAM, AIM, AIS

Mary Ann Cook, CPCU, MBA, AU, AAI

Susan Crowe, CPCU, MBA, AIC, ARe, ARM, API

Doug Froggatt, CPCU, AINS

Beth Illian, CPCU, AINS, AIS

Contents

Assignment 1
Personal Insurance Overview	1.1
Elements of Loss Exposures	1.3
Property Loss Exposures	1.5
Liability Loss Exposures	1.8
Personal Financial Planning Loss Exposures	1.12
Risk Management Process	1.17
Risk Management Techniques	1.21
Insurance as a Risk Financing Technique	1.27
Common Policy Provisions	1.32
Policy Analysis	1.38
Summary	1.42

Assignment 2
Automobile Insurance and Society	2.1
Compensation of Auto Accident Victims	2.3
No-Fault Automobile Laws	2.9
Automobile Insurance for High-Risk Drivers	2.13
Automobile Insurance Rate Regulation	2.15
Summary	2.21

Assignment 3
Personal Auto Policy: Liability, Med Pay, and UM Coverage	3.1
Overview of the Personal Auto Policy	3.3
Declarations	3.7
Definitions	3.10
Part A—Liability Coverage	3.14
Part A—Liability Coverage Case Study	3.23
Part B—Medical Payments Coverage	3.30
Part B—Medical Payments Coverage Case Study	3.34
Part C—Uninsured Motorists Coverage	3.42
UM/UIM Endorsements and State Variations	3.48
Part C—Uninsured Motorists Coverage Case Study	3.51
Summary	3.57

Assignment 4
PAP: Physical Damage, Duties After an Accident, Endorsements	4.1
Part D—Coverage for Damage to Your Auto	4.3
Part D—Coverage for Damage to Your Auto Case Study	4.11
Part E—Duties After an Accident or Loss	4.18
Part F—General Provisions	4.21
Common Endorsements to the Personal Auto Policy	4.26
Personal Auto Endorsements for Transportation Network Exposures	4.33
Personal Auto Coverage Case Study	4.36
Summary	4.45

Assignment 5
Homeowners Property Coverage	5.1
ISO Homeowners Coverage	5.3
Overview of Homeowners Form HO-3	5.6
HO-3 Section I—Property Coverages	5.10
HO-3 Section I—Perils Insured Against and Exclusions	5.17
HO-3 Section I—Conditions	5.22
2011 HO-3 Section I—Property Coverage Case Study	5.29
Summary	5.35

Assignment 6
Homeowners Liability, Conditions, Coverage Forms, and Endorsements	6.1
HO-3 Section II—Liability Coverages	6.3
HO-3 Section II—Exclusions	6.10
HO-3 Section II—Conditions	6.16
Determining Whether Homeowners Section II—Liability Coverages Covers a Claim	6.23
Coverage Variations in ISO Homeowners Forms	6.29
Commonly Used Endorsements that Modify the 2011 ISO Homeowners Policies	6.34
HO-3 Coverage Case	6.43
Summary	6.49

Assignment 7
Other Residential Insurance	7.1
Dwelling Policies	7.3
Dwelling Coverage Case Study	7.13
Mobilehome Coverage	7.19
The National Flood Insurance Program	7.24
FAIR and Beachfront and Windstorm Plans	7.32
Summary	7.36

Assignment 8
Other Personal Property and Liability Insurance	8.1
Inland Marine Floaters	8.3
Personal Watercraft Insurance	8.7
Personal Umbrella Liability Insurance	8.15
Umbrella Coverage Case Study	8.20
Summary	8.29

Assignment 9
Life Insurance Planning	9.1
Premature Death Loss Exposures	9.3
Determining the Amount of Life Insurance to Own	9.7
Types of Life Insurance	9.12
Sources of Life Insurance	9.18
Common Life Insurance Contractual Provisions and Riders	9.21
Life Insurance Case Study	9.27
Summary	9.33

Assignment 10
Retirement Planning	10.1
The Retirement Loss Exposure and Achieving Financial Goals	10.3
Individual Retirement Accounts	10.9
Types of Tax-Deferred Retirement Plans	10.12
Employer-Sponsored Retirement Plans	10.16
Individual Annuities	10.18
Social Security Program (OASDHI)	10.21
Summary	10.27

Assignment 11
Disability and Health Insurance
Planning   11.1

Disability and Health-Related
Personal Loss Exposures   11.3

Disability Income Insurance   11.6

Health Insurance Plans   11.15

Government-Provided Health
Insurance Plans   11.21

Long-Term Care Insurance   11.27

Summary   11.34

Index   1

Direct Your Learning

Personal Insurance Overview

Educational Objectives

After learning the content of this assignment, you should be able to:

▶ Summarize the three elements of loss exposures.

▶ Describe the property loss exposures that individuals and families might face in terms of each of the following:
- The assets exposed to loss
- The causes of loss
- The financial consequences of loss

▶ Describe the liability loss exposures that individuals and families might face in terms of each of the following:
- The assets exposed to loss
- The causes of loss
- The financial consequences of loss

▶ Describe the personal financial planning loss exposures that individuals and families might face in terms of each of the following:
- The assets exposed to loss
- The causes of loss
- The financial consequences of loss

▶ Demonstrate how the six steps of the risk management process can guide individuals and families in their risk management decisions.

▶ Describe how risk control and risk financing techniques are used by individuals and families.

▶ Explain how personal insurance is used as a risk management technique.

▶ Summarize the contents of the six common categories of policy provisions of a property-casualty insurance policy.

▶ Describe the primary methods of insurance policy analysis.

Outline

Elements of Loss Exposures

Property Loss Exposures

Liability Loss Exposures

Personal Financial Planning Loss Exposures

Risk Management Process

Risk Management Techniques

Insurance as a Risk Financing Technique

Common Policy Provisions

Policy Analysis

Summary

Personal Insurance Overview

ELEMENTS OF LOSS EXPOSURES

Individuals and families sustain significant property and liability losses each year, as well as losses that affect their personal financial planning. Homes accidentally catch fire and are destroyed, individuals involved in automobile accidents are sued, and wage earners are disabled and lose income. All of these events have financial consequences for individuals and families. To what extent could they have identified the presence of risk in their lives and better managed those exposures?

Individuals and families incur losses when assets they own, such as a home or an auto, or assets they generate, such as earning power, experience a reduction in value. Additionally, they could expose their assets to loss through their activities if they cause another person to suffer injury or loss. The chance that a tree will fall on a home and damage the roof is an example of a **loss exposure**. An actual loss need not occur for a loss exposure to be present; rather, simply the possibility of loss must exist. Every loss exposure has three elements:

- Asset exposed to loss
- Cause of loss
- Financial consequence of loss

To the extent that individuals and families understand the conditions or situations that present the possibility of loss to their assets, the causes of loss, and the financial consequences of loss, the better they can manage their own personal loss exposures. See the exhibit "The Loss Exposure 'Equation'."

> ### The Loss Exposure 'Equation'
> The "product" of the elements "equals" a loss exposure. Remove any one of the three elements, and a loss exposure is no longer present.
>
> Loss exposure = Asset exposed to loss × Cause of loss × Financial consequence of loss

[DA00076]

Loss exposure
Any condition or situation that presents a possibility of loss, whether or not an actual loss occurs.

Asset Exposed to Loss

The first element of a loss exposure is an asset exposed to loss. Most individuals and families seek to achieve a standard of living that provides them with comfort and security. In the course of achieving this desired standard of living, people accumulate assets. However, asset accumulation can be jeopardized when assets are exposed to loss.

An asset exposed to loss can be any item with value that is exposed to a possible reduction in that value due to loss. For example, individuals and families own (or have furnished for their use) assets that can be exposed to loss, such as homes, personal property, and money; additionally, they may operate automobiles and watercraft. Other assets exposed to loss can include those that can generate, accrue, or sustain value, such as a worker's income, a couple's retirement investment portfolio, or a wage earner's good health.

Cause of Loss

Cause of loss (peril)
The actual means by which property is damaged or destroyed.

A cause of loss is another element of a loss exposure. A **cause of loss** (or peril) is the means by which an asset can be reduced in value. See the exhibit "Cause of Loss and Multiplier Effect."

> ### Cause of Loss and Multiplier Effect
> Sometimes one cause of loss can have a multiplier effect, demonstrating the unpredictable nature of causes of losses. For example, a fire burns down a three-unit rental dwelling owned by a retired couple. The couple suffers not only the loss of the dwelling but also the loss of rental income they rely on as their primary source of monthly income. Additionally, consider a homeowner whose vacation property is vandalized. Because a broken rear window in the house goes unnoticed for several days, a subsequent rainstorm causes extensive water damage to the owner's hardwood floor.

[DA00077]

Individuals and families should, to the extent possible, identify and guard against causes of loss that could present the possibility of damage to or a reduction in value of their assets. Fire, wind, hail, lightning, theft, vandalism, auto collision, loss of employment, and long-term illness are all examples of causes of loss that can occur to assets.

Financial Consequence of Loss

The third element of a loss exposure is the financial consequence of loss. An asset exposed to loss is affected by a cause of loss, generating a financial consequence.

The financial consequences of a loss depend on the type of asset exposed to loss, the cause of loss, and the severity of the loss. In the case of a primary wage earner who suffers a short-term illness and returns to work after a brief period of disability, the financial consequences, although they may be significant to the wage earner, are not severe. A primary wage earner who suffers a long-term illness and is unable to return to work for many months because of disability is likely to suffer a severe financial consequence as a result of the loss. Similarly, an individual whose auto sustains a dented bumper as the result of a collision suffers the minor financial consequence of having the bumper repaired. However, if that individual is sued by another motorist who claims that she was seriously injured in that same accident, the financial consequences of loss could be severe.

PROPERTY LOSS EXPOSURES

Virtually all individuals and families have property. Property used, stored, enjoyed, or displayed is property that may be exposed to loss. Such property may include a family's house, an individual's television, or a child's framed photograph. Losses to property can result in serious financial consequences to those who suffer the losses.

All property is subject to **property loss exposures**. Property may be destroyed, damaged, stolen, or lost, or may otherwise suffer a decrease in value because of a particular cause of loss (or peril).

Individuals and families face countless situations in their daily lives that present the possibility of a property loss that has financial consequences. For example, an individual's belongings could be destroyed by a flood, or a family's home and its contents could be destroyed by a tornado. These situations, and many more, are loss exposures that individuals and families might face.

Property loss exposures can be examined in terms of three loss exposure elements:

- Assets exposed to loss
- Causes of loss
- Financial consequences of loss

Property loss exposure
A condition that presents the possibility that a person or an organization will sustain a loss resulting from damage (including destruction, taking, or loss of use) to property in which that person or organization has a financial interest.

Assets Exposed to Loss

Assets exposed to loss are any items of property that have value. A common method of classifying property uses two broad categories— **real property** and **personal property**. Much like the term "real estate," real property includes land, buildings, attached structures, plants growing on the land, and anything embedded in the land, such as minerals. All other property, such as a bicycle or a sofa or a computer, is classified as personal property. Individuals and families can be faced with loss exposures by owning or having a legal interest in one or both of these types of property. See the exhibit "Examples of Assets (Property) Exposed to Loss."

Real property (realty)
Tangible property consisting of land, all structures permanently attached to the land, and whatever is growing on the land.

Personal property
All tangible or intangible property that is not real property.

Examples of Assets (Property) Exposed to Loss

Real Property	Land, buildings, other structures attached to the land (swimming pool, storage shed, flagpole), whatever is growing on the land (trees, crops), and anything embedded in the land (foundations, underground pipes)
Personal Property	Dwelling contents, high-value articles (jewelry, silverware), rare or unique property (antiques, art work), business personal property, motor vehicles, trailers, watercraft, and aircraft

[DA00140]

Real Property

Individuals and families face property loss exposures that can arise from several types of owned real property. All real property is tangible property having a physical form that can be seen or touched.

For example, a single-family home purchased by an individual could pose a significant real property loss exposure. The land also indicates an additional real property loss exposure, as may any foundations or underground pipes. Any sheds attached to the land, or anything growing on it, such as trees, also could present real property loss exposures.

Personal Property

Listing all the specific kinds of personal property that individuals and families can own that are exposed to loss would be virtually impossible, when one considers the scope of the personal property definition. A general sampling of some personal property loss exposures includes those experienced by homeowners, renters, or condominium owners, who likely own furniture, televisions, and other electronic entertainment equipment. Additional household personal property can include computers, appliances, dishes, carpets, sports equipment, clothing, tools, books, jewelry, cameras, and digital recording devices. A homeowner could park a car in the driveway (the car is personal property) or have a boat at a vacation home (the boat is personal property). Additionally, personal property can include intangible property such as patents or copyrights (which are also often referred to as intellectual property). See the exhibit "Insuring and Pricing Personal Property Loss Exposures—Personal Property Categories."

Personal Insurance Overview 1.7

Insuring and Pricing Personal Property Loss Exposures—Personal Property Categories

For the purpose of identifying, insuring, and pricing personal property loss exposures, personal property can be divided into these categories:

Dwelling contents—the broadest category of personal property. A dwelling's contents may include furniture, appliances, draperies, electronics, kitchenware, groceries, clothing, sports equipment, tools, toys, and many other items common to the use of a dwelling as a home. Such items are generally insured as a group rather than individually.

High-value personal property—items of personal property worth considerable sums of money. Examples include jewelry, silverware, furs, and firearms. These items may be partially covered under the category of dwelling contents. However, they usually require a more specific type of insurance, because many property insurance policies limit the maximum amount of coverage available under specific loss conditions (for example, jewelry coverage is more limited for a theft loss under a homeowners policy than for a fire loss), for this category of personal property.

Rare or unusual property—items whose value comes from their unique characteristics. These items may often be one of a kind or one of a very few in existence in terms of like kind and quality and are not easily replaced. Examples of this type of property are antiques, works of art, coin or stamp collections, and other collectibles. Such items should be specifically listed for insurance purposes because most insurance policies limit the amount that an insurer will pay for this type of personal property.

Business personal property—personal property, such as office furniture and computer equipment, used for business purposes. Because most personal insurance policies limit or exclude coverage for business personal property, additional insurance coverage may be necessary.

Motor vehicles, trailers, watercraft, and aircraft—mobile property typically excluded (or covered only up to a certain limit) in policies covering dwellings and their contents. Because these items present unique loss exposures, they should be separately insured using the appropriate coverage form.

To keep the cost of personal insurance reasonable, personal insurance policies are designed to cover the loss exposures faced by the average person or family. If personal policies included unlimited coverage for all types of personal property, premiums needed to provide such coverage would be higher than most people could afford or would be willing to pay. For example, the cost to insure individual, expensive jewelry items against theft is not automatically included in homeowners policy premiums. Insurance professionals can help individuals and families understand the relationship between cost and coverage by explaining that, in order to keep insurance premiums reasonable for the average consumer, it is fair for those persons who own valuable or unusual items to pay an additional premium to insure them.

[DA00139]

Causes of Loss

Many causes of loss (or perils) can damage or destroy both real and personal property. In terms of real property, causes of loss faced by individuals and families include fire damage to a dwelling or storage shed, lightning damage to a tree, earthquake damage to a swimming pool, and wind damage to roof shingles. Personal property causes of loss can include theft of a car or damage to a car in an accident, disappearance of luggage and its contents while the owner is on vacation, and loss of a diamond that falls from its setting in a ring. Even damage to a motorboat that collides with a dock is a personal property loss. Any loss that results from the countless possible causes of loss that can affect an individual's or a family's property has consequences in terms of asset value.

Financial Consequences of Loss

When property is damaged or destroyed, individuals and families sustain certain financial consequences. Financial consequences of loss can include one or more of these outcomes:

- Reduction in value of property—The difference between the value of the property before the loss (preloss value) and after the loss (post-loss value). For instance, if an individual severely damages the front bumper of an auto by colliding with a tree, the auto would be worth less after the accident than it was worth before the accident.
- Increased expenses—Expenses in addition to normal living expenses that are necessary because of the loss. For example, increased living expenses could include the expenses an individual incurs following a dwelling fire, such as the cost of renting a hotel room, while the dwelling is temporarily uninhabitable.
- Lost income—Loss of income that results if property is damaged. For example, if a hurricane damages a home rented to others, the owner might not be able to collect rent on the property until the house is repaired or replaced.

LIABILITY LOSS EXPOSURES

Individuals and families face a potential reduction in their assets from the possibility of being sued or being held responsible for someone else's injury.

Whether through owning property, driving a car, or entering into contracts with others, all individuals and families face personal **liability loss exposures**. Even if a liability claim is successfully defended, and therefore does not result in payment of **damages**, the party against whom the claim was made nonetheless incurs defense costs, other claim-related expenses, and potentially adverse publicity, all of which may produce a financial loss. The three elements of personal liability loss exposures are the assets exposed to loss, causes of loss, and financial consequences of loss.

Liability loss exposure
Any condition or situation that presents the possibility of a claim alleging legal responsibility of a person or business for injury or damage suffered by another party.

Damages
Money claimed by, or a monetary award to, a party who has suffered bodily injury or property damage for which another party is legally responsible.

Assets Exposed to Loss

The assets exposed to loss in a liability loss exposure are money or other financial assets. A liability loss can result from property ownership or from the actions of individuals or family members. For example, if an individual is at fault in an auto accident, he or she must pay damages for vehicle repairs or replacement, medical expenses, and other costs stemming from the accident. As another example, if a renter breaches a lease, the landlord can sue for lost rental income and the asset that is exposed to loss is the renter's money or financial assets. If a house guest trips and breaks her leg on an unsafe sidewalk, the homeowner may be required to pay damages for her resulting medical expenses and perhaps the wages she loses while she recuperates.

Damages awarded in a liability judgment can take the form of general, special, and punitive damages. **General damages** are monetary awards to compensate victims for losses, such as pain and suffering, that do not involve specific measurable expenses. **Special damages** are a form of compensatory damages that compensate for specific, identifiable expenses associated with the injured person's loss, such as medical expenses or lost wages. **Punitive, or exemplary, damages** are awarded by a court to punish a defendant for a reckless, malicious, or deceitful act or to deter similar conduct; they need not bear any relationship to a party's actual damages. Punitive damages are generally awarded against companies, although they may be used against individuals.

Causes of Loss

The cause of loss associated with a liability loss exposure is the claim of liability or the filing of a lawsuit. The settlement of disputes between individuals and the indemnification for wrongs committed against individuals are within the scope of **civil law**. By contrast, criminal law deals with conduct that endangers the public welfare, such as the crimes of murder, rape, and fraud. Because such criminal acts are generally not the subject of insurance, civil law provides the legal foundation of insurance. Several types of claims fall under civil law, but the most common personal liability claims involve **tort** liability, contractual liability, and statutory liability.

These are examples of circumstances in which liability may be claimed or a suit filed:

- Breach of a legal duty, if that breach causes harm to another, such as injuries caused by an auto accident
- Breach of contract, such as a failure to pay rent on an agreed date
- Failure to adhere to requirements set out in statutes, regulations, or local ordinances, such as failing to provide a safe sidewalk at a residence

---

General damages

A monetary award to compensate a victim for losses, such as pain and suffering, that does not involve specific, measurable expenses.

Special damages

A form of compensatory damages that awards a sum of money for specific, identifiable expenses associated with the injured person's loss, such as medical expenses or lost wages.

Punitive damages (exemplary damages)

A payment awarded by a court to punish a defendant for a reckless, malicious, or deceitful act to deter similar conduct; the award need not bear any relation to a party's actual damages.

Civil law

A classification of law that applies to legal matters not governed by criminal law and that protects rights and provides remedies for breaches of duties owed to others.

Tort

A wrongful act or an omission, other than a crime or a breach of contract, that invades a legally protected right.

Tort Liability

An individual may face a claim for tort damages on the basis of any act of negligence, intentional torts, or absolute liability. See the exhibit "Sources of Tort Liability."

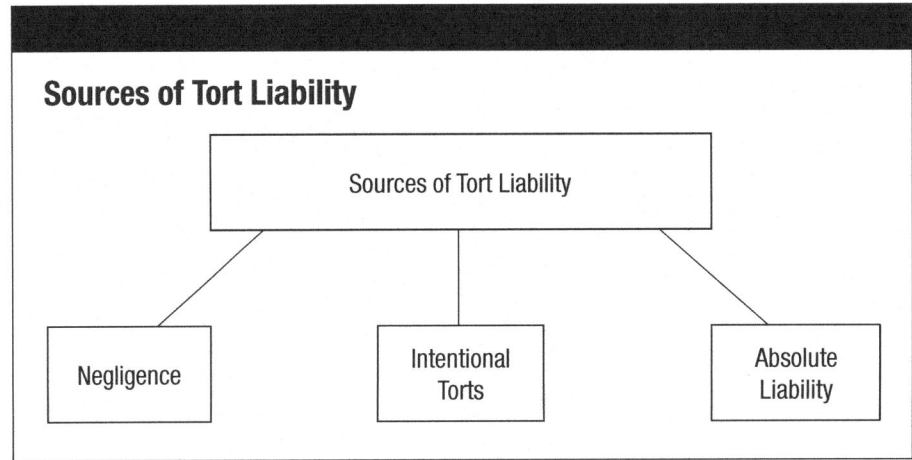

[DA00135]

Negligence
The failure to exercise the degree of care that a reasonable person in a similar situation would exercise to avoid harming others.

Negligence is the most common cause of liability losses. To prove that negligence has occurred, an injured party must prove that all four legal elements of negligence have occurred:

- A duty to act. (For example, a family has a duty to maintain its premises so as not to cause injury to a guest.)
- A breach of that duty. (For instance, if a family allows a child to leave a ball on the front entry steps of its home, it may have breached its duty to keep the premises safe.)
- An injury or damage occurs. (For example, a guest trips on the ball that was left on the steps and breaks his leg.)
- The breach of duty is the direct cause of the injury or damage in an unbroken chain of events. (In this example, the direct cause of the guest's broken leg is the ball that the child left on the steps.)

Regardless of whether the harm that results is intended, an intentional act can create liability. These are some examples of these acts, known as intentional torts:

- Libel is a written or printed untrue statement that damages a person's reputation. For example, if Ted prints an article in a local community newsletter falsely claiming that his neighbor, Paul, has been convicted of drunken driving, Ted may be guilty of libel.
- Slander is an oral untrue statement that damages a person's reputation. For instance, if, at a parent-teacher meeting, Susan publicly and falsely accuses a local pharmacist of selling illegal drugs to teenagers, she may be guilty of slander.

- Assault is the intentional and unlawful threat of bodily harm. For example, if Mary threatens to hit Betty, and Betty believes that Mary is ready and willing to carry out her threat, Mary has assaulted Betty.
- Battery is unlawful physical contact with another person. Continuing the previous example, if Mary hits Betty, she has committed battery. Betty may sue Mary for damages resulting from assault and battery.
- Trespass is the unauthorized possession or use of land. If Jacob parks his car in Chris's yard without Chris's permission, Jacob may be guilty of trespass.
- Nuisance is the violation of a person's right to enjoy use of property without disruption from outside sources. For instance, if a person persistently hosts noisy parties that last late into the night, the neighbors may seek an injunction against such activities under civil law.

Absolute liability is liability that does not involve proving negligence. For example, if a person keeps a pet alligator in a cage in his back yard and the alligator bites a neighbor, the owner of the alligator could be held liable regardless of whether negligence can be proved.

Contractual Liability

The possibility of contractual liability arises when an individual enters into a contract or an agreement. Leases for homes and apartments, as well as rental agreements for autos, power tools, and other equipment, typically contain provisions that transfer the financial consequences of liability losses from the owner of the property to the renter. For example, an apartment lease may require the tenant to assume liability for any injury or damage to others, even in instances in which the owner of the property is at fault.

Statutory Liability

Statutory liability exists because of the passage of a statute or law. Most important to individuals and families are the laws dealing with liability arising out of automobile accidents. These laws vary by state and change the legal basis of liability regarding negligence.

Financial Consequences of Loss

Because the asset exposed to loss in a liability loss exposure is money or other financial assets, the financial consequences of a liability loss can be serious. When a liability claim occurs, an individual or a family can suffer two major financial consequences:

- Costs of investigation and defense
- Money damages awarded if the defense is not successful or if the claim is settled out of court

Many liability claims are settled before they reach court. In such cases, parties to the claim negotiate the amount paid in damages, and the costs of investigation and defense generally are reduced. Because settling out of court usually is less expensive than a potentially long trial, insurance companies often try to reach out-of-court settlements. In theory, the financial consequences of a liability loss exposure are limitless. In practice, financial consequences are limited to the total wealth of the responsible party. Although some jurisdictions limit the amounts that can be taken in a claim, liability claims can result in the loss of most or all of a person's assets, as well as in a claim on future income.

PERSONAL FINANCIAL PLANNING LOSS EXPOSURES

Prudent personal financial planning is essential to the long-term security of individuals and families. One component of a personal financial plan entails accounting for circumstances that may unexpectedly affect spending or income.

Personal financial planning loss exposures
Life, health, and retirement related loss exposures.

Certain **personal financial planning loss exposures** can cause significant financial difficulty for individuals and families. The three elements of personal financial planning loss exposures are the assets exposed to loss, causes of loss, and financial consequences of loss. Primary examples of personal financial planning loss exposures include retirement loss exposures, premature death exposures, poor health and disability exposures, and unemployment exposures.

Retirement Loss Exposures

The assets exposed to loss when an individual retires are regular employment income and the related benefits, such as health insurance. The primary risk associated with retirement is that the accumulated assets a family or individual has allocated for retirement will insufficiently compensate for the loss of income and benefits. Therefore, although the immediate cause of loss related to retirement loss exposures usually is voluntary retirement, actual retirement-related loss stems from failure to maintain resources sufficient to sustain a desired lifestyle or from an underestimation of the length of the retirement period.

Historically, most workers retired voluntarily by age sixty-five. However, the age at which workers may collect full Social Security benefits is gradually increasing, from age sixty-five and two months in 2003 to age sixty-seven in 2027. This age increase has provided workers with additional incentive to remain in the workforce beyond age sixty-five. Additionally, an increasing percentage of the workforce is maintaining employment beyond full-retirement age, often in a part-time capacity, to help mitigate the financial risks associated with retirement.

If replacement income from Social Security benefits, private retirement plans, and personal savings is inadequate, the retired worker's standard of living may be reduced significantly. If the retired worker lives unusually long, incurs catastrophic medical expenses, or requires long-term care in a nursing facility, the financial consequences of retirement may result in insufficient income to sustain the worker and his or her family. See the exhibit "2007 Employment Status of the Civilian Noninstitutional Population (Total)."

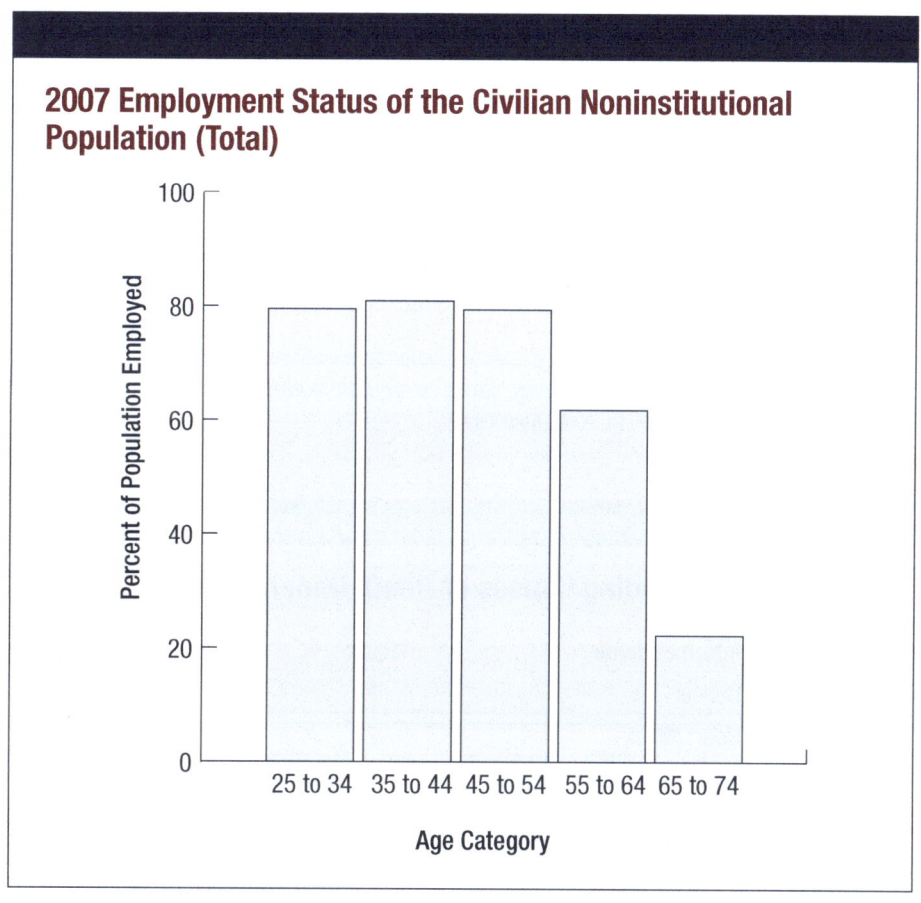

Source: www.bls.gov/cps/cpsaat3.pdf (accessed February 21, 2008) [DA00115]

Premature Death Loss Exposures

A death is considered premature if it occurs before an individual reaches his or her life expectancy. The assets exposed to loss as the result of an individual's premature death include the expected income on which his or her family or heirs rely. The causes of loss associated with premature death include accident, illness, or the intentional taking of life. If replacement income from life insurance, financial assets, or existing income from other sources does not meet the needs of the deceased individual's family, it is likely to experience considerable financial hardship. The financial consequences of premature death, particularly if the individual was the family's primary wage earner, can be catastrophic. See the exhibit "Number of Deaths and Death Rates, All Races, Both Sexes, 2005."

Number of Deaths and Death Rates, All Races, Both Sexes, 2005

Age Range	Death Rate (per 100,000)
15-24	81.35
25-34	104.45
35-44	191.50
45-54	436.95
55-64	935.75
65-74	2178.80
75-84	5433.45

Source: "Deaths: Final Data for 2005," Centers for Disease Control, January 2008, www.cdc.gov/nchs/data/nvsr/nvsr56/nvsr56_10.pdf (accessed February 21, 2008). [DA00082]

Deaths in 2004—Leading Causes of Death Under Age 65

Informal Name	Rank
Cancer	1
Heart Attack	2
Accidents	3
Stroke	4
Diabetes	5
Emphysema, etc.	6
Systemic Infection	7
Kidney Disease	8
Flu and Pneumonia	9
Alzheimer's	10

Source: National Center for Health Statistics, National Vital Statistics Reports, vol. 55, no. 19, August 21, 2007. [DA00083]

Health and Disability Loss Exposures

The assets exposed to loss as a result of an individual's poor health or disability include income if the person is unable to work, as well any individual or family savings and other financial assets, which may be depleted by health-related expenditures. The causes of loss associated with health and disability loss exposures are chronic illness or physical or mental disability. Loss exposures from disability and poor health may result from conditions present at birth, those that are hereditary, or those that are caused by accidents. There are four types of disability:

- **Temporary partial disability**—A broken finger may reduce a computer programmer's efficiency at the keyboard but does not prevent him or her from using the computer.
- **Temporary total disability**—Surgery may render an employee unable to work for a short period of time.
- **Permanent partial disability**—A worker who sustains a back injury lifting boxes in the organization's warehouse may still be able to perform clerical work even if he or she can no longer engage in strenuous physical labor.
- **Permanent total disability**—A disabled person may be completely unable to perform any productive work for the remainder of his or her life. In addition to severe injuries and illnesses, certain psychiatric conditions, such as schizophrenia, can result in permanent total disability.

The financial consequences of poor health and disability can vary substantially. For example, the ramifications of temporary partial disability are not as serious as those associated with permanent total disability. In many circumstances, an individual may incur catastrophic medical expenses as a result of poor health or disability. Lacking health insurance or savings to pay such expenses, a sick or injured person will be exposed to financial insecurity, which may be compounded by reduction or elimination of income if the person is unable to work. The inability to pay large medical bills is a prevalent cause of personal bankruptcy. See the exhibit "Percentage of Persons With Work Disability."

Temporary partial disability (TPD)

A disability caused by a work-related injury or disease that temporarily limits the extent to which a worker can perform job duties; the worker is eventually able to return to full duties and hours.

Temporary total disability (TTD)

A disability caused by a work-related injury or disease that temporarily renders an injured worker unable to perform any job duties for a period of time.

Permanent partial disability (PPD)

A disability caused by a work-related injury or disease that impairs the injured employee's earning capacity for life, but the employee is able to work at reduced efficiency.

Permanent total disability (PTD)

A disability caused by a work-related injury or disease that renders an injured employee unable to ever return to gainful employment.

Percentage of Persons With Work Disability

Age Range	Percentage of Population*
16 to 24 years old	4.7 %
25 to 34 years old	6.4 %
35 to 44 years old	8.7 %
45 to 54 years old	12.9 %
55 to 64 years old	21.4 %

* In March 2005, 19,656,000 persons were classified as having a work disability if they had a health problem or a disability that prevented them from working or that limited them from the kind or amount of work they could do.

Source: U.S. Census Bureau, unpublished data, http://www.census.gov/hhes/www/disability/disability.html [DA00084]

Data on Disabilities for the Civilian Noninstitutionalized Population 16-64 Years Old

Sex and Disability Status	Number	Percentage of Population
Both Sexes—Sensory, physical, or mental disability	22,361,913	13.0%
Men—Sensory, physical, or mental disability	10,884,719	12.9%
Women—Sensory, physical, or mental disability	11,477,194	13.1%

Source: U.S. Census Bureau, 2006 American Community Survey [DA00085]

Unemployment

The assets exposed to loss by unemployment include income and employer-provided benefits. The causes of loss in cases of unemployment may be voluntary (when the worker chooses to end his or her employment) or involuntary (when the employer chooses to terminate the employee). If unemployment is involuntary, it may be caused by circumstances beyond the control of the employer, such as structural or technological changes in the economy, or the employer may terminate an employee for performance-related or other organization-specific reasons.

The financial consequences of loss due to unemployment are loss of earnings and other employer-provided benefits, such as health insurance and monetary contributions toward retirement. Unless they have adequate replacement income or accumulated savings on which to draw, unemployed individuals and their families likely will experience a financial hardship during a period of unemployment.

In addition, if the unemployment was caused by adverse overall economic conditions, the only positions available to an unemployed individual may be those with reduced or limited work hours (a condition often referred to as underemployment). The resulting reduced income may be insufficient for maintaining the worker's previous standard of living. A long period of unemployment can substantially reduce or exhaust an unemployed worker's savings. Additionally, a recent study by the National Bureau of Economic Research (NBER) indicates that job layoffs may adversely affect the unemployed worker's long-term health.[1]

RISK MANAGEMENT PROCESS

Individuals and families should use the risk management process to determine the best techniques for managing their loss exposures.

Often, significant, life-altering events such as marriage, having children, starting a new job, or making a major purchase (a home or car, for example) require individuals and families to evaluate the risks they face and the best ways to manage them. They may accomplish this by using the **risk management process**. Although this process was developed for organizations, individuals and families also can follow its steps to guide their risk management decisions. See the exhibit "The Risk Management Process."

Risk management process
The method of making, implementing, and monitoring decisions that minimize the adverse effects of risk on an organization.

The Risk Management Process

- Step 1: Identifying loss exposures
- Step 2: Analyzing loss exposures
- Step 3: Examining feasibility of risk management techniques
- Step 4: Selecting the appropriate risk management techniques
- Step 5: Implementing selected risk management techniques
- Step 6: Monitoring results and revising the risk management program

[DA00095]

Step 1: Identifying Loss Exposures

Organizations use a wide variety of methods to identify their loss exposures. By contrast, individuals and families usually rely on friends, family members, and their insurance agent to help them identify their loss exposures. Friends and family members can help identify loss exposures by sharing their own loss histories and experience. The insurance agent may provide checklists that focus on common sources of loss exposures and use his or her own experience and training to help individuals and families determine areas that they may need to address with risk management techniques.

Two of the most common property and liability loss exposures that individuals and families must address are connected to home and automobile ownership. They are often also subject to a significant number of other liability loss exposures, such as an individual's liability stemming from a physical altercation at work.

Step 2: Analyzing Loss Exposures

Step two of the risk management process, analyzing loss exposures, entails estimating the likely significance of possible losses identified in step one. Together, these two steps constitute the process of assessing loss exposures, and they are therefore often considered the most important components of the risk management process.

When organizations analyze the loss exposures they have identified, they focus on four dimensions:

- Loss frequency—the number of losses (such as fires, auto accidents, or liability claims) within a specific time period
- Loss severity—the amount, in dollars, of a loss for a specific occurrence
- Total dollar losses—the total dollar amount of losses for all occurrences during a specific period
- Timing—when losses occur and when loss payments are made

Individuals and families may also use these components to guide their analysis. For example, a family could analyze its automobile loss exposures in this manner:

- Loss frequency—During the previous year, family members were responsible for two auto accidents and also filed a claim for a broken windshield.
- Loss severity—The loss severity for each of the auto claims was $11,500, $2,200, and $300, respectively.
- Total dollar losses—The total of the three losses for the policy year is $14,000.
- Timing—Generally, these kinds of property losses are settled in a matter of days or weeks. However, an automobile liability claim for hundreds of thousands of dollars filed by a person injured in one of the accidents may require years to resolve.

Only a properly assessed loss exposure can be appropriately managed. Once a loss exposure has been assessed, the best ways to manage it may become immediately apparent. The remaining steps of the risk management process flow from this assessment.

Step 3: Examining the Feasibility of Risk Management Techniques

Loss exposures can be addressed through **risk control** techniques and **risk financing** techniques. Risk control techniques minimize the frequency or severity of losses; for example, an individual can avoid automobile loss exposures by not purchasing or driving an auto. Risk financing techniques, such as insurance, generate funds to finance losses that risk control techniques cannot reduce or prevent. See the exhibit "Risk Management Techniques."

Risk control

A conscious act or decision not to act that reduces the frequency and/or severity of losses or makes losses more predictable.

Risk financing

A conscious act or decision not to act that generates the funds to pay for losses and risk control measures or to offset variability in cash flows.

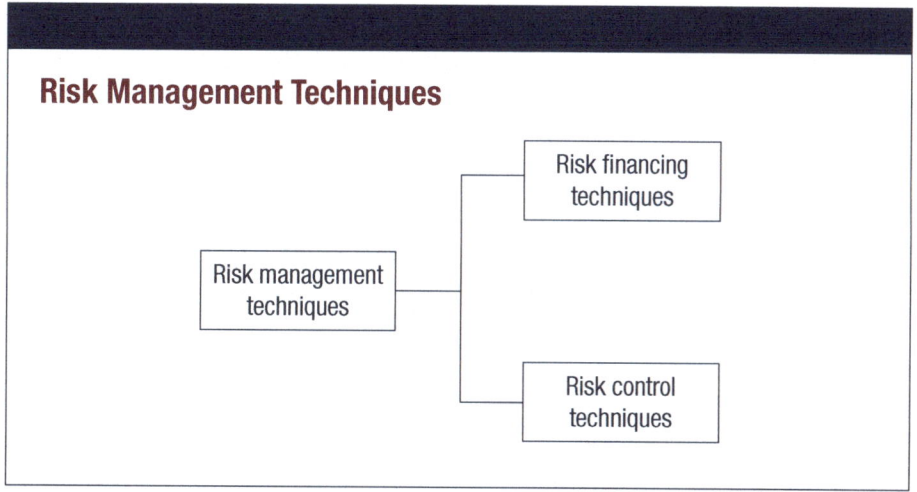

[DA00096]

Risk management techniques are not usually used in isolation. Unless entirely avoiding a loss exposure, individuals should typically apply at least one risk control technique and one risk financing technique to each of their significant loss exposures. The risk control technique alters the estimated frequency and severity of loss, and the financing technique pays for losses that occur despite the controls.

This step of the risk management process entails determining the feasibility of risk management techniques. Individuals and families should examine all available risk control and risk financing techniques and determine which are feasible for them. After making this determination, they use the next step in the process to determine which of the feasible techniques is the most appropriate for each loss exposure.

Unlike organizations, most individuals and families have access to a limited number of feasible risk control and risk financing techniques, the most prevalent of which is the purchase of insurance. For some loss exposures, such as a fire exposure to a home, this method is mandated by the mortgage lender. In this case, the individual or family has a choice of buying suitable homeowners insurance or not buying the home.

Step 4: Selecting the Appropriate Risk Management Techniques

Once loss exposures have been identified and analyzed and possible risk management techniques considered, individuals and families can select the techniques that best prevent or reduce losses and that will adequately finance losses that occur. Selecting the most appropriate combination of risk management techniques is usually based on quantitative financial considerations as well as qualitative, nonfinancial considerations.

Most households choose risk management techniques by using financial criteria. That is, they choose the most effective techniques that will have the greatest positive (or least negative) effect on their assets. Households must compare the potential costs of completely untreated loss exposures with the costs of possible risk management techniques when considering whether a technique is economical.

A household's nonfinancial goals can constrain its financial goals, leading to the selection of risk management techniques that, although best for that family, might be inconsistent with its value maximization goal. For example, a family may install a home alarm system. The cost of the system's initial installation and associated monthly monitoring fees may exceed the resulting insurance premium savings. However, the additional nonfinancial benefit of the peace of mind the family experiences from feeling safer may outweigh the measure's financial costs.

Step 5: Implementing the Selected Risk Management Techniques

Implementing risk management techniques may involve any of these measures:

- Purchasing loss reduction devices, such as smoke alarms or flame-retardant roofing
- Contracting for loss prevention services, such as burglar alarm services
- Funding retention programs, such as maintaining a savings account to fund the loss exposures of small-value items that could be retained in a household operating budget
- Implementing and continually reinforcing loss control programs, such as keeping flammable materials away from heat sources
- Selecting agents or brokers, insurers, and other insurance providers who can suggest ways to deal with specific loss exposures (particularly out-of-the-ordinary loss exposures, such as coin collections and home entertainment centers)

- Requesting insurance policies and paying premiums for loss exposures that an individual does not want to retain (or is required to have by statute or by a lender), such as homeowners, automobile, and liability loss exposures
- Creating and updating a list of possessions that may be subject to loss

Implementing risk management techniques does not necessarily end with the initial implementation of a selected technique. For example, if a family purchases or builds a vacation home, it almost certainly will also decide to purchase property insurance. However, additional details, such as the exact placement of fire extinguishers, the terms and cost of insurance and noninsurance contract revisions, selection of an insurer, the timing of insurance premium payments, and the actual deposit of funds in a savings account for a retention program or to cover deductibles, must be addressed as the program is implemented.

Step 6: Monitoring Results and Revising the Risk Management Program

Individuals and families must monitor and periodically review their risk management program to ensure that it is achieving expected results. They also should adjust it to accommodate changes in loss exposures and in the availability or cost-effectiveness of alternative risk management techniques.

A risk management program should be adjusted as life-changing events occur. For example, if a family member acquires a driver's license, the family's auto loss exposures should be re-evaluated. Similarly, new dependents added to the family, or children leaving the home to attend college, can significantly alter a family's financial situation. Additionally, if individuals engage in new hobbies with significant loss exposures (such as coin collecting or the acquisition of expensive art), they should adopt additional risk management techniques to deal with these exposures. These techniques could include the use of safety deposit boxes or the purchase of insurance to safeguard these assets.

RISK MANAGEMENT TECHNIQUES

Individuals and families can manage the risks they face by using risk management techniques.

All risk management techniques fall into one of two categories: risk control or risk financing. Individuals and families may use both kinds of techniques to manage risks and ensure their well-being, financial stability, and security. See the exhibit "Risk Management Techniques."

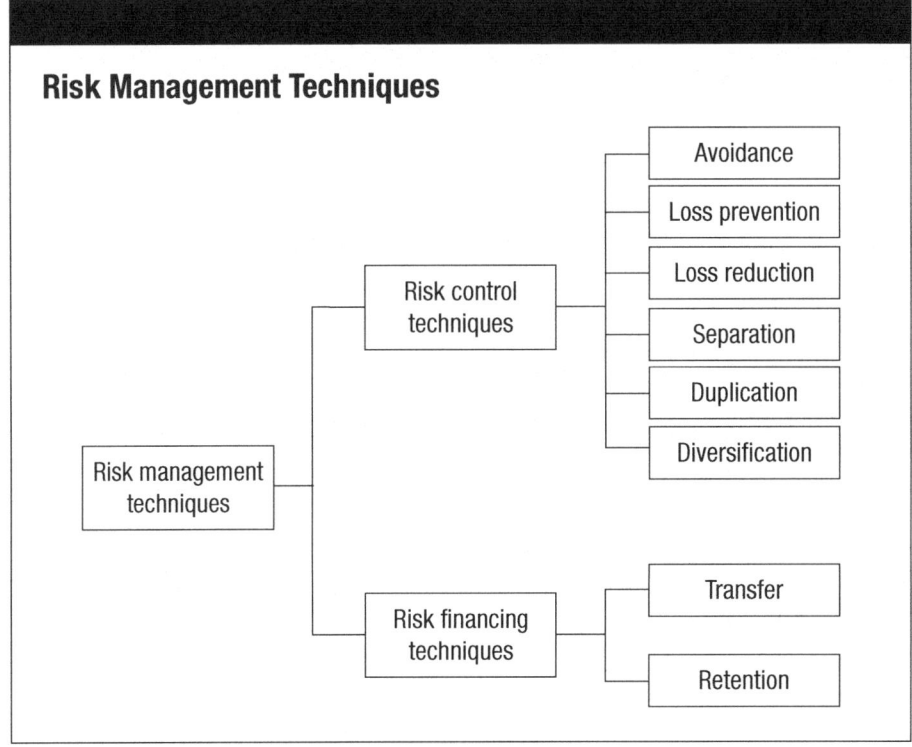

[DA00137]

Risk Control Techniques

Risk control techniques fall into one of six broad categories:

- Avoidance
- Loss prevention
- Loss reduction
- Separation
- Duplication
- Diversification

Each of these techniques aims to reduce either loss frequency or loss severity, or to make losses more predictable. Although some of these techniques, such as separation and duplication, are more appropriate for organizations, individuals and families can consider one or more of them as they review their specific loss exposures.

Avoidance

The goal of **avoidance** is not simply to reduce loss frequency, but to eliminate any possibility of loss. For example, an individual living in a city may decide not to purchase a car in order to avoid automobile loss exposures. Additionally, if an individual is concerned about dying in an airplane crash, he or she can choose not to travel by air. However, by avoiding air travel, the

Avoidance

A risk control technique that involves ceasing or never undertaking an activity so that the possibility of a future loss occurring from that activity is eliminated.

individual increases the loss exposure to injury or death from the other means of transport chosen in its place. In some cases, avoidance is at least impractical, if not impossible. For instance, while automobile loss exposures may be avoided by not driving a car, most individuals and families require a car for daily activities.

Loss Prevention

Generally, a **loss prevention** measure is implemented to break the sequence of events that leads to the loss. Determining effective loss prevention measures usually requires carefully studying how particular losses are caused.

As is the case with avoidance, a loss prevention measure may reduce the frequency of losses from one loss exposure but increase the frequency or severity of losses from other loss exposures. For example, a family living in a high-crime area may reduce the probability of theft by installing security devices in its home. Those security devices, however, might make it impossible for firefighters to enter the home or could trap a family member inside the home if a fire occurred.

> **Loss prevention**
> A risk control technique that reduces the frequency of a particular loss.

Loss Reduction

An individual or family may also use **loss reduction** techniques. For example, by installing fire-resistant shingles, a family could expect reduced losses from a fire compared to the fire losses it could experience with standard shingles. Some loss reduction measures can prevent losses as well as reduce them. For example, using a burglar alarm in a home is generally considered a loss reduction measure because the alarm is activated only when a burglary occurs. However, because burglar alarms also act as a deterrent, they can prevent loss as well as reduce it.

> **Loss reduction**
> A risk control technique that reduces the severity of a particular loss.

Separation

Separation is appropriate if a family can operate with only a portion of its assets left intact. For example, a family may store some of its jewelry in a safe at its home and store the remainder in a bank's safety deposit box. The intent of separation is to reduce the severity of an individual loss at a single location. However, by creating multiple locations, separation may increase loss frequency.

> **Separation**
> A risk control technique that isolates loss exposures from one another to minimize the adverse effect of a single loss.

Duplication

Examples of **duplication** include maintaining a second set of records (such as copies of wills placed in a safety deposit box); spare parts for autos, household appliances, or yard machinery; and copies of keys.

> **Duplication**
> A risk control technique that uses backups, spares, or copies of critical property, information, or capabilities and keeps them in reserve.

Diversification

Diversification closely resembles duplication and separation. Families use diversification when they allocate their assets among a mix of stocks and bonds from companies in different industry sectors. A family might diversify investments by purchasing stock in a bank and stock in a pharmaceutical manufacturer and other unrelated industries. Because these are unrelated industries, any losses from one stock may be more than offset by profits in the other industries.

As with separation and duplication, diversification can increase loss frequency. However, by spreading risk, diversification reduces loss severity and can make losses more predictable.

Risk Financing Techniques

Risk financing can help individuals and families recover from loss or damage that might otherwise cause them significant financial impairment. Traditionally, risk financing measures generally have been categorized as either retention techniques or transfer techniques.

Retention

Usually, a family deliberately uses **retention** only to treat loss exposures that are within its financial means, such as when it selects a $1,000 deductible on collision insurance for its vehicles. For instance, although most individuals and families are offered insurance by retailers for the repair or replacement of new appliances (stoves, dishwashers, washers, dryers, and so forth), many choose instead to retain these risks, because the loss of an appliance would not be catastrophic and the repair or replacement cost is relatively minimal. If individuals and families do not plan to treat loss exposures or are unaware of them, they retain them by default. Retention is the default risk financing technique that results if an individual or family fails to identify or transfer a risk.

Most families and individuals do not retain losses on a pre-planned, structured basis. They generally pay for retained losses with reserve savings or may change budgeting priorities to pay for them. Retention can be planned or unplanned; complete or partial; or funded or unfunded.

Planned retention is a deliberate assumption of loss that has been identified and analyzed and may be chosen because it is the most cost effective or convenient technique, or because no other alternatives are available.

Unplanned retention is the inadvertent, unplanned assumption of a loss exposure that has not been identified or accurately analyzed. For example, many individuals and families inadvertently retain flood losses because they do not anticipate that rain associated with the remnants of a hurricane will endanger their property. An individual or a family also may inadvertently retain losses if

---

Diversification
A risk control technique that spreads loss exposures over numerous projects, products, markets, or regions.

Retention
A risk financing technique by which losses are retained by generating funds within the organization to pay for the losses.

they select inadequate insurance policy limits. For example, if an insured with an auto liability limit of $100,000 is at fault in an auto accident that seriously injures another party, the insured may be liable for more than $100,000 in damages and may be required to pay the amount in excess of that figure. The excess amount, therefore, represents an unplanned retention.

Retention is complete if a loss exposure is entirely retained. Partial retention entails retaining a portion of a loss exposure and transferring the unretained portion through insurance or another risk financing technique. With insurance, the deductible represents the portion of the loss that the insured retains.

Funded retention is a pre-loss arrangement intended to ensure that funding is available to pay for losses that do occur. Unfunded retention is the lack of advance funding for losses.

Transfer

Insurance is the most prevalent form of risk **transfer**. The insurance buyer substitutes a small, certain financial cost, the insurance premium, for the possibility of a large, uncertain financial loss, which is paid by the insurer. Although insurance is only one approach to risk transfer, it is frequently the only method of risk transfer available to individuals and families.

Some risk transfer techniques, however, do not involve insurance. An example of such a noninsurance risk transfer is a hold-harmless agreement, which is a noninsurance contractual provision that obligates one of the parties to the contract to assume the legal liability of another party to the contract. A hold-harmless agreement may be included in an apartment lease, for instance.

Hedging is a noninsurance risk transfer technique in which one asset (money) is paid to offset the risk associated with another asset. For example, if a family agrees to pay a particular price for all of its home fuel oil in advance of the heating season, it is "hedging" against the possibility that fuel costs will increase during the season. See the exhibit "Examples of Risk Management Techniques Used by Individuals and Families."

Insurance

A risk management technique that transfers the potential financial consequences of certain specified loss exposures from the insured to the insurer.

Transfer

In the context of risk management, a risk financing technique by which the financial responsibility for losses and variability in cash flows is shifted to another party.

Examples of Risk Management Techniques Used by Individuals and Families

Risk Management Technique	Loss Exposure	Treatment
Risk Control Techniques		
• Avoidance	Death by airline accident	Drive instead
	Fire damage to home	Do not purchase home
	Theft of automobile	Do not purchase auto
	Storm damage to watercraft	Do not purchase speedboat
• Loss Prevention	Liability suit caused by injury on slippery floors	Install rugs
	Liability suit caused by fall on steep stairways	Install handrails
• Loss Reduction	Home fire	Install fire-resistant shingles and fire extinguishers
	Home burglary	Install burglar alarm
• Separation	Theft of valuables	Some valuables remain at home, others are stored in a safety deposit box
• Duplication	Loss of keys	Make duplicate set of keys
	Destruction by fire of valuable documents	Make additional copies
• Diversification	Steep reduction in value of a major family investment	Diversify investment into a variety of suitable assets
Risk Financing Techniques		
• Retention	Wear and tear on vehicles and clothing	Budget for acceptable loss exposures
• Transfer	Property damage due to fire or auto liability suit	Transfer risks to another individual or entity (often transferred by purchasing insurance)

[DA00136]

INSURANCE AS A RISK FINANCING TECHNIQUE

Personal insurance is a risk transfer technique individuals and families use to finance their personal loss exposures.

All individuals and families have personal loss exposures. Although some of these loss exposures may be managed through noninsurance transfers and retention, the most prevalent risk management technique is the purchase of personal insurance. Personal insurance transfers the financial consequences of loss exposures to an insurer or to a government agency.

Personal insurance consists of three layers: social programs of insurance, which are government provided (such as Social Security benefits); group insurance (such as group health and life insurance sold to a company's employees); and individual insurance (such as auto and homeowners insurance). Individuals may elect to manage a loss exposure with insurance, may be required to purchase insurance as a condition of a mortgage or automobile loan, and also may automatically participate in government-provided insurance. See the exhibit "Three Layers of Personal Insurance."

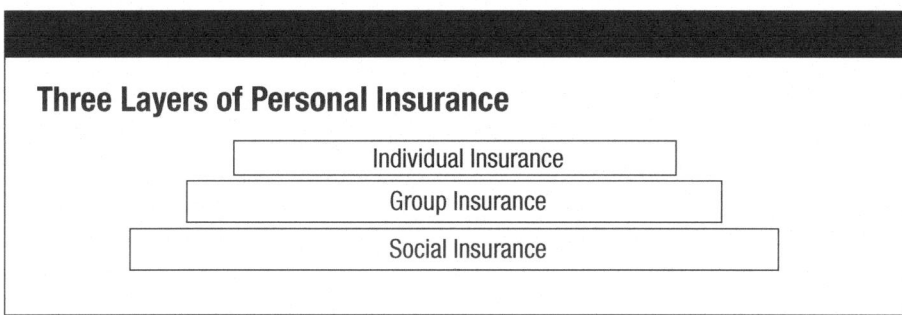

[DA00204]

The most widely purchased kinds of insurance from these three layers address these loss exposures:

- Property and liability loss exposures
- Retirement loss exposures
- Premature death loss exposures
- Health and disability loss exposures
- Unemployment loss exposures

Property and Liability Loss Exposures

Property loss exposures stem from a legal interest in both real property and personal property. Liability loss exposures originate from the possibility of being sued or being held responsible for someone else's injury.

Auto insurance (an example of individual insurance) covers auto-related property and liability loss exposures. An individual's purchase of automobile insurance reduces the financial uncertainty associated with a collision loss and also may satisfy a requirement of the loan used to pay for the auto. More importantly, the policy's liability coverage mitigates the financial effect of a liability injury suit, whose associated costs could far exceed the cost of the automobile itself.

Homeowners insurance (an example of individual insurance) protects against real and personal property loss exposures as well as liability loss exposures. By obtaining homeowners insurance, a family purchasing a home reduces the financial uncertainty associated with home-related property and liability loss exposures and satisfies the requirements of the mortgage company that is financing the home's purchase.

For liability protection beyond that offered by homeowners and auto policies, individuals and families can purchase umbrella liability protection. For example, an umbrella policy could be purchased with a limit of $1 million. The umbrella would apply above the liability limits of the homeowners and auto policies. This type of excess liability policy also provides liability coverage not available in the underlying coverages, subject to an insured's self-insured retention, such as $1,000.

Because the prevalence of insured homes and automobiles allows insurers to accurately predict loss costs and to use premiums from all insureds to pay for the losses of the relative few, insurance is the most effective way for individuals and families to manage many of their property and liability loss exposures. See the exhibit "Insurance Deductibles."

Insurance Deductibles

In order to minimize the cost of insurance and encourage insureds to protect and care for their insured property, insurers require the insured to retain a predetermined portion of the cost of a covered loss in the form of a deductible. For example, insureds may purchase automobile insurance with a $500 or $1,000 deductible for collision insurance. That is, the insured bears the cost of a loss up to the deductible amount. By participating in the loss, insureds may be more careful, and this participation keeps the price of insurance lower than otherwise.

[DA05645]

Retirement Loss Exposures

The assets exposed to loss when an individual retires are regular employment income and the related benefits of employment, such as health insurance. Many individuals and families maintain savings plans and pension plans to help them prepare for retirement. Some may choose through an insurance mechanism to convert their savings to annuities, which guarantee a monthly payment for life. See the exhibit "Retirement Accounts."

> **Retirement Accounts**
>
> Families and individuals also can mitigate the financial uncertainty associated with retirement loss exposures by participating in individual retirement accounts (IRAs), Roth IRAs, and 401(k) savings plans. These retirement accounts are not considered insurance, but their value, which is often aided by contributions from employers, can help individuals and families augment other sources of retirement income.

[DA00203]

Additionally, the federal government's Social Security program (an example of social insurance) provides financial benefits to retirees and their families. Although participants can begin drawing Social Security benefits at age sixty-two, they are not eligible to receive their entire allotted monthly benefit until they reach full retirement age. Under law, the full retirement age of sixty-five started steadily increasing in 2003. By 2027, the full retirement age will be age sixty-seven. See the exhibit "Retirement Benefit Trends."

> **Retirement Benefit Trends**
>
> Many workers are opting to work beyond their full retirement age and postpone drawing on Social Security benefits because they fear that those benefits may not adequately sustain their standard of living. Because of these concerns, workers also opt to participate in employer-sponsored group pension plans, defined benefit plans, and defined contribution plans. Recently, however, there has been a decline in the number of employers offering defined benefit plans. Instead, they prefer to contribute to defined contribution plans or 401(k) plans, which do not present as much economic risk to the employer since the employee assumes any investment risk. Often, employees are fully vested (have immediate rights to the monies, which they can transfer if there is a change in employment). Although these plans are not insurance, they do help to mitigate retirement-related loss exposures.

[DA00206]

Premature Death Loss Exposures

A death is considered premature if it occurs before an individual reaches his or her life expectancy. The assets exposed to loss as the result of an individual's premature death include the expected income on which his or her family or heirs rely. Premature death of a family member is a potentially devastating personal loss exposure that should receive high priority in an individual or family financial plan. One of the most effective ways for families to manage the premature death loss exposure is to purchase a life insurance policy (an example of individual insurance).

Individuals and families use life insurance as a risk management technique for many of the same reasons that they use property-casualty insurance. The basic principle of insurance is that the financial losses of the few are drawn from the paid premiums of the many. Life insurance beneficiaries are compensated by the premiums paid by insureds in the life insurance pool.

The amount of life insurance that an individual or family should purchase can be determined by the needs-based approach or the human life value approach. The needs-based approach attempts to estimate a family's future financial needs to determine the life insurance compensation they will require. This value is calculated after also accounting for any Social Security or other applicable benefits the family will receive. The human life value approach does not attempt to estimate a family's future financial needs. Instead, it uses the estimated present value of the insured's financial contribution to the family to determine the income that the family could lose in the event of the insured's premature death. Courts often use the human life value approach to determine appropriate compensation for a wage earner's family for its loss. Often, the needs-based approach and the human life value approach are used together to determine the amount of life insurance a family should purchase.

Health and Disability Loss Exposures

Health and disability insurance reduces the financial uncertainty associated with an individual or family member's illness or disability. Many employers contribute a portion of the premiums for their employees' health and disability insurance.

Individual and group health and disability insurance may be more important to an individual or a family than life insurance. If a person becomes critically ill or disabled, the cost of hospital care, medicines, and care-giving could become a severe financial burden to his or her family. The illness or disability might also prevent his or her spouse from obtaining employment to help replace his or her income, because the spouse might be required to become a full-time caregiver.

Workers compensation
A system that pays lost wages, medical and vocational rehabilitation expenses, and death benefits to injured workers or their dependents for employment-related injuries and diseases.

Three prominent government programs (social insurance programs) that also provide health and disability benefits are Medicare, Medicaid, and **workers compensation**. Medicare provides coverage for medical expenses of most individuals age sixty-five and older, while Medicaid provides health and disability insurance for low-income individuals.

Individuals and families also may consider purchasing long-term health care insurance to help mitigate the potentially high costs of extended medical care or custodial care they may require later in life in a nursing home or hospital, or in their home. Long-term care insurance premiums may be costly, however, especially for older individuals.

Unemployment Loss Exposures

The assets exposed to loss by unemployment include income and employer-provided benefits. All state governments sponsor unemployment compensation programs that pay benefits to covered individuals who are involuntarily unemployed. The benefits help workers purchase necessities and maintain their pre-unemployment standard of living. Unemployment benefits provide an amount that is approximately two-thirds of the hourly worker's previous income.

States derive unemployment benefits from the taxes or premiums they assess employers. Generally, unemployed workers receive unemployment benefits for a particular number of weeks or until they secure employment. The state may legislate an increase in the number of weeks over which the unemployed can collect benefits, depending on economic conditions or state unemployment rates. In especially depressed economic conditions, the federal government may assist the states. Additionally, labor unions often provide unemployment compensation for members who have been laid off or are on strike. See the exhibit "Insurance Available for Personal Loss Exposures."

Insurance Available for Personal Loss Exposures

Loss Exposure	Personal Insurance	Group Insurance	Social Insurance
Automobiles	Personal auto	*	
Property: home and contents	Homeowners	*	
Personal liability	Homeowners/umbrella	*	
Valuable items: Jewelry, coin collections, and fine art	Homeowners (property endorsement or personal articles floater)	*	
Damage to property from rising waters			National Flood Insurance
Retirement	Personal savings/annuities		Social Security (including Medicare and Medicaid)
Premature death	Individual life	Group life	Social Security
Health and disability	Individual health	Group health	Social Security and workers compensation
Unemployment	Personal savings	Union benefits (in some circumstances)	State unemployment funds (reinforced by the federal government)

* May be available on a group basis

[DA00205]

COMMON POLICY PROVISIONS

Every insurance policy is composed of numerous policy provisions.

Policy provision
Any phrase or clause in an insurance policy that describes the policy's coverages, exclusions, limits, conditions, or other features.

Some **policy provisions** are common to most insurance policies, whereas others are unique to specific policies. Despite the wide variation in property-casualty insurance policy provisions, they typically fall into one of six categories, depending on the purpose they serve. Each of the policy provisions must be examined during policy analysis to determine its exact effect on coverage. See the exhibit "Property-Casualty Insurance Policy Provisions."

Property-Casualty Insurance Policy Provisions

Policy Provision Categories	Description	Effect on Coverage
Declarations	Unique information about the insured; list of forms included in policy	Outline who or what is covered, and where and when coverage applies
Definitions	Words with special meanings in policy	May limit or expand coverage based on definitions of terms
Insuring Agreements	Promise to make payment	Outline circumstances under which the insurer agrees to pay
Conditions	Qualifications on promise to make payment	Outline steps insured needs to take to enforce policy
Exclusions	Limitations on promise to make payment	Limit insurer's payments based on excluded persons, places, things, or actions
Miscellaneous Provisions	Wide variety of provisions that may alter policy	Deal with the relationship between the insured and the insurer or establish procedures for implementing the policy

[DA00214]

Declarations page (declarations, or dec.)
An insurance policy information page or pages providing specific details about the insured and the subject of the insurance.

Declarations

Insurance policy **declarations** typically contain not only the standard information that has been "declared" by both the insured and the insurer, but also information unique to the particular policy. The declarations (commonly referred to as the information page or declarations page) typically appear as the first page (or one of the first pages) in an insurance policy and contain these items:

- Policy or policy number
- Policy inception and expiration dates (policy period)
- Name of the insurer
- Name of the insurance agent
- Name of the insured(s)
- Names of persons or organizations whose additional interests are covered (for example, a mortgagee, a loss payee, or an additional insured)
- Mailing address of the insured
- Physical address and description of the covered property or operations
- Numbers and edition dates of all attached forms and endorsements
- Dollar amounts of applicable policy limits
- Dollar amounts of applicable deductibles
- Premium

In some cases, other policy forms or **endorsements** also contain information that qualifies as part of the declarations. This information is often referred to as a "schedule." For example, an endorsement to a homeowners policy may list descriptions of and limits of coverage for valuable pieces of personal property that need special insurance treatment. See the exhibit "Homeowners Policy Declarations."

Endorsement
A document that amends an insurance policy.

Definitions

Words and phrases defined within an insurance policy have special, defined meanings when they are used within that particular policy. The **definitions** section defines the terms used throughout the entire policy or form. In personal insurance policies, the definitions section usually precedes the policy's other sections. Boldface type or quotation marks typically are used to distinguish words and phrases defined elsewhere in the policy. Undefined words and phrases are interpreted according to these rules of policy interpretation:

Definitions
A section of an insurance policy that defines terms used throughout the policy form.

- Everyday words are given their ordinary meanings.
- Technical words are given their technical meanings.
- Words with an established legal meaning are given their legal meanings.
- Consideration is also given to the local, cultural, and trade-usage meanings of words, if applicable. Many of the definitions that appear in insurance policies are intended to resolve real or perceived ambiguity regarding the use of those terms in previous policies.

Homeowners Policy Declarations

Homeowners Policy Declarations

POLICYHOLDER: David M. and Joan G. Smith
(Named Insured) 216 Brookside Drive
Anytown, USA 40000

POLICY NUMBER: 296 H 578661

POLICY PERIOD: **Inception:** March 30, 20XX
Expiration: March 30, 20XX

Policy period begins 12:01 A.M. standard time at the residence premises.

FIRST MORTGAGEE AND MAILING ADDRESS:

Federal National Mortgage Assn.
C/O Mortgagee, Inc.
P.O. Box 5000
Businesstown, USA 55000

We will provide the insurance described in this policy in return for the premium and compliance with all applicable policy provisions.

SECTION I COVERAGES	LIMIT
A—Dwelling	$ 120,000
B—Other Structures	$ 12,000
C—Personal Property	$ 60,000
D—Loss of Use	$ 36,000

SECTION I DEDUCTIBLE: $ 250
(In case of loss under Section I, we cover only that part of the loss over the deductible amount shown above.)

SECTION II COVERAGES	LIMIT	
E—Personal Liability	$ 300,000	Each Occurrence
F—Medical Payments to Others	$ 1,000	Each Person

CONSTRUCTION: Masonry Veneer **NO. FAMILIES:** One **TYPE ROOF:** Approved

YEAR BUILT: 1990 **PROTECTION CLASS:** 7 **FIRE DISTRICT:** Cook Township

NOT MORE THAN 1000 FEET FROM HYDRANT

NOT MORE THAN 5 MILES FROM FIRE DEPT.

FORMS AND ENDORSEMENTS IN POLICY: HO 00 03, HO 04 61

POLICY PREMIUM: $ 350.00 **COUNTERSIGNATURE DATE:**   **AGENT:** A.M. Abel

Copyright, ISO Properties, Inc. [DA00215]

Personal Auto Policy Definitions

Example of PP 00 01 01 05 Definitions

J. "Your covered auto" means:
   1. Any vehicle shown in the Declarations.
   2. A "newly acquired auto".
   3. Any "trailer" you own.
   4. Any auto or "trailer" you do not own while used as a temporary substitute for any other vehicle described in this definition which is out of normal use because of its:
      a. Breakdown;
      b. Repair;
      c. Servicing;
      d. Loss; or
      e. Destruction.

   This Provision (J.4.) does not apply to Coverage For Damage To Your Auto.

K. "Newly acquired auto":
   1. "Newly acquired auto" means any of the following types of vehicles you become the owner of during the policy period:
      a. A private passenger auto; or
      b. A pickup or van, for which no other insurance policy provides coverage, that:
         (1) Has a Gross Vehicle Weight Rating of 10,000 lbs. or less; and
         (2) Is not used for the delivery or transportation of goods and materials unless such use is:
            (a) Incidental to your "business" of installing, maintaining or repairing furnishings or equipment; or
            (b) For farming or ranching.

Includes copyrighted material of Insurance Services Office, Inc., with its permission. Copyright, ISO Properties, Inc., 2003. [DA00326]

Insuring Agreements

Following the declarations, and possibly preceded by a section containing definitions, the body of most insurance policies begins with an **insuring agreement**. The insuring agreement is the promise of coverage the insurer makes to the insured and is essentially what the insured is buying.

The term "insuring agreement" is usually applied to statements that introduce a policy's coverage section. However, the term also can describe statements introducing coverage extensions, additional coverages, supplementary

> **Insuring agreement**
> A statement in an insurance policy that the insurer will, under described circumstances, make a loss payment or provide a service.

payments, and so forth. Even unlabeled statements within declarations, definitions, exclusions, or conditions can serve as insuring agreements.

Policies typically contain an insuring agreement for each coverage they provide. Consequently, package policies contain multiple insuring agreements. For example, the Insurance Services Office (ISO) Personal Auto Policy (PAP) typically provides liability, medical payments, uninsured motorists, and damage to "your" auto coverages. Therefore, the PAP contains an insuring agreement for each of these four coverages. See the exhibit "Personal Auto Policy Liability Insuring Agreement (from PP 00 01 01 05)."

Personal Auto Policy Liability Insuring Agreement (from PP 00 01 01 05)

PART A – LIABILITY COVERAGE

INSURING AGREEMENT

A. We will pay damages for "bodily injury" or "property damage" for which any "insured" becomes legally responsible because of an auto accident. Damages include prejudgment interest awarded against the "insured". We will settle or defend, as we consider appropriate, any claim or suit asking for these damages. In addition to our limit of liability, we will pay all defense costs we incur. Our duty to settle or defend ends when our limit of liability for this coverage has been exhausted by payment of judgments or settlements. We have no duty to defend any suit or settle any claim for "bodily injury" or "property damage" not covered under this policy.

B. "Insured" as used in this Part means:

1. You or any "family member" for the ownership, maintenance or use of any auto or "trailer".

2. Any person using "your covered auto".

3. For "your covered auto", any person or organization but only with respect to legal responsibility for acts or omissions of a person for whom coverage is afforded under this Part.

4. For any auto or "trailer", other than "your covered auto", any other person or organization but only with respect to legal responsibility for acts or omissions of you or any "family member" for whom coverage is afforded under this Part. This Provision (B.4.) applies only if the person or organization does not own or hire the auto or "trailer".

Includes copyrighted material of Insurance Services Office, Inc., with its permission. Copyright, ISO Properties, Inc., 2003. [DA00216]

Conditions

The insurer's promises in the insuring agreement are enforceable only if an insured event occurs and only if the insured has fulfilled its contractual duties as specified in the **policy conditions**. Some policy conditions are found in a section of the policy titled "Conditions," whereas others are found in the forms, endorsements, or other documents that constitute the policy.

Policy condition
Any provision that qualifies an otherwise enforceable promise made in the policy.

Examples of common policy conditions include the insured's obligation to pay premiums, report losses promptly, provide appropriate documentation for losses, cooperate with the insurer in any legal proceedings, and refrain from jeopardizing the insurer's rights to recover from responsible third parties. If the insured does not adhere to the policy's conditions, then the insurer may be released from any obligation to perform some or all of its otherwise enforceable promises.

Exclusions

The primary function of **exclusions** is not only to limit coverage but also to clarify the coverages granted by the insurer. Specifying what the insurer does not intend to cover is a way of clarifying what the insurer does intend to cover. Exclusions have six purposes:

Exclusion
A policy provision that eliminates coverage for specified exposures.

- Eliminate coverage for uninsurable loss exposures—Some loss exposures (such as war) possess few if any of the ideal characteristics of an insurable loss exposure. Exclusions allow insurers to preclude coverage for these loss exposures.

- Assist in managing moral and morale hazards—Exclusions enable insurers to limit coverages for causes of loss over which the insured had some control. For example, some exclusions assist in managing morale hazards by making insureds themselves bear the losses that result from their own carelessness.

- Reduce likelihood of coverage duplications—In some cases, two insurance policies provide coverage for the same loss. Exclusions ensure that two policies work together to provide complementary, not duplicate, coverage and that insureds are not paying duplicate premiums. For example, assume Karim has both a personal auto policy and a homeowners policy. If Karim leaves his laptop computer in his car and the car is stolen, he can submit a claim for the laptop under his homeowners insurance. Therefore, the loss of the laptop does not need to be covered under his personal auto policy.

- Eliminate coverages not needed by the typical insured—Exclusions allow insurers to exclude coverage for loss exposures not faced by the typical insured. This means that all insureds would not have to share the costs of covering the loss exposures that relatively few insureds have. For example, the typical individual does not own or operate private aircraft or rent portions of the family home for storage of others' business property.

Therefore, homeowners policies typically exclude coverage for such loss exposures.

- Eliminate coverages requiring special treatment—Exclusions eliminate the coverages that require rating, underwriting, loss control, or reinsurance treatment substantially different from what is normally required by the insurance policy. As an example, many standard policies covering valuable personal property exclude coverage for loss exposures involving property exhibited at a convention or trade fair.
- Assist in keeping premiums reasonable—Exclusions allow insurers to preclude risks that would otherwise increase costs. By keeping costs down, insurers can offer premiums that a sufficiently large number of insurance buyers consider reasonable. For example, a personal auto policy excludes coverage for mechanical breakdown and road damage to tires.

Miscellaneous Provisions

In addition to declarations, definitions, insuring agreements, conditions, and exclusions, insurance policies often contain miscellaneous provisions that specify the relationship between the insured and the insurer or help establish working procedures for implementing the policy. However, even if the insured does not follow the procedures specified in the miscellaneous provisions, the insurer may still be required to fulfill its contractual promises.

Miscellaneous provisions often are unique to particular types of insurers, as in these examples:

- A policy issued by a mutual insurer is likely to describe each insured's right to vote in the election of the board of directors.
- A policy issued by a reciprocal insurer is likely to specify the attorney-in-fact's authority to implement its powers on the insured's behalf.

POLICY ANALYSIS

Each pre-loss question posed or post-loss claim filed by an insured is a unique situation that may require a review of policy provisions.

Insurance professionals should conduct pre-loss policy analysis to prepare themselves to answer an insured's coverage questions and to ensure that the policy being sold is appropriate for the insured's loss exposures. Insureds should conduct pre-loss policy analysis to verify that the policy they're purchasing adequately addresses their loss exposures. After a loss, the insurer must analyze the policy to determine whether it covers the loss and, if necessary, the extent of coverage the policy provides.

Pre-Loss Policy Analysis

Pre-loss policy analysis almost exclusively relies on scenario analysis to determine the extent of coverage (if any) the policy provides for the losses generated by a given scenario. For insureds, the primary source of information for generating scenarios for analysis is their past loss experience. Particularly if the insured has never suffered a loss that triggered insurance coverage, friends, neighbors, co-workers, and family members can also provide information about their experiences with losses and the claim process. Such information can help an insured formulate scenarios for pre-loss policy analysis.

Another source of information for the insured's scenario analysis is the insurance producer or customer service representative consulted in the insurance transaction. Such insurance professionals need to be able to accurately interpret coverage questions raised. Producers may have specialized knowledge of the loss exposures covered under the policy. They also understand the alternative ways insurance policies may describe the same coverage and may be aware of any policy provisions that depart from customary wording. For example, homeowners who have read news articles about toxic mold may consult their insurance producers to determine whether their homeowners insurance policy covers mold, fungus, or wet rot.

One of the limitations of scenario analysis is that, because the number of possible loss scenarios is theoretically infinite, it is impossible to account for every possibility. For example, most insurance professionals or insureds would not have envisioned the terrorist attacks of September 11, 2001. Alternatively, the insured or insurance professional may recognize the possibility of an event but underestimate the extent of potential loss. For example, the damage Hurricane Andrew caused in 1992 was unprecedented, as was the extent of flooding New Orleans experienced following Hurricane Katrina in 2005. These events prompted insurers to fundamentally change the methods used to evaluate these types of risks.

Post-Loss Policy Analysis

When an insured reports a loss, the insurer must determine whether the loss triggers coverage and, if so, the extent of that coverage. The primary method of post-loss policy analysis is the DICE (an acronym representing the policy provision categories: declarations, insuring agreements, conditions, and exclusions) method, which is a systematic review of all the categories of property-casualty policy provisions. See the exhibit "DICE Decision Tree."

The DICE method entails following four steps to determine whether a policy provides coverage. The first step is an examination of the declarations page to determine whether the information provided by the insured precludes coverage. For example, an insured may report to the property insurer that a fire occurred at the insured premises on May 5. The declarations page contains both the policy inception and expiration dates (delineating the policy

DICE Decision Tree

To determine whether a policy covers a loss, many insurance professionals apply the DICE method. ("DICE" is an acronym for categories of policy provisions: declarations, insuring agreement, conditions, and exclusions.) The DICE method has four steps:

1. Review of the declarations page to determine whether it covers the person or the property at the time of the loss
2. Review of the insuring agreement to determine whether it covers the loss
3. Review of policy conditions to determine compliance
4. Review of policy exclusions to determine whether they preclude coverage of the loss

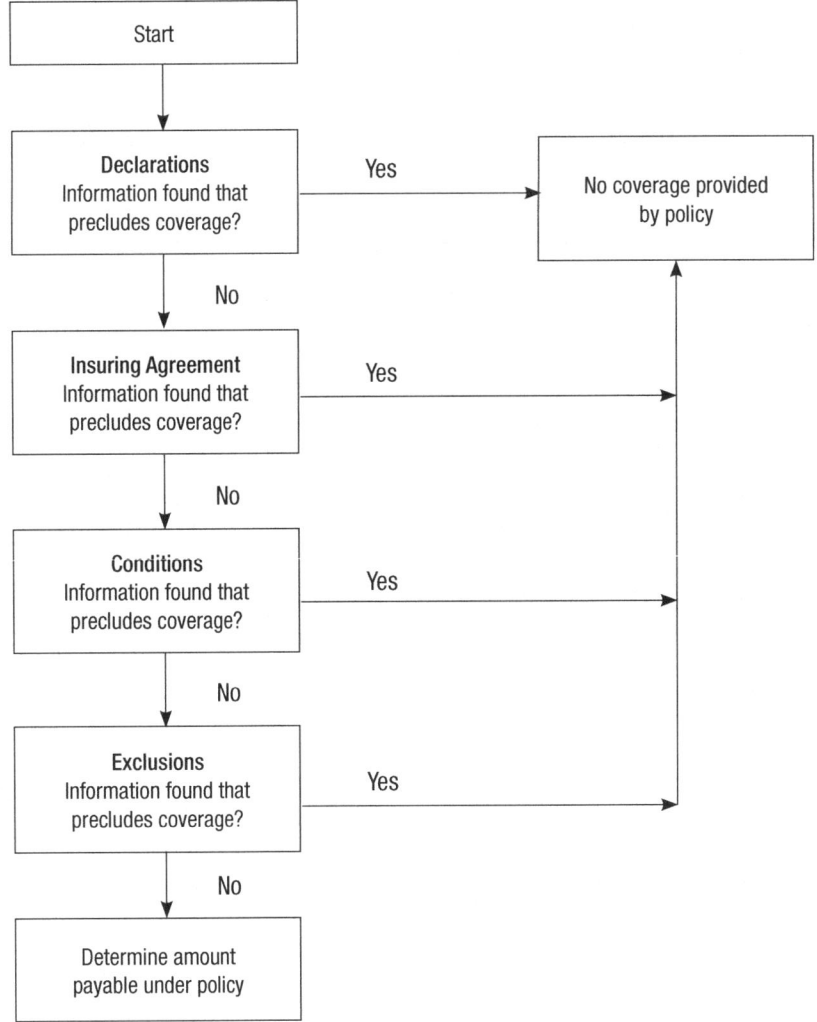

Each of these four steps is used in every case. Other categories of policy provisions should be examined. For example, endorsements and terms defined in the policy should be reviewed in relation to the declarations, insuring agreement, exclusions, and conditions.

period). If the policy period ended on April 30, then the policy would not provide coverage for this loss.

If nothing in the declarations precludes coverage, the insurance professional would move to the second step in the DICE method, an analysis of the insuring agreement. For example, in the homeowners policy, the insurer agrees to provide coverage in exchange for the insured's payment of the premium. If the premium is not paid, the policy would not cover the claim. The insuring agreement or agreements often contain policy provisions regarding the covered property or events, covered causes of loss, and coverage territories. If these provisions contain specially defined terms, those definitions should be analyzed. If a provision in an insuring agreement precludes coverage, the claim will be denied.

If nothing in the insuring agreement precludes coverage, the insurance professional proceeds to the third step of the DICE method, analyzing conditions. Policy conditions specify the duties of the insurer and the insured. Examples of common policy provisions include the insured's obligation to report losses promptly, provide appropriate documentation for losses, and cooperate with the insurer in any legal proceedings. Violating a condition can change the coverage on an otherwise-covered claim. Examining the policy conditions can help the insurance professional clarify these important points:

- Whether fulfillment of certain conditions, such as premium payment conditions, is required for there to be an enforceable policy
- Whether coverage will be denied if an insured party breaches a policy condition
- Whether coverage triggers and coverage territory restrictions affect the loss
- Whether conditions concerning the rights and duties of both parties to maintain the insurance policy apply (for example, the insurer's right to inspect covered premises, the rights of either or both parties to cancel the policy, and the insurer's right to make coverage modifications)
- Whether the post-loss duties of the insured and the insurer affect coverage
- Whether conditions have been or need to be adhered to regarding claim disputes
- Whether subrogation and salvage rights and conditions must be considered

One breach of a condition that can occur under a homeowners policy is the concealment of a material fact. For example, assume an insured has a primary business running a furniture refinishing operation in his home. If he fails to disclose this fact when obtaining his homeowners coverage, in violation of one of the policy's coverage conditions, the policy would not cover a fire caused by flammable rags used to polish furniture.

If the insured has complied with all of the policy's conditions, the insurance professional performs the final step of the DICE method, analyzing policy exclusions and any other policy provisions not already analyzed, including endorsements and miscellaneous provisions. This is the fourth and final step of the DICE method. Exclusions, which can appear anywhere in the policy, state what the insurer does not intend to cover. The primary function of exclusions is not only to limit coverage but also to clarify the coverages granted by the insurer. They also eliminate coverage for uninsurable loss exposures (such as intentional acts) and can be used to reduce the likelihood of coverage duplications, eliminate coverages not needed by the typical insured, eliminate coverages requiring special treatment, or assist in keeping premiums reasonable. For example, an exclusion in a homeowners policy precludes coverage for claims resulting from earth movement caused by an earthquake, landslide, or subsidence that damages a dwelling or its contents.

After using the DICE method to determine whether the claim is covered, the insurer must then determine how much is payable under that insurance policy. The amount payable under a given insurance policy can be affected not only by the value of the loss but also by policy limits and deductibles, or self-insured retentions. For property insurance, the amount payable is affected by several factors. The valuation provision indicates how the property will be valued for claim purposes, which could be on the basis of its replacement cost, its depreciated actual cash value, or some other valuation method. The amount payable is also affected by applicable policy limits and can be limited by a coinsurance provision or other insurance-to-value provisions. Some policies designate a deductible to be subtracted from the amount otherwise payable. For liability insurance, the valuation of a covered loss is established by the courts or, more commonly, by a negotiated settlement. The amounts payable for both property and liability insurance losses can also be affected by other insurance.

SUMMARY

The three elements of loss exposures are assets exposed to loss, causes of loss, and financial consequences of loss. If individuals and families understand the conditions or situations that present the possibility of loss occurrence, how losses occur, and the consequences of loss, then they will be in better position to manage their own personal loss exposures.

Individuals and families face a number of loss exposures in terms of the assets exposed to loss, the causes of loss to which property is exposed, and the financial consequences of loss. Assets exposed to loss can include both real property and personal property. Many causes of loss exist, including fire, theft, and collision, and they result in various financial consequences to property. These financial consequences include a reduction in value of property, increased expenses, and lost income.

A liability loss occurs because of an injury to another person or property. When a person who has an asset exposed to loss commits a breach of legal duty or a breach of contract, or fails to adhere to statutes, he or she may be responsible for related damages. Financial consequences of personal liability loss exposures can include damages paid to the plaintiff, settlement costs, legal fees, and court costs.

Important personal financial planning loss exposures include insufficient income during retirement, premature death, poor health or disability, and unemployment. Depending on the circumstances, these loss exposures can have significant financial consequences for an individual or family.

The risk management process consists of six steps:

1. Identifying loss exposures
2. Analyzing loss exposures
3. Examining the feasibility of risk management techniques
4. Selecting the appropriate risk management techniques
5. Implementing the selected risk management techniques
6. Monitoring results and revising the risk management program

Individuals and families use risk control and risk financing techniques to manage their risks. Risk control techniques can be categorized as avoidance, loss prevention, loss reduction, separation, duplication, and diversification. Risk financing can be accomplished through retention or transfer. The most prevalent risk transfer technique is insurance.

A variety of personal insurance policies are used by individuals and families to manage their personal risks that arise from homeowner and automobile loss exposures and other property and liability exposures. Additional loss exposures arise from retirement, premature death, poor health and disability, and unemployment. The insurance available for these loss exposures includes retirement-related policies, life insurance policies, health and disability insurance policies, and unemployment compensation policies.

Every insurance policy is composed of numerous policy provisions. Each provision falls into one of six categories, depending on the purpose it serves:

- Declarations
- Definitions
- Insuring agreements
- Conditions
- Exclusions
- Miscellaneous provisions

Insureds and insurers should analyze an insurance policy before a loss occurs in order to ensure that the policy adequately covers the loss exposures it is intended to address. The primary method of pre-loss policy analysis is scenario analysis. After a loss occurs, an insurer uses the DICE method to determine whether the insurance policy provides coverage.

ASSIGNMENT NOTE

1. "Laid-off Workers Face Increased Premature Death Risk: Study," CBC News, December 2007, www.cbc.ca/health/story/2007/12/06/layoffs-death.html (accessed January 10, 2008).

Direct Your Learning

Automobile Insurance and Society

Educational Objectives

After learning the content of this assignment, you should be able to:

- Evaluate each of the following approaches to compensating automobile accident victims:
  - Tort liability system
  - Financial responsibility laws
  - Compulsory insurance laws
  - Uninsured motorists coverage
  - Underinsured motorists coverage
  - No-fault insurance
- Describe no-fault automobile laws in terms of each of the following:
  - Types of no-fault laws
  - Benefits required by no-fault laws
- Explain how high-risk drivers may obtain auto insurance.
- Describe automobile insurance rate regulation in terms of each of the following:
  - Rating factors
  - Matching price to exposure
  - Competition
  - Other regulatory issues

Outline

Compensation of Auto Accident Victims

No-Fault Automobile Laws

Automobile Insurance for High-Risk Drivers

Automobile Insurance Rate Regulation

Summary

Automobile Insurance and Society

COMPENSATION OF AUTO ACCIDENT VICTIMS

Under the legal system in the United States, persons who are injured or who incur property damage losses as the result of auto accidents that are the fault of other drivers are entitled to compensation and damages.

Automobile insurers and state governments have designed these approaches to compensating auto accident victims:

- Tort liability system
- Financial responsibility laws
- Compulsory insurance laws
- Uninsured motorists coverage
- Underinsured motorists coverage
- No-fault insurance

Tort Liability System

The tort liability system, which is based on fault, is the traditional and most commonly used method of seeking compensation for injured auto accident victims in the U.S. Most tort liability cases arise out of negligence. If a driver operates an auto in a negligent manner that results in bodily injury to another person or in damage to another's property, the operator can be held legally liable for damages incurred by the injured person. To avoid legal liability, auto owners and operators must exercise a high degree of care to protect others from harm.

Under the tort liability system, injured auto accident victims must prove that another party was at fault before they can collect damages from that party. The amount of damages can be determined through negotiations between the two parties or through a lawsuit and court settlement.

The major advantage of the tort liability system is that it provides a remedy for victims of negligent or irresponsible drivers who cause accidents. Injured victims are compensated for their costs, and the costs are allocated to the responsible party. The tort liability system may also act as an incentive for drivers to act responsibly in order to avoid lawsuits.

The disadvantages of the tort liability system include these considerations:

- Substantial time delays in reaching a settlement either through negotiation or through the courts
- Significant legal and administrative costs related to settling lawsuits or pursuing a case to judgment
- Punitive damage awards by juries that may be considered excessive

Financial Responsibility Laws

Financial responsibility laws require motorists to provide proof of financial responsibility (such as liability insurance) under these circumstances:

- After an auto accident involving bodily injury or property damage exceeding a certain dollar amount
- After a conviction for certain serious offenses, such as drunk driving or reckless driving, or after losing a driver's license because of repeated violations
- Upon failure to pay a final judgment that results from an auto accident

Motorists who fail to provide the required proof of financial responsibility can face suspension of their driver's license and vehicle registration. Proof of financial responsibility can include an insurance policy, a certificate of deposit, a surety bond, or a certificate of self insurance, depending upon the jurisdiction.

Financial responsibility laws provide some protection to victims of auto accidents against irresponsible drivers. These laws work in conjunction with the tort liability system to ensure that at-fault drivers will not only be held liable for accidents they cause, but also that they have a mechanism in place to pay for the financial consequences of those accidents.

Some potential disadvantages of financial responsibility laws include these considerations:

- Most financial responsibility requirements become effective only after an accident, a conviction, or a judgment.
- Financial responsibility laws do not guarantee payment to all accident victims. Persons injured by uninsured drivers, hit-and-run drivers, or drivers of stolen cars might not be compensated.
- Injured persons might not be fully indemnified for their injuries even when injured by motorists who can prove financial responsibility. Most financial responsibility laws set minimum financial requirements, which may not fully compensate a victim.

Financial responsibility law
Law enacted to ensure that motorists have the financial ability to pay for any property damage or bodily injury they might cause as a result of driving or owning an auto.

Compulsory Auto Insurance Laws

Most states have enacted **compulsory auto insurance laws** that require auto liability insurance for all motorists to drive legally within the state. In lieu of auto insurance, a motorist can post a bond or deposit cash or securities to guarantee financial responsibility in the event of an auto accident. In addition, many states require the insurer to verify insurance coverage and/or to notify the state if a policy is canceled or is not renewed. Other states may require insurers to submit information regarding the automobile insurance policies they have issued within that jurisdiction.

One advantage of compulsory insurance laws, as compared to financial responsibility laws, is that motorists must provide proof of financial responsibility before an accident occurs. By requiring proof of financial responsibility prior to an accident, compulsory insurance laws go beyond financial responsibility laws by ensuring that accident victims are compensated for their losses. Compulsory insurance laws work in conjunction with the tort liability system to ensure compensation for victims of auto accidents that are the fault of other drivers.

These are frequently cited disadvantages of compulsory insurance:

- Compulsory insurance laws do not guarantee compensation to all accident victims. Accidents and resulting injuries can be caused by drivers who do not comply with the law, such as hit-and-run drivers, drivers whose insurance has lapsed, out-of-state drivers with no insurance, drivers of stolen cars, or drivers of fraudulently registered vehicles.
- Compulsory insurance laws provide incomplete protection. The required minimum amount of insurance may not meet the full needs of accident victims. In some states, the required minimum limit for bodily injury coverage is as low as $10,000 or $20,000 per person.
- Compulsory insurance laws may not reduce the number of uninsured motorists. Some drivers do not insure their vehicles because insurance is too costly. Others let coverage lapse after demonstrating proof of insurance to satisfy vehicle registration requirements.
- Insurers argue that compulsory laws restrict their freedom to select profitable insureds. In addition, insurers fear that state regulators might deny needed rate increases, resulting in underwriting losses.
- Consumer advocates argue that if insurers are allowed to increase rates to compensate for accepting all applicants for insurance, rates might become unfairly high for good drivers. In effect, good drivers could be subsidizing rates for the high-risk drivers that insurers are required to insure.
- Compulsory insurance laws do not prevent or reduce the number of automobile accidents. This argument expresses one of the most serious problems associated with automobile insurance.

> **Compulsory auto insurance law**
>
> Law that requires the owners or operators of automobiles to carry automobile liability insurance at least equal to certain minimum limits before the vehicle can be licensed or registered.

Several states have implemented measures intended to respond to the disadvantages of compulsory insurance. Such measures include low-cost policies; no pay, no play laws; and unsatisfied judgment funds.

Low-cost auto insurance is intended to decrease the number of uninsured drivers by making minimal liability coverage available at a reduced cost. In New Jersey, for example, a basic policy offers $15,000 in personal injury protection, up to $250,000 in medical benefits for catastrophic injuries, and $5,000 property damage liability. Uninsured motorists, underinsured motorists, and physical damage coverages are not available. In Colorado, a low-cost plan provides **first party** medical expense or personal injury protection coverage with a maximum benefit of $25,000. A program in California offers bodily injury liability coverage up to $10,000 per person and $20,000 per accident.[1] Low-cost insurance programs are intended to provide some level of protection at a reduced cost to assist lower-income drivers in purchasing the insurance coverage required to comply with compulsory auto insurance laws.

No pay, no play laws prohibit uninsured drivers from initiating lawsuits for noneconomic damages, such as pain and suffering.[2] Only a few states have such laws, and some of those laws apply not only to uninsured drivers, but also to those driving under the influence of alcohol or using a vehicle while committing a felony.

A few other states have established **unsatisfied judgment funds**, which have these characteristics:

- An injured person can receive compensation from the fund after having obtained a judgment against a negligent driver and proving that the judgment cannot be collected.
- The maximum amount paid is generally limited to the state's minimum compulsory insurance requirement. In addition, most funds reduce the amount paid by any amount the injured person has collected from other collateral sources of recovery, such as workers compensation benefits or insurance.
- The negligent driver is not relieved of legal liability when the unsatisfied judgment fund compensates the insured person. The negligent driver's license is revoked until the driver reimburses the fund.

Unsatisfied judgment funds offer the advantage of providing injured accident victims some protection against irresponsible motorists. In addition, states with such funds attempt to keep uninsured drivers off the road by suspending their driver's licenses until they reimburse the unsatisfied judgment fund.

Uninsured Motorists Coverage

Uninsured motorists (UM) coverage compensates an insured for bodily injury caused by an uninsured motorist, a hit-and-run driver, or a driver whose insurer is insolvent. UM insurance is mandatory in many states and optional

---

First party
The insured in an insurance contract.

Unsatisfied judgment fund
A fund designed to provide a source of recovery for victims of motor vehicle accidents when an at-fault motorist is unable to pay any judgment.

Uninsured motorists (UM) coverage
Coverage that provides a source of recovery for occupants of a covered auto or for qualifying pedestrians who are injured in an accident caused by an at-fault motorist who does not have the state minimum liability insurance or by a hit-and-run driver.

in the rest. Most states require that all automobile liability policies contain UM coverage unless the insured voluntarily waives the coverage in writing.

Because compulsory insurance laws have not substantially reduced the number of uninsured drivers, there is the potential for unreimbursed losses if a driver is involved in an auto accident with an uninsured at-fault driver. UM coverage is an approach to compensating such auto accident victims that can be used to provide some financial protection against uninsured drivers.

UM coverage, however, has several disadvantages:

- As with other compensation methods, an injured person may not be fully compensated for his or her economic loss. Unless the insured has purchased higher UM limits, the maximum paid for a bodily injury claim is limited to the state's financial responsibility or compulsory insurance law requirement.
- Before an injured person can collect under UM coverage, the uninsured motorist's legal responsibility for the accident must be established. This can be difficult to establish in some cases and may involve legal proceedings, adding to the expense.
- Property damage is excluded in many states. In such states, for example, if a negligent uninsured motorist fails to stop for a red light and damages another car, the owner of the damaged car would collect nothing under the UM coverage. In some states, UM property damage coverage can be added at the insured's option.
- The victim is paying for insurance to protect against the failure of others to act responsibly. In effect, UM insurance provides coverage similar to the liability insurance that the negligent party failed to buy.

Underinsured Motorists Coverage

Underinsured motorists (UIM) coverage provides additional limits of protection to the victim of an auto accident when the negligent driver's insurance limits are insufficient to pay for the damages. UIM coverage can be added by endorsement to an automobile insurance policy and in some states is included automatically.

Although underinsured motorists insurance is sometimes combined with uninsured motorists insurance, the two coverages should not be confused. They do not overlap or duplicate each other. An insured can collect under one coverage or the other, depending on the situation, but not both. UM coverage applies when bodily injury is caused by an uninsured motorist, a hit-and-run driver, or a driver whose insurer is insolvent. In contrast, UIM coverage applies only when the at-fault driver has liability insurance with lower liability limits than the limits provided by the injured person's UIM coverage. UIM coverage can be triggered based on whether the losses are greater than the at-fault driver's liability limits (a damages trigger) or when

Underinsured motorists (UIM) coverage
Coverage that applies when a negligent driver has liability insurance at the time of the accident but has limits lower than those of the injured person's coverage.

those liability limits are lower than the injured person's UIM coverage (a limits trigger).

As with UM coverage, underinsured motorists coverage assists in compensating auto accident victims who would not be fully compensated otherwise. In this way, UIM coverage addresses one of the disadvantages of compulsory auto insurance. While limits may still be insufficient, it does offer some level of increased protection.

A disadvantage is that even the underinsured coverage may be insufficient to cover all costs. Also, the victim is paying for insurance to protect against the failure of others to act responsibly and to carry sufficient liability limits.

No-Fault Automobile Insurance

No-fault automobile insurance is another approach for compensating auto accident victims. Many states have no-fault auto insurance laws that restrict the filing of lawsuits against at-fault drivers. Other states allow some type of first-party automobile insurance but do not restrict lawsuits.

Under a no-fault system, an injured person does not need to establish fault and prove negligence in order to collect payment for damages. In addition, certain no-fault laws place some restrictions on an injured person's right to sue a negligent driver who causes an accident. In some states, when a claim is below a certain monetary threshold, the injured motorist collects for injuries under his or her own insurance policy.

No-fault laws were developed to avoid the costly and time-consuming process of determining legal liability for auto accidents under the tort liability system. By eliminating the need to prove fault, no-fault laws allow accident victims to receive benefits much sooner after an accident and, as a result, may allow for a quicker recovery from injuries. Because no-fault laws limit the number of lawsuits that result from auto accidents, the burden on the state's court system is reduced, as are overall costs.

No-fault laws were developed to correct what was perceived as serious defects in the tort liability system based on fault. Proponents of such laws cite these as advantages of no-fault laws:

- They eliminate the need to determine fault. Following an auto accident, determining who is at fault is often difficult, especially when more than one driver has contributed to the accident.
- They eliminate inequities in claim payments. Those who favor no-fault laws argue that the tort liability system results in claim payment inequities. Small claims may be overpaid, and claims involving serious injuries may be underpaid.
- They expand the limited scope of the tort system. Many persons injured in auto accidents or the beneficiaries of those killed in auto accidents do

> **No-fault automobile insurance**
>
> Insurance that covers automobile accident victims on a first-party basis, allowing them to collect damages from their own insurers regardless of who was at fault.

not collect, or collect less than their full economic loss, under the current tort liability system.
- They decrease the proportion of premium dollars used for claim investigation and legal costs. Under the tort liability system, a large proportion of the liability coverage premium dollar is used to pay for attorneys, claim investigation expenses, and other costs of determining fault.
- They reduce delays in payments. Many claims take months or even years to settle under the tort liability system, which often involves lengthy court trials and delays in the legal system.

Supporters of the tort liability system, however, present various potential disadvantages of no-fault laws:

- Assertions of premium savings and expense reductions are overstated and unreliable. Auto insurance premiums have not decreased significantly and, in some cases, have increased in states that have implemented no-fault plans.
- No-fault insurance may penalize safe drivers. The rating system used for no-fault insurance may unfairly allocate accident costs to the drivers who are not responsible for the accidents, thus increasing premiums for good drivers.
- No-fault benefits do not include payment for pain and suffering. Attorneys representing injured auto accident victims argue that the dollar amount of medical expenses and lost wages does not always represent the true loss to the victim, because the amount does not include damages for pain and suffering.
- No-fault benefits may increase fraud. In states with stated monetary thresholds, some physicians, lawyers, and other professionals abuse the system by inflating fees charged for services or charging for unnecessary services and procedures so that the claim exceeds the threshold. These actions lead to higher auto insurance costs for all policyholders.[3]

NO-FAULT AUTOMOBILE LAWS

Roughly one-half of the states in the United States have auto no-fault laws, which allow auto accident victims to collect first-party benefits from their own insurers.

No-fault laws authorize or mandate auto no-fault insurance—often referred to as personal injury protection (PIP)—and they define the benefits that insurers can or must provide. Thus, insurers in no-fault states often avoid the costly and time-consuming process of determining legal responsibility for auto accidents and instead handle claims quickly so that injured persons can be compensated for their medical expenses and lost wages.

No-fault laws

State statutes that require motorists to purchase (or require insurers to make available) insurance that provides minimum first-party benefits to injured persons regardless of fault.

Types of No-Fault Laws

Early proponents of no-fault insurance anticipated a system using a pure no-fault law. Under this system, an injured person would not need to establish fault and prove negligence in order to collect payment for damages, regardless of the injury's severity. A pure no-fault system would abolish use of the tort liability system for bodily injuries resulting from auto accidents. Opponents of a pure no-fault system argue that it would unfairly eliminate the right to certain legal actions; consequently, no state has yet enacted a pure no-fault law. Instead, certain states have enacted differing versions of no-fault laws, which prescribe one of three basic types of no-fault plans:

- Modified no-fault plans
- Add-on plans
- Choice no-fault plans

Modified No-Fault Plans

About half of the states with no-fault laws have modified no-fault plans. In contrast to pure no-fault plans, modified no-fault plans place some restrictions on the right to sue an at-fault driver but do not entirely eliminate the right.

Under a modified no-fault plan, injured motorists collect economic losses (such as medical expenses and lost wages) from their own insurers through the PIP benefits mandated by the plan. After collecting economic losses through their no-fault coverage, injured persons can sue at-fault drivers for any economic losses that exceed the no-fault coverage limits. For example, in a state that has a modified no-fault plan, John carries the minimum PIP medical coverage limit of $10,000 set by the plan. He is injured by an at-fault driver and incurs $25,000 in medical expenses. Because John's economic losses exceed the $10,000 limit, he has the right to sue the at-fault driver for the $15,000 of medical expenses that exceed the PIP medical coverage limit.

Additionally, injured motorists can sue at-fault drivers for noneconomic losses (such as pain and suffering, emotional distress, and disfigurement) if their injuries exceed a threshold stated in the law. The threshold can be either a **monetary threshold** (also called a dollar threshold) or a **verbal threshold**.

Monetary threshold (dollar threshold)

In a no-fault system, a dollar limit in total medical expenses an injured victim must exceed before he or she is permitted to sue the other party.

Verbal threshold

In a no-fault system, the designated criteria that are verbally "set forth in the statute that limit the right to sue."

When a monetary threshold applies, an injured motorist (or his or her survivors) can sue for noneconomic losses if the economic losses exceed a stated dollar amount. For example, in a state that has a modified no-fault plan with a monetary threshold of $5,000, Sally is injured by an at-fault driver. She incurs $3,000 in medical expenses and loses $4,000 in wages. Because Sally's economic losses exceed the $5,000 threshold, she has the right to sue the at-fault driver for any noneconomic losses she might have suffered.

When a verbal threshold applies, an injured motorist (or his or her survivors) can sue for noneconomic losses if his or her injuries meet a verbal description of serious injuries. Examples of injuries commonly described in verbal thresholds include death, permanent disfigurement or scarring, significant and permanent loss of a bodily function, and significant and permanent injury. Verbal thresholds sometimes specify a minimum disability period (the number of days the injured person has been disabled because of the accident) before the injured person can sue for damages.

Add-On Plans

An **add-on plan** is appropriately named because it adds no-fault benefits to auto insurance policies, but it differs from a modified no-fault plan because it places no restrictions on the injured person's right to sue a negligent party for damages. An add-on plan offers the insured the option of collecting for economic losses through his or her own insurer. For example, one state's add-on plan allows optional first-party coverage for medical expenses and loss of income, but the insured retains the right to seek compensation from the negligent driver. Under this law, all insurers that sell auto insurance in that state must offer every auto policyholder this coverage, but policyholders are not obligated to purchase it. In some other states with add-on plans, no-fault benefits must be purchased by all insureds.

Add-on plan

In a no-fault system, a plan that provides certain personal injury protection (PIP)-type benefits such as medical payments and disability coverages to injured victims, without regard to fault.

Choice No-Fault Plans

Under a **choice no-fault plan**, when an auto insurance policy is purchased or renewed, the insured can choose whether to be covered on a modified no-fault basis or not. In most states with choice no-fault plans, insureds who choose not to be covered on a modified no-fault basis must purchase add-on no-fault coverages. The modified no-fault option provides premium reductions in return for limitations on the right to sue for damages for certain types of auto injuries. If modified no-fault coverage is not selected, the insured retains full rights to seek compensation from the negligent party, but the insurer charges a higher premium. See the exhibit "Right to Sue in No-Fault Plans."

Choice no-fault plan

In a no-fault system, a plan that gives the insured the option, at the time an auto insurance policy is purchased or renewed, of choosing whether to be covered on a no-fault basis.

Right to Sue in No-Fault Plans

Type of Plan	Restrictions on Right to Sue?
Modified No-Fault Plans	Yes
Add-On Plans	No
Choice No-Fault Plans	Only if modified no-fault is selected

[DA00589]

Benefits Required by No-Fault Laws

Benefits required by no-fault laws typically include these:

- Medical expenses—usually subject to a limit
- Rehabilitation expenses—usually paid in addition to medical expenses
- Loss of earnings—a proportion of the insured person's lost earnings (usually subject to a maximum amount and time limit)
- Expenses for essential services—benefits paid for expenses incurred in obtaining services for necessary household tasks the injured person normally performs but now cannot
- Funeral expenses—usually paid up to a certain limit (sometimes included in the medical expense limit)
- Survivors' loss benefits—periodic income payments that partially compensate certain survivors for the death of a covered auto accident victim

Insurers provide no-fault benefits by adding an endorsement to an auto insurance policy, typically called a PIP endorsement (or, in some states, "basic reparations"). The coverage provided by no-fault insurance is called **personal injury protection (PIP) coverage**. PIP endorsements vary by state, and in some states the no-fault laws specify precise policy language to be used in the endorsement.

Nearly all no-fault laws specify coverage only for bodily injury. No-fault laws generally exclude property damage for several reasons: property damage amounts are relatively small and damages are usually confined to vehicles; the amount of damage to property can usually be determined without difficulty; and auto insurers can usually settle claims for damage to their insureds' property quickly. See the exhibit "Efforts to Combat PIP Fraud."

> **Personal injury protection (PIP) coverage**
> Coverage that pays benefits, regardless of fault, for medical expense, income loss, and other benefits, resulting from bodily injury to occupants of a covered auto.

Efforts to Combat PIP Fraud

PIP coverage in some states has been exploited by fraud rings. Fictitious pain clinics and corrupt medical and legal professionals have collaborated to assist many insureds in filing fraudulent PIP claims. Legislatures in various states are exploring revisions to no-fault laws that will curtail such claims. Among changes being considered is one that would reduce time frames for reporting auto accidents (sometimes sixty days) to allow insurers to review treatment plans earlier and avoid unnecessary treatments. Some states impose precertification guidelines for treatment of certain injuries, particularly soft tissue damage. The use of verbal rather than monetary thresholds helps avoid driving up medical costs unnecessarily.

[DA05496]

Some states require that insurers offer (for an additional premium) optional benefits higher than the minimum prescribed by no-fault laws. Additionally, some states require insurers to provide optional deductibles, allowing insureds to reduce or eliminate certain no-fault benefits for a reduced premium.

No-fault laws typically allow the no-fault insurer to collect payment (through **subrogation**) from at-fault parties to the extent that no-fault benefits were paid. Often, the insurer can require reimbursement of benefits it has paid to the insured if the insured subsequently recovers from the responsible party through legal action. Provisions for recovery under a no-fault law are described in the law and vary among states.

AUTOMOBILE INSURANCE FOR HIGH-RISK DRIVERS

High-risk drivers include those who habitually violate traffic laws, those who have been responsible for an excessive number of traffic accidents, and those who have been convicted of certain serious offenses, such as reckless driving, driving with a suspended license, or driving under the influence of alcohol or drugs. Insuring these individuals is extremely difficult for private insurers because of the high probability of a high-risk driver seriously injuring or killing other persons and causing extensive property damage.

Private insurers willingly insure drivers with average and above average driving records. Increasingly, private insurers also willingly accept some drivers with below average driving records in specialized high-risk driver programs. For those drivers who cannot obtain insurance from private insurers in this voluntary market, states have created mechanisms to make insurance available in a **residual market** (also called the shared market).

Voluntary Market Programs

Some insurers in the voluntary market offer insurance programs for high-risk drivers (often called nonstandard insurance programs). In contrast to insurers in the residual market, these voluntary insurers accept their own applications, service their policies, pay their claims and expenses, and retain full responsibility for their own underwriting results.

Because high-risk drivers are more likely to have accidents than other drivers, insurers that offer high-risk driver programs in the voluntary market may impose special restrictions and take other measures to reduce the risk to an acceptable level. Consequently, insurance in high-risk driver programs generally has several common characteristics:

- In many cases, private insurers limit coverage amounts to those that comply with the state's financial responsibility or compulsory insurance requirement. In some cases, private insurers offer optional higher limits.
- Medical payments coverage may be limited.
- Collision insurance may be available only with a high deductible.
- Premiums are substantially higher than premiums charged for average and above-average drivers.

Subrogation
The process by which an insurer can, after it has paid a loss under the policy, recover the amount paid from any party (other than the insured) who caused the loss or is otherwise legally liable for the loss.

Residual market
The term referring collectively to insurers and other organizations that make insurance available through a shared risk mechanism to those who cannot obtain coverage in the admitted market.

Safe driver insurance plan (SDIP)
Plan that allows for lower basic premiums for accident-free driving records and a surcharge for accidents.

Many voluntary insurers offering high-risk driver programs encourage insureds to drive responsibly through **safe driver insurance plans (SDIPs)**. Under these plans, premium credits are given to insureds who have no auto accidents or traffic convictions within a specified time period; however, insureds who incur traffic convictions or have at-fault accidents must pay higher premiums.

Residual Market Programs

States have developed various programs for high-risk drivers in the residual market, including these:

- Automobile insurance plans
- Joint underwriting associations (JUAs)
- Other programs

Automobile Insurance Plans

Automobile insurance plan
Plan for insuring high-risk drivers in which all auto insurers doing business in the state are assigned their proportionate share of such drivers based on the total volume of auto insurance written in the state.

Most states offer an **automobile insurance plan**, often called an assigned risk plan, for high-risk drivers who cannot obtain auto insurance in the voluntary market. Under a state's automobile insurance plan, all auto insurers doing business in the state are assigned their proportionate share of high-risk drivers based on the total volume of auto insurance written in the state. For example, an insurer that writes 10 percent of all the auto insurance in a state would be assigned 10 percent of the state's high-risk drivers.

Although state automobile insurance plans vary, they usually have common characteristics:

- Applicants must show that they have been unable to obtain auto liability insurance within a certain number of days (usually sixty) of the application.
- The minimum limits of insurance offered are at least equal to the state's financial responsibility or compulsory insurance requirement. (Most plans offer optional higher limits, as well as medical payments and physical damage coverages.)
- Certain applicants may be ineligible for coverage, such as those who do not have a valid driver's license, those convicted of a felony within the preceding thirty-six months, and habitual violators of state and local laws.
- Premiums are generally higher than premiums in the voluntary market. High-risk drivers are rated on the basis of their driving records and are charged accordingly.

While states use the term "assigned risk" to describe automobile insurance plans, most insurers no longer use or recommend that term. Insurers prefer to avoid negative characterization of their high-risk drivers for marketing purposes. Such insureds' driving habits may improve over time, and insurers may want to retain this newly profitable business.

Joint Underwriting Associations (JUAs)

Instead of offering an automobile insurance plan, several states have established **joint underwriting associations (JUAs)** to make auto insurance available to high-risk drivers. A JUA sets the insurance rates and approves the policy forms to be used for high-risk drivers. Although JUAs vary by state, generally a limited number of insurers are designated as servicing insurers to handle high-risk business.

Agents and brokers submit applications of high-risk drivers to the JUA or to a designated servicing insurer. The servicing insurer usually receives applications, issues policies, collects premiums, settles claims, and provides other necessary services.

In a state that offers a JUA, all auto insurers pay a proportionate share of total underwriting losses and expenses based on each insurer's share of voluntary auto insurance written in the state, a portion of which can be used to compensate the servicing insurers. For example, an insurer that writes 12 percent of all of the voluntary auto insurance in a particular state must pay 12 percent of the underwriting losses experienced by the JUA and 12 percent of the expenses, even though it is not required to insure high-risk drivers.

> **Joint underwriting association (JUA)**
> Organization that designates servicing insurers to handle high-risk auto insurance business; all auto insurers in the state are assessed a proportionate share of the losses and expenses based on their percentage of the voluntary auto insurance premiums written in the state.

Other Programs

A few states have enacted laws to establish a special **reinsurance facility** for high-risk drivers. Under this pool arrangement, insurers accept all auto insurance applicants who have a valid driver's license; the insurers issue policies, collect premiums, and settle claims. However, if an applicant for auto insurance is considered a high-risk driver, the insurer has the option of assigning the driver's premiums and losses to the reinsurance facility while continuing to service the policy. All auto insurers doing business in the state share any underwriting losses and the expenses of the reinsurance facility in proportion to the total auto insurance that they write in that state.

One state (Maryland) has established a state fund mechanism that provides insurance to high-risk applicants. Under this program, the state owns the fund but requires all private insurers to subsidize any losses; the private insurers, in turn, can recover those losses by surcharging their own insureds.

> **Reinsurance facility**
> A state-wide reinsurance pool to which insurers can assign premiums and losses for high-risk drivers; original insurers service the policies, but all insurers in the pool share the losses and expenses of the facility in proportion to the total auto insurance they write in that state.

AUTOMOBILE INSURANCE RATE REGULATION

All of the states in the United States require drivers to comply with state compulsory auto insurance laws or financial responsibility laws in exchange for the privilege to legally operate an auto. For most drivers, purchasing auto insurance is the only practical way to meet those requirements; therefore, the public often perceives purchasing insurance as a right rather than a privilege. Auto insurers are in business to make a profit, and this goal of profitability can conflict with the public's perceived right to buy insurance. Government regulation of insurance rates helps resolve this conflict.

State rating laws vary, but they generally require insurers to use rates that are adequate to pay all claims and expenses, reasonable (not excessive) for the exposure presented, and not unfairly discriminatory. In requiring adequate and reasonable rates, regulators must balance the concerns of insurers and consumers. Unfair discrimination occurs when an insurer applies different standards or treatment to insureds that present objectively similar loss potential. An example of unfair discrimination in auto insurance rating would be charging higher-than-normal rates for an applicant based solely on the applicant's race, religion, or ethnic background.

In applying the preceding requirements, auto insurance rate regulation is concerned with several issues:

- Rating factors
- Matching price to exposure
- Competition
- Other regulatory issues

Rating Factors

Rating systems vary by state and also by insurer. The rating of personal auto insurance is often computerized, but insurers decide which rating factors will be automated. All rating factors and discounts and credits reflect a change in the frequency and/or severity of a loss or in some way affect the cost of providing insurance.

Primary Rating Factors

Primary rating factors are the major factors that most states and insurers use for determining the cost of personal auto insurance. Although these factors have been used for many years in rating auto insurance, several states no longer permit the use of some factors that they consider unfairly discriminatory, such as age and gender. Primary rating factors include these:

- Territory—Determined by where the auto is normally used and garaged (parked overnight), territory is usually defined by the location of the insured's residence. Rural territories often have lower rates than urban territories because loss frequency and claim expenses tend to be higher in cities. Road conditions, state safety laws, and the extent of traffic regulation are territorial factors that affect the frequency and severity of auto accidents.
- Use of the auto—Insurers normally classify each insured auto for its principal use. Typical "use" categories include pleasure, driving to work or school, business, and farm use. Rates are generally lowest for farm and highest for business use, reflecting typical accident statistics.

- Age—Young drivers have less driving experience and tend to be involved in accidents more frequently than older drivers. Therefore, rates for younger drivers are often higher than those for more experienced drivers.
- Gender—In the past, women have tended to have fewer accidents than men in the same age categories, particularly among youthful drivers, so rates are often lower for women than for men. However, this tendency is changing as women's driving habits change.
- Marital status—Young married men tend to have fewer accidents than young unmarried men, and rates often reflect this tendency for this category of insureds.

Other Rating Factors

In addition to primary rating factors, other factors also affect loss statistics. Typically, these factors are not essential in determining the rating classification. Other rating factors that personal auto insurers use include these:

- Driving record—Almost all insurers use an applicant's driving record to determine whether the individual presents an acceptable exposure and, if acceptable, at what rate. Many insurers have safe driver insurance plans (SDIPs) that base premiums on the insured's driving record.
- Driver education—A premium discount may be provided for young drivers who complete an approved driver education course, usually including road experience. Also, some insurers offer premium discounts to drivers age fifty-five and older who successfully complete defensive driver training courses. Driver training can help reduce the frequency and severity of auto losses.
- Good student—Students who maintain good grades may be offered premium discounts because, theoretically, they have fewer accidents than poor or average students.
- Multi-car policy—Most insurers give a multi-car discount when more than one auto is insured under the same policy. This discount is based on the assumption that two or more autos owned by the same insured will not be driven as often as a single auto. Additionally, it is less costly for the insurer to cover additional autos under the same contract, so savings may be passed to the insured.
- Years of driving experience—Generally, drivers with more years of experience make fewer mistakes and have fewer accidents.
- Credit-based insurance score—Some insurers consider an applicant's insurance score. This numerical ranking is similar to a credit score, but without income data, and is based on information from an individual's financial history. Actuarial research indicates that insureds with low insurance scores submit more claims than insureds with high insurance scores. Some states consider insurance scores unfairly discriminatory and do not allow them as a rating factor.

- Type of auto—The performance, age, and damageability of an auto can affect the rates for physical damage coverage on it. For example, a new sports car would cost more to insure for collision coverage and possibly for liability coverage than an older station wagon because the sports car would be more expensive to repair, might be damaged more easily, and is more likely to be operated in an unsafe manner.
- Deductibles—Insureds who choose higher deductibles for collision and other physical damage coverage on their autos can receive a credit, sometimes a significant one, because the insured retains a portion of covered losses.
- Liability limits—Rates are generally based on the minimum liability limits required by the state, and premiums increase if the insured chooses higher limits. (However, doubling liability limits does not mean doubling the premium, and higher limits are often a bargain compared to minimum limits.)

Other Discounts and Credits

Some insurers also give discounts or credits for certain automobile features or practices of the insured that reduce insurer costs:

- Anti-theft devices can reduce the frequency of theft losses.
- Passive restraints (airbags) can reduce the severity of injuries.
- Reduced auto use by a student who attends a school that is more than a specified distance from home and does not garage an insured auto at school can reduce the frequency of losses.
- Having more than one type of policy with the same insurer (called a multi-policy or multi-account discount) reduces administrative costs.
- Multiple years of continuous coverage with the insurer (called a renewal or anniversary discount) reduces acquisition costs.

Factors That Affect Auto Insurance Rates

Primary factors:
- Territory
- Use of auto
- Age
- Gender
- Marital status

Other factors:
- Driving record
- Driver education
- Good student
- Multi-car policy
- Years of driving experience
- Credit-based insurance score
- Type of auto
- Deductibles
- Liability limits

[DA05737]

Matching Price to Exposure

Insurers often divide auto insurance applicants into homogeneous classes, or rating categories, such as "preferred," "standard," and "nonstandard," that reflect different levels of exposure to loss. For example, applicants with good driving records and rating factors that suggest they present minimal loss exposure are categorized as preferred. By offering lower rates to this category of insureds, insurers hope to attract and retain good customers. Conversely, applicants with poor driving records or rating factors that suggest they present greater loss exposure are categorized as nonstandard and are charged higher rates. Usually insurers also have a standard rating category for drivers that fall between these two extremes and present an average loss exposure.

Regulators usually approve these rating categories because policyholders receive equitable treatment based on the loss exposures they present.

Competition

Competition for profitable automobile business is often intense among insurers. When insurers are making a profit, they often compete with each other by lowering rates. However, insurers cannot decrease rates to the point at which they can no longer cover the costs of claims and expenses. In times of high underwriting losses and low profits, insurers must raise rates, restrict the number and types of new applicants they will accept, or take other steps to become more profitable.

Because of this tendency of insurers to consider competitive cycles in pricing personal auto insurance, regulators monitor rates carefully to ensure adequacy and reasonableness. Insurance regulators monitor rates primarily through rate filings, which are the documentation that an insurer files with a state to request a change in existing rates. Insurers' rates must always meet the state requirements that rates must be adequate, reasonable, and not unfairly discriminatory.

Other Regulatory Issues

Many other regulatory issues, such as these, affect auto insurance coverages and rates:

- Rising healthcare costs
- Environmental issues
- Vehicle modifications

Rising Healthcare Costs

Increases in automobile insurance rates can often be linked to that portion of the premium linked to healthcare costs. One component of auto insurance coverage is personal injury protection (PIP), which pays the healthcare bills for individuals injured in auto accidents.

Each year, more than two million American motorists suffer personal injuries from auto accidents, with about 38,000 dying in auto accidents.[4] Costs for treating these accident victims are rising rapidly, translating into higher auto insurance premiums. Costs for treating an auto accident victim range from $6,000 to $9,000 and can total tens of thousands of dollars.[5]

The increasing cost of healthcare in the U.S. places great strains on all systems used to finance healthcare coverage, including auto insurance as well as private employer-sponsored and public health insurance coverage. To illustrate, healthcare costs in the United States in 2007 totaled more than three times the 1990 total and over eight times the 1980 costs.[6] These costs directly affect not only the medical payments/PIP side of premiums, but also liability payments and uninsured motorists coverage.

Environmental Issues

Environmental issues can affect auto insurance coverages and rates because automobiles are a primary source of pollution emissions. Most environmental laws affecting auto insurance are state regulations. State emissions regulations, for example, increase auto costs and result in higher claim payments for more expensive autos.

As another example of environmental issues affecting auto insurance costs, California's "pay-as-you-drive" regulation enables insurers to offer consumers rates that are based on actual instead of estimated miles driven. This program provides financial incentives for California motorists to drive less, leading to lower-cost auto insurance, less air pollution through lower auto exhaust emissions, and a reduced dependence on foreign oil.[7] Because of increased concern about the environmental effects of auto use, the future may hold more state-based environmental regulations that not only curb pollution but also affect auto insurance rates.

Vehicle Modifications

The growing vehicle modification business adds performance parts and styling features that can affect auto insurance rates. Whatever the reason for the modifications (which can range from personal styling preferences to handicap access equipment), features must conform to local or regional vehicle standard regulations. However, compliance for some modifications is not always easy to detect or enforce. Such modifications as a lowered or raised suspension, increased engine size, and tinted windows can increase risk and insurance premiums because modifications can put insureds at a greater risk of collision. A modified vehicle can become untrustworthy and affect safety as well as auto insurance rates.

Even modifications that would appear to create safer vehicles, like improved brake systems, can increase insurance costs for several reasons:

- Modifications can increase auto values and, as a result, insurers' claim payments.
- Modified autos can attract thieves, also increasing insurers' claim payments.
- Auto performance modifications improve auto performance, which can result in more severe accidents.

SUMMARY

Victims of auto accidents caused by the negligence of another party are entitled to compensation and damages. Some of the approaches to compensating auto accident victims include these:

- Tort liability system
- Financial responsibility laws
- Compulsory insurance laws
- Uninsured motorists coverage
- Underinsured motorists coverage
- No-fault insurance

Roughly one-half of the states in the U.S. have no-fault laws that authorize or mandate one of three types of auto no-fault insurance plans: modified no-fault plans, add-on plans, and choice no-fault plans. These plans define the benefits that insurers can or must provide and define any restrictions on the right to sue the at-fault party.

Some high-risk drivers can purchase auto insurance from private insurers in the voluntary market that offer high-risk driver insurance programs. Other high-risk drivers can usually purchase insurance in residual market programs, which include automobile insurance plans, joint underwriting associations (JUAs), reinsurance facilities, and state funds. These programs share many common characteristics, and all require higher premiums than standard auto insurance to offset potential underwriting losses and expenses.

State insurance regulators require auto insurers to develop rates that are adequate to pay all claims and expenses, reasonable (not excessive) for the exposure presented, and not unfairly discriminatory. Insurers develop rating factors that conform to these requirements, and state regulators ensure that insurers apply rating categories that match the price of auto insurance to the appropriate level of loss exposure. Because insurers consider competitive cycles in pricing personal auto insurance, regulators monitor rates carefully to ensure adequacy and reasonableness. Other regulator and rating issues include the effects of rising healthcare costs on auto insurance rates, environmental issues, and vehicle modifications.

ASSIGNMENT NOTES

1. Insurance Information Institute, *Issues Updates*, November 2007, www.iii.org (accessed December 17, 2007).
2. Insurance Information Institute, *Issues Updates*, November 2007, www.iii.org (accessed December 17, 2007).
3. Insurance Information Institute, *No Fault Auto Insurance*, October 2007, www.iii.org (accessed January 28, 2008).
4. National Highway Traffic Safety Administration, www-nrd.nhtsa.dot.gov/Pubs/811162.PDF (accessed February 3, 2010).
5. Insurance Information Institute, http://huetherinsurance.com/PDF%20Files/Auto%20Rates%20on%20the%20Rise.pdf (accessed February 4, 2010).
6. The Kaiser Family Foundation, www.kaiseredu.org/topics_im.asp?imID=1&parentID=61&id=358 (accessed February 3, 2010).
7. "California Issues Regulations for Pay-As-You-Drive," *Insurance Journal*, www.insurancejournal.com/news/west/2009/09/10/103600.htm (accessed February 3, 2010).

Direct Your Learning

3

Personal Auto Policy: Liability, Med Pay, and UM Coverage

Educational Objectives

After learning the content of this assignment, you should be able to:

- Summarize the sections of the Personal Auto Policy.
- Identify the types of information typically contained on the Declarations page of the Personal Auto Policy.
- Define the words and phrases included in the Definitions section of the Personal Auto Policy.
- Summarize each of the provisions in Part A—Liability Coverage of the Personal Auto Policy.
- Given a case describing an auto liability claim, determine whether Part A—Liability Coverage of the Personal Auto Policy would cover the claim and, if so, the amount the insurer would pay for the claim.
- Summarize each of the provisions in Part B—Medical Payments Coverage of the Personal Auto Policy.
- Given a case describing an auto medical payments claim, determine whether Part B—Medical Payments Coverage of the Personal Auto Policy would cover the claim and, if so, the amount the insurer would pay for the claim.
- Summarize each of the provisions in Part C—Uninsured Motorists Coverage of the Personal Auto Policy.
- Describe underinsured motorists insurance in terms of:
  - Its purpose
  - The ways in which it can vary by state

Outline

Overview of the Personal Auto Policy

Declarations

Definitions

Part A—Liability Coverage

Part A—Liability Coverage Case Study

Part B—Medical Payments Coverage

Part B—Medical Payments Coverage Case Study

Part C—Uninsured Motorists Coverage

UM/UIM Endorsements and State Variations

Part C—Uninsured Motorists Coverage Case Study

Summary

Educational Objectives, continued

- Given a case describing an uninsured motorists claim, determine whether Part C—Uninsured Motorists Coverage of the Personal Auto Policy would cover the claim and, if so, the amount the insurer would pay for the claim.

Personal Auto Policy: Liability, Med Pay, and UM Coverage

OVERVIEW OF THE PERSONAL AUTO POLICY

Many auto owners in the United States use some form of the Insurance Services Office, Inc. (ISO) Personal Auto Policy (PAP) to insure their personal auto loss exposures.

The PAP is designed to insure private passenger autos—vehicles such as cars, vans, station wagons, and sport utility vehicles designed primarily for use on public roads—as well as pickup trucks and full-size vans.

The PAP consists of a Declarations page, an Agreement and Definitions page, and six separate sections. Almost all PAPs also include one or more endorsements to comply with state-specific requirements or to meet specific coverage needs of some insureds.

These are the six sections:

- Part A—Liability Coverage
- Part B—Medical Payments Coverage
- Part C—Uninsured Motorists Coverage
- Part D—Damage to Your Auto Coverage
- Part E—Insured Duties Following an Accident or Loss
- Part F—General Provisions

Declarations

The Declarations page includes general information, such as the name and mailing address of the insured. This page also provides the name of the insurer issuing the policy and the name and address of the producer, if applicable. Other information on the Declarations page includes the policy period, a description of the covered autos, limits of liability, premium and rating information, and any endorsements that may apply to the policy.

Agreement and Definitions

The Agreement and Definitions page of the PAP includes a general agreement stating that the insurer is providing the coverage subject to payment of premium and to the terms of the policy. The definitions section uses simple-to-understand language to define important words and phrases that are used throughout the policy.

Overview of Coverages

The PAP coverages may be summarized in this fashion:

- Part A—Liability Coverage protects the insured against claims or lawsuits for bodily injury or property damage arising out of the operation of an auto.
- Part B—Medical Payments Coverage compensates for reasonable and necessary medical and funeral expenses because of bodily injury to the insured caused by an auto accident.
- Part C—Uninsured Motorists Coverage pays damages if an insured is injured by an uninsured motorist, a hit-and-run driver, or a driver whose insurer is insolvent.
- Part D—Coverage for Damage to Your Auto compensates for physical damage to a covered auto and to certain nonowned autos. Also referred to as physical damage coverage, Part D includes other than collision and collision coverages. Some insureds elect not to include physical damage coverage on their policies.
- Part E—Duties After an Accident or Loss outlines the duties required of an insured after an accident or a loss, such as requirements for notifying the insurer of the details of any losses that happen.
- Part F—General Provisions contains information such as how changes to the policy can be made, provisions for cancellation and termination of the policy, and descriptions of the policy period and territory.

Endorsements

In addition to the PAP coverage form, the policy also includes state-specific endorsements. These endorsements are usually used to adapt the PAP to state-specific laws and regulations applying to auto insurance. Endorsements are also available to provide additional coverages that are desired by some policyholders but are not purchased by all policyholders. These endorsements are separate from the PAP coverage form but must be considered as part of the overall structure of a PAP. See the exhibit "Overview of the Personal Auto Policy."

Overview of the Personal Auto Policy

Insured Risk	Peril (Cause of Loss)	Consequences	Treatment
Personal Auto	Accident with another vehicle	Damage to the "Other" vehicle; Financial—cost of repairs	PAP—Part A: Liability Coverage
Personal Auto	Accident with another vehicle	Injury to driver and/or passengers; Financial—costs of medical	PAP—Part B: Medical Payments Coverage
Personal Auto	Accident with another vehicle	Injury from uninsured or underinsured motorist; Financial—costs of medical, loss of wages, pain and suffering	PAP—Part C: Uninsured Motorists Coverage
Personal Auto	Accident with another vehicle	Damage to "Your" vehicle; Financial—cost of repairs, loss of use	PAP—Part D: Damage to Your Auto Coverage
Personal Auto	Accident with another vehicle	Injury to passengers in "Your" vehicle; Financial—costs of medical, loss of wages, pain and suffering	PAP—Part A: Liability Coverage

Continued on next page

3.6 Survey of Personal Insurance and Financial Planning

Insured Risk	Peril (Cause of Loss)	Consequences	Treatment
Personal Auto	Accident with another vehicle	Injury to driver and passengers of "Other" vehicle; Financial—costs of medical, loss of wages, pain and suffering	PAP—Part A: Liability Coverage
Personal Auto	Accident with another vehicle	Property of persons not in vehicles: Financial—cost of repairs, cost of loss of use	PAP—Part A: Liability Coverage
Personal Auto	Accident with another vehicle, theft	Personal property damaged/lost while in vehicle; Financial—cost of repairs	Homeowners policy
Personal Auto	Accident with pedestrian	Injury to pedestrian; Financial—costs of medical, loss of wages, pain and suffering	PAP—Part A: Liability Coverage
Personal Auto	Vandalism	Damage to "Your" vehicle; Financial—cost of repairs	PAP—Part D: Damage to Your Auto Coverage
Personal Auto	Theft	Damage to / Loss of "Your" vehicle; Financial—cost of repairs or cost of replacement	PAP—Part D: Damage to Your Auto Coverage
Personal Auto	Single car accident	Damage to "Your" vehicle; Financial—cost of repairs	PAP—Part D: Damage to Your Auto Coverage
Personal Auto	Collision with an object	Damage to "Your" vehicle; Financial—cost of repairs	PAP—Part D: Damage to Your Auto Coverage
Personal Auto	Collision with an object	Damage to property of others; Financial—cost of repairs	PAP—Part A: Liability Coverage

[DA05800]

DECLARATIONS

Most insurance policies contain a declarations page that provides basic information about the parties involved and the specific coverage provided.

The Declarations page of the Personal Auto Policy (PAP) personalizes each policy by identifying the covered parties, vehicles, and policy period. The Declarations page includes a policy number and also indicates the name of the insurer and the insured, as well as the policy period. Also listed is a description of the insured autos, which coverages are provided, the limits of insurance for each coverage, and any endorsements that apply to the policy. Although each insurer designs its own declarations page, the information discussed here is typically included.

Insurer

The Declarations page shows the name of the insurer providing the coverage. If an agency or brokerage sold the policy, its name and contact information may also be included.

Named Insured

The Declarations page shows the name and mailing address of the policyholder or **named insured**. The named insured can be an individual, a married couple, or other parties. This is the party that is responsible for premium payment, can request cancellation of the policy, and receives any notices issued by the insurer. When a married couple purchases insurance, the husband's name, the wife's name, or both names may appear in the declarations.

Named insured
A person, corporation, partnership, or other entity identified as an insured party in an insurance policy's declarations page.

Policy Period

The **policy period** is the time during which the policy provides coverage. The policy period starts at 12:01 a.m. standard time at the address of the policyholder on the date the policy becomes effective and ends at 12:01 a.m. standard time on the date the policy expires. The policy period is usually six months or one year.

Policy period
The time frame, beginning with the inception date, during which insurance coverage applies.

Description of Insured Autos

The Declarations page identifies each of the autos and trailers specifically insured under the policy. This description usually includes each vehicle's year, make, model, and **vehicle identification number (VIN)**. It may also include body type, annual mileage, use of the vehicle, date of purchase, or other information about each vehicle.

Vehicle identification number (VIN)
A unique number that is assigned to each vehicle and that identifies certain vehicle characteristics.

Schedule of Coverages

This schedule indicates the coverages and limits that apply to each listed auto, along with the premium for each coverage. If Part D—Coverage for Damage to Your Auto applies, the deductibles are also shown separately for other than collision coverage and for collision coverage.

Applicable Endorsements

The Declarations page also lists any endorsements that are attached to the policy. For example, if the policyholder owns a snowmobile that is covered under the policy, the snowmobile endorsement would be listed along with the premium for the coverage. Most policies will also include at least one state-specific endorsement.

Lienholder

Whether it is owned or leased, a vehicle may be financed through a bank, savings and loan association, credit union, or other organization that holds the title to the vehicle until the loan is paid. In such a case, the name of the lender, loss payee, or lienholder is usually shown on the Declarations page.

Garage Location

If an insured auto will be kept garaged primarily at a location other than the insured's mailing address stated on the Declarations page, that separate location will also be listed in the declarations. This location is where the auto is principally parked overnight; it may be in a garage, but it may also be in a driveway or on the street. The garage location is used for rating purposes.

Rating Information

The rating class for the vehicle and any applicable credits and discounts may be shown. Some insurers offer premium discounts if, for example, multiple cars are insured under the policy, the insured has passed a driver training or defensive driving course or has a good academic record or grades, or the insured vehicle has passive restraints or anti-theft devices.

Signature

The signature of an authorized legal representative of the insurer is usually shown at the bottom of the Declarations page. Also included is the counter-signature date, which is the date when the policy was signed by the authorized legal representative. See the exhibit "Personal Auto Policy Declarations."

Personal Auto Policy Declarations

Personal Auto Policy Declarations

POLICYHOLDER: David M. and Joan G. Smith
(Named Insured) 216 Brookside Drive
Anytown, USA 40000

POLICY NUMBER: 296 S 468211

POLICY PERIOD: **FROM:** June 25, 20XX
TO: December 25, 20XX

But only if the required premium for this period has been paid, and for six-month renewal periods if renewal premiums are paid as required. Each period begins and ends at 12:01 A.M. standard time at the address of the policyholder.

INSURED VEHICLES AND SCHEDULE OF COVERAGES

	VEHICLE PREMIUM	COVERAGES	LIMITS OF INSURANCE	
1	20XX Toyota Camry		VIN XXX	
		Coverage A—Liability	$ 300,000 Each Occurrence	$ 203.00
		Coverage B—Medical Payments	$ 5,000 Each Person	$ 36.00
		Coverage C—Uninsured Motorists	$ 300,000 Each Occurrence	$ 61.80
				TOTAL $ 300.80
2	20XX Ford Focus		VIN XXX	
		Coverage A—Liability	$ 300,000 Each Occurrence	$ 203.00
		Coverage B—Medical Payments	$ 5,000 Each Person	$ 36.00
		Coverage C—Uninsured Motorists	$ 300,000 Each Occurrence	$ 61.80
		Coverage D—Other Than Collision	Actual Cash Value Less $ 100	$ 41.60
		—Collision	Actual Cash Value Less $ 250	$ 131.00
				TOTAL $ 473.40

POLICY FORM AND ENDORSEMENTS: PP 00 01, PP 03 06

COUNTERSIGNATURE DATE: June 1, 20XX

AGENT: A.M. Abel

Copyright, ISO Properties, Inc. [DA00174]

DEFINITIONS

Most insurance policies include a separate definitions section that explains both common terms and less frequently used insurance-specific wording to assist policyholders in understanding the coverage they have purchased.

The first page of the Personal Auto Policy (PAP) contains the definitions of several terms used throughout the policy. Because the PAP is designed for individuals who may not be familiar with insurance terminology, these definitions appear at the beginning of the policy for easy reference. In contrast, most commercial policy forms include the definitions at the end of the policy. See the exhibit "Personal Auto Policy Definitions."

Often, when a word or phrase that is included in the definitions section is used elsewhere in the policy, it is shown in quotation marks (for example, "bodily injury" or "property damage"). This punctuation indicates that specific definitions apply to these terms throughout the entire policy. The definitions are written in simple language designed to be easily understood by individuals who may not be familiar with insurance terminology.

The Definitions section of the PAP defines these words and phrases:

- You and your—The words "you" and "your" refer to the named insured shown on the Declarations page. "You" and "your" also include an unnamed spouse of the named insured—provided that the spouse is a resident of the same household. When an unnamed spouse of the named insured moves out of the household but remains married to the insured, the spouse is considered "you" for another ninety days or until the policy expires—whichever comes first. Coverage ceases if the spouse is named on another policy.
- We, us, and our—The words "we," "us," and "our" refer to the insurer providing insurance under the contract, generally the company named in the declarations.
- Leased vehicles—This definition clarifies what the policy includes when it refers to an owned auto. A leased private passenger auto, pickup, or van is deemed to be an owned auto if it is leased under a written agreement for a continuous period of at least six months. For example, a car that the insured leases for two years would be considered an owned auto under the PAP. However, a car rented during a two-week vacation would not be considered an owned auto.
- Bodily injury—Bodily injury is bodily harm, sickness, or disease, including death. This phrase is referred to in Part A—Liability Coverage and in Part B—Medical Payments Coverage, as well as in Part C—Uninsured Motorists Coverage, and defines some of the coverage for which payment will be made under the policy.
- Business—Business includes a trade, a profession, or an occupation. The definition of this term is important in understanding exclusions that apply to the coverage parts in the PAP.

Personal Auto Policy Definitions

PERSONAL AUTO
PP 00 01 01 05

PERSONAL AUTO POLICY

AGREEMENT

In return for payment of the premium and subject to all the terms of this policy, we agree with you as follows:

DEFINITIONS

A. Throughout this policy, "you" and "your" refer to:

1. The "named insured" shown in the Declarations; and
2. The spouse if a resident of the same household.

If the spouse ceases to be a resident of the same household during the policy period or prior to the inception of this policy, the spouse will be considered "you" and "your" under this policy but only until the earlier of:

1. The end of 90 days following the spouse's change of residency;
2. The effective date of another policy listing the spouse as a named insured; or
3. The end of the policy period.

B. "We", "us" and "our" refer to the Company providing this insurance.

C. For purposes of this policy, a private passenger type auto, pickup or van shall be deemed to be owned by a person if leased:

1. Under a written agreement to that person; and
2. For a continuous period of at least 6 months.

Other words and phrases are defined. They are in quotation marks when used.

D. "Bodily injury" means bodily harm, sickness or disease, including death that results.

E. "Business" includes trade, profession or occupation.

F. "Family member" means a person related to you by blood, marriage or adoption who is a resident of your household. This includes a ward or foster child.

G. "Occupying" means:

1. In;
2. Upon; or
3. Getting in, on, out or off.

H. "Property damage" means physical injury to, destruction of or loss of use of tangible property.

I. "Trailer" means a vehicle designed to be pulled by a:

1. Private passenger auto; or
2. Pickup or van.

It also means a farm wagon or farm implement while towed by a vehicle listed in **1.** or **2.** above.

J. "Your covered auto" means:

1. Any vehicle shown in the Declarations.
2. A "newly acquired auto".
3. Any "trailer" you own.
4. Any auto or "trailer" you do not own while used as a temporary substitute for any other vehicle described in this definition which is out of normal use because of its:
   a. Breakdown;
   b. Repair;
   c. Servicing;
   d. Loss; or
   e. Destruction.

   This Provision (**J.4.**) does not apply to Coverage For Damage To Your Auto.

K. "Newly acquired auto":

1. "Newly acquired auto" means any of the following types of vehicles you become the owner of during the policy period:
   a. A private passenger auto; or
   b. A pickup or van, for which no other insurance policy provides coverage, that:
      (1) Has a Gross Vehicle Weight Rating of 10,000 lbs. or less; and
      (2) Is not used for the delivery or transportation of goods and materials unless such use is:
         (a) Incidental to your "business" of installing, maintaining or repairing furnishings or equipment; or
         (b) For farming or ranching.
2. Coverage for a "newly acquired auto" is provided as described below. If you ask us to insure a "newly acquired auto" after a specified time period described below has elapsed, any coverage we provide for a "newly acquired auto" will begin at the time you request the coverage.

PP 00 01 01 05 © ISO Properties, Inc., 2003 Page 1 of 13

a. For any coverage provided in this policy except Coverage For Damage To Your Auto, a "newly acquired auto" will have the broadest coverage we now provide for any vehicle shown in the Declarations. Coverage begins on the date you become the owner. However, for this coverage to apply to a "newly acquired auto" which is in addition to any vehicle shown in the Declarations, you must ask us to insure it within 14 days after you become the owner.

If a "newly acquired auto" replaces a vehicle shown in the Declarations, coverage is provided for this vehicle without your having to ask us to insure it.

b. Collision Coverage for a "newly acquired auto" begins on the date you become the owner. However, for this coverage to apply, you must ask us to insure it within:

(1) 14 days after you become the owner if the Declarations indicate that Collision Coverage applies to at least one auto. In this case, the "newly acquired auto" will have the broadest coverage we now provide for any auto shown in the Declarations.

(2) Four days after you become the owner if the Declarations do not indicate that Collision Coverage applies to at least one auto. If you comply with the 4 day requirement and a loss occurred before you asked us to insure the "newly acquired auto", a Collision deductible of $500 will apply.

c. Other Than Collision Coverage for a "newly acquired auto" begins on the date you become the owner. However, for this coverage to apply, you must ask us to insure it within:

(1) 14 days after you become the owner if the Declarations indicate that Other Than Collision Coverage applies to at least one auto. In this case, the "newly acquired auto" will have the broadest coverage we now provide for any auto shown in the Declarations.

(2) Four days after you become the owner if the Declarations do not indicate that Other Than Collision Coverage applies to at least one auto. If you comply with the 4 day requirement and a loss occurred before you asked us to insure the "newly acquired auto", an Other Than Collision deductible of $500 will apply.

Copyright, ISO Properties, Inc., 2003. [DA00192]

- Family member—A family member is a person who is related to the named insured or spouse by blood, marriage, or adoption and who resides in the named insured's household. This definition also includes a ward or a foster child. This definition is important under the PAP, which is designed to provide coverage for the named insured and other family members.
- Occupying—Occupying is defined as in, upon, getting in, on, out, or off. This definition is used in connection with Part B—Medical Payments Coverage and Part C—Uninsured Motorists Coverage and clarifies the coverages provided.
- Property damage—Property damage is physical injury to, destruction of, or loss of use of tangible property. This phrase appears only in Part A—Liability Coverage and defines the coverage for which some payments will be made under the policy.
- Trailer—A trailer is a vehicle designed to be pulled by a private passenger auto, a pickup, or a van. This definition also includes a farm wagon or farm implement towed by a vehicle included in the definition of a trailer.

"Your covered auto" is one of two terms included in the definitions that have more detailed definitions than the other defined terms. This important definition applies to the vehicles that are covered under the PAP and includes four classes of vehicles:

- Any vehicle shown in the Declarations—Your covered auto includes any vehicle listed in the Declarations. Covered vehicles can include private passenger autos such as cars, minivans, station wagons, sport utility vehicles, or pickup trucks owned by the named insured.
- A newly acquired auto—Because the coverage for newly acquired autos is detailed and is different for liability and for physical damage coverages, it is defined separately.
- Any trailer you own—A trailer owned by the named insured is also a covered auto. As mentioned, a trailer is a vehicle designed to be pulled by a private passenger auto, pickup, or van.
- A temporary substitute auto or trailer—A temporary substitute vehicle is one that is used as a short-term substitute for another covered auto that is out of normal use due to breakdown, repair, servicing, loss, or destruction. A temporary substitute auto is covered under all PAP coverages except damage to your auto (physical damage). For physical damage coverage, temporary substitute vehicles are treated the same as other nonowned autos.

"Newly acquired auto," the other detailed definition, includes any of two types of vehicles that become an owned vehicle during the policy period:

- A private passenger auto.
- A pickup or van for which no other insurance policy provides coverage. To be covered as newly acquired autos, pickups and vans must have a Gross Vehicle Weight (GVW) Rating of 10,000 pounds or less. They also must not be used for the delivery or transportation of goods and materials unless such use is incidental to the business of installing, maintaining, or repairing furnishings or equipment or is for farming or ranching.

For liability, medical payments, uninsured motorists, or any other PAP coverage except the coverage for damage to your auto, a newly acquired auto automatically receives coverage equal to the broadest coverage indicated for any vehicle shown in the declarations. The definition of newly acquired auto includes two stipulations:

- An additional auto is automatically covered for fourteen days after the named insured becomes the owner. The insured must request coverage beyond fourteen days.
- A replacement auto is covered for the remainder of the policy period, even if the insured does not ask for coverage.

The definition of newly acquired autos is different for damage to your auto (physical damage) coverage than for the other PAP coverages. This is because some insureds drop physical damage coverage on older vehicles with a reduced value, but they might need the coverage when purchasing a newer vehicle. This definition also discusses coverage of newly acquired autos because such

Collision coverage
Coverage for direct and accidental loss or damage to a covered auto caused by collision with another object or by overturn.

Other than collision (OTC) coverage
Coverage for physical damage to a covered auto resulting from any cause of loss except collision or a cause of loss specifically excluded.

information is necessary to clarify which autos are covered. The physical damage definition of newly acquired auto has two provisions:

- An insured who carries **collision coverage** or **other than collision (OTC) coverage** on at least one auto receives automatic coverage on a newly acquired auto for fourteen days. The coverage that automatically applies is equal to the broadest coverage (that is, the smallest deductible) on any vehicle currently shown in the policy declarations. The insured must ask the insurer to add the auto to the policy within this time frame for coverage to apply beyond the fourteen-day automatic coverage period.
- An insured who does not carry collision or other than collision coverage on at least one auto receives automatic physical damage coverage on a newly acquired auto for four days, subject to a $500 deductible. The insured must ask the insurer to add the auto within this time frame for coverage to apply beyond the four-day automatic coverage period.

PART A—LIABILITY COVERAGE

Because the financial consequences of automobile liability loss are potentially far greater than any damage that could occur to an insured's auto, the Personal Auto Policy's Part A—Liability Coverage offers particularly valuable protection for the insured.

The Personal Auto Policy (PAP), from Insurance Service Office, Inc. (ISO), consists of a Declarations page, Definitions, and six separate parts. Part A—Liability Coverage provides protection against an insured's legal liability arising out of the ownership, maintenance, or use of an auto.

This section discusses these provisions of Part A:

- Insuring Agreement
- Supplementary Payments
- Exclusions
- Limit of Liability
- Out of State Coverage
- Financial Responsibility
- Other Insurance

Insuring Agreement

The Part A Insuring Agreement states the insurer's duty to pay damages and defense costs and defines the persons and organizations insured under Part A.

Damages and Defense Costs Covered

In the Insuring Agreement, the insurer agrees to pay damages for bodily injury or property damage for which an insured is legally responsible because of an auto accident. Damages may include both **compensatory damages** and punitive, or exemplary, damages. The policy limit(s) applicable to this coverage can be expressed either on a **split-limits basis** or a **single-limits basis**.

The damages covered also include any **prejudgment interest** awarded against the insured. Many states' laws allow plaintiffs (injured persons who file suit) to receive interest on a judgment from the time an accident occurs, or a lawsuit is filed, to the time the judgment is handed down. Prejudgment interest is added to the amount recovered to put the claimant in the same position as if he or she had received payment for damages at the time of the accident or suit.

Because prejudgment interest is considered to be part of the award for damages, it is subject to the applicable limit of liability for Part A. For example, assume an insured who is legally liable for bodily injury in an auto accident has a PAP with a $100,000 limit of liability. If the insured is found legally liable for injuring one person and ordered to pay a $50,000 judgment, plus $5,000 in prejudgment interest, the insured's PAP insurer will pay the full $55,000. However, if the judgment is for $95,000, plus $10,000 in prejudgment interest, the insured's PAP will pay only up to the $100,000 limit of liability.

In addition to agreeing to pay damages for which the insured is legally liable, subject to policy limits, the insurer also agrees to defend the insured and pay all legal costs the insured may incur in a liability suit—even if the combined costs exceed the limit of liability. In other words, the insurer is obligated to pay defense costs in addition to the policy limits. When a large claim is involved, the insurer cannot simply offer, or "tender," its policy limits and be relieved of any further duty to defend the insured. However, the insurer's duty to settle or defend ends when the limit of liability has been exhausted by the payment of judgments or settlements.

The insurer also has no obligation to defend any claim that is not covered under the policy. If, for example, a suit alleges only that the insured intentionally caused bodily injury, the insurer has no obligation to defend the insured because the PAP specifically excludes bodily injury (or property damage) intentionally caused by the insured. However, courts have often held that an insurer's duty to defend is broader than its duty to pay damages. Various rules of law define an insurer's duty to defend, but these rules are beyond the scope of this discussion.

Persons and Organizations Insured

As stated in its Insuring Agreement, Part A of the PAP provides liability coverage for four classes of persons or organizations: the named insured and family members, any person using the named insured's covered auto, any person or organization legally responsible for the acts of a covered person while using a covered auto, and any person or organization legally responsible for the named insured's or family member's use of any automobile or trailer.

Compensatory damages
A payment awarded by a court to reimburse a victim for actual harm.

Split-limits basis
Separate coverage limits that allow one limit for bodily injury to each person; a second, usually higher, limit for bodily injury to all persons in each accident; and a third limit for all property damage in each accident.

Single-limits basis
One coverage limit that applies to all damages arising from bodily injury or property damage or both, resulting from a single accident.

Prejudgment interest
Interest that may accrue on damages before a judgment has been rendered.

The named insured and family members are covered for the ownership, maintenance, or use of any auto or trailer. The named insured, referred to as "you" in the PAP, also includes the named insured's spouse if the spouse is a resident of the same household. Family members are persons related to the named insured by blood, marriage, or adoption, as well as wards or foster children, who live in the named insured's household. In addition, children who are temporarily away from home, such as those attending college, are still covered under their parents' policy. These insureds are protected, not only while driving covered autos, but also when operating borrowed autos, rented vehicles (autos or trucks), or any other auto, subject to the policy exclusions.

Any person using the named insured's covered auto is also covered under Part A. Unless otherwise noted the phrase "covered auto" is used in this discussion to mean "your covered auto" as defined in the PAP. The PAP definition of "your covered auto" includes any vehicle shown in the declarations; a "newly acquired auto" (as defined in the PAP); any "trailer"(as defined in the PAP) that the named insured owns; or any auto or "trailer" that the named insured does not own while used as a temporary substitute for any other covered auto that is out of normal use because of its breakdown, repair, servicing, loss, or destruction.

Part A also covers any person or organization legally responsible for the acts of a covered person while using a covered auto. Assume that, while driving his car to the post office to pick up a package for his employer, Bob negligently injures another person. If the victim sues Bob's employer, the employer is also covered under his PAP (because Bob is a covered person while driving his car, and the employer is responsible for his actions as an employee).

Coverage further extends to any person or organization legally responsible for the named insured's or family member's use of any automobile or trailer. This provision applies only if the person or organization does not own or hire the auto or trailer. For example, Cheryl, the named insured, injures a pedestrian while driving a car loaned to her by a local business to run errands for a nursing home. Because neither Cheryl nor the nursing home owns or has hired the car, Cheryl's PAP will defend both her and the nursing home against any allegation of liability for the injury to the pedestrian. However, the local business that loaned Cheryl the car would not be covered under Cheryl's PAP and would seek liability coverage under its own policy.

Supplementary Payments

Part A of the PAP contains a provision for payment of certain expenses that are considered to be **supplementary payments**, which, if paid, will not reduce the limit of liability. There are five supplementary payments in Part A:

- Cost of bail bonds—The insurer agrees to pay up to $250 for the cost of bail bonds (bail bond premiums) required because of an accident that results in bodily injury or property damage covered by the policy.
- Premiums on appeal bonds and bonds to release attachments—An insured ordered to pay a court-awarded judgment can appeal that decision to a higher court. An appeal bond guarantees that, if the appeal is lost, the insured will pay the original judgment and the cost of the appeal. During legal proceedings, the plaintiff may place an **attachment** on the insured's property, such as a vehicle. A release of attachment bond guarantees that the insured will pay any judgment, thereby permitting a release of the attachment on the insured's property.
- Interest accruing after a judgment—Interest that accrues after a judgment (called **postjudgment interest**) is also paid as a supplementary payment. For example, if the insured appeals a lawsuit, any interest that accrues after the judgment becomes payable to the plaintiff by the insurer. The insurer will pay this amount on behalf of the insured separately from the liability judgment, and the amount paid will not reduce the limit of liability.
- Loss of earnings because of attendance at trials—The insurer also pays up to $200 per day for an insured's loss of earnings (but not of other income) for attending a hearing or trial at the insurer's request.
- Other reasonable expenses incurred at the insurer's request—For purposes of defending a lawsuit, an insurer may make requests of the insured that result in expenditures. Any such reasonable expenses are also covered as supplementary payments. For example, an insured may incur travel and transportation expenses to testify at a trial at the insurer's request.

Supplementary payments
Various expenses the insurer agrees to pay under a liability insurance policy (in addition to the liability limits) for items such as premiums on bail bonds and appeal bonds, loss of the insured's earnings because of attendance at trials, and other reasonable expenses incurred by the insured at the insurer's request.

Attachment
The act of seizing property to secure a judgment.

Postjudgment interest
Interest that may accrue on damages after a judgment has been entered in a court and before the money is paid.

Exclusions

As with most insurance policies, the Part A—Insuring Agreement describes broad coverage that is narrowed by exclusions. PAP liability coverage is subject to several exclusions.

Intentional Injury

The PAP does not provide liability coverage for an insured who intentionally causes bodily injury or property damage. For example, if Sam becomes enraged when he is caught in a traffic jam and deliberately rams the vehicle in front of him, his responsibility for any intentional property damage to the other motorist's car would not be covered under his PAP.

Property Owned or Transported

Liability coverage does not apply to damage to property owned or being transported by an insured. For example, if Alice is transporting a friend's suitcase and clothing while she is driving on vacation and is at fault in an auto accident in which these items are damaged, the loss to the items is not covered under Alice's PAP.

Property Rented to, Used by, or in the Care of the Insured

Liability for property rented to, used by, or in the care of the insured is not covered under the PAP. For example, if Don rents glassware and china for a party and those items are later damaged in an accident involving his car, his liability for damage to the rented glassware and china is not covered. However, this exclusion does not apply to damage to a residence or private garage. Therefore, if Don accidentally backs his car into the side of a vacation house he is renting, his liability for the damage to the rented house would be covered.

Bodily Injury to an Employee of an Insured

The liability coverage also excludes bodily injury to an employee of an insured who is injured during the course of employment. Compensation for the employee's injury is usually provided under a workers compensation law. However, injury to a domestic employee injured in the course of employment is covered if workers compensation benefits are not required or are unavailable for that employee.

Public or Livery Conveyance

Public or livery conveyance
In case law, a method of transportation that is indiscriminately offered to the general public, such as a taxi or public bus.

A **public or livery conveyance** is one that is indiscriminately offered to the public (usually to carry people or property for a fee), such as a taxi or a bus. Part A liability coverage does not apply to an insured's ownership or operation of a vehicle while it is being used as a public or livery conveyance. This exclusion also applies to any period of time the vehicle is being used by an insured who is logged into a transportation network platform as a driver, whether or not passengers are in the vehicle. For example, if local taxicab drivers are on strike and Harry decides to capitalize on the situation by transporting persons in his car for a fee, Harry's PAP liability coverage does not apply to this activity. The exclusion does not apply to share-the-expense car pools.

Garage Business Use

Liability insurance does not apply to any insured while employed or engaged in the business of selling, repairing, servicing, storing, or parking vehicles designed for use mainly on public highways. This exclusion also applies to road testing and delivery of vehicles. For example, if an auto mechanic has an accident while road testing a customer's car, the mechanic's PAP liability coverage does not apply. The intent is to exclude a loss exposure that should be covered by a commercial auto policy, such as a garage policy, purchased by the owner of the business.

The garage business exclusion does not apply to the insured's covered auto when it is being driven by the named insured; a family member; or any partner, agent, or employee of the named insured or a family member. For example, if a mechanic injures someone while driving his covered auto (rather than a customer's auto) to a parts shop to pick up a part for his employer, the mechanic's PAP liability insurance would cover the loss.

Other Business Use

Liability coverage does not apply to any vehicle other than a private passenger auto, a pickup, a van, or a trailer (while it is being used with a covered vehicle) that is maintained or used in any business other than farming or ranching. The intent is to exclude liability coverage for commercial vehicles and trucks used in a business.

For example, if an insured drives a city bus or operates a large commercial truck, the insured's PAP liability coverage does not apply. Coverage for such vehicles is available through business auto policies.

Vehicle Used Without Reasonable Belief of Being Entitled

If an insured uses a vehicle without reasonable belief that he or she is entitled to do so, the liability coverage does not apply. For example, if Jake notices that the keys have been left in a stranger's car at a mall, takes the car for a ride, and causes an accident, his PAP does not provide liability coverage.

This exclusion does not apply when another family member (as defined) uses the owned auto of a named insured. For insurance purposes, it is assumed that a family member has permission to use another family member's car.

Nuclear Energy Liability Losses

The PAP excludes coverage of liability for bodily injury or property damage caused by an insured who is also covered by a nuclear energy liability policy. Almost anyone can become an insured under a nuclear energy liability policy because some of these policies have broad definitions of who an insured is and may include a member of the public. For example, if an individual accidentally drives his vehicle into a nuclear energy facility, causing the release of harmful radiation, he could potentially be considered an insured under that facility's nuclear energy liability policy and be covered for damages claimed by other parties exposed to radiation.

Vehicles With Fewer Than Four Wheels or Designed for Off-Road Use

Liability arising out of the ownership, maintenance, or use of any vehicle that has fewer than four wheels is excluded. Also excluded is liability coverage for any vehicle that is designed mainly for use off public roads, other than a non-owned golf cart, a vehicle being used by an insured in a medical emergency, or a trailer.

For example, any liability Fred might incur while driving a golf cart owned by the country club where he is playing golf would be covered. Although this provision excludes coverage for motorcycles, mopeds, and motorscooters, those vehicles can be covered by adding an endorsement to the PAP.

Other Vehicles Owned by Insured or Available for Insured's Regular Use

Any vehicle, other than a covered auto, owned by the named insured or made available for the named insured's regular use is also excluded. An insured can drive another person's auto on an occasional, as opposed to a regular, basis and still have coverage under his or her own policy. If the nonowned auto is furnished for the insured's regular use, the insured's liability coverage does not apply.

The intent of this exclusion is to encourage customers to accurately disclose the number of vehicles they own or regularly operate. Otherwise, the insured could insure and pay premiums for only one vehicle even though the insured drives several cars on a regular basis, substantially increasing the insurer's exposure.

Vehicles Owned by or Available for Family Member's Regular Use

A similar exclusion applies to vehicles (other than covered autos) owned by any family member or furnished or made available for the regular use of any family member. However, the exclusion does not apply to the named insured and spouse while maintaining or occupying such a vehicle. Therefore, the liability insurance under Bill's PAP would cover him while he is using a car owned by his daughter, who lives with him, which he has borrowed. If the daughter has insured her car, Bill would be covered by her policy on a primary basis, as well as his own policy on an excess basis.

Racing

PAP liability coverage does not apply to any vehicle that is located inside a racing facility for the purpose of preparing for, practicing for, or competing in any organized racing or speed contest.

Personal Vehicle Sharing

Liability coverage does not apply to any covered auto while it is enrolled in a personal vehicle sharing program under the terms of a written agreement. The exclusion also applies to any operation of the vehicle in connection with such programs by anyone other than the insured or the insured's "family members."

Personal vehicle sharing programs are similar in some ways to rental car companies. However, the vehicles are not owned by the company operating the program. Vehicle sharing programs manage the sharing of privately owned private passenger vehicles for use by those enrolled in the program.

Limit of Liability

Most PAPs are written on a split-limits basis, with the three types of limits stated in this order:

- Bodily injury to each person
- Bodily injury to all persons in each accident
- Property damage in each accident

For example, split limits of $100/$300/$50 mean that the insured has bodily injury liability limits of $100,000 per person and $300,000 for each accident, and a limit of $50,000 for property damage liability per accident.

Some policies are written with a single limit that applies per accident to the total of both bodily injury and property damage liability. For example, a policy might have a single limit of $300,000 for bodily injury and property damage liability. The Single Liability Limit endorsement modifies the policy to provide coverage on a single-limit basis.

The PAP states that the limits of liability for the policy will not be increased, regardless of the number of insured persons, claims made, vehicles or premiums shown, or vehicles involved in an auto accident. The most any claimant can recover for one accident is the applicable limit(s) stated in the declarations. For example, if Betty causes an accident while running an errand for her employer in her personal auto, the injured claimant might sue both Betty and her employer, because Betty was acting on her employer's behalf. Betty's insurer would handle the claim and respond to a lawsuit on behalf of both Betty and her employer. However, Betty's insurer would not pay more than the limits of liability on her PAP, even though it is responding on behalf of two parties. (Her employer might also have its own coverage.)

The Limit of Liability provision also states that no one is entitled to receive duplicate payments for the same elements of loss under Part A—Liability Coverage, Part B—Medical Payments Coverage, Part C—Uninsured Motorists Coverage, or any underinsured motorists coverage provided by the policy. This provision prevents insureds from collecting twice for one loss under different parts of the same policy.

Out of State Coverage

The PAP contains an Out of State Coverage provision that applies when an auto accident occurs in a state other than the one in which the covered auto is principally garaged. If the accident occurs in a state that has a financial responsibility law or a similar law that requires higher liability limits than the limits shown in the declarations, the PAP automatically provides the higher required limits for that accident.

In addition, if a state has a compulsory insurance law or a similar law that requires nonresidents to maintain coverage whenever they use a vehicle in that state, the PAP provides the required minimum amounts and types of coverage. This provision protects insureds when they are driving in other states by providing the benefits required by any state in which an accident occurs. For example, a driver who is not required to have "no-fault" personal injury protection (PIP) coverage in his or her home state would have PIP coverage when driving in a state that requires it.

Financial Responsibility

Many states' laws require insureds to demonstrate proof of financial responsibility after an accident or traffic violation has occurred. Under these laws, the PAP can be used to demonstrate proof of financial responsibility to the extent required by the state where the accident or traffic violation has occurred. In addition, if a financial responsibility law is changed to require higher minimum limits of liability, the PAP automatically complies with the new law.

Other Insurance

The Other Insurance provision of Part A addresses situations in which more than one auto policy covers a liability claim.

If the insured has other applicable liability insurance on an owned vehicle, the insurer pays only its pro rata share of the loss. The insurer's share is the proportion of the loss that the limit of liability bears to the total of all applicable limits. For example, Joseph accidentally injures another motorist while driving his owned auto and must pay damages of $60,000. Assume Joseph has a PAP with a $100,000 limit of liability with Insurer A and also has a PAP with a $50,000 limit of liability with Insurer B. If two auto liability policies cover the same owned vehicle, each insurer pays its pro rata share. Each insurer pays according to this formula:

$$\text{Insurer's share of damages} = \left(\frac{\text{Limit of liability of that insurer's policy}}{\text{Total limits of liability of all applicable policies}} \right) \times \text{Amount of damages}$$

$$\text{Insurer A's share} = \left(\frac{\$100,000}{\$150,000} \right) \times \$60,000 = \$40,000$$

$$\text{Insurer B's share} = \left(\frac{\$50,000}{\$150,000} \right) \times \$60,000 = \$20,000$$

If other liability insurance is available on a nonowned vehicle, including any vehicle used as a temporary substitute for a covered auto, the PAP coverage is excess over any other collectible insurance. For example, Ken borrows a car owned by Patti with her permission. Ken has a PAP with $100/$300/$50 liability limits, and Patti has a PAP with $50/$100/$25 liability limits. Ken negligently injures another motorist and must pay a judgment of $60,000. Patti's insurance is primary and Ken's is excess. Each insurer pays these amounts:

- Patti's insurer (primary)—$50,000 (Patti's per person limit)
- Ken's insurer (excess)—$10,000 (the excess over Patti's limit)

PART A—LIABILITY COVERAGE CASE STUDY

Knowing how to apply Part A—Liability Coverage of the Personal Auto Policy (PAP) to the facts of a case is an important skill. This case study helps the student make the transition from knowing policy language to knowing how to apply policy language to losses.

Liability insurance provided by the PAP covers a wide range of loss exposures. Coverage can extend to other users of autos covered by the PAP. The application of coverage depends on the circumstances of the loss.

Case Facts

Given the facts presented by the case, will the auto liability claim be covered? If so, what amount would the insurer pay for the claim?

George and Sam go to a party. They agree that George will not consume any alcohol at the party so that he can drive them both home safely in Sam's car. After several hours of Sam drinking alcoholic beverages, the two decide to leave the party. Although Sam's blood alcohol level exceeds the legal limit, he insists he is capable of driving and demands George return his car keys. George refuses and gets into the driver's seat of Sam's car. Sam sits in the passenger's seat. George proceeds to drive on the expressway toward Sam's home when he loses control of the vehicle, swerves off the road, and hits a bridge abutment. Sam is severely injured.

Both Sam and George notified their insurers within twenty-four hours and complied with all other policy conditions. To confirm the facts of this loss are accurate, the insurer relied on police reports, recorded statements from witnesses, medical records, and inspections of the accident scene and any vehicles involved.

Sam sues George for payment of costs related to his injuries. Sam's lawsuit against George does not come to trial until four years after the accident. Sam is then awarded $110,000 in damages. During the four years, $20,000 of prejudgment interest accumulates. In addition, the attorneys hired by the insurers to defend George in Sam's lawsuit charged $15,000.

Both Sam and George have PAPs. Sam's PAP has a $25,000 single limit of liability per occurrence. George's PAP has a $100,000 single limit of liability per occurrence. Neither PAP contains any endorsements that would affect liability coverage. See the exhibit "PAP Coverage Case Study Summary."

PAP Coverage Case Study Summary

Insureds	George and Sam each have PAP policies.
Types of policies and coverage limits	Sam's PAP—$25,000 liability limit per occurrence.
	George's PAP—$100,000 liability limit per occurrence.
Endorsements that affect the case	None.
Other policy information	No other relevant information.
Background	The insureds have complied with the policy conditions.

[DA05635]

Case Analysis Tools

To determine whether Sam's or George's PAP (or both, or neither) provide coverage for George's alleged liability, the insurance or risk management professional should have copies of the policy forms and any applicable endorsements that are indicated on the Declarations pages of the policies. See the exhibit "Personal Auto Policy Declarations."

To determine whether a policy covers a loss, many insurance professionals apply the DICE method. ("DICE" is an acronym for categories of policy provisions: declarations, insuring agreement, conditions, and exclusions.) The DICE method has four steps:

1. Review of the declarations page to determine whether it covers the person or the property at the time of the loss
2. Review of the insuring agreement to determine whether it covers the loss
3. Review of policy conditions to determine compliance
4. Review of policy exclusions to determine whether they preclude coverage of the loss

Each of these four steps is used in every case. Other categories of policy provisions should be examined. For example, endorsements and terms defined in the policy should be reviewed in relation to the declarations, insuring agreement, exclusions, and conditions.

Personal Auto Policy Declarations

Personal Auto Policy Declarations

POLICYHOLDER: Sam Insured
(Named Insured) 216 Brookside Drive
Anytown, USA 40000

POLICY NUMBER: 296 D 468211

POLICY PERIOD: **FROM:** June 15, 20XX
TO: Dec. 15, 20XX

But only If the required premium for this period has been paid, and for six-month renewal periods If renewal premiums are paid as required. Each period begins and ends at 12:01 A.M. standard time at the address of the policyholder.

INSURED VEHICLES AND SCHEDULE OF COVERAGES

	VEHICLE	COVERAGES	LIMITS OF INSURANCE		PREMIUM
1	20XX Toyota Camry		VINXXX		
		Coverage A—Liability	$ 25,000	Each Occurrence	$ 203.00
		Coverage B—Medical Payments	$ 5,000	Each Person	$ 36.00
		Coverage C—Uninsured Motorists	$ 20,000	Each Occurrence	$ 61.80
				TOTAL	$ 300.80

POLICY FORM AND ENDORSEMENTS: PP 00 01
COUNTERSIGNATURE DATE: June 15, 20XX
AGENT: A. M. Abel

Copyright, ISO Properties, Inc. [DA00237]

Determination of Coverage

To examine the policy forms to determine whether coverage applies to the losses, the insurance professional can apply the DICE method, which involves four steps.

The first DICE step is to determine whether the driver or vehicle is described on an insured's PAP Declarations page and whether the accident occurred during the policy period. In this case, two PAPs potentially provide coverage. Sam has his own PAP in which his car is listed as a covered auto. George also

Personal Auto Policy Declarations

Personal Auto Policy Declarations

POLICYHOLDER: (Named Insured)	George Insured 210 Brookside Drive Anytown, USA 40000

POLICY NUMBER: 296 D 468300

POLICY PERIOD: **FROM:** June 1, 20XX
TO: Dec. 1, 20XX

But only If the required premium for this period has been paid, and for six-month renewal periods If renewal premiums are paid as required. Each period begins and ends at 12:01 A.M. standard time at the address of the policyholder.

INSURED VEHICLES AND SCHEDULE OF COVERAGES

VEHICLE	COVERAGES	LIMITS OF INSURANCE	PREMIUM
1 20XX Ford Focus		VINXXX	
	Coverage A—Single Limit of Liability	$ 100,000 Each Occurrence	$ 245.00
	Coverage B—Medical Payments to Others	$ 5,000 Each Person	$ 25.00
	Coverage C—Uninsured Motorists	$ 100,000 Each Person	$ 61.80
		$ 300,000 Each Occurrence	
	Coverage D—Other Than Collision	Actual Cash Value Less $100	$ 41.60
	—Collision	Actual Cash Value Less $250	$ 131.00
		TOTAL	$ 504.40

POLICY FORM AND ENDORSEMENTS: PP 00 01

COUNTERSIGNATURE DATE: June 1, 20XX

AGENT: A. M. Abel

Copyright, ISO Properties, Inc. [DA00238]

has a PAP in which he is listed as the named insured. The accident occurred during the policy period of both policies.

The second DICE step is to determine whether the event has triggered coverage under one or both of the two PAPs' insuring agreements. In this policy provision, common to both Sam's and George's PAP, the insurer agrees to pay damages for bodily injury and property damage for which an insured is legally responsible because of an auto accident. Sam is a named insured under his policy. George is not shown as a named insured on Sam's policy, but he is an insured while using Sam's covered auto. Accidentally driving a car into a bridge abutment qualifies as an auto accident. Sam's demand that George pay him for his injuries and property damage as a result of the auto accident also helps trigger liability coverage under both PAP insuring agreements.

The third DICE step is to determine whether all policy conditions have been met. Both Sam and George notified their insurers promptly, and all other conditions, for both policies, were satisfied. See the exhibit "Part A—Liability Coverage."

Part A—Liability Coverage

PART A – LIABILITY COVERAGE
INSURING AGREEMENT

We will pay damages for "bodily injury" or "property damage" for which any "insured" becomes legally responsible because of an auto accident. Damages include prejudgment interest awarded against the "insured". We will settle or defend, as we consider appropriate, any claim or suit asking for these damages. In addition to our limit of liability, we will pay all defense costs we incur. Our duty to settle or defend ends when our limit of liability for this coverage has been exhausted by payment of judgments or settlements. We have no duty to defend any suit or settle any claim for "bodily injury" or "property damage" not covered under this policy.

Includes copyrighted material of Insurance Services Office, Inc., with its permission. Copyright, ISO Properties, Inc., 2003. [DA00240]

The fourth DICE step is to determine whether one or more exclusions preclude coverage the insuring agreements have granted. One exclusion in Sam's PAP (and none from George's PAP) may apply to this case. The exclusion eliminates coverage for the insured's use of a vehicle without having a reasonable belief that he or she is entitled to do so. Shortly before Sam entered the car, he told George he wanted his car keys back so he could drive. With his statement to George, Sam may have been attempting to rescind the permission he had earlier given George to drive his car.

A question a court may have to decide is whether George had a reasonable belief that he was still entitled to use Sam's car at the time of the accident. In making that determination, a judge or jury may consider whether George was aware of Sam's intoxicated state. It appears that he was, having been with Sam at the party.

Based on the preceding factors, the insurer determined that George had a reasonable belief that he was entitled to use Sam's car. This determination will make the exclusion inapplicable, thereby allowing liability coverage for

George to remain in effect in relation to Sam's demands for payment for his injuries.

Based on this application of the DICE method, both Sam's and George's PAP provide coverage for George's alleged liability.

Determination of Amounts Payable

Determining the amount payable for a loss under liability coverage may involve analyzing such issues as other insurance (two policies providing coverage) and the limit of liability available to pay losses.

Sam is not liable for the accident because he was not driving the car. However, under his insurance policy, George is considered an insured driver of Sam's covered auto. Therefore, George is provided liability coverage under Sam's policy. George is also provided liability coverage under his own policy. The Other Insurance provision of both PAPs addresses situations such as this when more than one policy covers the same liability claim. See the exhibit "Part A—Liability Coverage."

Part A—Liability Coverage

PART A—LIABILITY COVERAGE

OTHER INSURANCE

If there is other applicable liability insurance we will pay only our share of the loss. Our share is the proportion that our limit of liability bears to the total of all applicable limits. However, any insurance we provide for a vehicle you do not own, including any vehicle while used as a temporary substitute for "your covered auto", shall be excess over any other collectible insurance.

Includes copyrighted material of Insurance Services Office, Inc., with its permission. Copyright, ISO Properties, Inc., 2003. [DA00242]

If the other insurance (in this case, George's PAP) is available on a nonowned vehicle (Sam's car), the liability coverage from George's PAP is excess over any other collectible insurance (Sam's PAP). Therefore, for Sam's demand for payment for his bodily injuries, each insurer will pay up to these amounts:

- Sam's insurer (primary)—$25,000 (Sam's per occurrence limit)
- George's insurer (excess)—$100,000 (the excess over Sam's limit)

A total of $125,000 is available. See the exhibit "Part A—Liability Coverage."

Part A—Liability Coverage

PART A – LIABILITY COVERAGE

INSURING AGREEMENT

A. We will pay damages for "bodily injury" or "property damage" for which any "insured" becomes legally responsible because of an auto accident. Damages include prejudgment interest awarded against the "insured". We will settle or defend, as we consider appropriate, any claim or suit asking for these damages. In addition to our limit of liability, we will pay all defense costs we incur. Our duty to settle or defend ends when our limit of liability for this coverage has been exhausted by payment of judgments or settlements.

SUPPLEMENTARY PAYMENTS

We will pay on behalf of an "insured":

1. Up to $250 for the cost of bail bonds required because of an accident, including related traffic law violations. The accident must result in "bodily injury" or "property damage" covered under this policy.

2. Premiums on appeal bonds and bonds to release attachments in any suit we defend.

3. Interest accruing after a judgment is entered in any suit we defend. Our duty to pay interest ends when we offer to pay that part of the judgment which does not exceed our limit of liability for this coverage.

4. Up to $200 a day for loss of earnings, but not other income, because of attendance at hearings or trials at our request.

5. Other reasonable expenses incurred at our request.

These payments will not reduce the limit of liability.

Includes copyrighted material of Insurance Services Office, Inc., with its permission. Copyright, ISO Properties, Inc., 2003. [DA00239]

The Part A limit of liability is the most that the insurer will pay for damages and prejudgment interest for which the insured is legally responsible. Defense costs and other supplementary payments are payable in addition to the limit of liability.

The total of the $110,000 award and the $20,000 of prejudgment interest is $130,000. Between the two PAPs, only $125,000 of coverage is available. Therefore, George would have to pay $5,000 himself. In addition to the limit of liability, Sam's insurer (as the primary insurer) would pay the $15,000 attorney fees. See the exhibit "Determination of Amounts Payable."

> **Determination of Amounts Payable**
>
> Of the $110,000 damages plus $20,000 prejudgment interest:
>
> - Sam's PAP is primary and will pay $25,000 to Sam.
> - George's PAP is excess and will pay $100,000 to Sam.
> - George will personally pay $5,000 to Sam.
>
> Of the $15,000 defense attorney fees for George:
>
> - Sam's PAP is primary and will pay $15,000.

[DA00244]

PART B—MEDICAL PAYMENTS COVERAGE

Soon after an auto accident that involves bodily injury, medical bills become due. Establishing who is at fault and should pay those bills often takes time, sometimes years.

Part B—Medical Payments Coverage of the Personal Auto Policy (PAP) provides auto accident medical coverage up to a limited amount without requiring a determination of fault.

Part B includes these provisions:

- Insuring Agreement
- Exclusions
- Limit of Liability
- Other Insurance

Insuring Agreement

The Part B Insuring Agreement states the insurer's promise to pay reasonable and necessary medical and funeral expenses incurred by an insured because of bodily injury caused by an accident. The insurer agrees to pay only those expenses incurred for services rendered within three years from the date of the accident. The types of expenses payable include those for medical, surgical, x-ray, dental, and funeral services. Unless otherwise noted, the phrases "medical expenses" and "medical payments" as used in this discussion are meant to include all of these types of expenses.

Medical payments coverage applies without regard to fault; therefore, whether or not the insured is legally liable for the accident, medical payments benefits may be paid for both the insured and other injured occupants of the insured's covered auto. Two classes of insureds are covered under Part B:

- The named insured and "family members" (as defined in the PAP)—These individuals are covered for their medical expenses if they are injured while occupying a motor vehicle or as pedestrians when struck by a motor vehicle designed for use mainly on public roads. Examples of covered losses include injuries to the named insured in an auto accident, injury to a family member's hand when a neighbor's car door shuts on it, and injuries a family member suffers when struck by a car while crossing the street.

- Any other person while occupying a covered auto—Medical expenses of passengers in a covered auto are covered. For example, if Mary owns her car and is the named insured, all passengers in her car are covered for their medical expenses under her policy. However, if Mary is operating a vehicle she does not own, passengers in the car (other than family members) are not covered under her medical payments coverage. Passengers in the non-owned vehicle can seek protection under their own policies or under the medical payments coverage that applies to the nonowned vehicle.

Exclusions

Many of the exclusions under Part B—Medical Payments Coverage are similar to those under Part A—Liability Coverage. There are several medical payments exclusions.

Motorized Vehicles With Fewer Than Four Wheels

If the insured is injured while occupying a motorized vehicle with fewer than four wheels, medical payments coverage does not apply.

Public or Livery Conveyance

An insured who is injured while occupying a covered auto that is being used as a public or livery conveyance (such as a taxi or public bus) will not receive medical payments. This exclusion also applies to any period of time the vehicle is being used by an insured who is logged into a transportation network platform as a driver, whether or not passengers are in the vehicle. The exclusion does not apply to share-the-expense car pools.

Vehicles Used as a Residence or Premises

Injuries that occur while the vehicle is located for use as a residence or premises are excluded. For example, after his apartment building burns down, Steve decides to live in a van covered by his PAP while he looks for a new apartment. If Steve burns himself while cooking on a small stove in the van, the medical payments coverage will not pay for treatment of his injury.

Injury During the Course of Employment

Injuries that occur during the course of employment are excluded from medical payments coverage if workers compensation benefits are required or available. For example, if Rosa is injured while driving her car on company business and her employer provides workers compensation benefits, those benefits, rather than PAP medical payments coverage, would apply.

Other Vehicles Owned by Insured or Available for Insured's Regular Use

Medical payments coverage does not apply to an injury sustained by an insured while occupying, or when struck by, any vehicle (other than a covered auto) that is owned by the named insured or is furnished or available for his or her regular use. The underlying intent of this provision is to exclude medical payments coverage on vehicles the named insured owns or uses regularly but does not insure under the policy.

Vehicles Owned by or Available for Family Member's Regular Use

Medical payments coverage does not apply to an injury sustained by an insured while occupying, or when struck by, any vehicle (other than a covered auto) that is owned by or is furnished or available for the regular use of any family member of the named insured. However, this exclusion has an important exception: it does not apply to the named insured and spouse. For example, assume that John, who lives with his parents, owns a car and insures it under a policy separate from the policy that insures his parents' vehicles. The parents are injured while riding in John's car. Their medical expenses are covered under their own PAP (as excess over any medical payments coverage in the son's policy).

Vehicle Occupied Without Reasonable Belief of Being Entitled

If an insured sustains an injury while using a vehicle without a reasonable belief that he or she is entitled to do so, medical payments coverage does not apply. For example, Harry works at a hotel and, without permission, takes a guest's car from the garage for use on a brief errand. If Harry swerves off the road and is injured, neither Harry's PAP nor the guest's PAP will pay his medical expenses. As with Part A—Liability Coverage, this medical payments exclusion does not apply when another family member (as defined) uses the owned auto of a named insured. For insurance purposes, it is assumed that one family member has permission to use another family member's car.

Vehicles Used in the Business of an Insured

Coverage is excluded for bodily injury sustained by an insured while occupying a vehicle used in the insured's business. However, this exclusion does not apply to a private passenger auto, a pickup or van, or a trailer used with these vehicles. The intent underlying this provision is to exclude coverage of vehicles that should be insured under a commercial auto policy.

Bodily Injury From Nuclear Weapons or War

Injury from the discharge of a nuclear weapon (even if accidental) or from war, insurrection, rebellion, or revolution is excluded from medical payments coverage.

Nuclear Radiation

Bodily injury caused by nuclear reaction, radiation, or radioactive contamination is also excluded. For example, if an insured drives a covered auto near a public utility plant when an accidental release of radiation occurs, injuries resulting from the radiation exposure would not be covered.

Racing

Excluded from medical payments coverage is bodily injury an insured sustains while occupying any vehicle that is located inside a racing facility for the purpose of preparing for, practicing for, or competing in any organized racing or speed contest.

Personal Vehicle Sharing Program

If an insured sustains an injury while occupying a vehicle that is enrolled in a vehicle sharing program under the terms of a written agreement, medical payments coverage does not apply.

Limit of Liability

The limit of insurance for medical payments coverage is stated in the declarations. This limit, typically between $1,000 and $10,000, is the maximum amount that will be paid to each injured person in a single accident, regardless of the number of insured persons, claims made, vehicles or premiums shown on the policy, or vehicles involved in the auto accident. The intent is to prevent an insured person from collecting more than the stated medical payments limit for any one accident.

In addition, the Limit of Liability provision specifically states that no one is entitled to receive duplicate payments for the same elements of loss under Part B—Medical Payments Coverage, Part A—Liability Coverage, Part C—Uninsured Motorists Coverage, or any underinsured motorists coverage provided by the policy. For example, assume Janice has a limit of $5,000 for medical payments coverage, and she is injured by an uninsured motorist. Janice's medical bills are $5,000. Without this provision, Janice might be able to collect $10,000—that is, $5,000 under the medical payments coverage and another $5,000 under the uninsured motorists coverage—for the same bills.

Other Insurance

If the medical payments coverage of more than one insurance policy applies to a claim, each insurer pays its pro rata share based on the proportion that its limit of liability bears to the total of applicable limits. For example, Jeff is injured when he accidentally drives his car into a tree. His medical expenses are $6,000. Assume Jeff has a PAP with a medical payments limit of $5,000 with Insurer A and also has a PAP with a medical payments limit of $10,000 with Insurer B. If two automobile policies cover the same owned vehicle, each insurer pays its pro rata share.

Insurer A's pro rata share is calculated by multiplying the total amount of covered medical expenses ($6,000) by that proportion that the medical payments limit in Insurer A's policy ($5,000) bears to the sum of the medical payments limits in both policies ($15,000). The calculation of Insurer A's share can be shown in formula as follows:

$$\$6{,}000 \times \left(\frac{\$5{,}000}{\$15{,}000}\right) = \$2{,}000$$

Insurer B's pro rata share is calculated by multiplying the total amount of covered medical expenses ($6,000) by that proportion that the medical payments limit in Insurer B's policy ($10,000) bears to the sum of the medical payments limits in both policies ($15,000). The calculation of Insurer B's share can be shown in formula as follows:

$$\$6{,}000 \times \left(\frac{\$10{,}000}{\$15{,}000}\right) = \$4{,}000$$

With respect to a nonowned vehicle or a vehicle while used as a temporary substitute for the insured's covered auto, medical payments coverage under a PAP is excess over any other collectible auto insurance that pays medical or funeral expenses. For example, assume that David is driving his own car and Pam is his passenger. From Pam's perspective, David's car is a nonowned vehicle. David's car skids on a patch of ice and hits a tree. David's PAP has a $5,000 limit on medical payments coverage, and Pam's PAP has a medical payments limit of $10,000. If Pam's medical expenses are $6,000, David's insurer pays $5,000 as primary insurance and Pam's insurer pays the remaining $1,000 as excess insurance.

PART B—MEDICAL PAYMENTS COVERAGE CASE STUDY

Knowing how to apply Part B—Medical Payments Coverage of the Personal Auto Policy (PAP) to the facts of a case is an important skill. This case study helps the student make the transition from knowing policy language to applying it to losses.

Medical payments coverage provides insurance for many different loss exposures. Coverage can extend to passengers of the insured's covered auto. The circumstances of a given loss determine whether coverage applies.

Case Facts

Given the facts presented in this case, will the medical payments claims be covered? If so, what amount will each insurer pay for each claim?

Jerry, who is part owner of a pizza restaurant, delivers pizzas whenever the regular driver is unavailable. One evening when he was delivering pizzas using his own pickup truck, he invited his girlfriend, Sara, to ride with him, and she accepted. Realizing he was running late on a delivery, Jerry tried to save time by accelerating as he approached an intersection controlled by a traffic light that had already turned from green to yellow. The driver of a vehicle traveling in the opposite direction was turning left and had assumed that Jerry would stop for the light, which by that time had turned red. The two vehicles collided. Both Jerry and Sara were injured, and they received extensive medical care over the next several months. To confirm the facts of this loss are accurate, the insurer relied on police reports, recorded statements from witnesses, medical records, and inspections of the accident scene and any vehicles involved. Jerry incurred $12,000 in medical expenses, and Sara incurred $14,000 in medical expenses.

Jerry has his own PAP, which has a limit of $5,000 for medical payments coverage. Sara lives with her parents, who have a PAP with a $10,000 medical payments limit. Neither PAP contains any endorsements affecting medical payments coverage. The pizza restaurant's workers compensation policy covers its owners as well as its employees. Jerry and Sara have each made a claim for medical payments coverage under Jerry's policy, and Sara has made a claim for medical payments coverage under her parents' policy. See the exhibit "PAP Coverage Case Study Summary."

Case Analysis Tools

To determine whether Jerry's policy or Sara's parents' policy (both or neither) provide coverage for Jerry's or Sara's medical expenses incurred as a result of the auto accident, the insurance or risk management professional should have copies of the policy forms, any applicable endorsements indicated on the Declarations page of the policies, and the Declarations pages themselves. See the exhibit "Personal Auto Policy Declarations."

PAP Coverage Case Study Summary	
Insureds	Jerry has a PAP policy, and Sara's parents have a PAP policy.
Types of policies and coverage limits	Jerry's PAP—$5,000 medical payments coverage per person.
	Sara's parents' PAP—$10,000 medical payments coverage per person.
Endorsements that affect this case	None.
Other policy information	The pizza restaurant's workers compensation policy covers Jerry.
Background	The insureds have complied with the policy conditions of both policies.

[DA00254]

To determine whether a policy covers a loss, many insurance professionals apply the DICE method. ("DICE" is an acronym for categories of policy provisions: declarations, insuring agreement, conditions, and exclusions.) The DICE method has four steps:

1. Review of the declarations page to determine whether it covers the person or the property at the time of the loss
2. Review of the insuring agreement to determine whether it covers the loss
3. Review of policy conditions to determine compliance
4. Review of policy exclusions to determine whether they preclude coverage of the loss

Each of these four steps is used in every case. Other categories of policy provisions should be examined. For example, endorsements and terms defined in the policy should be reviewed in relation to the declarations, insuring agreement, exclusions, and conditions.

Determination of Coverage

To examine the policy forms to determine whether coverage applies to the losses, the insurance or risk management professional can apply the four steps of the DICE method to determine whether Jerry's policy covers Jerry's and Sara's medical expenses. The same method would be applied to determine whether Sara's medical expenses would be covered under her parents' policy.

The first DICE step is to determine whether the driver or vehicle is described on the insured's PAP Declarations page and whether the accident occurred during the policy period. In this case, Jerry is listed as named insured on his

Personal Auto Policy Declarations

Personal Auto Policy Declarations

POLICYHOLDER: Jerry Insured
(Named Insured) 216 Brookside Drive
Anytown, USA 40000

POLICY NUMBER: 296 D 468210

POLICY PERIOD: **FROM:** February 1, 20XX
TO: August 1, 20XX

But only If the required premium for this period has been paid, and for six-month renewal periods If renewal premiums are paid as required. Each period begins and ends at 12:01 A.M. standard time at the address of the policyholder.

INSURED VEHICLES AND SCHEDULE OF COVERAGES

	VEHICLE	COVERAGES	LIMITS OF INSURANCE		PREMIUM
1	20XX Ford F-150		VINXXX		
		Coverage A—Liability	$ 300,000	Each Occurrence	$ 203.00
		Coverage B—Medical Payments	$ 5,000	Each Person	$ 36.00
		Coverage C—Uninsured Motorists	$ 300,000	Each Occurrence	$ 61.80
				TOTAL	$ 300.80

POLICY FORM AND ENDORSEMENTS: PP 00 01
COUNTERSIGNATURE DATE: February 1, 20XX
AGENT: A. M. Abel

Copyright, ISO Properties, Inc. [DA00255]

own policy, and his pickup is listed as a covered auto. Further, the accident occurred during the policy period indicated on the Declarations page.

The second DICE step is to determine whether the event triggers coverage under the Insuring Agreement provision of a PAP's Part B. In this provision, the insurer promises to pay reasonable and necessary medical expenses incurred by an insured because of bodily injury caused by an accident. The Insuring Agreements in Jerry's and Sara's parents' policies are identical. See the exhibit "Part B—Medical Payments Coverage."

Personal Auto Policy Declarations

Personal Auto Policy Declarations

POLICYHOLDER: John and Jane Insured
(Named Insured) 210 Brookside Drive
Anytown, USA 40000

POLICY NUMBER: 296 D 468511

POLICY PERIOD: **FROM:** January 1, 20XX
TO: July 1, 20XX

But only if the required premium for this period has been paid, and for six-month renewal periods if renewal premiums are paid as required. Each period begins and ends at 12:01 A.M. standard time at the address of the policyholder.

INSURED VEHICLES AND SCHEDULE OF COVERAGES

	VEHICLE	COVERAGES	LIMITS OF INSURANCE		PREMIUM
1	20XX Honda Accord		VINXXX		
		Coverage A—Liability	$ 300,000	Each Occurrence	$ 203.00
		Coverage B—Medical Payments	$ 10,000	Each Person	$ 36.00
		Coverage C—Uninsured Motorists	$ 300,000	Each Occurrence	$ 61.80
				TOTAL	$ 300.80
2	20XX Ford Focus		VINXXX		
		Coverage A—Liability	$ 300,000	Each Occurrence	$ 203.00
		Coverage B—Medical Payments	$ 10,000	Each Person	$ 36.00
		Coverage C—Uninsured Motorists	$ 300,000	Each Occurrence	$ 61.80
		Coverage D—Other Than Collision	Actual Cash Value Less	$100	$ 41.60
		—Collision	Actual Cash Value Less	$250	$ 131.00
				TOTAL	$ 473.40

POLICY FORM AND ENDORSEMENTS: PP 00 01

COUNTERSIGNATURE DATE: January 1, 20XX

AGENT: A. M. Abel

Copyright, ISO Properties, Inc. [DA00256]

Part B—Medical Payments Coverage

PART B – MEDICAL PAYMENTS COVERAGE

INSURING AGREEMENT

A. We will pay reasonable expenses incurred for necessary medical and funeral services because of "bodily injury":

   1. Caused by accident; and
   2. Sustained by an "insured".

   ...

B. "Insured" as used in this Part means:

   1. You or any "family member":
      a. While "occupying"; or
      b. As a pedestrian when struck by; a motor vehicle designed for use mainly on public roads or a trailer of any type.
   2. Any other person while "occupying" "your covered auto".

Includes copyrighted material of Insurance Services Office, Inc., with its permission. Copyright, ISO Properties, Inc., 2003. [DA05636]

Jerry and Sara have incurred medical expenses as a result of the accident. To be covered, however, Jerry and Sara also have to fit the definition of an insured under the Insuring Agreement provision. This provision recognizes two classes of insureds: the named insured or "family members" (as defined in the policy) and any other person occupying a covered auto. As the named insured, Jerry fits the first class of insureds. Sara is within the second class of insureds in the definition because she was occupying the pickup, which is named in the declarations as a covered auto, at the time of the accident.

Sara may also obtain medical payments coverage through her family's PAP. Because she resides with her parents, she is covered under the Part B insuring agreement as a family member for injuries suffered while occupying any vehicle. Jerry is not an insured under Sara's family's policy.

The third DICE step is to determine whether the insureds have complied with all policy conditions—for example, that Jerry and Sara authorized the insurers to obtain medical reports and submitted proofs of loss. Also, because two policies are potentially applicable, they have notified both insurers of the accident. All other conditions for both policies were met.

The fourth DICE step is to determine whether one or more exclusions preclude the coverage the insuring agreements have granted. Two exclusions could apply here. See the exhibit "Part B—Medical Payments Coverage."

Part B—Medical Payments Coverage

PART B – MEDICAL PAYMENTS COVERAGE

EXCLUSIONS

We do not provide Medical Payments Coverage for any "insured" for "bodily injury":

...

8. Sustained while "occupying" a vehicle when it is being used in the "business" of an "insured". This Exclusion (8.) does not apply to "bodily injury" sustained while "occupying" a:
   a. Private passenger auto;
   b. Pickup or van; or
   c. "Trailer" used with a vehicle described in a. or b. above.

Includes copyrighted material of Insurance Services Office, Inc., with its permission. Copyright, ISO Properties, Inc., 2003. [DA00258]

The first exclusion in Jerry's PAP may apply to Jerry's and Sara's claims for medical payments coverage. The exclusion eliminates coverage for bodily injury sustained while the injured person is occupying a vehicle used in the insured's business. At the time of the accident, Jerry was using his pickup to deliver pizzas for the restaurant in which he has partial ownership. However, this exclusion has an exception: It does not apply to several types of vehicles, including pickups. Therefore, this exclusion would not preclude Jerry or Sara from receiving payment under Jerry's PAP. See the exhibit "Part B—Medical Payments Coverage."

Part B—Medical Payments Coverage

PART B – MEDICAL PAYMENTS COVERAGE

EXCLUSIONS

We do not provide Medical Payments Coverage for any "insured" for "bodily injury":

...

4. Occurring during the course of employment if workers' compensation benefits are required or available for the "bodily injury"

Includes copyrighted material of Insurance Services Office, Inc., with its permission. Copyright, ISO Properties, Inc., 2003. [DA00259]

Another exclusion involves Jerry's coverage alone. Injuries that occur during the course of employment are excluded from medical payments coverage if workers compensation benefits are required or available. Jerry is part owner of the pizza restaurant and was delivering pizza when the accident occurred. The restaurant's workers compensation policy was in force at the time of the accident, and it covered the restaurant's owners as well as its employees. Therefore, any claim by Jerry to his PAP insurer for medical payments coverage will likely be denied. This exclusion does not apply to Sara, and her claim is therefore covered under Jerry's policy.

No exclusions in Sara's family's PAP apply to Sara's claim under that policy. Therefore, Sara's claim under that policy would be covered, too.

Determination of Amounts Payable

Determining the amount payable for a loss under medical payments coverage may involve analyzing such issues as whether more than one insurance policy provides the coverage for the same injuries. Because Jerry is not covered under either PAP policy and Sara is covered under both, the task is to determine how much Sara can collect under both policies. The Other Insurance provision of the PAP addresses these situations. See the exhibit "Part B—Medical Payments Coverage."

Part B—Medical Payments Coverage

If there is other applicable auto medical payments insurance we will pay only our share of the loss. Our share is the proportion that our limit of liability bears to the total of all applicable limits. However, any insurance we provide with respect to a vehicle you do not own, including any vehicle while used as a temporary substitute for "your covered auto", shall be excess over any other collectible auto insurance providing payments for medical or funeral expenses.

Includes copyrighted material of Insurance Services Office, Inc., with its permission. Copyright, ISO Properties, Inc., 2003. [DA00260]

The pickup Sara was occupying at the time of the accident, owned by Jerry, is a nonowned auto under her family's medical payments coverage, making that coverage excess over Jerry's medical payments coverage. Jerry's policy has a $5,000 limit (which will pay first as primary coverage), and Sara's family policy has a $10,000 limit (which will pay second as excess coverage). The total amount of coverage available to Sara is $15,000. Consequently, all of the $14,000 in medical expenses will be covered. The first $5,000 will be paid by Jerry's PAP and remaining balance of $9,000 will be paid by her parents' PAP. See the exhibit "Determination of Amounts Payable."

> **Determination of Amounts Payable**
>
> Jerry's medical expenses are not covered under his own PAP or Sara's parents' PAP. However, he can make a claim for medical expenses under the restaurant's workers compensation policy.
>
> Sara is covered under Jerry's PAP, which has primary coverage up to $5,000. She is also covered under her parents' PAP, which has excess coverage up to $10,000, creating a combined coverage limit of $15,000 for her medical expenses. Therefore, with $14,000 in medical expenses the first $5,000 will be paid by Jerry's PAP, and the remaining $9,000 will be paid by her parents' PAP.

[DA05638]

PART C—UNINSURED MOTORISTS COVERAGE

It can be emotionally devastating when a family member is severely injured by another driver in an auto accident. It can also be financially devastating if the at-fault driver is uninsured.

Part C—Uninsured Motorists (UM) Coverage of the Personal Auto Policy (PAP) is intended to compensate an insured and the insured's family members for injuries caused by an at-fault uninsured motorist, a hit-and-run driver, or a driver whose insurer is insolvent. The UM provisions in the PAP are usually modified or completely replaced by state-specific endorsements because each state's UM law may require unique provisions. However, the basic PAP UM provisions, though seldom used without modification, provide a basic understanding of the usual elements of this coverage.

Part C includes these provisions:

- Insuring Agreement
- Exclusions
- Limit of Liability
- Other Insurance
- Arbitration

Insuring Agreement

In the Part C—Insuring Agreement, the insurer agrees to pay compensatory damages that the insured person is legally entitled to recover from the owner or operator of an uninsured motor vehicle because of bodily injury caused by an accident. Such compensatory damages could include medical expenses, rehabilitation expenses, lost wages, and other losses resulting from the insured's bodily injury. Because the insuring agreement limits coverage to compensatory damages, punitive, or exemplary, damages (which are meant to punish a driver for a reckless, malicious, or deceitful act) are not covered.

UM coverage compensates insureds for damages caused by uninsured motorists without their having to sue the uninsured driver. However, UM coverage applies only if the uninsured motorist is legally responsible for the accident.

Although the standard PAP provides UM coverage only for bodily injury claims, some states' UM coverage applies to property damage claims as well. In such states, the UM property damage coverage is subject to a deductible, such as $200 or $300.

Insured Persons

Three classes of persons are considered insureds under UM coverage:

- The named insured and family members—These individuals are covered if injured by an uninsured motor vehicle while occupying a covered auto or a vehicle that is not owned by the named insured or a family member. They are also covered as pedestrians.
- Any other person occupying a covered auto—Passengers in a covered auto have coverage for bodily injury caused by an uninsured motorist.
- Any person legally entitled to recover damages because of bodily injury to a person described in the preceding two paragraphs—For example, a surviving spouse of a person killed in an accident caused by an uninsured driver is covered.

Uninsured Motor Vehicles

Part C specifies the types of vehicles that are considered **uninsured motor vehicles**. An uninsured motor vehicle is a land motor vehicle or trailer of any type that meets any of these criteria:

- No bodily injury liability insurance or bond applies to the vehicle at the time of the accident.
- A bodily injury liability policy or bond is in force, but the limit for bodily injury liability is less than the minimum amount required by the financial responsibility law in the state where the named insured's covered auto is principally garaged.
- The vehicle is a hit-and-run vehicle, whose operator or owner cannot be identified, that hits (a) the named insured or any family member, (b) a vehicle that the named insured or any family member is occupying, or (c) the named insured's covered auto.
- A bodily injury liability policy or bond applies at the time of the accident, but the insurance or bonding company (a) denies coverage or (b) is or becomes insolvent. For example, if Tom has a valid claim against a negligent motorist whose liability insurer becomes insolvent before the claim is paid, Tom can collect for his bodily injury damages under the UM coverage of his PAP.

> **Uninsured motor vehicle**
> A land motor vehicle or trailer that is not insured for bodily injury liability, is insured for less than the financial responsibility limits, is a hit-and-run vehicle, or whose insurer denies coverage or becomes insolvent.

Part C also specifies certain vehicles that are not considered to be uninsured motor vehicles. If an insured is injured by one of these vehicles, UM coverage does not apply. As stated in Part C of the PAP, the definition of uninsured motor vehicle does not include any vehicle or equipment that meets any of these criteria:[1]

- It is owned by or furnished or available for the regular use of you or any "family member."
- It is owned or operated by a self-insurer under any applicable motor vehicle law, except a self-insurer which is or becomes insolvent.
- It is owned by any governmental unit or agency.
- It is operated on rails or crawler treads.
- It is designed mainly for use off public roads while not on public roads.
- It is located for use as a residence or premises.

Exclusions

As with most coverages, Part C is limited by exclusions. The UM coverage has these exclusions.

Owned But Not Insured Vehicle

This exclusion eliminates UM coverage for bodily injury sustained by an insured while occupying, or when struck by, any motor vehicle that is owned by that insured but not insured for UM under "this policy" (the PAP under which coverage is being sought). For example, if Madeline has not purchased UM coverage under "this policy" on a vehicle she owns, and if, while occupying it, she is struck by a vehicle driven by an uninsured, at-fault driver, Madeline's PAP would not provide any UM coverage for this accident. If Madeline has purchased UM coverage for this vehicle under another policy, the auto could be covered under that other policy.

Owned Vehicle With Primary UM Coverage in Other Policy

If a vehicle owned by the named insured of "this policy" has primary UM coverage in another policy, and a family member is injured by an uninsured motorist while occupying the vehicle, "this policy" would provide no UM coverage for the family member. For example, Susan insures a car she owns and uses in her business under a business auto policy that includes UM coverage. Susan's daughter would not have UM coverage under Susan's PAP while occupying that vehicle.

Claim Settlement That Prejudices Insurer's Right of Recovery

UM coverage does not apply to a claim that the insured settles without the insurer's consent if such a settlement prejudices the insurer's right to recover payment. In a legal context, "prejudice" means to injure or damage another party's right. The purpose of this exclusion is to protect the insurer's right to assert a subrogation action against the party who is legally responsible for the insured's injuries. For example, George, who has UM coverage on his vehicle, is involved in a serious auto accident. He agrees to accept a payment from the at-fault driver that is well below the driver's liability policy limits because he intends to make a UM claim against his own insurer for any additional damages. This exclusion allows George's insurer to deny his claim because by accepting the low payment from the at-fault driver, George prejudiced the insurer's right to recover full payment from the at-fault driver.

Public or Livery Conveyance

If a person is injured while occupying a covered auto when it is being used as a public or livery conveyance (such as a taxi or public bus), UM coverage does not apply. Most state forms include a reinforced public or livery conveyance exclusion that also excludes any period of time a covered auto is logged into a transportation network platform. For example, if Paul decides to supplement the family income by providing a part-time taxi service from the airport to local hotels, he would not have UM coverage while doing so. Because this exclusion applies only to "your covered auto," the insured and family members would be covered for UM while occupying a public or livery conveyance that is not "your covered auto." In addition, the exclusion contains an exception clarifying that the exclusion does not apply to a share-the-expense car pool.

Vehicle Used Without Reasonable Belief of Being Entitled

UM coverage does not apply to any person who uses a vehicle without a reasonable belief that he or she is entitled to do so. The exclusion contains an exception that states that the exclusion does not apply to family members.

No Benefit to Workers Compensation or Disability Benefits Insurer

UM coverage cannot directly or indirectly benefit any insurer or self-insurer under a workers compensation law or disability benefits law. In some states, if an injured employee receives workers compensation benefits, the workers compensation insurer has a legal right to recover the amount of the benefits from a negligent third party through subrogation. If an employee receives workers compensation benefits for an injury involving an uninsured, at-fault driver, the workers compensation insurer could sue the driver or attempt to make a claim under the injured employee's uninsured motorists coverage. This exclusion prevents the workers compensation insurer from obtaining reimbursement under the injured worker's UM coverage.

Punitive Damages

As stated in the Part C insuring agreement, UM coverage applies only to compensatory damages, which do not include punitive damages. For example, Debbie is struck by an uninsured vehicle driven by an at-fault driver and suffers serious injuries. Debbie is dissatisfied with the amount offered by her own UM insurer and sues the driver. The case goes to court, and the jury awards her punitive damages in addition to her compensatory damages. Debbie's own insurer would not pay the punitive damages amount under UM coverage.

Personal Vehicle Sharing Program

UM coverage does not apply to any insured who sustains an injury while occupying a vehicle enrolled in a personal vehicle sharing program under the terms of a written agreement. Coverage also does not apply while a covered auto is being used in connection with a personal vehicle sharing program by anyone other than the insured or a family member.

Limit of Liability

The minimum amount of UM coverage available under the PAP is set by the financial responsibility or compulsory insurance law of the state in which the insured auto is principally garaged. Higher limits can be purchased for an additional premium. The limit of liability for UM coverage is shown in the declarations. UM coverage is normally written on a split-limits basis, but coverage on a single-limit basis is available by endorsement.

The limits shown are the most that will be paid regardless of the number of insured persons, claims made, vehicles or premiums shown in the declarations, or vehicles involved in the accident. This provision is intended to prevent "stacking" of UM payments under a policy that covers more than one car owned by the named insured. Stacking refers to situations in which the insured maintains that, because the policy covers, and premiums have been paid for, two (or more) vehicles, he or she should collect up to the stated limit multiplied by the number of vehicles. For example, assume the insured owns three cars that are covered by a PAP with a UM limit of $25,000 per person. If the insured is injured by an uninsured motorist, the most the insured can recover is $25,000, not $75,000.

The UM section specifically states that no person will receive duplicate payments for any loss under Part A—Liability Coverage, Part B—Medical Payments Coverage, or Part C—Uninsured Motorists Coverage, or under any UM coverage provided by the policy. For example, if Christine is injured by a hit-and-run driver and incurs $5,000 in medical expenses, she cannot collect $5,000 under her medical payments coverage and then collect an additional $5,000 for the same expenses under her UM coverage. (She can, however, attempt to collect any additional damages under her UM coverage as long as they do not duplicate the expenses for which the insurer has already paid under her medical payments coverage.)

Likewise, the insurer will not make duplicate payment under the UM coverage if payment has been made by the person or organization legally responsible for the accident or if the injured person is entitled to receive payment under a workers compensation or disability benefits law.

Other Insurance

If other applicable UM insurance is available under one or more policies, these provisions apply to the payment for damages:

- The total amount paid will be no more than the highest limit of any of the policies that provide coverage. For example, Susan has two policies that both provide her UM coverage. One policy has a per-person limit of $100,000 and the other policy has a per-person limit of $250,000. The most she will be paid, regardless of how high her damages are, will be $250,000.
- Coverage for an accident involving a vehicle the named insured does not own, including any vehicle while being used as a temporary substitute for a covered auto, is provided on an excess basis over any collectible insurance providing coverage on a primary basis.
- For example, assume that Louis has UM coverage with limits of $50,000/$100,000 under his PAP. (These limits indicate $50,000 per person and $100,000 per accident for bodily injury. No property damage limit is given because UM coverage usually does not include property damage.) He is injured by an uninsured motorist while riding in Gayle's car. Gayle has $25,000/$50,000 of UM coverage. If Louis is entitled to $35,000 for his bodily injuries, Gayle's insurer pays the first $25,000 as primary insurer of her owned vehicle, and Louis's insurer pays the remaining $10,000 as excess insurance (because Louis does not own the vehicle).
- If "this policy" and another policy (or policies) provide coverage on a primary basis, each policy will contribute proportionally to the insured's recovery. Each insurer's share is equal to the proportion its UM limit bears to the total amount available under all applicable coverages provided on a primary basis.
- For example, John has two policies that both provide him UM coverage on a primary basis. The policy with Insurer A has a per-person UM limit of $100,000, and the policy with Insurer B has a per-person UM limit of $50,000. While driving his own vehicle, John is injured by an uninsured motorist, and his damages are $60,000. If two automobile policies cover the same vehicle on a primary basis, each insurer pays its pro rata share. Each insurer pays according to the following formula:

    Insurer A: ($100,000 ÷ $150,000) × $60,000 = $40,000

    Insurer B: ($50,000 ÷ $150,000) × $60,000 = $20,000

- If "this policy" and another policy (or policies) provide coverage on an excess basis, each policy will contribute proportionally to the insured's recovery, based on the excess limits each policy provides.

Arbitration

If the insurer and insured cannot agree on whether the insured is entitled to recover damages from an uninsured motorist or on the amount of damages, the dispute can be settled by **arbitration**. However, arbitration does not include disputes involving coverage, such as whether the driver of the covered auto had a reasonable belief he was entitled to use the auto.

If the insurer and insured consent to arbitration, each party selects an arbitrator, and the two arbitrators select a third arbitrator. If the two arbitrators cannot agree on a third arbitrator within thirty days, either party can request that the selection be made by a judge of a court having jurisdiction. Each party pays the expenses it incurs, and both parties share the expenses of the third arbitrator.

A decision agreed to by two of the three arbitrators is binding as to whether the insured is legally entitled to recover damages and the amount of damages. However, this decision is binding only if the amount of damages does not exceed the minimum limit for bodily injury specified by the state's financial responsibility law. If the amount of damages exceeds that limit, either party can demand the right to a trial within sixty days of the arbitrators' decision. Otherwise, the arbitrators' decision is binding.

Arbitration
An alternative dispute resolution (ADR) method by which disputing parties use a neutral outside party to examine the issues and develop a settlement, which can be final and binding.

UM/UIM ENDORSEMENTS AND STATE VARIATIONS

In most states, it is possible to supplement uninsured motorists (UM) coverage with underinsured motorists (UIM) coverage to address shortcomings of UM.

UIM coverage is an outgrowth of UM coverage. UIM coverage goes beyond UM coverage. It is important in situations in which a negligent driver is insured for at least the minimum required financial responsibility limits but the policy's liability limits are insufficient to pay the insured's damages.

Purpose of Coverage

An increasing number of insureds who have UM coverage with high coverage limits are involved in accidents with at-fault motorists who are insured at or slightly above the minimum state-required limits. Because in such situations the at-fault motorists are insured for at least the minimum state-required limits, they are not considered uninsured motorists under UM coverage provisions. Although a person who has been injured or whose vehicle has been damaged can seek recovery from the negligent motorist, any amount recovered may represent far less than the injured person's full damages.

For example, a victim may receive a $75,000 judgment against an at-fault motorist who has insurance for only $25,000 (the minimum required by the state's financial responsibility law) and no other assets to make up the difference. Unless the victim has UIM coverage, the most she can recover is $25,000. UIM coverage always applies to damages for bodily injury and, in some states, also includes damages for property damage.

In some states, the Underinsured Motorists Coverage Endorsement (PP 03 11) of Insurance Services Office, Inc. (ISO) can be added to the Personal Auto Policy (PAP) to provide coverage as a supplement to the UM coverage in the PAP. In several states, however, insurers use either a state-specific UIM endorsement or a single, state-specific endorsement providing both UM and UIM coverages that replaces the UM coverage of the standard PAP.

State Variations

Regardless of the policy provisions used by an insurer, individual states' UM/UIM statutes govern who is protected and under what circumstances. Where the insured's vehicle is registered or principally garaged determines which state's laws apply. Insurance and risk management professionals must be familiar with the laws in their states regarding both UM and UIM coverage. However, they should generally avoid applying court decisions related to UM to UIM cases. Courts (even in the same jurisdiction) do not always come to the same conclusion, especially in states where UIM coverage is optional but UM coverage is mandated.

Mandatory or Optional Coverage

Some states mandate that UIM coverage be provided on all auto liability policies. Other states allow insureds to reject UIM coverage, but typically only if the named insured rejects the coverage in writing.

Mandatory or optional limits for UIM coverage also vary by state. Many states require that the UIM limit equal the UM coverage limit, which, for many states, must also equal the PAP's bodily injury liability limit. In some states, the UM limit can be reduced, but not below the state's minimum financial responsibility limit.

Limits Trigger or Damages Trigger

Some states' UIM endorsements contain a "limits trigger." Other states' endorsements contain a "damages trigger." In general, a trigger is something that must occur or exist in order for coverage to apply. In states that apply the limits trigger, the endorsement applies when the negligent driver carries liability limits below the limits provided by the UIM coverage of the injured party.

For example, suppose Tom has an auto liability policy with a $100,000 UIM limit and Lynn has an auto liability policy with a single limit of $50,000, both of which exceed the minimum financial responsibility limits in her state. The two are involved in an auto accident, and Lynn is liable for Tom's damages. If Tom's damages are $60,000, he will collect $50,000 from Lynn's insurer and $10,000 under his UIM coverage. His UIM protection applies even if the limits of Lynn's policy are greater than the minimum required by the state. The key criterion for UIM protection with a limits trigger is that the liability limits of the other party's policy are less than the insured's UIM limits.

In states that apply a damages trigger, the UIM endorsement applies when the negligent driver carries liability insurance limits that are lower than the injured party's actual damages.

For example, assume Anne has purchased UIM coverage with a $50,000 single limit. Randy has purchased auto liability coverage with a $100,000 single limit. Randy causes an accident in which Anne is injured. If Anne's damages are $150,000, her UIM coverage will be triggered because Randy's policy limit is less than Anne's damages. However, if Anne's damages are $75,000, her UIM coverage will not be triggered because her damages are less than Randy's limit. The key criterion for coverage to apply under UIM coverage with a damages trigger is that the liability limits of the other party's policy are less than the insured's damages.

Stacking

Another UIM variation among states relates to stacking, which is the application of two or more limits to a single auto accident. Stacking may involve two or more separate policies (interpolicy stacking). The UIM policy limit of one policy would be added to (stacked on) the UIM limit of the other policy.

For example, when a husband and wife have separate policies, both policies may apply when either or both of them are injured by an underinsured motorist. If the UIM limit of the husband's policy is $25,000 and the UIM limit of the wife's policy is $50,000, when the policies' limits are stacked, the insured will be able to collect up to $75,000.

Some states allow interpolicy stacking by endorsement. Other states do not.

Stacking can also occur within a single policy that covers more than one vehicle (intrapolicy stacking). Some states allow intrapolicy stacking by endorsement. In some states, the insured can choose between stacking or nonstacking but must pay a higher premium for a policy that allows stacking. Other states prohibit intrapolicy stacking. They require that the maximum to be paid for an accident is the single (unstacked) UIM limit shown on the Declarations page, regardless of the number of insureds, claims made, vehicles or premiums shown on the Declarations page, or vehicles involved.

PART C—UNINSURED MOTORISTS COVERAGE CASE STUDY

Applying Part C—Uninsured Motorists (UM) Coverage of the Personal Auto Policy (PAP) to auto accidents is similar to applying liability coverages. This case study helps the student make the transition from knowing policy language to applying it to losses.

The PAP's UM coverage covers losses caused by another driver in a wide range of circumstances. The circumstances of a loss are critical to determining whether UM coverage applies.

Case Facts

Given the facts presented in this case, will the uninsured motorist claims of the insureds be covered? If so, what amount would the insurer pay for each of the insureds' claims?

Harry and Amanda, a married couple, insure their vehicles under a PAP, which lists them both as named insureds. Amanda was driving to work when one of her car's front tires suddenly lost air. Amanda stopped the car on the side of the road and was inspecting the tire when she was struck by another vehicle and severely injured. The driver of the other car, Rocky, panicked and fled the scene. To confirm the facts of this loss are accurate, the insurer relied on police reports, recorded statements from witnesses, medical records, and inspections of the accident scene and any vehicles involved.

Rocky did not have auto liability insurance or enough assets to pay for all of the injuries he caused. Amanda incurred $100,000 in medical bills and significant pain and suffering. While Amanda was in the hospital, Harry was deprived of her companionship. Amanda and Harry have $250,000 in uninsured motorists coverage per occurrence on their PAP, and she believed that this coverage would pay the remainder of her medical bills. Therefore, when Rocky's attorney offered $5,000 to settle her claim against Rocky, she agreed and signed a release of her claim against Rocky.

After and in addition to receiving the $5,000 from Rocky's attorney, Amanda has demanded that their own insurer pay her a total of $200,000 for her UM claim, which would include consideration of her medical bills as well as the other pain and suffering. Harry has demanded their insurer pay him $10,000 for his UM claim. Their PAP does not contain any endorsements affecting UM coverage. For the purposes of this case study, assume that the policy conditions have been met. See the exhibit "PAP Coverage Case Study Summary."

PAP Coverage Case Study Summary

Insureds	Amanda and Harry are each insured under their PAP.
Types of policies and coverage limits	Amanda's and Harry's PAP has $250,000 UM coverage per occurrence.
Endorsements that affect the case	None
Other policy information	No other relevant information
Background	The insureds have complied with all policy conditions.

[DA00264]

Case Analysis Tools

To determine whether Harry and Amanda's PAP provides coverage for the injuries they incurred that were caused by Rocky's negligence, the insurance or risk management professional should have copies of the policy forms, any applicable endorsements that are indicated on the Declarations page of the policy, and the Declarations page itself. See the exhibit "Personal Auto Policy Declarations."

Determination of Coverage

To examine the policy forms to determine whether coverage applies to the losses, the insurance or risk management professional can apply the four steps of the DICE method.

The first DICE step is to determine whether the driver or vehicle is described on the Declarations page of Harry and Amanda's PAP and whether the accident occurred during the policy period. Because Amanda is listed as the named insured on the PAP with Harry, she qualifies as an insured under that policy. The accident occurred during the policy period. See the exhibit "Part C—Uninsured Motorists Coverage."

The second DICE step is to determine whether the event triggers coverage under the uninsured motorists insuring agreement of Harry and Amanda's PAP. In this policy provision, the insurer agrees to pay compensatory damages that an insured is legally entitled to recover from the owner or operator of an uninsured motor vehicle because of bodily injury caused by an accident. A court probably would find Rocky liable for Amanda's injuries. Because Rocky had no liability coverage in effect at the time of the accident, Amanda should be able to establish with her insurer that she is legally entitled to recover from the operator of an uninsured motor vehicle.

Personal Auto Policy Declarations

Personal Auto Policy Declarations

POLICYHOLDER: Harry and Amanda Insured
(Named Insured) 400 Brookside Drive
Anytown, USA 40000

POLICY NUMBER: 296 D 467211

POLICY PERIOD: **FROM:** June 15, 20XX
TO: Dec. 15, 20XX

But only If the required premium for this period has been paid, and for six-month renewal periods If renewal premiums are paid as required. Each period begins and ends at 12:01 A.M. standard time at the address of the policyholder.

INSURED VEHICLES AND SCHEDULE OF COVERAGES

	VEHICLE	COVERAGES	LIMITS OF INSURANCE		PREMIUM
1	20XX Isuzu Rodeo		VINXXX		
		Coverage A—Liability	$ 250,000	Each Occurrence	$ 203.00
		Coverage B—Medical Payments	$ 5,000	Each Person	$ 36.00
		Coverage C—Uninsured Motorists	$ 250,000	Each Occurrence	$ 61.80
				TOTAL	$ 300.80
2	20XX Ford Mustang		VINXXX		
		Coverage A—Liability	$ 250,000	Each Occurrence	$ 203.00
		Coverage B—Medical Payments	$ 5,000	Each Person	$ 36.00
		Coverage C—Uninsured Motorists	$ 250,000	Each Occurrence	$ 61.80
		Coverage D—Other Than Collision	Actual Cash Value Less	$100	$ 41.60
		—Collision	Actual Cash Value Less	$250	$ 131.00
				TOTAL	$ 473.40

POLICY FORM AND ENDORSEMENTS: PP 00 01

COUNTERSIGNATURE DATE: June 15, 20XX

AGENT: A. M. Abel

Copyright, ISO Properties, Inc. [DA00265]

> **Part C—Uninsured Motorists Coverage**
>
> PART C – UNINSURED MOTORISTS COVERAGE
>
> INSURING AGREEMENT
>
> A. We will pay compensatory damages which an "insured" is legally entitled to recover from the owner or operator of an "uninsured motor vehicle" because of "bodily injury":
>
>   1. Sustained by an "insured"; and
>   2. Caused by an accident.
>
>   The owner's or operator's liability for these damages must arise out of the ownership, maintenance or use of the "uninsured motor vehicle".

Includes copyrighted material of Insurance Services Office, Inc., with its permission. Copyright, ISO Properties, Inc., 2003. [DA00268]

Harry is also entitled to UM coverage from this accident. The insuring agreement of the couple's PAP includes in its definition of "insured" any person legally entitled to recover damages because of bodily injury to another insured. Harry is legally entitled to damages resulting from Amanda's bodily injuries, which could include his loss of companionship and quality of life with her. However, his claim is dependent upon Amanda's claim. If her UM claim is denied, his will be as well.

The third DICE step is to determine whether the parties have complied with all policy conditions, including, for example, Amanda's timely reporting of the loss to her insurer and authorization of release of her medical records to the insurer. See the exhibit "Part C—Uninsured Motorists Coverage."

> **Part C—Uninsured Motorists Coverage**
>
> PART C – UNINSURED MOTORISTS COVERAGE
>
> EXCLUSIONS
>
>   ...
>
>   B. We do not provide Uninsured Motorists Coverage for "bodily injury" sustained by any "insured":
>
>   1. If that "insured" or the legal representative settles the "bodily injury" claim and such settlement prejudices our right to recover payment.

Includes copyrighted material of Insurance Services Office, Inc., with its permission. Copyright, ISO Properties, Inc., 2003. [DA00269]

The fourth DICE step is to determine whether one or more exclusions preclude the coverage the insuring agreement has granted. An exclusion that could apply in this situation involves a claim settlement that prejudices an insurer's right of recovery.

By settling with Rocky for a minimal amount with the expectation that she could recover the remaining amount of her damages from her insurer, Amanda may have prejudiced her insurer's right to recover from Rocky. The insurer has a legal right to recover from Rocky any payments it makes to Amanda, because he caused her injuries. However, when she settled with Rocky, Amanda signed a release that terminated her insurer's right of recovery. If the insurer could have proven that Rocky had assets sufficient to reimburse it for the amounts it would have paid Amanda, it could have claimed that it was prejudiced by her settlement; therefore, this exclusion may eliminate her coverage. Assume for the purposes of this case study that Amanda's insurer decided that, because Rocky had so few assets, it would be unable to prove that its right of recovery against Rocky was prejudiced by her settlement with him and that it, therefore, did not assert that exclusion.

Determination of Amounts Payable

Before settling with Rocky, Amanda could have sued him in order to get a court to determine the appropriate amount of compensation for her injuries. However, litigation is a costly and lengthy process that sometimes produces unexpected results. Amanda and her insurer may instead have opted to negotiate for an appropriate amount of compensation to be paid under her UM coverage. If they could not agree on an amount, they could submit the matter to arbitration. See the exhibit "Part C—Uninsured Motorists Coverage."

Part C—Uninsured Motorists Coverage

PART C – UNINSURED MOTORISTS COVERAGE

ARBITRATION

   A. If we and an "insured" do not agree:

   ...

       2. As to the amount of damages which are recoverable by that "insured"; from the owner or operator of an "uninsured motor vehicle" then the matter may be arbitrated.

   ...

   C. ...A decision agreed to by at least two of the arbitrators will be binding as to:

   ...

       2. The amount of damages. This applies only if the amount does not exceed the minimum limit for bodily injury specified by the financial responsibility law of the state in which "your covered auto" is principally garaged. If the amount exceeds that limit, either party may demand the right to a trial.

Includes copyrighted material of Insurance Services Office, Inc., with its permission. Copyright, ISO Properties, Inc., 2003. [DA00270]

The Arbitration provision in Part C allows an arbitration panel to render a decision on the amount payable to an insured. However, this decision is binding only if the amount of damages does not exceed the minimum limit for bodily injury specified by the state's financial responsibility law. In this case, Amanda was seriously injured; therefore, the arbitration panel will likely find that she is entitled to an amount substantially larger than the minimum limit specified by the state. Under the policy, that decision would be nonbinding. If Amanda believes the amount rendered by the arbitration panel is inadequate, she can still pursue other remedies.

As noted, Amanda's husband, Harry, also has a claim under the UM coverage of their PAP. He is entitled to compensation for loss of companionship and quality of life with Amanda due to her injuries. Therefore, it is appropriate for the arbitration panel to also award Harry an amount for his damages. See the exhibit "Limit of Liability."

Limit of Liability

LIMIT OF LIABILITY

A. The limit of liability shown in the Declarations for each person for Uninsured Motorists Coverage is our maximum limit of liability for all damages, including damages for care, loss of services or death, arising out of "bodily injury" sustained by any one person in any one accident. Subject to this limit for each person, the limit of liability shown in the Declarations for each accident for Uninsured Motorists Coverage is our maximum limit of liability for all damages for "bodily injury" resulting from any one accident.

This is the most we will pay regardless of the number of:

1. "Insureds";
2. Claims made;
3. Vehicles or premiums shown in the Declarations; or
4. Vehicles involved in the accident.

Includes copyrighted material of Insurance Services Office, Inc., with its permission. Copyright, ISO Properties, Inc., 2003. [DA00271]

However, even with the additional amount for Harry's damages, the most the insurer would pay for the sum of damages recoverable by Amanda and Harry would be the applicable limit of liability. That is, they cannot each collect up to the limit separately. This is because the limit is the most the insurer will pay for bodily injury resulting from any one accident regardless of the number of insureds, claims made, vehicles shown in the declarations, or vehicles involved in the accident.

After reviewing the facts of the accident, the medical records, and the policy documents, Harry and Amanda's insurer agrees to their demands of $200,000 for her and $10,000 for him. See the exhibit "Determination of Amounts Payable."

> **Determination of Amounts Payable**
>
> Of the $250,000 UM policy limit per occurrence, Amanda and Harry's insurer paid them a total of $210,000 based on Amanda's demand to the insurer and Harry's loss of companionship, for which he received $10,000. They also recovered $5,000 from Rocky.

[DA05639]

SUMMARY

The Personal Auto Policy (PAP) is used to insure autos owned by individuals and families, such as cars, vans, and station wagons. The PAP includes a Declarations page, an Agreement and Definitions section, and six coverage sections. The PAP may also include one or more endorsements that modify or expand the coverage provided.

The PAP Declarations page provides specific information regarding the insurer, the named insured, the policy number and the policy period, insured vehicles, the coverages provided, and a list of any endorsements that may apply to the policy. Also included in the declarations are the identification of insured vehicles' lienholders, if any; vehicles' garage locations if other than at the insured's address; rating information; and the signature of an authorized legal representative of the insurer.

The Definitions section of the Personal Auto Policy provides a useful reference tool and contains definitions for many terms used throughout the policy. The definitions are written in an easy-to-read format to allow for a clear understanding of the insurance terms used in the policy.

Part A—Liability Coverage of the PAP pays damages for bodily injury or property damage for which the insured is legally responsible because of an auto accident. The Insuring Agreement of Part A provides a broad grant of coverage, which can be either extended or narrowed by the following policy provisions: Supplementary Payments, Exclusions, Limit of Liability, Out of State Coverage, Financial Responsibility, and Other Insurance.

Knowing how to apply liability coverages to the facts of a case is an important skill. This is accomplished by first determining whether a loss is covered and, if so, determining how much an insurer should pay for the loss.

Part B—Medical Payments Coverage of the PAP provides auto accident medical coverage that pays reasonable and necessary medical and funeral expenses, regardless of who is at fault for an auto accident. The coverage granted by the

Insuring Agreement in Part B is limited by Exclusions, Limit of Liability, and Other Insurance provisions in the same part.

Applying medical payments coverages to the facts of a case is accomplished by first determining whether a loss is covered. If the policy covers the loss, the next step is to determine how much the insurer should pay.

Part C—Uninsured Motorists Coverage pays for bodily injury to an insured who is injured by an uninsured motorist, a hit-and-run driver, or a driver whose insurer becomes insolvent. The coverage is limited by a set of exclusions and is further modified by the Limit of Insurance, Other Insurance, and Arbitration provisions in Part C.

UIM coverage is an outgrowth of UM coverage. Unlike UM coverage, UIM coverage applies in situations in which a negligent driver is insured for at least the minimum required financial responsibility limits but has liability limits that are insufficient to pay the insured's damages.

As with most coverages, it is valuable to know how to apply UM coverage to the facts of a case. This case study helps the student make the transition from knowing policy language to applying it to losses.

ASSIGNMENT NOTE

1. Includes copyrighted material of Insurance Services Office, Inc., with its permission. Copyright, ISO Properties, Inc., 2003.

Direct Your Learning

4

PAP: Physical Damage, Duties After an Accident, Endorsements

Educational Objectives

After learning the content of this assignment, you should be able to:

- Summarize each of the provisions in Part D—Coverage for Damage to Your Auto of the Personal Auto Policy.
- Given a case describing an auto physical damage claim, determine whether Part D—Coverage for Damage to Your Auto of the Personal Auto Policy would cover the claim and, if so, the amount the insurer would pay for the claim.
- Describe the insured's duties following a covered auto accident or loss as shown in Part E of the Personal Auto Policy.
- Summarize each of the general provisions in Part F of the Personal Auto Policy.
- Describe the Personal Auto Policy endorsements that are used to handle common auto loss exposures.
- Describe the Personal Auto Endorsements that are used to handle exposures related to transportation network companies.
- Given a case describing an auto claim, determine whether the Personal Auto Policy would cover the claim and, if so, the amount the insurer would pay for the claim.

Outline

Part D—Coverage for Damage to Your Auto

Part D—Coverage for Damage to Your Auto Case Study

Part E—Duties After an Accident or Loss

Part F—General Provisions

Common Endorsements to the Personal Auto Policy

Personal Auto Endorsements for Transportation Network Exposures

Personal Auto Coverage Case Study

Summary

PAP: Physical Damage, Duties After an Accident, Endorsements

4

PART D—COVERAGE FOR DAMAGE TO YOUR AUTO

The most expensive investment for many people, aside from their residence, is their automobile. Insurance is a way to protect that investment.

Part D of the Personal Auto Policy (PAP) provides **physical damage coverage** for damage to or theft of a covered auto.

Part D includes these provisions:

- Insuring Agreement
- Transportation Expenses
- Exclusions
- Limit of Liability
- Payment of Loss
- No Benefit to Bailee
- Other Sources of Recovery
- Appraisal

Insuring Agreement

In the Part D insuring agreement, the insurer promises to pay for any direct and accidental loss to "your covered auto" or a "non-owned auto" as defined in the PAP, minus the **deductible** shown on the PAP Declarations page. Direct and accidental losses to an auto fall into two categories: collision losses and other than collision (OTC) losses.

Collision Coverage

The PAP declarations indicate whether a named insured has bought collision coverage for a specified auto as well as the amount of the premium for that coverage. Collision is defined in the PAP as the upset of or impact of "your covered auto" or a "non-owned auto" with another vehicle or object. Examples of collision losses covered under Part D of the PAP include those resulting from a car colliding with another car, hitting a tree, overturning after a driver loses control, or being damaged when a passenger in a parked car opens a car door, striking the insured vehicle parked next to it.

Physical damage coverages
There are four kinds: comprehensive—pays for loss to covered auto or its equipment from any cause not excluded, except collision or overturn; specified causes of loss—provides named peril coverage; collision—covers loss to a covered auto or its equipment by collision with another object or by overturn; and towing—provides coverage for towing and labor performed at the place of disablement.

Deductible
A portion of a covered loss that is not paid by the insurer.

Collision losses are paid regardless of fault, as in these examples:

- If Frank is responsible for an accident that damages his car, his collision coverage will pay for any physical damage to his own car, minus any deductible that applies.
- If the driver of another car causes the accident that damages Frank's car, Frank can collect either from the other driver (or the driver's insurer) or from his own insurer. If Frank collects from his own insurer, his insurer has the right to recover payment from the driver who caused the accident (or the driver's insurer). This recovery is referred to as subrogation.

If two or more autos that have collision coverage under the same policy are damaged in the same collision, only the highest deductible applies. For example, Bob owns three cars, all of which are covered under the same PAP. While turning into his driveway during a winter storm, Bob's car skids on the snow and collides with both of his other cars. Bob's PAP includes a $250 collision deductible on two of the cars and a $500 collision deductible on the third car. In settling this loss, Bob's PAP insurer will apply a single $500 deductible to the total damage to all three cars.

Other Than Collision Coverage

Similar to collision coverage, other than collision (OTC) coverage is effective only if the declarations indicate that it is provided for that auto. The distinction between collision coverage and OTC coverage is relevant: many motorists purchase only OTC coverage because it is less expensive than collision coverage. Also, the OTC coverage often has a lower deductible than that of collision coverage.

OTC coverage insures auto physical damage losses that are not caused by collision and are not specifically excluded in the policy. This coverage was previously referred to as "comprehensive," and many insurance professionals still use that label. The term was changed because "comprehensive" implies coverage for everything; however, like virtually all other coverages, OTC coverage is subject to exclusions.

While collision is specifically defined in the PAP, OTC is not. However, the policy does list certain causes of loss that are considered OTC:

- Missiles or falling objects
- Fire
- Theft or larceny
- Explosion or earthquake
- Windstorm
- Hail, water, or flood
- Malicious mischief or vandalism
- Riot or civil commotion

- Contact with a bird or animal
- Breakage of glass

The causes of loss covered by OTC are not limited to those specifically listed. Any "direct and accidental loss" that is not due to collision and is not specifically excluded would be covered as an OTC loss. For example, if a covered auto is used to take an injured person to the hospital, resulting in blood stains to the covered auto's upholstery, OTC coverage would apply. The same coverage would apply to exterior damage to a covered auto when it is splattered with paint while parked next to a house being painted.

Two points about OTC are especially important. First, colliding with a bird or an animal is an OTC loss. Such a loss is therefore subject to the OTC deductible, which is usually lower than the collision deductible. Second, if glass breakage is caused by a collision, the insured can elect to have the glass breakage covered as part of the collision loss. As a result, the deductible for collision coverage would also apply to the glass breakage. If the insured instead elects to have the glass breakage covered under OTC, both deductibles could apply.

Nonowned Autos

The Part D coverages also apply to a "non-owned auto." Therefore, if Lois borrows a car that belongs to her friend Sean, any physical damage coverage that applies to Lois's covered auto also applies to the borrowed vehicle. (However, Lois's coverage would be excess over any physical damage coverage Sean has on his car.)

An insured can occasionally drive a rented or borrowed auto, and the insured's physical damage insurance will cover the vehicle. However, if the insured regularly drives a rented or borrowed vehicle, or if one is made available for an insured's regular use, the insured's coverage does not apply. For example, if Rosa is in an accident while driving a company car furnished by her employer or a car made available for her regular use in a carpool, the Part D coverages of her PAP do not apply. The determining factor is not how frequently Rosa drives a nonowned auto, but whether the nonowned auto is made available for her regular use.

The definition of nonowned auto also includes any auto or trailer that is being used as a temporary substitute for a covered auto or trailer that is out of normal use because of its breakdown, repair, servicing, loss, or destruction. For example, if a mechanic loans Jim a car to use while his is being repaired, Jim's physical damage insurance applies to the loaner car.

If a nonowned auto is damaged by a covered cause of loss, the PAP provides the broadest coverage applicable to any covered auto shown in the declarations. For example, Oscar owns two cars that are insured by his PAP. One car is covered for both collision and OTC, while the second car is covered only for OTC. If Oscar borrows his neighbor's car, it is covered by Oscar's PAP for both collision and OTC.

Deductibles

Deductibles require the insured to share covered losses with the insurer. Part D requires deductibles for three reasons: to reduce small claims, to hold down premiums, and to encourage insureds to be careful in protecting their cars against damage or theft.

A deductible of $100, $250, $500, or some higher amount specified in the policy declarations typically applies to each covered collision loss. A separate, often lower, deductible applies to OTC losses. For example, a PAP may have a $500 collision deductible and a $250 OTC deductible.

Transportation Expenses

Transportation expenses

Additional coverage in the Personal Auto Policy for substitute transportation costs incurred as the result of a covered physical damage loss.

Part D also provides an additional coverage known as **transportation expenses**. Following a covered physical damage loss to a covered auto, the insurer will reimburse the insured for temporary transportation expenses, such as auto rental fees or taxi fares, up to $20 per day, to a maximum of $600 for each covered loss. The same limits apply to a nonowned auto when the insured is legally responsible to the auto's owner for the owner's transportation expenses. A nonowned rental car is also subject to the transportation expense limits when the car's owner claims a loss of income because the car cannot be rented while it is being repaired and the named insured is legally responsible for the renter's loss of income.

The transportation expense coverage provided by the PAP applies only to expenses incurred when the cause of loss is covered by the policy. For example, if the insured did not purchase collision coverage, the policy would not apply to transportation expenses incurred due to a collision. Or if an insured has to rent a car because of mechanical difficulty, the rental car expenses are not covered.

Transportation expenses are not subject to a dollar-amount deductible. However, they are subject to a waiting period, which is essentially a deductible stated in time rather than in dollars. While a forty-eight-hour waiting period applies to total theft losses under OTC coverage, a twenty-four-hour waiting period applies to loss by other perils under both collision and OTC.

Because stolen cars often require repairs after they are recovered, transportation expenses coverage extends until the time the stolen auto is returned to use (or the insurer pays for the auto). For example, Luisa's covered auto is stolen and recovered seventeen days later. Her car has been damaged, and repair parts must be ordered. Luisa's car is in the repair shop a total of twenty days. Her PAP, which includes OTC coverage, will pay Luisa's transportation expenses for thirty-five days (17 + 20 − 2), where the two days is the waiting period, up to $20 per day, but subject to a maximum of $600.

Exclusions

A number of exclusions narrow the broad coverage in the PAP Part D insuring agreement.

Public or Livery Conveyance

Physical damage insurance does not apply while the vehicle is used as a public or livery conveyance, such as a taxi or a bus. This includes any period of time the vehicle is being used by any person who is logged into a transportation network platform, whether or not there are passengers in the vehicle. As with comparable exclusions under other coverages of the PAP, this exclusion does not apply to a share-the-expense car pool.

Wear and Tear, Freezing, Breakdown, and Road Damage to Tires

Damage "due and confined to" wear and tear, freezing, mechanical or electrical breakdown or failure, and road damage to tires is excluded. This exclusion eliminates coverage for losses that either occur inevitably or can often be prevented by regular maintenance or the exercise of care. This exclusion does not apply if the damage results from the total theft of a covered auto or a nonowned auto. If the tires on Bill's covered auto are damaged beyond repair because he strikes a pothole, the cost of replacing the tires would not be covered. However, if a thief damages the tires by driving the wrong way across the spikes in a parking lot, the tire loss would be covered because it results from the car's theft.

As an illustration of how the policy language of "due and confined to" applies, consider an electrical failure resulting from a short-circuit. The electrical failure causes a fire, destroying the car. The ensuing loss to the car would be covered, and the exclusion would be confined to the electrical component that failed.

Radioactive Contamination or War

Loss due to radioactive contamination, discharge of a nuclear weapon, war (declared or undeclared), civil war, insurrection, rebellion, or revolution is excluded. For example, if a covered auto is damaged from radioactive contamination because of a nuclear accident at a public utility plant, the damage is excluded.

Electronic Equipment

Loss to any electronic equipment that reproduces, receives, or transmits audio, visual, or data signals is excluded. This includes radios and stereos, tape decks, compact disk systems, navigation systems, internet access systems, personal computers, video entertainment systems, telephones, televisions, two-way mobile radios, scanners, and citizens band radios. However, the exclusion does not apply to electronic equipment that is permanently installed in "your covered auto" or a nonowned auto. When such electronic equipment is permanently installed, the high theft potential is reduced.

Media and Accessories

Tapes, records, disks, and other media used with sound, video, or data equipment are not part of the auto and are therefore not covered under the PAP. For example, the theft of videotapes or computer software from an insured's car is not covered even if the car is locked.

Government Destruction or Confiscation

The PAP excludes coverage for a total loss to a covered auto or nonowned auto due to destruction or confiscation by governmental or civil authorities. However, this exclusion does not apply to the interests of any loss payees (such as banks or other lending institutions) in the covered auto.

Trailer, Camper Body, or Motor Home

If the policy contains an appropriate endorsement, a trailer, camper, or motor home may be shown in the declarations as a covered auto. Physical damage loss to a trailer, camper, or motor home that is not shown in the declarations is excluded. However, the exclusion does not apply to a nonowned trailer. Also not excluded is a camper body or trailer acquired during the policy period if the insurer is asked to cover it within fourteen days after the insured becomes the owner.

Nonowned Auto Used Without Reasonable Belief of Being Entitled

As with other coverages, the PAP provides no physical damage coverage for loss to a nonowned auto when it is used by the insured or a family member who does not reasonably believe that he or she is entitled to use it.

Radar and Laser Detection Equipment

Loss to equipment designed to detect radar or laser beams is excluded. The exclusion is based on the theory that these devices promote unsafe driving.

Customizing Equipment

Many pickup trucks and vans are customized with special equipment, such as furniture, bars, or murals. Part D excludes loss to any custom furnishings or equipment in or on any pickup or van. However, if a covered auto is a pickup, the customized equipment exclusion does not apply to a cap (a hard cover over the bed of a pickup), a cover (usually made of canvas or other cloth to cover a pickup bed), or bedliner (a layer of resilient plastic over the floor and sides of a pickup bed).

Nonowned Auto Used in Garage Business

Also excluded under Part D is loss to a nonowned auto maintained or used in the business of selling, repairing, servicing, storing, or parking vehicles designed for use on public highways, including road testing and delivery. For example, if Ross is employed as an auto mechanic and damages a customer's car while road-testing it, the physical damage loss to the car is not covered under Ross's PAP. This commercial loss exposure should be insured by the repair shop.

Racing

Loss to a covered auto or a nonowned auto is excluded if the auto is damaged while located in a facility designed for racing if the auto is being used to prepare for, practice for, or compete in any prearranged racing or speed contest.

Rental Vehicles

If an insured's PAP provides physical damage coverage for an owned auto, the policy also provides physical damage coverage for nonowned vehicles—including rental vehicles. However, the exclusion states that the PAP will not pay for loss to, or loss of use of, a rental auto if the rental agreement includes a damage waiver or if applicable state law precludes the rental company from recovering from the insured for the loss.

Auto rental companies usually offer their customers a damage waiver at substantial extra cost. If purchased, this waiver eliminates or substantially reduces the individual's financial obligation to the rental company for damage to the car in an auto accident. Physical damage protection for rental autos is also provided as a benefit by some credit card companies, provided their card is used to charge the rental.

Personal Vehicle Sharing Program

Any loss that occurs while enrolled in a personal vehicle sharing program under the terms of a written agreement is excluded. Also excluded is any loss to or loss of use of a nonowned auto used by the insured or any family member in connection with a personal vehicle sharing program if the provisions of the program preclude recovery of the loss from the insured.

Limit of Liability

The insurer's limit of liability for a physical damage loss to a covered auto is the lower of either the **actual cash value (ACV)** of the damaged or stolen property or the amount necessary to repair or replace the property with other

Actual cash value (ACV)
Cost to replace property with new property of like kind and quality less depreciation.

property of like kind and quality. In determining ACV, an adjustment is made for depreciation and physical condition of the damaged property.

When a vehicle sustains only a partial loss (such as a damaged fender), the insurer usually pays the cost of repairing it, less any applicable deductible. However, if the damage to the vehicle is extensive and the cost of repairs exceeds the vehicle's ACV, the car may be declared a total loss. In such a case, the amount the insurer will pay is limited to the ACV of the damaged vehicle, less any applicable deductible.

The insurer's maximum obligation for electronic equipment that reproduces, receives, or transmits audio, visual, or data signals and that is permanently installed but not in the locations used by the original manufacturer of the auto, is limited to $1,000. Also, the maximum amount paid for physical damage to a nonowned trailer is $1,500.

Payment of Loss

The insurer has the option of paying for the loss in money or repairing or replacing the damaged or stolen property. If a stolen auto is returned to the insured, the insurer pays the cost to return it and also pays for any damage resulting from the theft. However, the insurer has the right to keep all or part of the stolen property and pay the insured an agreed or appraised value. Payment for the loss includes the applicable sales tax for the damaged or stolen property.

No Benefit to Bailee

The No Benefit to Bailee provision states that the policy will not benefit, either directly or indirectly, any bailee (a person who assumes custody of the property of others for business purposes). If one of Midtown Parking Garage's employees negligently damages Donna's car by a covered cause of loss while it is in Midtown's custody, Donna's PAP insurer will pay for the damage to her car. The No Benefit to Bailee provision preserves the right of Donna's insurer to recover from Midtown if the garage was negligent. Although Donna receives prompt recovery, Midtown does not benefit from Donna's insurance.

Other Sources of Recovery

If a loss is covered by sources of recovery other than the PAP, the PAP insurer will pay only its share of the loss: the proportion that its limit of liability bears to the total applicable limits.

For example, an insured trailer with an ACV of $3,000 is destroyed by a fire in the insured's garage. The insured's OTC coverage applies to the loss. The PAP insurer's limit of liability for the loss is $3,000, the ACV of the trailer. The insured's homeowners insurance also covers the fire loss to the trailer, subject in this case to a $1,000 sublimit. The total of the applicable limits is

$4,000 ($3,000 + $1,000). The PAP insurer's proportional share of the loss is $3,000/$4,000, or 75 percent. Thus, the PAP insurer's share is 75 percent of $3,000 ($2,250). The loss payment would be reduced by the amount of the insured's OTC deductible.

Any physical damage coverage provided by the PAP for a nonowned auto is excess over any other collectible source of recovery. Other sources of recovery could include coverage provided by the owner of the nonowned auto, any other applicable physical damage insurance, and any other source of recovery that applies to the loss.

For example, if Andy borrows Barry's car and damages it, Barry's physical damage insurance applies first, and Andy's insurance is excess, subject to his deductible. If Barry's collision deductible is $200 and Andy's collision deductible is $100, and the damage is $1,000, Barry's policy pays $800 ($1,000 – $200) and Andy's policy pays $100 ($200 – $100). The remaining $100 would have to be paid either by Andy or by Barry. If Andy acted negligently and Barry's car was damaged as a result, Barry's insurer may choose to subrogate against Andy for the $800 it paid to repair Barry's car. Andy's insurer will not pay the $800 under Part A—Liability Coverage because of the exclusion for property damage to property used by or in the care of the insured.

Appraisal

In the event of a disagreement on the amount of loss, either party may demand an **appraisal** of the loss. According to the Appraisal provision in the PAP, each party selects a competent and impartial appraiser. The two appraisers then select an "umpire." If the appraisers cannot agree on the ACV and the amount of loss, any differences are submitted to the umpire. A decision by any two of the three is binding on all. Each party pays its chosen appraiser and shares equally the expenses of the appraisal and the umpire. If the insurer agrees to an appraisal, it does not waive any of its rights under the policy (that is, the policy conditions and exclusions would still apply).

Appraisal
A method of resolving disputes between insurers and insureds over the amount owed on a covered loss.

PART D—COVERAGE FOR DAMAGE TO YOUR AUTO CASE STUDY

Applying Part D—Coverage for Damage to Your Auto of the Personal Auto Policy (PAP) to auto accidents involves unique coverage issues not associated with the other parts of the PAP. Several types of losses often occur in a single accident.

Part D—Coverage for Damage to Your Auto can extend to a wide range of loss exposures that includes claims for other than collision and loss of use. The circumstances of each accident will determine whether coverage for a particular claim applies.

Case Facts

Given the facts presented in this case, will the other than collision and loss of use claims be covered? If so, what amounts will the insurer pay for each claim?

Joe drove his car to the grocery store. When he returned to where he had parked his car, he discovered it had been stolen. Joe called his insurer and the police to inform them of the theft. Four days later, the police found his car. However, stolen from the vehicle were all four wheels, a factory-installed compact disk (CD) player, and several compact disks. Five days later, all the stolen parts had been replaced, the car was back in use, and Joe had incurred these costs to replace the stolen parts (including labor):

- Four wheels (rims and tires)—$1,200
- CD player—$500
- Estimated cost of replacing the stolen disks—$150

While his car was out of use, Joe rented a substitute auto for $30 a day, totaling $270 for the nine-day period.

To confirm the facts of this loss were accurate, the insurer relied on police reports, recorded statements from the insured and witnesses, rental car receipts, repair invoices, and appraisal of the covered auto.

Joe has his own PAP and, as part of that policy, paid a premium for other than collision (OTC) coverage for the car that was stolen. The OTC coverage is subject to a $500 deductible. His loss of use coverage is limited to $20 a day, not to exceed a maximum of $600. He has submitted a claim for the losses he incurred as a result of the theft. His PAP does not contain any endorsements that would affect coverage for damage to his car. See the exhibit "Overview of Joe's Policy."

Overview of Joe's Policy

Insured	Joe
Type of policy and coverage limits	Joe's PAP—$500 deductible for other than collision and for loss of use; $20 per day for a maximum of $600.
Endorsements that affect the case	None.
Other policy information	No other relevant information.
Background	The insured has complied with the policy conditions.

[DA00321]

Case Analysis Tools

To determine whether Joe's policy provides coverage for the damages to his auto, the insurance or risk management professional should have copies of the policy forms, any applicable endorsements that are indicated on the Declarations page of the policy, and the Declarations page itself. See the exhibit "Joe's Policy Declarations."

Joe's Policy Declarations

Personal Auto Policy Declarations

POLICYHOLDER: Joe Insured
(Named Insured) 816 Brookside Drive
Anytown, USA 41234

POLICY NUMBER: 286 D 465211

POLICY PERIOD: **FROM:** June 18, 20XX
TO: Dec. 18, 20XX

But only If the required premium for this period has been paid, and for six-month renewal periods If renewal premiums are paid as required. Each period begins and ends at 12:01 A.M. standard time at the address of the policyholder.

INSURED VEHICLES AND SCHEDULE OF COVERAGES

	VEHICLE	COVERAGES	LIMITS OF INSURANCE	PREMIUM
1	20XX Honda Civic		VINXXX	
		Coverage A—Liability	$ 300,000 Each Occurrence	$ 203.00
		Coverage B—Medical Payments	$ 5,000 Each Person	$ 36.00
		Coverage C—Uninsured Motorists	$ 300,000 Each Occurrence	$ 61.80
		Coverage D—Other Than Collision	Actual Cash Value Less $500	$ 41.60
		—Collision	Actual Cash Value Less $500	$ 131.00
			TOTAL	$ 473.40

POLICY FORM AND ENDORSEMENTS: PP 00 01

COUNTERSIGNATURE DATE: June 18, 20XX

AGENT: A. M. Abel

Copyright, ISO Properties, Inc. [DA00313]

Determination of Coverage

To examine the policy forms to determine whether coverage applies to the losses, the insurance or risk management professional can apply the four steps of the DICE method to determine whether Joe's PAP provides coverage for his car. See the exhibit "DICE Analysis."

> **DICE Analysis**
>
> A DICE analysis is a logical method to approach a coverage determination for most types of loss. DICE is an acronym for these policy parts:
>
> - Declarations
> - Insuring agreements
> - Conditions
> - Exclusions
>
> The claim representative reviews the policy language in a logical order to determine whether coverage applies and, if it does, what dollar limit amounts may apply.
>
> DICE analysis involves four steps:
>
> - Review the declarations page to determine whether it covers the person or the property at the time of loss.
> - Review the insuring agreement to determine whether it covers the loss.
> - Review the policy conditions to determine compliance.
> - Review the policy exclusions to determine whether they preclude coverage of the loss.
>
> By carefully performing the four steps described and reviewing policy terms and any other policy endorsements with the facts of the loss, the claim representative can determine what—if any—coverage may apply to a loss.

[DA05891]

The first DICE step is to determine whether the driver or vehicle is described on the insured's PAP Declarations page and whether the theft occurred during the policy period. Joe is listed as the named insured on his own PAP. The car that was stolen is listed as a covered auto. The theft occurred during the policy period.

The second DICE step is to determine whether the event triggers coverage under the PAP's physical damage insuring agreement. See the exhibit "Personal Auto Policy Liability Insuring Agreement."

In this policy provision, the insurer agrees to pay for any direct and accidental loss to "your covered auto" or a "non-owned auto," less the deductible shown on the declarations page.

The theft of the car is a direct and accidental loss from Joe's perspective. Because the loss is not the result of a collision or any other excluded cause of

> **Personal Auto Policy Liability Insuring Agreement**
>
> PART D – COVERAGE FOR DAMAGE TO YOUR AUTO
>
> INSURING AGREEMENT
>
> We will pay for direct and accidental loss to "your covered auto" or any "non-owned auto", including their equipment, minus any deductible shown in the Declarations.
>
> ...
>
> We will pay for loss to "your covered auto" caused by:
>
> 1. Other than "collision" only if the Declarations indicate that Other Than Collision Coverage is provided for that auto.

Copyright, ISO Properties, Inc., 2003. [DA05646]

loss, it falls under OTC coverage. As established in the first DICE step, Joe's car is a covered auto for physical damage coverage, thus satisfying another requirement stated in the insuring agreement.

The third DICE step is to determine whether all policy conditions (for example, Joe's timely reporting of his loss to his insurer) have been complied with. For the purposes of this case study, the student should assume that they have been.

The fourth DICE step is to determine whether one or more exclusions preclude coverage the insuring agreements have granted. See the exhibit "Personal Auto Policy Exclusions, Electronic Equipment."

> **Personal Auto Policy Exclusions, Electronic Equipment**
>
> PART D – COVERAGE FOR DAMAGE TO YOUR AUTO
>
> EXCLUSIONS
>
> We will not pay for:
>
> ...
>
> 4. Loss to any electronic equipment that reproduces, receives or transmits audio, visual or data signals. This includes but is not limited to:
>
>   ...
>
>   c. Compact disk systems;
>
>   ...
>
>   This exclusion (4.) does not apply to electronic equipment that is permanently installed in "your covered auto" or any "non-owned auto".

Copyright, ISO Properties, Inc., 2003. [DA05640]

Two exclusions may apply in this case. The first involves electronic equipment. Loss to any electronic equipment that reproduces, receives, or transmits audio, visual, or data signals is excluded. The CD player stolen from Joe's car would fall into that category. However, the exclusion does not apply to electronic equipment that is permanently installed in the car, as Joe's CD player was. Therefore, the stolen CD player is covered.

The second exclusion eliminates coverage for tapes, records, disks, or other media used with sound, video, or data equipment. The compact disks that were stolen from Joe's car would be considered media as defined by the policy; therefore, Joe's insurer would not pay for the cost of replacing them. See the exhibit "Personal Auto Policy Exclusions, CDs."

Personal Auto Policy Exclusions, CDs

PART D – COVERAGE FOR DAMAGE TO YOUR AUTO

EXCLUSIONS

We will not pay for:

...

5. Loss to tapes, records, disks or other media used with equipment described in Exclusion **4**.

Copyright, ISO Properties, Inc., 2003. [DA05641]

In summary, Joe's OTC coverage applies to the stolen wheels and CD player but not to the disks. Also, because Joe incurred temporary transportation expenses resulting from a covered loss to a covered auto, the Transportation Expenses coverage in Part D of the PAP covers his cost of renting a temporary substitute auto (subject to the per day and total limits).

Determination of Amounts Payable

Determining the amounts payable for Joe's loss under Part D of the PAP involves application of the Limit of Liability provision, the OTC deductible, and the Transportation Expenses coverage provision. See the exhibit "Personal Auto Policy Limit of Liability."

The insurer's limit of liability for a physical damage loss is the lower of the actual cash value of the damaged or stolen property or the amount necessary to repair or replace the property with other property of like kind and quality.

Because the car was recovered with only a few of its parts stolen, it is considered a partial, rather than a total, loss. The insurer will pay Joe the cost of replacing the covered stolen parts (the wheels and the CD player) because it is less than the car's actual cash value.

> **Personal Auto Policy Limit of Liability**
>
> PART D – COVERAGE FOR DAMAGE TO YOUR AUTO
>
> LIMIT OF LIABILITY
>
> A. Our limit of liability for loss will be the lesser of the:
>
>   1. Actual cash value of the stolen or damaged property; or
>
>   2. Amount necessary to repair or replace the property with other property of like kind and quality.
>
>   However, the most we will pay for loss to:
>
>   ...
>
>   2. Electronic equipment that reproduces, receives or transmits audio, visual or data signals, which is permanently installed in the auto not used by the auto manufacturer for installation of such equipment, is $1,000.

Copyright, ISO Properties, Inc., 2003. [DA05643]

The Limit of Liability provision also limits the coverage for stolen electronic equipment to $1,000 if the equipment was permanently installed in a location not used by the original manufacturer. However, Joe's CD player was factory-installed and had a value of only $500; therefore, the $1,000 limit does not affect the amount payable.

The total covered physical damage loss can now be calculated as $1,200 (for replacement of wheels) plus $500 (for replacement of CD player), or $1,700. The OTC deductible of $500 is subtracted from this amount to arrive at a payment of $1,200.

Although Joe's cost of renting a temporary substitute auto is insured under the Transportation Expenses coverage, that coverage is limited to $20 a day, not to exceed a maximum of $600. Moreover, because this was a total theft of the car, the policy imposes a two-day waiting period before reimbursement of Joe's transportation expenses begins. The car was out of service for a total of nine days—four days for the police to find the car and another five days to replace all the stolen parts. Therefore, following the two-day waiting period, Joe will receive reimbursement of up to $20 per day for his transportation expenses for seven days. The insurer will reimburse Joe for $140 of the $270 he spent to rent a temporary substitute auto. See the exhibit "Personal Auto Policy Transportation Expenses."

Joe will receive a total claim payment of $1,340, consisting of $1,200 for the stolen auto parts and $140 for his temporary transportation expenses. See the exhibit "Determination of Amounts Payable."

> **Personal Auto Policy Transportation Expenses**
>
> PART D – COVERAGE FOR DAMAGE TO YOUR AUTO
>
> TRANSPORTATION EXPENSES
>
> A. In addition, we will pay, without application of a deductible, up to a maximum of $600 for:
>
>   1. Temporary transportation expenses not exceeding $20 per day incurred by you in the event of a loss to "your covered auto". We will pay for such expenses if the loss is caused by:
>
>   a. Other than "collision" only if the Declarations indicate that Other Than Collision Coverage is provided for that auto.
>
>   ...
>
> B. Subject to the provisions of Paragraph A., if the loss is caused by:
>
>   1. A total theft of "your covered auto" or a "non-owned auto", we will pay only expenses incurred during the period:
>
>   a. Beginning 48 hours after the theft; and
>
>   b. Ending when "your covered auto" or the "non-owned auto" is returned to use or we pay for its loss.

Copyright, ISO Properties, Inc., 2003. [DA05642]

> **Determination of Amounts Payable**
>
> - For the other than collision claim that included cost to replace the wheels and the compact disk player, the insurer will pay $1,200, which includes subtracting the $500 deductible.
> - The cost to replace the compact disks is excluded.
> - For the Transportation Expense loss of use claim, the insurer will pay $140.
> - The total payment from the insurer is $1,340.

[DA05644]

PART E—DUTIES AFTER AN ACCIDENT OR LOSS

The Personal Auto Policy (PAP) contains a section outlining several important duties with which the insured must comply in order for the policy to provide coverage.

Before an insurer is obligated to pay for an accident or loss covered under the Personal Auto Policy (PAP), the insured must comply with certain requirements, such as notifying the insurer when a loss has occurred, cooperating in the investigation and settlement of the claim, and performing several other duties. Part E of the PAP specifies these general duties the insured must perform after an accident or a loss.

The insurer has no obligation to provide coverage if the insured's failure to comply with these requirements is prejudicial to the insurer (that is, if the insured's action is detrimental to the insurer). For example, if an insured does not promptly notify the insurer when a loss occurs, the insurer may not be required to provide coverage under the PAP. The insured must also perform additional duties if seeking protection under Part C—Uninsured Motorists Coverage or Part D—Coverage for Damage to Your Auto. See the exhibit "Part E—Duties After an Accident or Loss."

Part E—Duties After an Accident or Loss

General Duties	Additional Duties for Uninsured Motorists Coverage	Additional Duties for Physical Damage Coverage
Provide prompt notice to the insurer	Notify police if a hit-and-run driver was involved in the accident or loss	Take reasonable steps to prevent further loss
Cooperate with the insurer	Submit legal papers to the insurer	Notify police if the covered auto is stolen
Submit legal papers to the insurer		Permit inspection and appraisal of the damaged property
Submit to a physical exam if requested		
Agree to an examination under oath		
Authorize release of pertinent medical records to the insurer		
Submit a proof of loss		

[DA00169]

General Duties

A person seeking coverage under the PAP must perform specified general duties after an accident or a loss in order to receive payment under all of the policy's coverages:

- Provide prompt notice to the insurer—The insurer must be notified promptly of how, when, and where the accident or loss happened. The notice also should include the names and addresses of any witnesses and injured persons. Notice to the insurer can be initiated with a phone call or a fax to the insurer's claim department.

- Cooperate with the insurer—The person seeking coverage must cooperate with the insurer in the investigation, settlement, or defense of any claim or suit related to the accident or loss. Cooperation can include providing details of the loss, names of witnesses to the accident or loss, police reports, and other important information related to the settlement and appropriate defense of the claim.
- Submit legal papers to the insurer—The person seeking coverage must promptly submit to the insurer copies of any notices or legal documentation received in connection with the accident or loss. This submission assists the insurer in fairly settling the claim and in defending any legal case that may arise.
- Submit to physical examination—The person seeking coverage must agree to submit to a physical examination conducted by a doctor chosen by the insurer upon request. The insurer pays for such examinations.
- Agree to examination under oath—The person seeking coverage must agree to an examination under oath if required by the insurer.
- Authorize release of medical records—The person seeking coverage must authorize the insurer to obtain medical reports and other pertinent records related to the claim.
- Submit proof of loss—The person seeking coverage must submit a **proof of loss** when required by the insurer. The insured swears to the contents of this statement and its contents.

Proof of loss
A statement of facts about a loss for which the insured is making a claim.

Additional Duties for Uninsured Motorists Coverage

A person seeking coverage under Part C—Uninsured Motorists Coverage must perform additional duties:

- Notify police—The person seeking coverage must promptly notify police if a hit-and-run driver was involved in the accident. This requirement is designed to discourage the filing of fraudulent claims.
- Submit legal papers—If the person seeking coverage sues the uninsured motorist, the insured must submit to the insurer a copy of the legal documentation related to the suit. This requirement ensures that the insurer has as much information as possible to prepare its legal case if a covered party enters into a lawsuit with a third party.

Additional Duties for Physical Damage Coverage

Additional duties are also required under Part D—Coverage for Damage to Your Auto:

- Prevent further loss—The person seeking coverage must take reasonable steps after a loss to protect a covered auto or nonowned auto and its

equipment from further loss. The insurer will pay the reasonable expenses the insured incurs to protect the vehicle from further damage. For example, the insurer will pay for a tow truck to transport the damaged auto to another location for safekeeping.
- Notify police—If a covered auto or nonowned auto is stolen, the person seeking coverage must promptly notify police of the theft. Prompt notification may increase the possibility that the stolen vehicle will be recovered.
- Permit inspection and appraisal—The person seeking coverage must permit the insurer to inspect and appraise the damaged property before its repair or disposal. For small losses, the insurer sometimes waives its right to inspect and appraise the damaged auto and instead allows the person seeking coverage to submit two or three repair estimates that serve as the basis for the loss settlement.

PART F—GENERAL PROVISIONS

The Personal Auto Policy includes terms and conditions that apply throughout the policy. These are contained in Part F of the policy.

Part F—General Provisions is the final part of the Personal Auto Policy (PAP). It contains general provisions and conditions that apply to the entire policy. These conditions include items that specify aspects of PAP coverage, such as how the insurer handles changes in the policy or policy cancellations.

Bankruptcy of Insured

This provision states that if the insured declares bankruptcy or becomes insolvent, the insurer is not relieved of any obligations under the policy. For example, if the insured is sued for an amount exceeding the policy limits and declares bankruptcy in an attempt to escape payment of the rest of the judgment, the insurer is still required to pay the part of the judgment covered by insurance.

Changes in the Policy

This provision indicates that the policy contains all the agreements between the named insured and the insurer. The terms of the policy cannot be changed or waived except by an endorsement issued by the insurer. If a change requires a premium adjustment, the adjustment is made in accordance with the manual rules of the insurer. Changes during the policy term that can result in a premium increase or decrease include changes in these elements:

- The number, type, or use of insured vehicles
- The operators using insured vehicles

- The place of principal garaging of insured vehicles
- The coverage provided, deductibles, or limits of liability

Liberalization Clause
A policy condition providing that if a policy form is broadened at no additional premium, the broadened coverage automatically applies to all existing policies of the same type.

Another portion of this provision, sometimes referred to as a **liberalization clause**, automatically provides broadened coverage under some conditions. According to this provision, if the insurer makes a change to the PAP that broadens its coverage without an additional premium, the change automatically applies to the insured's existing policy on the date the revision is effective in the insured's state. This provision does not, however, apply to changes that include both broadenings and restrictions of coverage or those that are implemented in a general program revision either by a new edition of the policy or by an amendatory endorsement.

Fraud

This provision says that no coverage exists for any insured who makes fraudulent statements or engages in fraudulent conduct in connection with any accident or loss for which a claim is made. For example, if an insured deliberately abandons a covered auto and then reports the car as stolen, the insurer does not cover the insured for that claim.

Legal Action Against the Insurer

According to this policy provision, no legal action can be brought against the insurer until the insured has fully complied with all of the policy terms. In addition, under Part A—Liability Coverage, no legal action can be brought against the insurer unless the insurer agrees in writing that the insured has an obligation to pay damages or the amount of the insurer's obligation has been finally determined by a judgment after a trial. No person or organization has any right under the policy to involve the insurer in any action to determine the liability of an insured unless all policy conditions have been met.

Insurer's Right to Recover Payment

The policy provision regarding an insurer's right to recover payment is often called the subrogation clause. If the insurer makes a loss payment to a person who has the right to recover damages from a third party that either caused or is legally liable for the loss, the insurer has a legal right of subrogation against that third party. For example, Joe, who is insured with Insurer A, is involved in an accident with Mary, who is insured with Insurer B. It is determined that Mary is legally liable for the accident and for Joe's injuries. If Insurer A makes payments to Joe, it can recover those payments from Mary or from Insurer B. The covered person must do whatever is necessary to enable the insurer to exercise its subrogation rights. In addition, the person to whom the loss payment was made is not allowed to do anything after the loss that would prejudice or impede the insurer's right of subrogation.

The subrogation provision does not apply to physical damage coverages in regard to any person who is using a covered auto with a reasonable belief that he or she is entitled to do so. For example, if Sue borrows Irene's car with her permission and damages the car in a collision, Irene's collision coverage will pay for the damage to the car. According to the terms of this provision, Irene's insurer cannot subrogate against Sue or her insurer.

Finally, if a person receives a loss payment from an insurer and also recovers damages from another party, that person is required to hold the proceeds of the second recovery in trust for the insurer and to reimburse the insurer to the extent of the insurer's loss payment.

Policy Period and Territory

The PAP applies only to accidents and losses that occur during the policy period shown on the Declarations page and within the policy territory.

The policy territory includes the United States, U.S. territories and possessions, Puerto Rico, and Canada. The policy also applies to a covered auto while being transported among ports of the U.S., Puerto Rico, or Canada. Coverage does not apply anywhere outside the policy territory. It is important to note that the policy territory does not include Mexico. Under Mexican law, a motorist from the U.S. who has not purchased valid insurance from a Mexican insurer and is involved in an accident can be detained in jail, have his or her car impounded, and be subject to other penalties. Motorists who are planning to drive into Mexico should purchase the Limited Mexico Coverage endorsement.

Termination

The PAP contains a provision that applies to **policy termination** by either the insured or insurer. The termination provision consists of four parts:

- Cancellation
- Nonrenewal
- Automatic termination
- Other termination provisions

All states have laws that restrict the insurer's right to cancel or nonrenew an auto policy, such as provisions for the number of days' notice that an insured must be given prior to cancellation. In many states, these laws differ from the termination provision in the PAP. Changes mandated by state laws are usually incorporated into the policy by means of a state endorsement that must be attached to all auto policies issued in that state. Whenever state laws and policy provisions conflict, state law supersedes the policy provisions.

Policy termination
The ending of the contractual relationship between the insured and insurer by cancellation, expiration, or nonrenewal.

Cancellation

Under the cancellation provision, the named insured normally can cancel anytime during the policy period by returning the policy to the insurer or by giving advance written notice of the date the **cancellation** is to become effective.

The insurer has more limited cancellation rights. If the policy has been in force for fewer than sixty days and is not a renewal or continuation policy, the insurer can cancel by mailing a cancellation notice to the named insured. Thus, the insurer has sixty days to investigate and determine whether a new applicant meets the insurer's underwriting standards. If the cancellation is for nonpayment of premium, the insurer must give the named insured at least ten days' notice; in all other cases, at least twenty days' notice must be given.

After the policy has been in force for sixty days, or if it is a renewal or continuation policy, the insurer can cancel the policy only for one of three reasons:

- The premium has not been paid.
- The insured's driver's license has been suspended or revoked during the policy period (or since the last annual anniversary of the original effective date if the policy is for other than one year).
- The policy has been obtained by a material misrepresentation. For example, if an insured knowingly provides false information to the insurer, the insurer has the right to cancel that person's coverage after the correct information is discovered.

Nonrenewal

This policy provision outlines the terms under which a policy is not renewed. Rather than cancel a policy, the insurer may decide to let the policy remain in force during the policy period but not to renew the policy for another term. If the insurer decides not to renew, the named insured must be given at least twenty days' notice before the end of the policy period. The conditions under which the insurer can nonrenew vary according to the length of the policy period:

- If the policy period is less than six months, the insurer has the right to nonrenew every six months, beginning six months after the policy's original effective date.
- If the policy period is six months or longer, but less than a year, the insurer has the right to nonrenew at the end of the policy period.
- If the policy period is one year or longer, the insurer has the right to nonrenew at each anniversary of the policy's original effective date. For example, after the policy has been in effect for at least one year, an insurer may decide to nonrenew a policy due to excessive loss amounts.

Cancellation

Termination of a policy, by either the insurer or the insured, during the policy term.

Automatic Termination

Under the automatic termination provision, if the insurer offers to renew the policy but the named insured does not accept the offer, the policy automatically terminates at the end of the current policy period. Failure to pay the renewal premium means that the named insured has not accepted the insurer's offer to renew the policy. That is, once the named insured is billed for another period, the premium must be paid, or the policy automatically terminates on its expiration date. Although in practice some insurers allow a short period of time for an insured to pay an overdue premium, the policy itself provides no grace period.

If the named insured obtains other insurance on a covered auto, the PAP coverage on that auto automatically terminates on the effective date of the other insurance. Suppose, for example, that Dennis has a PAP from Insurer X covering his sedan. He subsequently buys a sports car and purchases a new auto policy from Insurer Z covering both the sports car and the sedan. Dennis's PAP from Insurer X automatically terminates on the effective date of his new policy from Insurer Z, even if he does not notify his PAP insurer. If Dennis becomes involved in a serious accident while driving his sedan, he cannot claim coverage under both policies.

Other Termination Provisions

The policy contains three additional termination provisions:

- The insurer may choose to deliver the cancellation notice rather than mail it. However, proof of mailing (to the named insured at the address as shown in the declarations) of any cancellation notice is considered sufficient proof of notice.
- If the policy is canceled, the named insured may be entitled to a premium refund. Any premium refund is computed according to the insurer's manual rules. Making or offering to make the refund is not a condition of cancellation.
- The effective date of cancellation stated in the cancellation notice becomes the end of the policy period.

Transfer of Insured's Interest in the Policy

This provision stipulates that the named insured's rights and duties under the policy cannot be assigned to another party without the insurer's written consent. This means that if the insured sells his or her vehicle, he or she cannot transfer the insurance policy to the new owner of the vehicle. However, if the named insured dies, the coverage is automatically continued to the end of the policy period for both the surviving spouse (if he or she is a resident of the same household at the time of the named insured's death) and the legal representative of the deceased person (but only with respect to the representative's legal responsibility to maintain or use a covered auto).

Two or More Auto Policies

If two or more auto policies issued to the named insured by the same insurer apply to the same accident, the insurer's maximum limit of liability is the highest applicable limit of liability under any one policy. The intent of this provision is to prevent the "stacking" (adding together) of policy limits when two or more auto policies are issued by the same insurer.

COMMON ENDORSEMENTS TO THE PERSONAL AUTO POLICY

Insurance professionals should be aware that, while the Personal Auto Policy (PAP) provides extensive coverage, additions or modifications may be necessary in some scenarios.

Because the unmodified Insurance Services Office, Inc. (ISO) PAP contains eligibility restrictions, coverage exclusions, and coverage limitations, it does not completely meet every customer's auto insurance needs. However, several policy endorsements provide coverage additions or modifications for customers who have coverage needs beyond the unendorsed PAP. See the exhibit "Frequently Used Personal Auto Endorsements."

Miscellaneous Type Vehicle Endorsement

The unmodified PAP excludes coverage for vehicles that have fewer than four wheels and vehicles designed for off-public-road use. The Miscellaneous Type Vehicle Endorsement (PP 03 23 01 05) provides coverage for a motor home, a motorcycle or similar type of vehicle, an all-terrain vehicle, a dune buggy, or a golf cart, none of which are included in the PAP's definition of covered auto. The endorsement clarifies the PAP provisions to apply to miscellaneous type vehicles rather than to private passenger vehicles, vans, or pickup trucks. The endorsement schedule lists each covered vehicle and the corresponding applicable coverages, limits of liability, and premiums.

An optional passenger hazard exclusion, which excludes liability coverage for bodily injury to any person occupying the covered vehicle, can be activated as part of the endorsement. For example, a motorcycle owner who never carries passengers can elect this exclusion in exchange for a lower premium.

Part D (physical damage) of the endorsement excludes coverage for loss to clothing or luggage, business or office equipment, sales samples, or articles used in exhibits. It also limits the amount paid for physical damage losses to the lowest of these values:

- The stated amount shown in the schedule or declarations
- The actual cash value of the stolen or damaged property
- The amount necessary to repair or replace the property (less any deductible)

Frequently Used Personal Auto Endorsements

Endorsement Name	Exposure Covered
Miscellaneous Type Vehicle Endorsement	Covers motor homes, motorcycles, and other vehicles with fewer than four wheels that are designed for off public road use
Snowmobile Endorsement	Provides coverage for snowmobiles other than vehicles propelled by airplane-type propellers or fans
Trailer/Camper Body Coverage (Maximum Limit of Liability)	Covers trailers or camper bodies, including related facilities or equipment
Extended Non-Owned Coverage	Provides liability and medical payments coverages for drivers of vehicles furnished or made available for the regular use of the named insured and/or family members
Named Non-Owner Coverage	Provides liability, medical payments, uninsured, and underinsured motorists coverages for drivers who do not own an auto but regularly or occasionally drive another person's vehicle or a rental vehicle
Auto Loan/Lease Coverage	Amends physical damage coverage for leased vehicles or vehicles with outstanding loan amounts to include an unpaid amount due on the lease or loan
Limited Mexico Coverage	Provides excess liability coverage over Mexican auto insurance for an insured who is involved in an accident or loss in Mexico within twenty-five miles of the United States border on a trip of ten days or less
Excess Electronic Equipment Coverage	Increases the $1,000 limit that applies to electronic equipment installed in the vehicle in locations not intended for that purpose by the auto manufacturer
Coverage for Damage to Your Auto (Maximum Limit of Liability)	Covers each described vehicle for a stated amount of insurance as indicated in the endorsement schedule that applies to collision and OTC losses
Optional Limits Transportation Expenses Coverage	Increases the limit for Coverage for Transportation Expenses under Coverage D (physical damage)
Towing and Labor Costs Coverage	Covers the towing of a disabled covered or nonowned auto, including costs for labor performed at the place of disablement.

[DA00170]

The determination of actual cash value includes an adjustment for the depreciation and physical condition of the damaged vehicle.

Snowmobile Endorsement

Coverage for snowmobiles can be added to the PAP by attaching a Snowmobile Endorsement (PP 03 20 01 05). A snowmobile is defined as a land motor vehicle propelled solely by wheels, crawler-type treads, belts, or similar mechanical devices and designed for use mainly off public roads on snow or ice. Under this definition, a vehicle propelled by airplane-type propellers or fans is not considered a snowmobile.

Available snowmobile coverages include liability, medical payments, uninsured motorists, collision, and other than collision. Each covered snowmobile is listed in a schedule that states the applicable coverages, limits of liability, and premiums.

The liability coverage for snowmobiles has several exclusions and modifications:

- Coverage does not apply if the snowmobile is used in any business.
- Coverage does not apply when the snowmobile is used in a race or speed contest or in practice or preparation for a race, regardless of whether the race is prearranged or organized.
- Coverage is excluded for any person or organization, other than the named insured, while renting or leasing a snowmobile.
- A passenger hazard exclusion can be activated that excludes liability for bodily injury to any person while occupying or being towed by the snowmobile.

The provisions of this endorsement regarding the amount paid for physical damage losses are the same as those of the Miscellaneous Type Vehicle Endorsement.

Trailer/Camper Body Coverage (Maximum Limit of Liability)

Under the Trailer/Camper Body Coverage (Maximum Limit of Liability) (PP 03 07 01 05) endorsement, coverage is extended to direct and accidental loss to a trailer or camper body described in the policy declarations or the schedule of the endorsement. The endorsement also provides coverage for related facilities or equipment, including, but not limited to, cooking, dining, plumbing, or refrigeration facilities, as well as awnings or cabanas. Loss to clothing or luggage, business or office equipment, and sales samples or articles used in exhibitions is excluded. The PAP exclusions for electronic equipment and media, radar detectors, and custom furnishings or equipment still apply. If necessary, such items can be covered under other PAP endorsements.

The provisions of this endorsement regarding the amount paid for physical damage losses are the same as those of the Miscellaneous Type Vehicle Endorsement.

Extended Non-Owned Coverage—Vehicles Furnished or Available for Regular Use

The unendorsed PAP excludes liability and medical payments coverage for vehicles furnished or made available for the regular use of the named insured and family members. This exclusion can be eliminated by adding the Extended Non-Owned Coverage—Vehicles Furnished or Available for Regular Use (PP 03 06 01 05) endorsement to the PAP. The endorsement's coverage applies only to the individual(s) named in the endorsement schedule. However, coverage can be extended to the named individual's family members. (Such an extension is indicated by a checkbox on the endorsement.)

The liability coverage provided by the endorsement is excess over any other applicable insurance on the nonowned vehicle. The endorsement schedule also indicates separate premiums for liability and for medical payments coverage.

The endorsement provides liability coverage for any vehicle furnished or available for the regular use of the named individual and for family members who are indicated in the schedule. For example, if Alice is furnished with a company car by her employer, this endorsement would provide liability and/or medical payments coverage on an excess basis.

Named Non-Owner Coverage

People who do not regularly own an auto or who occasionally drive another person's vehicle or a rental vehicle can secure coverage for the loss exposures arising out of their use of a nonowned auto by purchasing a PAP with the Named Non-Owner Coverage (PP 03 22 01 05) endorsement. This endorsement is used in conjunction with the PAP to provide liability coverage, medical payments coverage, uninsured motorists coverage, and underinsured motorists (but not physical damage) coverage for a driver who does not own an auto.

This coverage applies only to a person who is actually named in the endorsement. The named insured's spouse or other resident family members are not automatically covered. Coverage for family members can be included by indicating such coverage on the endorsement schedule.

The liability insurance under a PAP with the named nonowner endorsement is excess over any other applicable liability insurance on the nonowned auto. The endorsement provides important protection to the named insured who drives a nonowned auto with inadequate liability limits or perhaps no insurance at all.

The endorsement provides the named insured with liability, medical payments, uninsured motorists, and underinsured motorists coverage on a newly acquired vehicle for up to fourteen days. Coverage automatically terminates when the named insured purchases separate insurance on the vehicle. Unlike the Extended Non-Owned Coverage—Vehicles Furnished or Available for Regular Use Endorsement, named non-owner coverage is designed for individuals who only occasionally use another person's vehicle.

Auto Loan/Lease Coverage

If an insured under the PAP leases or has an outstanding loan for a vehicle that experiences a total loss, the balance of the loan or lease may exceed the vehicle's actual cash value. However, the lending institution or leasing company still will require the outstanding balance on the vehicle, even though it has been destroyed. The Auto Loan/Lease Coverage (PP03 35 01 05) endorsement amends the Part D (physical damage) coverage of the PAP so that, in the event of the loss, coverage is included for the unpaid amount due on the lease or loan. In such a situation, the endorsement provides coverage for the difference between the outstanding loan amount and the amount that would have been paid based on the limit of liability as stated in the unendorsed policy (actual cash value or the amount necessary to repair or replace the property with like kind and quality). This allows the insured to satisfy any outstanding loan or lease payments.

Under the Auto Loan/Lease endorsement, none of these would be included in any loss payment:

- Lease or loan payments that were overdue at the time of loss
- Penalties imposed under a lease for excessive use, abnormal wear and tear, or high mileage
- Security deposits not refunded by a lessor
- Costs for extended warranties; credit life insurance; or health, accident, or disability insurance purchased with the loan or the lease
- Balances transferred from previous loans or leases

The endorsement schedule includes a description of the covered auto(s) and premiums for other than collision and/or collision coverage. See the exhibit "Auto Loan/Lease Coverage Example."

Limited Mexico Coverage

The unendorsed PAP does not provide any coverage in Mexico; however, the Limited Mexico Coverage (PP 03 21 01 05) endorsement can be added to the PAP. This endorsement extends the PAP coverages to an insured who is involved in an accident or loss in Mexico within twenty-five miles of the United States border on a trip of ten days or less.

> **Auto Loan/Lease Coverage Example**
>
> Karl has a forty-eight-month loan on a two-year-old vehicle whose actual cash value is $31,000. The vehicle is totally destroyed in an accident. At the time of the loss, Karl's loan amount is $33,450, of which $595 is the remaining cost of an extended warranty. An unendorsed PAP would pay Karl the $31,000 actual cash value. If the policy includes the Auto Loan/Lease Coverage endorsement, the payment would be $32,855 (the $33,450 loan amount less the $595 warranty cost).

[DA05772]

The coverage provided by this endorsement does not meet Mexico's auto liability insurance requirements. The endorsement is effective only if primary liability coverage is also purchased from a licensed Mexican insurer. Mexican insurance usually can be purchased from a licensed agent at the border. The stipulations requiring a Mexican insurance policy are displayed in boldface print at the top of the endorsement under a "Warning" header.

The liability insurance provided by the endorsement is excess over the Mexican insurance and over any other valid and collectible insurance. The major advantage of the endorsement is that it provides additional liability insurance beyond that provided by the Mexican policy, as well as providing the other standard PAP coverages, such as physical damage coverage.

Excess Electronic Equipment Coverage

The unendorsed PAP excludes coverage for loss to any electronic equipment that is not permanently installed in the insured vehicle and also excludes coverage for loss to tapes, records, disks, or other media. The PAP also includes a $1,000 limit on electronic equipment that reproduces, receives, or transmits audio, visual, or data signals that are permanently installed in locations not intended for that purpose by the auto manufacturer. This includes navigation systems, Internet access systems, audio equipment, and other similar electronic equipment. The Excess Electronic Equipment Coverage (PP 03 13 01 05) endorsement can be used to increase the limit on such equipment from $1,000 to a limit shown in the endorsement schedule. The endorsement schedule also includes a description of the covered vehicle and the limit of liability and premiums for excess electronic equipment.

The Excess Electronic Equipment Coverage endorsement also provides coverage for direct and accidental loss to tapes, records, disks, or other media owned by the named insured or the named insured's family member. Coverage is provided for the lesser of the actual cash value or the amount necessary to repair or replace the stolen or damaged property, subject to a maximum limit of $200 for all such media. The media must be in or upon the covered auto or any nonowned auto at the time of loss.

Coverage for Damage to Your Auto (Maximum Limit of Liability)

The Coverage for Damage to Your Auto (Maximum Limit of Liability) (PP 03 08 06 94) endorsement to the PAP allows owners of high-value antique cars or restored show cars to establish the car's insurable value when the policy is written by inserting a stated amount of insurance in the policy. Under this endorsement (often called a "stated amount" endorsement), each vehicle is described, and a stated amount of insurance is shown that applies to collision loss and other than collision loss.

Even though the endorsement indicates a stated amount of insurance, it may not provide coverage for that amount in the event of a total loss to the vehicle. Rather, the insurer's maximum limit of liability for a covered loss is limited to the lowest of these values:

- The stated amount shown in the schedule or in the declarations
- The actual cash value of the stolen or damaged property
- The amount necessary to repair or replace the property with other property of like kind and quality

If, for example, the stated amount of insurance is less than the vehicle's actual cash value or the amount necessary to repair or replace the property, the stated amount is used as the basis of the loss settlement. However, if the stated amount of insurance is greater than the vehicle's actual cash value or the amount necessary to repair or replace the property, the lower amount is the basis for payment. In any case, the amount paid is reduced by any applicable deductible shown in the endorsement schedule or policy declarations.

When determining the vehicle's actual cash value in the event of a total loss, an adjustment is made for depreciation and the physical condition of the vehicle. This endorsement also states that if a repair or replacement of the vehicle results in better than like kind or quality, the insurer will not include the amount of betterment in any loss payment.

Optional Limits Transportation Expenses Coverage

The temporary transportation expenses associated with the loss of use of an auto can be significant when the owner has to rent a substitute auto until his or her owned auto is repaired or replaced. The PAP provides coverage up to a limit of $20 per day for such temporary transportation expenses. Depending on the prices charged by local rental car providers and the type of transportation needed, the cost could exceed this limit.

Increased limits for loss of use are available under the Optional Limits Transportation Expenses Coverage Endorsement (PP 03 02). The endorsement allows the insured to increase coverage to one of three limits, which can be applied to the costs of a substitute vehicle for the period reasonably required to repair or replace the auto:

- $30 per day, subject to a maximum of $900
- $40 per day, subject to a maximum of $1,200
- $50 per day, subject to a maximum of $1,500

Towing and Labor Costs Coverage

Available in limits of $25, $50, or $75, the Towing and Labor Costs Coverage Endorsement (PP 03 03) provides coverage for the costs of towing the covered auto when it is disabled. The cost of labor performed to repair the auto at the place of disablement is also covered up to the limit. A single limit per disablement applies whether it is used for towing or labor costs. However, a separate limit applies to each disablement. Thus, if a vehicle is disabled five times during the policy period, the limit is reinstated for each incident. See the exhibit "Variation on the ISO PAP."

> ### Variation on the ISO PAP
>
> Many insurers choose to use only ISO PAP forms when providing personal auto insurance coverage to their insureds. However, some insurers may choose to offer a non-ISO policy that responds to an insured's unique needs. For example, such a policy can provide enhanced vehicle disablement coverage.
>
> This coverage applies in the event the covered auto is disabled because of a covered loss that occurs beyond a certain distance (such as fifty miles) from the insured's residence. In such a circumstance, the coverage applies to commercial transportation fees for the occupants of the auto to return home or the costs to reach their destination and the cost of extra meals and lodging needed when the loss results in delays.

[DA05771]

PERSONAL AUTO ENDORSEMENTS FOR TRANSPORTATION NETWORK EXPOSURES

More and more people use their personal autos to drive for **transportation network companies (TNCs)**. Personal auto policies (PAPs) are not designed to provide coverage in these situations and typically include a public livery or conveyance exclusion. This issue has raised coverage questions and given rise to the need to define appropriate coverage for such operations.

Drivers who use their personal autos on behalf of TNCs face some of the same exposures as other drivers as well as additional exposures associated with driving passengers for hire. Therefore, TNC drivers require **liability coverage**, **medical payments coverage**, uninsured/underinsured motorists, and physical damage coverage (collision and comprehensive). Typically, these coverages

Transportation network company
A company that uses a mobile application or website to connect riders with drivers and arrange transportation in a personal auto for a fee.

Liability coverage
Coverage that protects the insured from damages owed because of legal liability to another party. For auto policies, it protects insureds against liability arising out of the ownership or operation of automobiles.

Medical payments coverage
Coverage that pays necessary medical expenses incurred within a specified period by a claimant (and in certain policies, by an insured) for a covered injury, regardless of whether the insured was at fault.

are excluded under a PAP when a driver is transporting a passenger for a fee, so drivers turn to a commercial auto policy for coverage—either one they purchase (such policies are prohibitively expensive for many TNC drivers) or one provided by the TNC.

Many TNCs provide coverage through a commercial auto policy to drivers when they are transporting passengers for that TNC; however, depending on TNC business policies and state regulations, this coverage may begin at different points in the TNC transaction (for example when a driver has logged on to the network versus when a passenger has accepted a ride), and coverage may be limited before a passenger enters the auto. Another concern is that commercial auto limits are generally higher than those carried by individuals under a PAP. To clarify when coverage under a driver's PAP ends and to address potential coverage gaps, Insurance Services Office, Inc. (ISO) has developed endorsements to the PAP. Although ISO has made these coverage forms available for use with the PAP, not all insurers will choose to write such coverage, and TNC-related operations may be unacceptable according to insurers' underwriting guidelines.

Public or Livery Conveyance Exclusion Endorsement

ISO's Public or Livery Conveyance Exclusion Endorsement (PP 23 40) reinforces the public or livery conveyance exclusion in the PAP, which excludes coverage when a personal auto is used to transport people for a fee (for example, as a taxi). Parts A, B, C, and D of the PAP all contain similar exclusions. This endorsement adds a "transportation network platform" definition and explains that the exclusion applies to any period of time the insured has logged in to such a platform as a driver, whether or not a passenger is in the vehicle. So, for example, if Juan drives for a TNC and has logged in to its network to show that he is available to provide rides, his PAP coverage ends. Juan may then have a coverage gap as he drives to pick up a passenger before the TNC's commercial coverage begins.

The Public or Livery Conveyance Exclusion Endorsement is designed to be attached to all PAPs unless one of the ISO transportation network driver endorsements is attached. It reinforces the public or livery exclusion under Part A—Liability Coverage, Part B—Medical Payments Coverage, and Part D—Coverage for Damage to Your Auto. It does not specifically apply to Part C—Uninsured Motorists Coverage; this is primarily addressed in state-specific uninsured motorists endorsements, which generally include the reinforced public or livery conveyance exclusion.

Transportation Network Driver Coverage (No Passenger) Endorsement

The optional Transportation Network Driver Coverage (No Passenger) endorsement (PP 23 41) replaces the public or livery conveyance exclusion in the standard PAP with wording from the Public or Livery Conveyance Exclusion endorsement. It includes an exception that covers share-the-expense car pooling and operation of an auto without passengers while the driver is logged in to a "transportation network platform." It also includes a schedule, which names the specific transportation network platform, describes the covered vehicle, and states the applicable coverages and premium.

The exceptions apply to Parts A, B, C, and D. They provide coverage after an insured has logged in to a transportation network platform but before a passenger is occupying the vehicle. This eliminates any coverage gap between the time the driver signs in to the TNC's network and when he or she picks up a passenger. Insurers charge an additional premium for this endorsement.

Limited Transportation Network Driver Coverage (No Passenger) Endorsement

The Limited Transportation Network Driver Coverage (No Passenger) endorsement (PP 23 45) is similar to the Transportation Network Driver Coverage endorsement; both provide coverage when the insured is logged in to a transportation network platform but has not yet picked up a passenger. The limited version's coverage ends once the driver accepts a passenger, which occurs before the passenger enters the vehicle. Both versions exclude coverage when a passenger is occupying the vehicle. This option limits the loss exposure further than the Transportation Network Driver Coverage (No Passenger) endorsement does, so the insurer charges less additional premium.

Depending on state regulations and the coverage provided by the TNC, commercial coverage may begin once a driver logs in to the TNC platform or accepts a request. In other situations, commercial coverage may not begin until a passenger is in the car. It is important for insurance professionals to be knowledgeable about the TNCs operating in their coverage territories so that they can understand the loss exposures and recommend appropriate coverage for personal lines customers. Coverage may also be available in the surplus lines market, while other insurers offer coverage through proprietary forms. See the exhibit "How Personal Auto Policy Endorsements Apply to Transportation Network Coverage."

How Personal Auto Policy Endorsements Apply to Transportation Network Coverage

	Insured logs on to the transportation network platform.	Insured accepts a passenger's request.	Passenger enters insured's auto.
Public or Livery Conveyance Exclusion	Personal auto policy coverage ends.		
Limited Transportation Network Driver Coverage (No Passenger)	Personal auto policy coverage still applies.	Personal auto policy coverage ends.	
Transportation Network Driver Coverage (No Passenger)	Personal auto policy coverage still applies.	Personal auto policy coverage still applies.	Personal auto policy coverage ends.

[DA12655]

PERSONAL AUTO COVERAGE CASE STUDY

Knowing how to apply the Personal Auto Policy (PAP) to the facts of a case is a critical skill. This case study can help the student begin to make the transition from knowing policy language to knowing how to apply policy language to losses.

This case study helps the student to apply the coverage parts of the PAP to a given set of facts.

Case Facts

Given the facts presented in this case, will the auto claim be covered? If so, what amount would the insurer pay?

Wanda was driving the family minivan home from a shopping trip to the local mall with her two young children and one of the children's friends. As the van entered an intersection, it was struck by an oncoming vehicle operated by David. It was subsequently determined that David, a part-time circulation manager for a local newspaper, disregarded a red traffic signal when he entered the intersection. David had been returning from visiting a prospective customer to discuss placement of advertising in the newspaper. Wanda and the three children were injured, and her van sustained major damage. Wanda and her children were transported to local hospitals by ambulance, and all four were admitted for further treatment. The youngest child required several months of physical rehabilitation following his release from the hospital. The ten-year-old friend who was a passenger in Wanda's van was treated in the emergency room and released. David was not injured in the accident. Wanda and David both live in a state that does not have a no-fault law.

To confirm that facts about an accident are accurate, insurers frequently rely on police reports, recorded statements from witnesses, medical records, and inspections of the accident scene and any vehicles involved. Both David and Wanda have PAPs. The student should assume that neither PAP contains any endorsements that would modify coverage.

Wanda and her family initiate a lawsuit against David for the total cost of their injuries, $408,500 ($100,000 for Wanda; $53,900 for her older child; and $254,600 for her younger child). The court rules in Wanda's favor and awards the full amount as damages. David was required to take three days off from work to testify at the trial. The medical costs for the passenger in Wanda's vehicle were $2,750. The repair costs for Wanda's minivan were $16,943. The cost to repair front-end damage on David's sedan was $5,450.

David's PAP has Coverage A limits of $500,000 per person and $1 million per accident, with Coverage D deductibles of $500 for Other than Collision and $1,000 for Collision. Wanda's family PAP has Coverage A limits of $250,000 per person and $500,000 per accident, with Coverage D deductibles of $500 for Other than Collision and $500 for Collision. See the exhibit "Case Facts."

Case Facts

Insureds	David M. Jones (David's PAP)
	Raymond George (Wanda's family PAP)
Types of policies and coverage limits	David's PAP:
	Coverage A—$ 500,000 per person
	$ 1 million per accident
	Coverage D deductibles—$ 500 Other Than Collision
	$ 1,000 Collision
	Wanda's PAP:
	Coverage A—$ 250,000 per person
	$ 500,000 per accident
	Coverage D deductibles—$ 500 Other Than Collision
	$ 500 Collision
Endorsements that affect the case	None
Other policy information	No other relevant information
Background	The insureds have complied with the policy conditions.

[DA00606]

Case Analysis Tools

To determine whether David's PAP, Wanda's PAP, or both provide coverage for the injuries to Wanda, her children, and the ten-year-old passenger in her car, as well as the damage to the two vehicles, the insurance or risk management professional should have copies of the policy forms and any applicable endorsements indicated on the Declarations pages of the policies. See the exhibit "Personal Auto Policy Declarations."

Personal Auto Policy Declarations

POLICYHOLDER: David M. Jones
(Named Insured) 39 Lee Street
Anytown, USA 33333

POLICY NUMBER: ABC 1234

POLICY PERIOD: **FROM:** May 10, 20X1
TO: May 10, 20X2

But only if the required premium for this period has been paid, and for six-month renewal periods if renewal premiums are paid as required. Each period begins and ends at 12:01 A.M. standard time at the address of the policyholder.

INSURED VEHICLES AND SCHEDULE OF COVERAGES

	VEHICLE	COVERAGES	LIMITS OF INSURANCE		PREMIUM
1	2011 Ford Taurus		VINXXX		
		Coverage A—Liability			
		Bodily Injury	$ 500,000	**Each Person**	
			$1,000,000	**Each Accident**	$ 506.00
		Property Damage	$ 500,000	**Each Accident**	$ 192.00
		Coverage B—Medical Payments	$ 5,000	**Each Person**	$ 56.00
		Coverage D—Other Than Collision	Actual Cash Value Less	$ 500	$ 87.00
		—Collision	Actual Cash Value Less	$1,000	$ 278.00
				TOTAL	$1,119.00

Loss Payee: National Bank, Anytown, PA

POLICY FORM AND ENDORSEMENTS: PP 00 01

COUNTERSIGNATURE DATE: May 1, 20X1

AGENT: P. Revere

Copyright, ISO Properties, Inc. [DA00275]

Personal Auto Policy Declarations

Personal Auto Policy Declarations

POLICYHOLDER: Raymond George
(Named Insured) 349 Green Street
Anytown, USA 33333

POLICY NUMBER: ABC 1234

POLICY PERIOD: **FROM:** September 30, 20X1
TO: September 30, 20X2

But only if the required premium for this period has been paid, and for six-month renewal periods if renewal premiums are paid as required. Each period begins and ends at 12:01 A.M. standard time at the address of the policyholder.

INSURED VEHICLES AND SCHEDULE OF COVERAGES

	VEHICLE	COVERAGES	LIMITS OF INSURANCE		PREMIUM
1	2011 Chrysler Town & Country Van		VINXXX		
		Coverage A—Liability			
		Bodily Injury	$ 250,000	Each Person	
			$ 500,000	Each Accident	$ 432.00
		Property Damage	$ 100,000	Each Accident	$ 97.00
		Coverage B—Medical Payments	$ 5,000	Each Accident	$ 47.00
		Coverage D—Other Than Collision	Actual Cash Value Less	$500	$ 97.00
		—Collision	Actual Cash Value Less	$500	$ 345.00
				TOTAL	$ 1,018.00

Loss Payee: Chrysler Financial Services, Anytown, USA

1	2009 Mazda Tribute		VIN XXX		
		Coverage A—Liability			
		Bodily Injury	$ 250,000	Each Person	
			$ 500,000	Each Accident	$ 396.00
		Property Damage	$ 100,000	Each Accident	$ 103.00
		Coverage B—Medical Payments	$ 5,000	Each Person	$ 48.00
		Coverage D—Other Than Collision	Actual Cash Value Less	$500	$ 86.00
		—Collision	Actual Cash Value Less	$500	$ 237.00
				TOTAL	$ 870.00

Loss Payee: None

TOTAL POLICY PREMIUM $ 1,888.00

POLICY FORM AND ENDORSEMENTS: PP 00 01

COUNTERSIGNATURE DATE: August 12, 20X1

AGENT: N. Hale

To determine whether a policy covers a loss, many insurance professionals apply the DICE method. ("DICE" is an acronym for categories of policy provisions: declarations, insuring agreement, conditions, and exclusions.) The DICE method has four steps:

1. Review of the declarations page to determine whether it covers the person or the property at the time of the loss
2. Review of the insuring agreement to determine whether it covers the loss
3. Review of policy conditions to determine compliance
4. Review of policy exclusions to determine whether they preclude coverage of the loss

Each of these four steps is used in every case. Other categories of policy provisions should be examined. For example, endorsements and terms defined in the policy should be reviewed in relation to the declarations, insuring agreement, exclusions, and conditions.

Determination of Coverage

To examine the policy forms to determine whether coverage applies to the losses, the insurance professional can apply the DICE method, which involves four steps.

The first step of the DICE method is to determine whether the drivers or vehicles are described on the insured's PAP Declarations page and whether the accident occurred during the policy period. In this case, two PAPs potentially provide coverage. David, who is single, has his own PAP in which he is listed as the named insured on the Declarations page, and his car is listed as a covered auto. Wanda also has a PAP that lists her husband, Raymond, as the named insured on the Declarations page and lists the minivan as a covered auto. Wanda is considered an insured under this policy because the PAP definition of an insured includes "the spouse if a resident of the same household." The accident occurred during the policy period of both policies. See the exhibit "Definitions."

The second step of the DICE method is to determine whether the event has triggered coverage under either of the PAPs' insuring agreements. In the Coverage Part A—Liability Coverage policy provision, the insurer agrees to pay damages for bodily injury and property damage for which an insured is legally responsible because of an auto accident. In this case, David's collision with Wanda's vehicle would be considered an auto accident. Also, Wanda's lawsuit naming David and demanding payment for injuries as a result of the auto accident helps trigger liability coverage under the PAP. The damage to the two vehicles would be covered under Coverage Part D—Coverage for Damage to Your Auto. This accident meets the policy's definition of collision, which includes "impact with another vehicle." Both policies would have to indicate on the Declarations page that collision coverage is provided for the described auto. See the exhibit "Part D—Coverage For Damage To Your Auto."

Definitions

A. Throughout this policy, "you" and "your" refer to:

1. The "named insured" shown in the Declarations; and

2. The spouse if a resident of the same household.

If the spouse ceases to be a resident of the same household during the policy period or prior to the inception of this policy, the spouse will be considered "you" and "your" under this policy but only until the earlier of:

1. The end of 90 days following the spouse's change of residency;

2. The effective date of another policy listing the spouse as a named insured; or

3. The end of the policy period

Includes copyrighted material of Insurance Services Office, Inc., with its permission. Copyright, ISO Properties, Inc., 1997. [DA00277]

Part D—Coverage For Damage To Your Auto

INSURING AGREEMENT

A. We will pay for direct and accidental loss to "your covered auto" or any "non-owned auto", including their equipment, minus any applicable deductible shown in the Declarations. If loss to more than one "your covered auto" or "non-owned auto" results from the same "collision", only the highest applicable deductible will apply. We will pay for loss to "your covered auto" caused by:

1. Other than "collision" only if the Declarations indicate that Other Than Collision Coverage is provided for that auto.

2. "Collision" only if the Declarations indicate that Collision Coverage is provided for that auto.

If there is a loss to a "non-owned auto", we will provide the broadest coverage applicable to any "your covered auto" shown in the Declarations.

B. "Collision" means the upset of "your covered auto" or a "non-owned auto" or their impact with another vehicle or object.

Includes copyrighted material of Insurance Services Office, Inc., with its permission. Copyright, ISO Properties, Inc., 1997. [DA00290]

The third DICE step is to determine whether all policy conditions have been met. For the purposes of this case study, the student should assume that they are.

The fourth step of the DICE method is to determine whether one or more exclusions preclude coverage that the insuring agreements have granted. In this case, the "other business use" exclusion under the Liability Coverage should be considered. This provision excludes the maintenance or use of any vehicle while the insured is employed or otherwise engaged in any business.

However, this exclusion would not apply to this situation because it contains an exception for the use of a private passenger auto. Because David was using his personal vehicle to make sales calls, the insurer determined that this exclusion did not apply. See the exhibit "Exclusions."

Exclusions

...

7. Maintaining or using any vehicle while that "insured" is employed or otherwise engaged in any "business" (other than farming or ranching) not described in Exclusion **A.6.**

   This Exclusion (**A.7.**) does not apply to the maintenance or use of a:

   a. Private passenger auto;

   b. Pickup or van; or

   c. "Trailer" used with a vehicle described in **a.** or **b.** above.

Includes copyrighted material of Insurance Services Office, Inc., with its permission. Copyright, ISO Properties, Inc., 1997. [DA00291]

One exclusion contained under Coverage D might have applied to Wanda's vehicle if the van had been equipped with any custom furnishings or equipment. Items such as special carpeting or insulation, furniture, height-extending roofs, or custom murals, paintings, or other decals or graphics are not covered.

Determination of Amounts Payable

Determining the amount payable for a loss under liability coverage involves analyzing the limit of liability available to pay losses and supplementary payments.

In this case, the court awarded Wanda and her family $408,500 as total damages payable due to bodily injury caused by David. The damages for Wanda were $100,000; for her older child, $53,900; and, for her younger child, $254,600.

Because the limits of liability on David's PAP are $500,000 per person and $1 million for any one accident, these damages are fully covered under David's policy. In addition, attorneys' fees to defend David in the suit brought by

Wanda and her family totaled $93,000. Under the Coverage Part A Insuring Agreement of David's PAP, this amount is paid in addition to the limit of liability and will be paid for the full amount. David was also required to take three days off from work to testify at the trial, and his insurer paid him $216 for loss of earnings. The Supplementary Payments provision of Coverage Part A provides coverage for up to $200 a day for loss of earnings to attend hearings or trials, but only if the insured attends at the insurer's request. This payment does not reduce the limit of liability available under Coverage Part A. See the exhibit "Part A—Liability Coverage."

Part A—Liability Coverage

INSURING AGREEMENT

A. We will pay damages for "bodily injury" or "property damage" for which any "insured" becomes legally responsible because of an auto accident. Damages include prejudgment interest awarded against the "insured". We will settle or defend, as we consider appropriate, any claim or suit asking for these damages. In addition to our limit of liability, we will pay all defense costs we incur. Our duty to settle or defend ends when our limit of liability for this coverage has been exhausted by payment of judgments or settlements. We have no duty to defend any suit or settle any claim for "bodily injury" or "property damage" not covered under this policy.

Includes copyrighted material of Insurance Services Office, Inc., with its permission. Copyright, ISO Properties, Inc., 1997. [DA00289]

The $2,750 in medical bills for the children's friend who was riding in Wanda's vehicle at the time of the accident would be paid under Coverage Part B—Medical Payments of Wanda's PAP. Medical payments coverage applies without regard to fault; therefore, regardless of whether the insured is legally liable for the accident, medical payments benefits may be paid for both the insured and other injured occupants of the insured's covered auto. In this case, the ten-year-old passenger would fall under the category of "any other person while occupying your covered auto." See the exhibit "Part B—Medical Payments Coverage."

For the damage to the vehicles, David's insurer would pay $4,450 (the $5,450 in damage to his car minus the $1,000 deductible that applies to collision coverage). The damage to Wanda's vehicle would be covered by David's insurer as property damage under Part A. However, instead of waiting for the court to determine whether David was liable for the damage, Wanda could file a claim with her insurer. Wanda's insurer would pay the $16,943 to repair the van minus the $500 deductible that applies to collision coverage (a total of $16,443). However, when David is found to be at fault for this accident, Wanda's insurer may have rights of subrogation against David's insurer. The PAP contains a provision titled "Our Right to Recover Payment"

> **Part B—Medical Payments Coverage**
>
> INSURING AGREEMENT
>
> A. We will pay reasonable expenses incurred for necessary medical and funeral services because of "bodily injury":
>
>   1. Caused by accident; and
>   2. Sustained by an "insured".
>
>   We will pay only those expenses incurred for services rendered within 3 years from the date of the accident.
>
> B. "Insured" as used in this Part means:
>
>   1. You or any "family member":
>   a. While "occupying"; or
>   b. As a pedestrian when struck by;
>   a motor vehicle designed for use mainly on public roads or a trailer of any type.
>   2. Any other person while "occupying" "your covered auto".

Includes copyrighted material of Insurance Services Office, Inc., with its permission. Copyright, ISO Properties, Inc., 2003 [DA00295]

that indicates if the insurer makes a payment to a person who has a right to recover damages from a third party, those rights are transferred to the insurer. Also, if Wanda were to recover damages from David or his insurer, she would be required to reimburse her insurer for the amount paid under her PAP. See the exhibit "Our Right To Recover Payment."

> **Our Right To Recover Payment**
>
> A. If we make a payment under this policy and the person to or for whom payment was made has a right to recover damages from another we shall be subrogated to that right. That person shall do:
>
>   1. Whatever is necessary to enable us to exercise our rights; and
>   2. Nothing after loss to prejudice them.
>
>   However, our rights in this Paragraph (A.) do not apply under Part D, against any person using "your covered auto" with a reasonable belief that that person is entitled to do so.
>
> B. If we make a payment under this policy and the person to or for whom payment is made recovers damages from another, that person shall:
>
>   1. Hold in trust for us the proceeds of the recovery; and
>   2. Reimburse us to the extent of our payment.

Includes copyrighted material of Insurance Services Office, Inc., with its permission. Copyright, ISO Properties, Inc., 1997. [DA00293]

Amounts Payable

David's PAP	Wanda's PAP
COVERAGE A—Bodily Injury Wanda's injuries—$100, 000 Older child's injuries—$53,900 Younger child's injuries — $254,600 TOTAL—$408, 500 Defense costs—$93,000 Loss of earnings—$216	COVERAGE B—Medical Payments Injuries to children's friend riding in car — $2,750
Coverage D—Collision Damage to David's vehicle—$4,450 ($5,450–$1,000 deductible)	Coverage D—Collision * Damage to Wanda's vehicle—$16, 443 ($16,943—$500 deductible) * Subject to subrogation recovery from David's insurer

[DA00294]

SUMMARY

Under Part D—Coverage for Damage to Your Auto of the PAP, the insurer agrees to pay for direct and accidental loss to a covered auto or nonowned auto, less the applicable deductible. The coverage granted by the insuring agreement is extended or limited by other Part D provisions.

It is important to know how to apply physical damage coverages to the facts of a case. This is accomplished by first determining whether a loss is covered and, if so, determining how much an insurer should pay for the loss.

Part E of the PAP outlines duties that the insured must perform after a loss. If the failure of the insured to comply with the stated duties is deemed prejudicial to the insurer, the insurer can deny coverage. In such a case, the insurer would have no obligation to make any payment for loss.

The General Provisions part of the PAP contains provisions and conditions that apply to the entire policy, rather than to specific coverage parts. These provisions include bankruptcy of the insured, changes in the policy, fraud, legal action against the insurer, insurer's right to recover payment (subrogation), policy period and territory, termination, transfer of the insured's interest in the policy, and two or more auto policies.

The unendorsed PAP is designed to insure vehicles such as private passenger autos, vans, or pickup trucks owned and/or used by individuals and families. Some insureds, however, have coverage needs that go beyond the basic PAP and require endorsements to customize their insurance coverage.

More drivers are using their personal autos as part of TNCs to provide passengers with rides for a fee. ISO has developed several endorsements that clarify when PAP coverage begins and ends for TNC drivers.

Knowing how to apply the PAP to the facts of a case is a critical skill. This is accomplished by first determining whether a loss is covered and, if so, determining how much the insurer should pay for the loss.

Direct Your Learning

5

Homeowners Property Coverage

Educational Objectives

After learning the content of this assignment, you should be able to:

▸ Describe how individuals and families can use the Insurance Services Office, Inc., (ISO) 2011 Homeowners insurance program to address their personal risk management needs.

▸ Describe the Homeowners 3—Special Form (HO-3) in terms of:
- Its structure and the coverages it provides
- The role of endorsements in modifying it
- The factors considered in rating it

▸ Describe what is insured by each of these coverages contained in the 2011 Homeowners 3—Special Form (HO-3) policy:
- Coverage A—Dwelling
- Coverage B—Other Structures
- Coverage C—Personal Property
- Coverage D—Loss of Use
- Additional Coverages

▸ Describe what is covered and what is excluded by these provisions in the 2011 Homeowners 3—Special Form (HO-3) policy:
- Perils Insured Against for Coverages A and B
- Perils Insured Against for Coverage C
- Section I—Exclusions

▸ Summarize each of the 2011 Homeowners 3—Special Form (HO-3) policy provisions in Section I—Conditions.

▸ Given a scenario describing a homeowners property claim, determine whether the 2011 HO-3 policy Section I—Property Coverages would cover the claim and, if so, the amount the insurer would pay for the claim.

Outline

ISO Homeowners Coverage

Overview of Homeowners Form HO-3

HO-3 Section I—Property Coverages

HO-3 Section I—Perils Insured Against and Exclusions

HO-3 Section I—Conditions

2011 HO-3 Section I—Property Coverage Case Study

Summary

Homeowners Property Coverage 5

ISO HOMEOWNERS COVERAGE

The Insurance Services Office, Inc. (ISO) Homeowners insurance program's policy forms are designed to meet the personal risk management needs of individuals and families.

The parties eligible for coverage under the ISO 2011 Homeowners (HO) insurance program fall into three general categories:

- Individuals and families who own a private home in which they reside—This is typically a single-family dwelling, but sometimes an eligible two to four-family dwelling. A mobile home is not eligible for unendorsed coverage. Dwelling and mobile home insurance policies are available for insuring residences that are not eligible for homeowners policies.
- People who rent or lease the premises in which they reside—The residence might be an apartment, a house (either a single-family house or other type), a mobile home, a trailer home, a house trailer, or a condominium unit.
- Individuals and families who own private condominium units used for residential purposes—Most insurers provide homeowners policies to people who own and live in condominium units. However, some insurers also provide such coverage when the insureds own but do not live in the condominium as long as the condominium unit is used as a residence by one family or by one or two tenants.

To address these parties' needs, the ISO Homeowners program offers six policy forms:

- Homeowners 2—Broad Form (HO-2)
- Homeowners 3—Special Form (HO-3)
- Homeowners 4—Contents Broad Form (HO-4)
- Homeowners 5—Comprehensive Form (HO-5)
- Homeowners 6—Unit-Owners Form (HO-6)
- Homeowners 8—Modified Coverage Form (HO-8)

Individuals and families should select a form based on their risk management needs and whether they meet the form's eligibility requirements. See the exhibit "How the ISO Homeowners Program Policy Forms Address Personal Risk Management Needs."

How the ISO Homeowners Program Policy Forms Address Personal Risk Management Needs

ISO Policy Form	Example of Personal Risk Management Need Addressed
HO-2—Broad Form	Meets most needs of owner-occupants for dwelling, other structures, and personal property coverage at a lower premium than the HO-3 or HO-5 coverages.
HO-3—Special Form	Meets the needs of owner-occupants of dwellings who want coverage on their dwellings and other structures that is broader than the HO-2 offers.
HO-4—Contents Broad Form	Meets the needs of tenants and other apartment or dwelling occupants who do not require coverage on the dwelling.
HO-5—Comprehensive Form	Meets the needs of owner-occupants of dwellings who want the broadest coverage available among ISO's forms for their dwellings, other structures, and personal property.
HO-6—Unit-Owners Form	Meets the needs of owners of condominium units and cooperative apartment shares.
HO-8—Modified Coverage Form	Meets the needs of owner-occupants of dwellings who may not meet insurer standards required for other policy forms.

[DA00300]

The HO-2—Broad Form (HO 00 02), simply known as the HO-2, provides named perils coverage for dwellings, other structures, and personal property. The HO-2 is designed to meet the risk management needs of owner-occupants of dwellings.

Forms HO-2, HO-3, HO-5, and HO-8 can be issued only to the owner-occupant of a one-, two-, three-, or four-family dwelling. Rules prohibit issuance to owners who do not occupy the dwelling. Further, the forms may not be issued to cover dwellings on farm premises. Persons purchasing a dwelling under a long-term installment contract, without legal title to the property, are eligible in the same manner as titled owners and occupants under a life estate arrangement. Also, a dwelling under construction is eligible if the named insured is the intended owner-occupant.

The HO-3—Special Form (HO 00 03), called the HO-3, provides special form coverage on dwellings and other structures (rather than the named perils coverage provided by the HO-2). Special form coverage, also known as open perils coverage, protects property against direct physical loss that is not otherwise excluded by the coverage form. Note that the HO-3 provides named perils coverage for personal property, as does the HO-2. The HO-3 is designed to meet the risk management needs of owner-occupants of dwellings who want broader coverage on their dwellings and other structures.

The HO-4—Contents Broad Form (HO 00 04), or HO-4, provides coverage for a tenant's personal property on a named perils basis. The HO-4 does not provide coverage for dwellings or other structures. This policy form is designed to meet the risk management needs of tenants and other occupants of apartments or dwellings. For example, a young woman who has recently graduated from college, started a new job, and moved into an apartment should obtain an HO-4 if she is no longer an official resident of her parents' insured household and would like her own personal property and liability insurance protection. Form HO-4 can be issued to a tenant who maintains a residence in any kind of structure. Persons who maintain a residence in a building that they own but that is not a one- or two-family dwelling are also eligible.

A homeowners policy (other than HO-4) may also be issued in the name of a trust and trustee(s) when legal title to a one-, two-, three-, or four-family dwelling or condominium unit is held solely by the trust and when the trustee, beneficiary, or grantor regularly resides there. If a portion of the premises is used for other-than-private-residential occupancy, eligibility rules permit (1) not more than two roomers or boarders per family unit and (2) an incidental business occupancy, such as an office, private school, or studio. Occasional rental of the premises to others is also allowed.

The HO-5—Comprehensive Form (HO 00 05), known as the HO-5, provides open perils coverage on dwellings, other structures, and personal property. The HO-5 is designed to meet the risk management needs of owner-occupants of dwellings who would like the broadest coverage available among ISO's forms for their property. A homeowner who desires the broadest available coverage for his home and contents, and is willing to pay the increased premium for it, should select the HO-5.

The HO-6—Unit-Owners Form (HO 00 06), or HO-6, provides coverage for personal property on a named perils basis, with limited dwelling coverage (unit improvements and betterments). The HO-6 is designed to meet the risk management needs of the owners of condominium units and cooperative apartment shares. The HO-6 is similar to the HO-4, but it includes special provisions for loss exposures inherent in condominium and cooperative unit ownership. For example, a couple that purchases a vacation unit in a seaside condominium community should obtain additional homeowners coverage under an HO-6.

Only owners of condominium units and cooperative apartment shareowners are eligible for the HO-6, although the insured is not required to be an occupant of the unit. If a two-, three-, or four-family dwelling is co-owned by the families who reside there, one of the owner-occupant forms may be issued in the name of one of the owner-occupants, with the others named on an Additional Insured Endorsement (HO 04 41) to cover each party's interest in the building. The other parties may be issued an HO-4 for their personal property. This combination of coverages gives all co-owners complete homeowners coverage.

Functional replacement cost

The cost of replacing damaged property with similar property that performs the same function but might not be identical to the damaged property.

The HO-8—Modified Coverage Form (HO 00 08), called the HO-8, provides coverage for a dwelling, other structures, and personal property on a limited, named perils basis. A special valuation clause specifies that damage will be covered on a **functional replacement cost** basis. The HO-8 is designed to meet the risk management needs of owners-occupants of dwellings that may not meet insurer underwriting standards required for other policy forms (such as when the replacement cost of a dwelling significantly exceeds the dwelling's market value). For example, a couple may own a historic home in a city where local property values, including the value of the historic home, are far below replacement cost. This couple may opt for homeowners coverage under an HO-8.

Apply Your Knowledge

A homeowner wishes the broadest possible coverage for his home and contents. Which of the six ISO Homeowners program forms would be most appropriate for his coverage needs?

Feedback: The HO-5—Comprehensive Form (HO 00 05), known as the HO-5, provides open perils coverage on dwellings, other structures, and personal property and is designed to meet the risk management needs of owner-occupants of dwellings who would like the broadest coverage available among ISO's forms for their property.

OVERVIEW OF HOMEOWNERS FORM HO-3

The Homeowners 3—Special Form (HO-3) provides insurance coverage for the majority of owner-occupied dwellings. The HO-3 form, coupled with available endorsements, is designed to meet the needs of individuals and families.

A widely used homeowners policy form is the Insurance Services Office, Inc. (ISO) Homeowners 3—Special Form (HO 00 03), commonly referred to as the HO-3. Learning the basic structure and coverages of an HO-3 policy is the basis for understanding a variety of HO forms. The HO-3 policy is designed for the owner-occupants of a one- to four-family dwelling, as opposed to owners who do not occupy the dwelling. It provides coverage for a house, its contents, and the occupants' liability and is designed to be broad enough to cover the property and liability insurance needs of most families. To meet an insured's specific needs, the HO-3 policy can be modified by endorsement. As with other homeowners policies, insurers charge a premium for coverage under the HO-3 that is based on homeowners rating factors and adjustments.

Structure of Homeowners Form HO-3

The HO-3 policy structure consists of these primary components:

- Declarations
- Agreement and Definitions
- Section I—Property Coverages
- Section II—Liability Coverages
- Endorsements

Sections I and II are both subject to exclusions and conditions. Section I includes perils insured against, while Section II offers additional coverages. See the exhibit "Policy Structure for the ISO Homeowners 3—Special Form."

Policy Structure for the ISO Homeowners 3—Special Form

Declarations
Agreement
Definitions
Section I—Property Coverages
    Coverage A—Dwelling
    Coverage B—Other Structures
    Coverage C—Personal Property
    Coverage D—Loss of Use
    Additional Coverages
Section I—Perils Insured Against
Section I—Exclusions
Section I—Conditions
Section II—Liability Coverages
    Coverage E—Personal Liability
    Coverage F—Medical Payments to Others
Section II—Exclusions
Section II—Additional Coverages
Section II—Conditions
Section I and II Conditions
Endorsements (if applicable)

Copyright, ISO Properties, Inc. [DA00350]

Declarations

The declarations provide essential information about the insured, the property covered, and the limits of coverage by answering these questions:

- Who is the policyholder?
- Where is the policyholder's residence?
- What are the coverage limits?
- What is the premium?
- What is the Section I deductible?
- What is the effective date of the policy?
- Which forms and endorsements apply to the policy?
- Who is the mortgage holder?

Agreement and Definitions

The agreement (also known as the insuring agreement) is usually the first sentence in the policy form. It establishes the basis for the contract and specifies what the insurer and the insured will do. The insurer agrees to provide coverage, and the insured agrees to pay the premium and comply with the policy conditions.

Definitions follow the agreement and continue for several pages. Definitions clarify what is and is not covered under the policy. Defined words have special meanings when they are used within the policy; a defined word or phrase might have a meaning that is different, narrower, or broader than the dictionary definition. Words or phrases defined in this section appear in the policy within quotation marks. For example, the terms "you" and "your" refer to the named insured shown in the policy declarations and his or her resident spouse, even if the spouse is not named.

If a word is used within a policy and no definition is provided, it is given the common definition provided by a dictionary.

Section I—Property Coverages

Section I—Property Coverages, the first of two major coverage sections in the HO-3 policy, specifies the property covered, the perils insured against, and the exclusions and conditions that affect property coverages and losses.

Section I is divided into four property coverages plus a group of Additional Coverages:

- Coverage A—Dwelling applies to the dwelling on the "residence premises" listed on the Declarations page. It also applies to structures attached to the dwelling, such as a garage or deck.
- Coverage B—Other Structures applies to structures on the residence premises, other than the dwelling building, that are not attached to the dwelling, such as storage sheds, detached garages, and swimming pools.

- Coverage C—Personal Property applies to the contents of the insured premises and to personal property owned or used by an insured anywhere in the world, such as personal luggage or borrowed skis that are stolen.
- Coverage D—Loss of Use applies to the insured's exposure to financial loss, apart from the property damage itself, if the premises where the insured resides are damaged so badly they are unfit for use.
- Additional Coverages apply to certain direct property losses or consequential expenses that are not covered by Coverages A, B, C, or D. An example of an Additional Coverage that insures direct property loss is Trees, Shrubs, and Other Plants. An example of an Additional Coverage that covers a consequential expense is Debris Removal.

Section II—Liability Coverages

Section II—Liability Coverages is divided into two parts:

- Coverage E—Personal Liability applies to third-party coverage for those who are injured or whose property is damaged by an insured, generally for a basic limit of $100,000.
- Coverage F—Medical Payments to Others covers the necessary medical expenses incurred by others (not an insured) within three years of an injury.

Role of Endorsements

As a self-contained insurance policy, the homeowners policy is a single document that forms a complete contract. The HO-3 meets the majority, but not all, of the homeowners insurance needs of most individuals and families. Many endorsements are available to modify the HO-3 policy. These have been developed for use nationwide and approved by the states. Endorsements can increase or decrease limits, add or remove coverages, change definitions, clarify policy intent, or recognize specific characteristics that require a premium increase or decrease.

For example, the Personal Property Replacement Cost Loss Settlement endorsement (HO 04 90 05 11) provides replacement cost coverage on personal property, awnings, carpeting, household appliances, and outdoor equipment. These items are covered on an actual cash value basis on an unendorsed HO-3 form.

Additional endorsements are available for condominiums, home businesses, mobile homes, additional perils, increased amounts of coverage, or a guard against inflation.

Factors Considered in Rating

Homeowners policy rating factors and adjustments can vary by insurer. However, they typically use a framework designed by ISO that includes the development of a base premium and adjustments. Insurers may make additional adjustments, outside the ISO framework, before arriving at the final premium.

A homeowners policy premium is determined by first developing the base premium. The base premium is based on factors such as the dwelling location, public protection class (classification used to rate the quality of community fire protection), construction factors, coverage amount, and the policy form selected.

Base premium adjustments are applied to reflect variations in the risk management requirements and loss exposures of individuals and families. Base premium adjustments can result from endorsements, deductible changes, and unusual construction types.

Final adjustments are applied to develop the final premium. These can include claim history, insurance score, and package policy credits. Final premium adjustments typically vary by insurer; for example, insurers may use one of the final adjustments (for example, claim history) on a consistent basis while not using others. See the exhibit "Rating Homeowners Policies."

Rating Homeowners Policies

    Base premium factors
+ Base premium adjustments
+ Final adjustments
    Final homeowners premium

[DA00301]

HO-3 SECTION I—PROPERTY COVERAGES

The Insurance Services Office, Inc. (ISO) 2011 Homeowners 3—Special Form (HO-3) provides coverage for a house and its contents. It is designed to cover the property loss exposures that most individuals and families face.

Section I—Property Coverages of the HO-3 policy provides four basic property coverages and twelve Additional Coverages:

- Coverage A—Dwelling
- Coverage B—Other Structures
- Coverage C—Personal Property
- Coverage D—Loss of Use

Coverage A—Dwelling

Coverage A applies to the dwelling on the residence premises listed on the Declarations page. "Residence premises" includes not only a one-family dwelling, but also a two-, three-, or four-family dwelling where the named insured resides in at least one of the units. It also applies to structures (such as a garage or a deck) attached to the dwelling and to materials and supplies located on or next to the covered dwelling and used to construct or repair the dwelling. Coverage does not apply to the land at the residence premises. See the exhibit "Residence Premises Endorsements."

> **Residence Premises Endorsements**
>
> The definition of "residence premises" in the homeowners form has led to some confusion regarding its interpretation. For example, if someone purchased a home and repaired it before moving in, an insurer could argue that the insured did not reside there and deny coverage. The Insurance Services Office, Inc. (ISO) Residence Premises Definition Endorsement (to be attached to all homeowners forms other than the HO-6 and Mobilehome forms, which have their own similar endorsements) changes the language of the definition to require residency at the inception date of the policy. This means that if an insured must move out of the home during the policy term—for example, because of renovations to the home or a long-term-care stay—the homeowners coverage will continue until the policy renewal. At policy renewal, coverage should be reviewed if the insured no longer resides at the premises on the inception date of the new policy term.
>
> Additionally, ISO has introduced an optional related endorsement. The Broadened Residence Premises Endorsement provides for a starting date and an end date to the residency requirement. For example, if an insured purchases a new home and does not plan to reside there for the first three months, this endorsement could be used to temporarily remove the residency requirement for that time period.

[DA12653]

Coverage B—Other Structures

Coverage B—Other Structures applies to structures on the residence premises that are not attached to the dwelling and are separated from it by "clear space." A fence, utility line, or similar connection linking another structure with the dwelling does not make it an attached structure.

An additional amount equal to 10 percent of the Coverage A limit is available for other structures. This 10 percent limit applies collectively to all "other structures" at the residence premises.

Coverage B has three important exclusions:

- A structure rented to anyone who is not a resident of the dwelling. However, a structure that is rented to others for use as a private garage is covered.
- A structure from which any business is conducted.
- A structure used to store business property. However, a structure containing business property is covered if the business property is solely owned by an insured or a tenant of the dwelling, provided that the business property does not include gaseous or liquid fuel, other than fuel in a permanently installed fuel tank of a vehicle or craft parked or stored in the structure.

Coverage C—Personal Property

Coverage C—Personal Property applies to items the insured owns or uses, anywhere in the world. It can also cover loss of or damage to personal property of others while that property is on the residence premises if the named insured requests such coverage after a loss. Coverage C can also cover loss of or damage to personal property of a guest or residence employee while it is in any residence occupied by an insured.

The standard limit for Coverage C is 50 percent of the Coverage A limit, and it applies in addition to that limit. The Coverage C limit can be increased simply by changing the amount appearing on the Declarations page and charging an additional premium.

Only 10 percent of the Coverage C limit or $1,000 (whichever is greater) is available for property usually located at a residence other than the one listed on the Declarations page. This same limitation applies to property kept by an insured in a self-storage warehouse.

The 10 percent or $1,000 limitation does not apply to personal property removed from the residence premises because the house is being repaired, renovated, or rebuilt and is not fit to live in or to store property in. An insured who is moving from one principal residence to another will have the full limit of Coverage C available at both locations for thirty days.

Special Limits of Liability

Some categories of personal property are subject to sublimits, called special limits of liability, within the Coverage C limit. Items within these categories pose a higher-than-average risk of loss (for example, jewelry) or are types of property not contemplated in homeowners insurance premiums (for example, business property). The special limits for three personal property categories (jewelry and furs; firearms and related items; and silverware, goldware, platinumware, and pewterware) apply only when loss is caused by theft. The special limits for eight other categories of personal property apply when loss is caused by any covered peril. See the exhibit "Special Sublimits Within Coverage C."

Special Sublimits Within Coverage C

Personal Property	Special Limit of Liability
Liability Sublimits Applicable to All Covered Perils	
Money and precious metals, including stored value cards, such as gift cards	$200
Securities, documents, records, and stamps, including cost to research and replace information that has been lost	$1,500
Watercraft, including trailers, equipment, and motors	$1,500
Trailers (other than used with watercraft)	$1,500
Portable electronic equipment	$1,500
Antennas, tapes, wires, records, disks, or other media	$250
Property Used Primarily for Business Purposes	
On the residence premises	$2,500
Away from the residence premises	$1,500
Sublimits Applicable to Theft (No Sublimit for Other Perils)	
Jewelry, furs, precious stones, and semiprecious stones	$1,500
Firearms and related items	$2,500
Silverware, goldware, platinumware, and pewterware	$2,500

[DA07598]

Property Not Covered

The HO-3 policy specifically excludes all coverage for some categories of personal property. In most cases, these items are usually insured through policies other than a homeowners policy:

- Articles separately described and specifically insured in this or other insurance. (For example, jewelry separately described on an endorsement or in a separate policy is Property Not Covered.)
- Animals, birds, or fish.
- Motor vehicles, parts, and electronic equipment that operates solely from the vehicle's electrical system. (Coverage is provided for vehicles not required to be registered, such as riding mowers and wheelchairs.)
- Aircraft and hovercraft.
- Property of a home-sharing occupant.
- Property of any other person occupying the residence as a result of any home-sharing host activities.
- Property of roomers and boarders unrelated to the insured.

- Property in an apartment rented to others. (Coverage for such property is provided as an Additional Coverage.)
- Property rented or held for rental to others off the residence premises.
- Business data, including drawings, stored either on paper or electronically.
- Credit cards or electronic fund transfer cards. (Coverage for such property is provided as an Additional Coverage.)
- Water or steam. (For example, there is no coverage for replacing water in a damaged swimming pool.)
- Property primarily used for home-sharing host activities.

Coverage D—Loss of Use

Coverage D applies to the insured's exposure to financial loss, apart from the property damage itself, if the residence premises are damaged so badly that they are not fit to live in. Coverage D applies only if the damage is the result of a loss that is covered under Section I—Property Coverages of the policy. The Coverage D limit is 30 percent of the Coverage A limit, and it applies in addition to the Coverage A limit. The limit can be increased by changing the amount on the Declarations page and paying an additional premium.

Three coverages are grouped under Coverage D:

- Additional living expense—If the insured must live elsewhere until the dwelling has been repaired, this pays for any necessary increase in living expenses required to maintain the household's normal standard of living.
- Fair rental value—If part of the residence is rented to others, the insurer will reimburse the insured the lost rental value (less expenses that do not continue) until repairs are made. Fair rental value arising from any home-sharing host activities is not covered.
- Loss of use due to civil authority—Even if an insured's property is undamaged, civil authorities may prohibit access to the home because of damage to neighboring property. In this case, the expenses of living elsewhere and lost rental income are covered for a maximum of two weeks.

Additional Coverages

The Additional Coverages insure against various types of losses that would not otherwise be covered under Section I of the policy. In addition to the basic descriptions of coverage provided in the bulleted list, the exhibit states whether each Additional Coverage creates an additional amount of insurance (as opposed to being payable within the applicable policy limit), whether each is subject to the policy deductible, and whether each must be triggered by another covered loss:

- Debris Removal—Covers reasonable expenses for removing debris of covered property that has been damaged by an insured peril or by ash, dust, or particles from a volcanic eruption that has caused direct loss to a covered building or property in the building. It also covers, subject to special conditions, the cost to remove fallen trees, not to exceed $500 for any one tree or $1,000 in any one loss.

- Reasonable Repairs—Covers reasonable costs incurred to protect covered property or repair other property damaged by an insured peril.
- Trees, Shrubs, and Other Plants—Covers loss caused by fire or lightning, explosion, riot or civil commotion, aircraft, vehicles not owned or operated by a resident, vandalism or malicious acts, or theft up to an additional 5 percent of the dwelling limit with a maximum of $500 for any one item. Property grown for business purposes is excluded.
- Fire Department Service Charges—Pays up to $500 for fire department charges incurred to save or protect insured property from a covered loss if the responding unit is from beyond the property's regular fire protection district.
- Property Removed—Covers property removed from premises endangered by an insured peril. While removed, the property is covered for direct loss by any cause (not limited to perils insured against) for up to thirty days.
- Credit Card, Electronic Fund Transfer Card or Access Device, Forgery, and Counterfeit Money—Pays up to $500 for legal obligations stemming from unauthorized use or theft of a credit card or an electronic fund transfer card or access device. It also covers loss due to forgery of a negotiable instrument or acceptance in good faith of counterfeit paper currency. There is no coverage for a card used by a resident of the household or by someone to whom the card was entrusted, and the insured must have complied with all terms of the issuing company. Losses arising from business use or dishonesty of the insured are excluded.
- Loss Assessment—Pays up to $1,000 for assessments charged by a corporation or an association of property owners for loss to collectively owned property caused by an insured peril.
- Collapse—Covers abrupt collapse of a building or part of a building resulting from an insured peril, hidden decay, insect or vermin damage, weight of contents or inhabitants, weight of rain, or defective material or construction. There is no coverage if the building was showing visible signs of deterioration before the collapse.
- Glass or Safety Glazing Material—Covers breakage of building glass, including breakage caused by earth movement. Direct physical loss to covered property caused solely by the broken glass is covered, but not resulting damage caused because the glass is broken (for example, rain damage). There is no coverage if the dwelling has been vacant for more than sixty days.
- Landlord's Furnishings—Pays up to $2,500 of the policy limit to cover damage caused by an insured peril other than theft to appliances, carpeting, and other household furnishings in apartments rented to others.

- Ordinance or Law—Pays up to 10 percent of the Coverage A limit to cover increased costs incurred due to the enforcement of any ordinance or law regulating the construction, demolition, remodeling, renovation, or repair of the insured building. There is no coverage for any costs relating to pollutants.
- Grave Markers—Covers grave markers, including mausoleums, for damage by an insured peril, up to $5,000.

Additional Coverages

Additional Coverages	Does this coverage create an additional limit?	Does the deductible apply?	Is this coverage dependent on another covered loss?
1. Debris Removal	Yes, if primary limits are exhausted, an additional 5 percent of the limit of liability is available.	Yes*	Yes, damage to covered property by a covered peril or volcanic eruption must occur.
2. Reasonable Repairs	No.	Yes*	Yes, damage to covered property by a covered peril must occur.
3. Trees, Shrubs, and Other Plants	Yes, up to $500 is provided for each item up to a total of 5 percent of the Coverage A limit.	Yes*	No.
4. Fire Department Service Charge	Yes, payment up to $500 is an additional limit.	No	No, there must be a threat of a covered peril, but there is no requirement that the peril actually occur.
5. Property Removed	No.	Yes*	No, the removed property is covered against direct loss from any cause.
6. Credit Card, Electronic Fund Transfer Card or Access Device, Forgery, and Counterfeit Money	Yes, an additional total of $500 is available for any series of acts committed by any one person. Defense coverage is also provided.	No	No.
7. Loss Assessment	Yes, for an additional $1,000.	Yes**	No, not to property of the insured. But there must be a loss from a covered peril to association property.
8. Collapse	No.	Yes *	No, other property need not be damaged, but the collapse must result from a covered peril.
9. Glass or Safety Glazing Material	No.	Yes*	No, other property need not be damaged, but the glass breakage must result from a covered peril.
10. Landlord's Furnishings	No.	Yes*	No.
11. Ordinance or Law	Yes, an additional limit of 10 percent of Coverage A is available.	Yes*	Yes, to the dwelling or an "other structure."
12. Grave Markers	No.	Yes*	No.

*Not a separate deductible. Only one deductible is subtracted from the total loss of a covered event.

** Only one deductible applies per unit to the total amount of any one loss, regardless of the number of assessments.

HO-3 SECTION I—PERILS INSURED AGAINST AND EXCLUSIONS

The Insurance Services Office, Inc. (ISO) Homeowners 3—Special Form (HO-3) protects policyholders against loss from a variety of perils to their homes, other structures, and personal property.

The HO-3 contains these divisions in Section I—Perils Insured Against:

- Coverage A—Dwelling and Coverage B—Other Structures are provided on a **special form coverage** basis, commonly referred to as open perils coverage.
- Coverage C—Personal Property is provided on a **named perils coverage** basis.

No covered perils are listed in Section I—Property Coverages for Coverage D—Loss of Use or for the policy's Additional Coverages, because Coverage D and three of the Additional Coverages apply only when other covered losses occur. The remaining Additional Coverages individually describe when coverage applies. Certain exclusions from coverage apply in Section I—Exclusions.

> **Special form coverage**
> Property insurance coverage covering all causes of loss not specifically excluded.
>
> **Named perils coverage**
> An insurance policy in which the covered causes of loss are listed or "named" in the policy.

Perils Insured Against for Coverages A and B

Insured perils for Coverage A—Dwelling and Coverage B—Other Structures are grouped together because both provide open perils coverage for real property with similar exposures to loss. Open perils coverage begins with this broad grant of coverage: "We insure against direct physical loss to property described in Coverages A and B."

This statement is followed by a list of excluded perils. Any peril not listed in these exclusions is covered. The excluded perils are these:

- Any peril excluded in Section I—Exclusions, discussed subsequently. Examples of excluded perils are flood, earthquake, and war.
- Collapse—However, collapse that results from some other cause is provided for under Section I—Property Coverages.
- Freezing of a plumbing, heating, air conditioning, or sprinkler system or a household appliance—If the insured fails to take reasonable precautions to prevent pipes and hoses from freezing and bursting, coverage is excluded for any resulting damage.
- Freezing, thawing, pressure, or weight of water or ice—Damage to external property (such as fences, pavement, patios, swimming pools, foundations, piers, and docks) caused by freezing, thawing, and water or ice pressure is excluded.
- Theft—Coverage is excluded for such loss that arises from home-sharing host activities or from theft in or to a dwelling under construction or

of construction materials and supplies until the dwelling is finished and occupied.
- Vandalism and malicious mischief—Coverage for vandalism, including ensuing losses such as fire damage, is excluded if the loss arises from home-sharing host activities or for dwellings that have been vacant for more than sixty consecutive days.
- Mold, fungus, or wet rot—Coverage for loss resulting from these causes is excluded unless the mold, fungus, or wet rot is hidden and results from an accidental leak of water or steam from a plumbing, heating, sprinkler, or air conditioning system; from a household appliance; or from a storm drain or water, steam, or sewer pipes off the residence premises. Sump pumps and roof drains are not considered part of the plumbing, heating, sprinkler, or air conditioning system or household appliance.
- Natural deterioration—Losses caused by wear and tear, marring, deterioration, mechanical breakdown, latent defect, inherent vice, smog, rust, other corrosion, and dry rot are excluded.
- Smoke from agricultural smudging or industrial operations—Damage that results from smoke caused by agricultural smudging or industrial operations is excluded. Agricultural smudging intentionally creates a dense smoke to protect plants from frost.
- Pollutants—The policy excludes coverage for damage to property caused by pollutants. An exception is made if the pollutants are released or escape as the result of any of the perils insured under Coverage C.
- Settling of the dwelling—Losses caused by settling, shrinking, bulging, or expansion of foundations, footings, patios, pavements, bulkheads, and the building structure are excluded.
- Animals—The HO-3 excludes damage caused by animals that an insured owns or keeps or by birds, rodents, or insects.

Unless the loss is otherwise excluded, the HO-3 covers water damage resulting from an accidental discharge or overflow of water or steam from a plumbing, heating, air conditioning, or sprinkler system; from a household appliance; or from a storm drain or water, steam, or sewer pipe off the residence premises. Coverage is provided for damage caused by the water, including the cost of tearing out and replacing any part of the building to make repairs. However, the loss to a damaged system or appliance is not covered.

Ensuing losses not specifically excluded by the HO-3 are covered. For example, settling of foundations is excluded, but if a settling foundation causes a water pipe to break, the ensuing water damage would be covered.

Perils Insured Against for Coverage C

Coverage C covers the contents of a home and other personal property. In contrast with the open perils coverage for Coverages A and B, Coverage C applies on a named perils basis, meaning that coverage applies only if covered property is damaged as a result of a cause of loss named in the policy. While open perils and named perils cover many of the same causes of loss, open perils coverage sometimes includes causes of loss that are not among the named perils.

For example, melting snow can back up beneath roof shingles because of the accumulation of frozen water (called an "ice dam") in the roof gutters. The water then enters the building, causing water damage to the building and personal property within. Ice dam is not a named peril under Coverage C, but it is a covered peril for purposes of Coverages A and B because it is not excluded. Therefore, any resulting water damage to the building is covered by Coverage A or B, but water damage to personal property in the building is not covered by Coverage C.

These are named perils that apply to Coverage C:

- Fire or lightning.
- Windstorm or hail—However, damage caused by rain, snow, sleet, sand, or dust is covered only if wind (including hurricane and tornado) or hail first damages the building, causing an opening in a roof or wall through which the cause of damage enters. Watercraft and their equipment are covered only while inside a fully enclosed building.
- Explosion.
- Riot or civil commotion—State laws commonly define a "riot" as a violent disturbance involving three or more (in some states, two or more) people. Civil commotion is a more serious and prolonged disturbance or violent uprising.
- Aircraft.
- Vehicles—For example, damage to personal property in the back seat of a car involved in an auto accident would be covered.
- Smoke—Sudden and accidental smoke damage to personal property, including damage by soot, fumes, or vapors from a boiler or furnace, is covered. Loss caused by smoke from agricultural smudging or industrial operations is excluded.
- Vandalism or malicious mischief—However, loss arising from home-sharing host activities is not included.
- Theft—Theft is generally understood to mean any unlawful taking of property. The theft peril states that it "includes attempted theft and loss of property from a known place when it is likely that the property has been stolen." Thus, for example, the peril includes damage to covered property that results from an attempted but unsuccessful theft, such as when thieves break through a door but flee before stealing anything because a burglar alarm sounds.
- Falling objects—Coverage is provided if a falling object breaks through the dwelling's roof or wall and damages the contents.

- Weight of ice, snow, or sleet—Coverage applies only for damage to property contained in a building.
- Accidental discharge or overflow of water or steam—The water or steam must be accidentally released by a plumbing, heating, air conditioning, or fire-protective sprinkler system or by a household appliance.
- Sudden and accidental tearing apart, cracking, burning, or bulging—Coverage applies if a hot water heating system, an air conditioning system, an automatic fire-protective sprinkler system, or an appliance for heating water suddenly and accidentally tears apart, cracks, burns, or bulges, resulting in a loss.
- Freezing—Damage resulting from the freezing of a plumbing, heating, air conditioning, or fire-protective sprinkler system or of a household appliance is covered provided that the insured has taken reasonable precautions to maintain the heat or has shut off and drained the system or appliance.
- Sudden and accidental damage from artificially generated electrical current—Loss to tubes, transistors, or electronic components or circuitry of appliances, computers, or home entertainment equipment is not covered.
- Volcanic eruption—This peril does not include loss caused by earthquake or tremors. Damage caused by airborne shock waves and ash, for example, is covered. An earthquake caused as a consequence of a volcanic eruption, however, is not covered.

Several noteworthy limitations apply to the theft peril. See the exhibit "Limitations Applicable to Theft Peril."

Limitations Applicable to Theft Peril

- Theft committed by an insured is excluded.
- Theft from a building under construction and theft of construction materials are excluded.
- Theft from a part of the insured premises rented to someone other than an insured is excluded.
- Theft of personal property from another residence the insured owns, rents, or occupies is excluded unless the insured is temporarily living there.
- Theft of property of an insured who is a student residing away from home (such as in a dormitory) is excluded unless the student has been there during the ninety days before the loss.
- Theft is excluded for watercraft, including furnishings and equipment, away from the residence premises.
- Theft of trailers, semi-trailers, and campers is excluded.
- Theft arising from home-sharing host activities is excluded.

[DA12648]

Section I—Exclusions

The HO-3 Section I exclusions apply to Coverages A, B, and C:

- Ordinance or law—This exclusion eliminates coverage for losses resulting from any ordinance or law that reduces the value of the property; requires testing for or cleaning up of pollutants; or requires demolition, construction, or debris removal. However, the HO-3 Additional Coverages section provides limited ordinance or law coverage for buildings or structures damaged as a result of an insured peril. The Additional Coverage applies to losses resulting from any ordinance or law that requires construction, demolition, remodeling, renovation, or repair beyond the typical repairs needed to restore the structures after a loss.
- Earth movement—Earthquakes and other types of earth movement, such as landslides, mudslides, mudflows, subsidence, and sinkholes, are excluded perils. This exclusion applies regardless of the cause of the earth movement, whether natural or otherwise. Damage caused by an ensuing fire or explosion is covered.
- Water—Coverage for losses caused by flood, surface water, waves, water, or waterborne material such as sewage that backs up through sewers and drains is excluded regardless of the cause of the water-related loss. Losses resulting from the "escape, overflow, or discharge" of "water or waterborne material from a dam, levee, seawall, or any other boundary or containment system" are also excluded. Ensuing losses from fire, explosion, or theft resulting from water damage are covered.
- Power failure—Damage resulting from a loss of electrical power or utility service because of a problem away from the insured residence premises is not covered. However, if power is interrupted by an insured peril that occurs on the premises, resulting losses are covered.
- Neglect—An insured is expected to use all reasonable means to protect property during and after a loss. The HO-3 provides no coverage for losses that result from the insured's failure to do so. Under an Additional Coverage, the insurer agrees to pay the cost of reasonable repairs to protect damaged property.
- War—Losses that result from war, including the discharge of nuclear weapons (on purpose or by accident), are excluded. This exclusion includes undeclared war, civil war, insurrection, rebellion, revolution, or military war-like action. Destruction, seizure, or use of insured property for military purposes is also excluded.
- Nuclear hazard—Losses that occur because of a nuclear hazard are excluded. A nuclear hazard is defined in Section I—Conditions as any "nuclear reaction, radiation, or radioactive contamination."
- Intentional loss—The HO-3 excludes any loss arising out of an act any insured commits or conspires to commit with the intent to cause a loss.
- Governmental action—Property described in Coverages A, B, and C is not covered against destruction, confiscation, or seizure by order of any

governmental or public authority. This exclusion does not preclude coverage for governmental action taken to prevent the spread of fire.

Section I—Exclusions contains three additional exclusions that apply only to Coverage A—Dwelling and Coverage B—Other Structures:

- Weather is an excluded peril only if it contributes to any of the previously excluded perils. For example, torrential rain that causes a mudslide would not be a covered peril, because earth movement (mudslide) is excluded. However, if the weight of rainwater that has collected on a roof causes the roof to collapse, coverage is provided under the Collapse form of Additional Coverage.
- Acts or decisions—including the failure to act or decide—of any person, group, organization, or government body are excluded.
- Damage that results from faulty planning, zoning, surveying, design specifications, workmanship, construction, renovation, materials, and maintenance is excluded. However, if faulty construction of a chimney in the insured's house results in a fire, the damage caused by the fire would be covered.

HO-3 SECTION I—CONDITIONS

Eighteen major conditions apply to the Section I coverages in the Insurance Services Office, Inc. (ISO) Homeowners 3—Special Form (HO-3). Both the insured and the insurer must meet these conditions.

Section I—Conditions of the ISO HO-3 policy describes the conditions that must be met by both the insured and the insurer and provides a majority of the information required for the insured and insurer to comply with the mutual "promise" made in the insuring agreement.

Insurable Interest and Limit of Liability

The Insurable Interest and Limit of Liability condition limits the maximum payment for any single loss to the applicable limits shown on the Declarations page, regardless of the number of insureds who have an insurable interest in the property. This condition further limits loss payment to any insured to the extent of that insured's insurable interest in the property at the time of the loss.

Deductible

The Deductible condition specifies that the policy deductible applies on a per-loss basis and that only the highest deductible applies when two or more apply to a loss. Before the 2011 revision, this condition had appeared after the Definitions section, but now follows the Insurable Interest and Limit of

Liability condition in the Conditions section. This placement reinforces the policy's intent that the deductible only applies to Section I losses.

Additionally, the minimum deductible for the ISO Homeowners program is $500. This is an increase from the previous minimum deductible amount under Section I, which was $250.

Your Duties After Loss

The Your Duties After Loss condition lists the insured's duties after a property loss. Because the cooperation of an insured is essential to the investigation, settlement, or defense of any claim, this condition clarifies that the insurer can deny coverage when an insured fails to fulfill the contractual duties listed.

In any given claim settlement, the insurer's claims representative might not require the performance of all of the listed items. However, this clause entitles the representative to require performance of any of the duties that may be helpful in the claim settlement process. These are the listed duties:

- Give prompt notice
- Notify the police
- Notify the credit card, electronic fund transfer card company, or access device company
- Protect the property from further damage
- Cooperate with the insurer
- Prepare an inventory
- Verify the loss
- Sign a sworn proof of loss

Loss Settlement

The Loss Settlement condition establishes the process for determining the amount to be paid for a property loss. There are two settlement methods, with the first method established for Coverage C—Personal Property and other miscellaneous items, and the other established for Coverage A—Dwelling and Coverage B—Other Structures.

The deductible amount shown on the Declarations page is subtracted once from the total of all losses payable under Section I and caused by a single loss event. (Two additional coverages do not have the deductible applied to them—one dealing with fire department service charges and the other with credit cards and other types of money cards.)

Losses to personal property listed under Coverage C—Personal Property, as well as awnings, carpeting, appliances, antennas, outdoor equipment, structures that are not buildings, and grave markers or mausoleums, are settled at the lesser of two amounts:

- Actual cash value (ACV) at the time of the loss
- The amount required to repair or replace the items

The loss settlement for buildings depends on how the limit of insurance compares to the replacement cost value of the damaged buildings at the time of the loss. These are the methods for determining the loss settlement for a building:

- If the limit of insurance is 80 percent or more of the replacement cost, the insurer will pay for the replacement cost of the damage up to the limit of coverage.
- If the limit of insurance is less than 80 percent of the replacement cost, the insurer will pay the greater of two amounts. The first amount is the ACV of the damage. The second is the proportion of the cost to repair or replace the damage that the limit of insurance bears to 80 percent of the replacement cost. This second method is sometimes easier to understand as a formula.

$$\text{Loss payment} = \frac{\text{Limit of insurance}}{80\% \times \text{Replacement cost}} \times \text{Replacement cost of the loss}$$

Except for small losses, which are generally considered to be under $2,500, the insurer will not pay more than the ACV until repairs are completed. An insured who has not decided whether a structure should be rebuilt can seek loss settlement on an ACV basis. Should the insured then decide to complete the repairs, he or she has up to 180 days after the loss to notify the insurer of intent to complete the repairs and make settlement on a replacement cost basis rather than on the ACV basis. See the exhibit "Loss Settlement Examples."

The insured is not required to rebuild a damaged or destroyed building on the same location. However, if the building is rebuilt on different premises, the insurer will pay no more than it would have if the building were repaired or replaced at the original premises. Regardless of the method used to determine the loss settlement amount, the limit of coverage shown on the Declarations page is the maximum amount that will be paid for any loss.

The Additional Limits of Liability for Coverages A, B, C, and D endorsement increases the Coverage A—Dwelling limit to equal the current replacement cost of the dwelling if that amount exceeds the limit appearing on the Declarations page. The limits of liability for Coverage B—Other Structures, Coverage C—Personal Property, and Coverage D—Loss of Use will be increased by the same percentage applied to Coverage A.

> **Loss Settlement Examples**
>
> These are examples of how the loss settlement for a dwelling would be determined. (These simple examples ignore any deductible that might apply.)
>
> Example 1—Dwelling limit equals or exceeds 80 percent of the replacement cost: An insured has a home with a $200,000 replacement cost and an HO-3 with a Coverage A limit of $180,000. Lightning strikes the central air conditioning unit and destroys it beyond repair. The unit has a replacement cost of $5,000 and is five years old. The dwelling is insured for more than 80 percent of replacement cost ($180,000 is 90 percent of $200,000).
>
> The insured would receive $5,000 to replace the unit.
>
> Example 2—Dwelling limit is less than 80 percent of the replacement cost: If this same insured has an HO-3 with a Coverage A limit of $100,000 (50 percent of the replacement cost), the insured's coverage would be below the 80 percent replacement cost requirement, and the second loss settlement method would be used. The insured would then receive the greater of the following:
>
> - The ACV of the air conditioner. The ACV would be the $5,000 replacement cost minus depreciation. If a central air conditioner has a useful life of ten years and is now five years old, this air conditioner would depreciate by 50 percent. The ACV would equal $2,500.
> - The limit is calculated:
>
> $100,000 ÷ (80% × $200,000) × $5,000 = $3,125
>
> The insured would receive the greater amount of $3,125.

[DA00299]

Loss to a Pair or Set

Often, items that are in pairs or sets are more valuable together than they are individually. Because of the increased value of pairs or sets, the Loss to a Pair or Set condition establishes the amount an insurer will pay if an item that is part of a pair or set is damaged or lost.

For example, Cindy has a custom-made brass lantern on each side of her driveway. The matching lanterns were recently fabricated at a cost of $2,000. As a pair, the lanterns have an ACV of $2,000. One lantern, by itself—not part of a pair—would have an ACV of $300 or could be exactly reproduced for $1,500. If one of Cindy's lanterns is stolen, the insurer has two options:

- Replace the missing lantern for $1,500 and restore the pair to its original value
- Pay Cindy the difference between the ACV of the lanterns as a pair and the ACV of the remaining single lantern ($1,700)

Replacing the missing lantern for $1,500 is the logical choice for the insurer in this case. However, if the missing lantern could not be replaced, the insurer might have no choice other than to pay $1,700 to compensate Cindy for the value lost. Whichever solution is chosen, the deductible will be subtracted from the final amount of the loss.

Appraisal

If the insured and the insurer cannot agree on the amount of a loss, the Appraisal condition outlines a method for resolving the disagreement. This method, commonly called the appraisal process, follows this procedure:

- The insurer and the insured each choose an appraiser to prepare an estimate of the value of the loss. Each party pays for its own appraiser.
- If the estimates differ, the two appraisers submit their differences to an umpire. The umpire is an impartial individual (often another appraiser or a judge) who resolves the differences. An agreement by any two of the three will set the amount of loss. The insurer and the insured share the cost of the umpire.

Other Insurance and Service Agreement

If two or more insurance policies cover the same loss, the Other Insurance and Service Agreement condition states that the loss will be shared proportionally by all policies.

This example demonstrates how the share is apportioned between two policies:

John has an HO-3 with an $80,000 Coverage A—Dwelling limit. Maryanne, John's wife, did not realize that John had purchased a homeowners policy. She also purchased a homeowners policy with a $120,000 Coverage A—Dwelling limit.

A fire destroys the couple's home, which has a $100,000 replacement cost at the time of the loss. After the fire, John and Maryanne discover that two policies exist to cover their home, with a total of $200,000 in coverage available ($80,000 from John's policy plus $120,000 from Maryanne's policy).

The two policies will share the loss proportionally:

- The insurer that issued John's policy will pay 40 percent of the loss ($80,000 ÷ $200,000 = 0.40), or $40,000.
- The insurer that issued Maryanne's policy will pay 60 percent of the loss ($120,000 ÷ $200,000 = 0.60), or $60,000.

An insured home or item of personal property might also be covered by a service plan, property restoration plan, home warranty, or service warranty agreement. The homeowners policy makes it clear in the Other Insurance and Service Agreement condition that homeowners insurance coverage applies as excess over any amounts payable under any such agreement.

Our Option

Insurers usually settle claims by paying the value of the loss, and the insured is responsible for repairing or replacing the property. However, the Our Option condition reserves the right for the insurer to repair or replace damaged property with similar property, should it choose to do so. Sometimes insurers exercise this right because they can purchase repairs or obtain replacement items at a deep discount. Repairing or replacing property is the insurer's option. The insured cannot require the insurer to repair or replace damaged property.

Loss Payment

As provided for in the Loss Payment condition, the insurer will adjust all losses with the insured or the insured's spouse (unless another person is named in the policy or is legally entitled to receive payment). A loss is payable sixty days after the insurer receives a proof of loss and either an agreement has been reached by the insurer and the insured or a court judgment or an appraisal award has been entered. (Time periods may vary according to state requirements.)

Abandonment of Property

The Abandonment of Property condition provides that if the insured abandons the property after it is damaged or destroyed, the insurer need not take responsibility for it. For example, after collecting insurance proceeds for a loss, an insured might prefer to walk away from a burned-out home in a neighborhood where property values have declined and turn the property over to the insurer, rather than remain liable for the damaged building. However, the insurer is not obligated to accept the property.

Mortgage Clause

The Mortgage Clause condition establishes these rights of the mortgagee listed on the Declarations page:

- If a loss occurs to property covered by Coverage A—Dwelling or Coverage B—Other Structures, the loss is payable jointly to the mortgagee and the insured. Typically, the mortgagee relies on this right to ensure that the insured uses the money to repair the property. The mortgagee is satisfied as long as the property is repaired and the insured continues to make mortgage payments.

- A mortgagee has rights that are independent of the insured's rights. If the insurer denies the insured's loss (if, for example, arson by the insured is discovered), the mortgagee retains the right to collect from the insurer its insurable interest in the property.

- An insurer must mail notice of cancellation or nonrenewal of a policy to the mortgagee (in addition to notice sent to the insured) at least ten days before the cancellation or nonrenewal.

No Benefit to Bailee

The No Benefit to Bailee condition states that a bailee who holds the property of an insured is responsible for the care of that property. For example, a dry cleaner who negligently damages an insured's clothing cannot avoid responsibility for the damage because the insured has coverage under the homeowners policy.

Loss Payable Clause

In the Loss Payable Clause condition, the insurer agrees to include the named loss payee when a claim is paid involving that personal property. For example, the Loss Payable Clause condition applies to a homeowner who uses leased or rented furniture. The homeowner might be asked to name the furniture leasing company as an additional insured for this property. This information would appear in the policy declarations. Ordinarily, this means that a claim draft would be payable to both the named insured and the loss payee. The loss payee is also entitled to notification if the policy is canceled or nonrenewed. See the exhibit "Other Section I Conditions."

Other Section I Conditions

Suit Against Us—Bars an insured from bringing legal action against the insurer unless the insured has complied with all policy provisions. Any legal action must be started within two years of the loss.

Recovered Property—Provides that if the insurer pays a claim for the loss of property, and the property is later recovered, the insured has the option of taking the property and returning the claim payment or keeping the claim payment and allowing the insurer to take over the property.

Volcanic Eruption Period—All volcanic eruptions that occur within a seventy-two-hour period are considered to be one volcanic eruption. If multiple eruptions should occur within that period, only one coverage limit and one deductible would apply.

Policy Period—Specifies that coverage applies only to losses that occur during the policy period.

Concealment or Fraud—States any insured who conceals or misrepresents any material information, engages in fraudulent conduct, or makes false statements relating to the insurance is not covered under the policy. This condition applies whether the conduct occurred before or after a loss.

Nuclear Hazard Clause—Defines the nuclear hazard, for which coverage is excluded in the Section I—Exclusions. Excluded nuclear hazards encompass any radiation, contamination, explosion, or smoke resulting from a nuclear reaction. A direct loss by fire resulting from the nuclear hazard is covered.

[DA07730]

2011 HO-3 SECTION I—PROPERTY COVERAGE CASE STUDY

Knowing how to apply the Insurance Services Office, Inc. (ISO) Homeowners 3—Special Form (HO-3) policy to the facts of a case is an important skill. This case study will help you make the transition from knowing policy language to applying policy language to personal property losses to determine whether coverage applies. As you progress through this case study, you can check your understanding of the coverage provided by answering the Knowledge to Action questions.

Case Facts

Marvin and Lashonda own a single-family home, which is insured under an unendorsed HO-3 policy with a $300,000 dwelling limit. A carport is attached to the rear of the home, where Marvin stores a small fishing boat and trailer. On February 2, 20X1, as the couple is cooking dinner, visitors unexpectedly arrive. Marvin and Lashonda forget to remove a pot from the stove, the pot overheats, and a fire ensues. The fire department is called, and the couple and their guests safely escape. The fire, smoke, and water damage destroy the kitchen and several adjoining rooms and damage the carport area, which is adjacent to the kitchen. The boat and trailer are destroyed by the heat and fire. Kitchen furnishings and appliances are destroyed. The couple must temporarily live in a nearby hotel for one month until their home is safe to occupy. Marvin and Lashonda report the loss to their insurer promptly. They are in compliance with all policy conditions, including Coverage A replacement cost provisions. See the exhibit "Summary of Marvin and Lashonda's Damages."

Summary of Marvin and Lashonda's Damages

$50,000	Value of structural damage to home because of the fire
$3,000	Value of Marvin's fishing boat and trailer (total loss)
$8,000	Value of structural damage to the carport
$3,500	Cost to live in a hotel while damage to home is repaired
$25,000	Value of damage to furnishings and appliances, including those items valued at a total loss

[DA07743]

Given the facts presented in the case, will the claim for fire and related damage be covered under the HO-3? If so, what amount will the insurer pay for the claim? When answering the questions in this case-based activity, consider only the information provided as part of this case.

Necessary Reference Materials

To determine whether the HO-3 policy provides coverage for the losses Marvin and Lashonda incurred as a result of the fire and the ensuing damage, you need copies of the HO-3 policy form and the Declarations page.

Overview of Steps

When examining the policy forms to determine whether coverage applies to the loss(es), you can apply the four steps of the DICE method. ("DICE" is an acronym for categories of policy provisions: declarations, insuring agreement, conditions, and exclusions.) Doing this involves analyzing these provisions and determining whether any information found at each step precludes coverage at the time the losses occurred. You should also examine other categories of policy provisions, such as the insured's duties, general provisions, endorsements (if applicable), and terms defined in the policy in relation to the declarations, insuring agreement, conditions, and exclusions.

Next, you should determine the amounts payable for the losses under the applicable policy or policies. Doing this involves analyzing the limits of insurance and any deductibles that apply. It also involves determining whether more than one policy provides coverage for the same loss.

Determination of Coverage

To determine whether HO-3 coverage applies for Marvin and Lashonda's submitted fire claim, you can move sequentially through the four steps of the DICE method of policy analysis.

DICE Analysis Step 1: Declarations

The first DICE step is to review the Declarations page of Marvin and Lashonda's policy to determine whether it covers the loss. See the exhibit "Excerpt From Marvin and Lashonda's Declarations Page."

Knowledge to Action

Action Task: Review the Declarations page in Marvin and Lashonda's policy.

According to your analysis of the excerpt of Marvin and Lashonda's Declarations page, is coverage applicable for the property and individuals in question during the coverage period?

Feedback: The Declarations page confirms Marvin and Lashonda as insureds for the premises damaged. The loss occurred during the policy period.

Excerpt From Marvin and Lashonda's Declarations Page

Homeowners Policy Declarations

POLICYHOLDER: Marvin and Lashonda Smith **POLICY NUMBER:** 296 H 578661
(Named Insured) 216 Brookside Drive
Anytown, USA 40000

POLICY PERIOD: **Inception:** March 30, 20XX Policy period begins 12:01 A.M. standard time
Expiration: March 30, 20X1 at the residence premises.

[DA07744]

DICE Analysis Step 2: Insuring Agreement

The second DICE step is to review Marvin and Lashonda's insuring agreement to determine whether it is applicable to the described loss.

Knowledge to Action

Action Task: Review the relevant portions of the insuring agreement in the HO-3 policy.

According to your analysis of the excerpt of the insuring agreement, did this loss trigger coverage under the HO-3 Insuring Agreement?

Feedback: Yes, coverage is triggered under the HO-3, in which the insurer agrees to pay for direct physical loss to property described in Coverages A and B (subject to certain exclusions) and for direct physical loss under Coverage C for certain named perils, including fire and subsequent smoke and water damage.

DICE Analysis Step 3: Conditions

The third DICE step is to review the policy conditions to determine whether they preclude coverage at the time of the loss. See the exhibit "HO-3 Policy Form (Unendorsed) With $500 Deductible."

> **HO-3 Policy Form (Unendorsed) With $500 Deductible**
>
> Marvin and Lashonda's Coverages
>
> Marvin and Lashonda Smith
> 216 Brookside Drive
> Anytown, USA
>
> Policy Period: From 03/30/X0 to 03/30/X1 (12:01 a.m. Standard time at the location of the residence premises)
>
> | Cov. A—Dwelling | $300,000 | Cov. B—Other Structures | $30,000 | Cov. C—Personal Property | $150,000 | Cov. D—Loss of Use | $90,000 |
> |---|---|---|---|---|---|---|---|

[DA07745]

Knowledge to Action

Action Task: Determine whether the HO-3 policy conditions preclude coverage for Marvin and Lashonda's loss.

According to your analysis of the excerpt of the HO-3 policy conditions, is coverage precluded for Marvin and Lashonda's loss?

Feedback: No, coverage is not precluded for Marvin and Lashonda's loss. They reported the claim promptly and are in compliance with all policy conditions. The $300,000 coverage under Coverage A meets the 80 percent Coverage A Replacement Cost provision.

DICE Analysis Step 4: Exclusions

The fourth DICE step is to review the policy exclusions to determine whether they exclude or limit coverage of the loss. See the exhibit "Special Limits of Liability."

Knowledge to Action

Action Task: Review the "Special Limits of Liability" exhibit to determine whether one or more exclusions exclude or limit coverage of Marvin and Lashonda's loss.

According to your review of the "Special Limits of Liability" exhibit, do one or more exclusions exclude or limit coverage of Marvin and Lashonda's loss?

Feedback: Yes, one coverage limitation in Marvin and Lashonda's HO-3 applies to Coverage C—Personal Property. Under Coverage C, a $1,500 limit applies per loss to watercraft, including trailers and related equipment. This limitation would apply to Marvin's fishing boat and trailer.

Special Limits of Liability

3. Special Limits Of Liability

The special limit for each category shown below is the total limit for each loss for all property in that category. These special limits do not increase the Coverage C limit of liability.

   a. $200 on money, bank notes, bullion, gold other than goldware, silver other than silverware, platinum other than platinumware, coins, medals, scrip, stored value cards and smart cards.

   b. $1,500 on securities, accounts, deeds, evidences of debt, letters of credit, notes other than bank notes, manuscripts, personal records, passports, tickets and stamps. This dollar limit applies to these categories regardless of the medium (such as paper or computer software) on which the material exists.

   This limit includes the cost to research, replace or restore the information from the lost or damaged material.

   c. $1,500 on watercraft of all types, including their trailers, furnishings, equipment and outboard engines or motors.

   d. $1,500 on trailers or semitrailers not used with watercraft of all types.

   e. $1,500 for loss by theft of jewelry, watches, furs, precious and semiprecious stones.

   f. $2,500 for loss by theft of firearms and related equipment.

   g. $2,500 for loss by theft of silverware, silver-plated ware, goldware, gold-plated ware, platinumware, platinum-plated ware and pewterware. This includes flatware, hollowware, tea sets, trays and trophies made of or including silver, gold or pewter.

   h. $2,500 on property, on the "residence premises", used primarily for "business" purposes.

   i. $500 on property, away from the "residence premises", used primarily for "business" purposes. However, this limit does not apply to loss to electronic apparatus and other property described in Categories j. and k. below.

   j. $1,500 on electronic apparatus and accessories, while in or upon a "motor vehicle", but only if the apparatus is equipped to be operated by power from the "motor vehicle's" electrical system while still capable of being operated by other power sources.

   Accessories include antennas, tapes, wires, records, discs or other media that can be used with any apparatus described in this Category j.

   k. $1,500 on electronic apparatus and accessories used primarily for "business" while away from the "residence premises" and not in or upon a "motor vehicle". The apparatus must be equipped to be operated by power from the "motor vehicle's" electrical system while still capable of being operated by other power sources.

   Accessories include antennas, tapes, wires, records, discs or other media that can be used with any apparatus described in this Category k.

[DA00338]

Determination of Amounts Payable

Now that you have completed the DICE analysis, you can determine the amounts payable. Doing this involves analyzing the limit(s) of insurance available to pay for the loss and any deductibles that apply. It also involves determining whether more than one policy provides coverage for the same loss.

Knowledge to Action

Under Coverage A, how much will Marvin and Lashonda receive for fire damage to their home?

Feedback: Under Coverage A, Marvin and Lashonda will receive $49,500 ($50,000 less the $500 deductible) for fire damage to the home (within the $300,000 Coverage A limit) at full replacement cost because the policy dwelling limit complies with policy replacement cost provisions (Note that for purposes of this case, the policy deductible is being applied here).

Under Coverage A, how much will Marvin and Lashonda receive for fire damage to their carport?

Feedback: Under Coverage A, Marvin and Lashonda will receive $8,000 for fire damage to their carport (considered part of the dwelling, not an "other structure"; within the $300,000 Coverage A limit).

Under Coverage C, before an adjustment is made for the depreciation and physical condition of the furnishings and appliances, how much would Marvin and Lashonda be entitled to receive for fire, smoke, and water damage to those items?

Feedback: Under Coverage C, Marvin and Lashonda would be entitled to receive $25,000 for fire, smoke, and water damage to furnishings and appliances (within the $150,000 coverage limit). However, the amount that they would actually receive would be reduced based on the actual cash value of the furnishings and appliances, which would reflect a diminished value based on the extent to which they've depreciated.

Under Coverage C, before an adjustment is made for the depreciation and physical condition of the boat and the trailer, how much would Marvin and Lashonda be entitled to receive for fire damage to each?

Feedback: Under Coverage C, Marvin and Lashonda will receive $1,500 for fire damage to the boat and trailer (leaving a $1,500 balance unpaid because of the special limit of liability; within $150,000 coverage limit). However, the amount that they would actually receive would be reduced based on the actual cash value of the boat and trailer, which would reflect a diminished value based on the extent to which they've depreciated.

Under Coverage D, how much will Marvin and Lashonda receive for the additional living expenses required for a one-month hotel stay while their home is made habitable?

Feedback: Under Coverage D, Marvin and Lashonda will receive $3,500 for their additional living expenses (within the $90,000 coverage limit).

SUMMARY

Individuals and families have a variety of personal risk management needs related to their homes and personal liability. The ISO Homeowners program offers a selection of homeowners forms to meet these various needs. The forms vary according to the types of property eligible for coverage and type of coverage provided.

The Homeowners 3—Special Form (HO 03) meets the needs of most homeowners and families. It includes several sections: Declarations, Agreement and Definitions, Section I—Property Coverages, and Section II—Liability Coverages. Endorsements can be added to modify the coverage provided. The premium for the coverage consists of a base premium and adjustments.

HO-3 Section I—Property Coverages contains four property coverages: Coverage A—Dwelling, Coverage B—Other Structures, Coverage C—Personal Property, and Coverage D—Loss of Use. Section I also includes twelve Additional Coverages, which provide limited coverage for various types of losses that would not otherwise be covered under Section I.

HO-3 provides open perils coverage for property described in Coverage A—Dwelling and Coverage B—Other Structures and named perils coverage for property described in Coverage C—Personal Property. Coverages A, B, and C are all subject to the Section I—Exclusions. Coverages A and B are also subject to several other exclusions that help to define the scope of open perils coverage.

HO-3 Section I—Conditions describes the eighteen major conditions applying to the property coverages that both the insured and the insurer must meet.

You should now be able to apply policy language to personal property losses to determine whether the losses are covered and, if so, the amount for which they are covered.

6

Direct Your Learning

Homeowners Liability, Conditions, Coverage Forms, and Endorsements

Educational Objectives

After learning the content of this assignment, you should be able to:

- Determine whether the 2011 Homeowners 3—Special Form (HO-3) policy provisions in the following Section II—Liability Coverages provide coverage for a given loss or loss exposure:
  - Coverage E—Personal Liability
  - Coverage F—Medical Payments to Others
  - Additional Coverages
- Determine whether one or more exclusions preclude the coverage provided by Section II of the 2011 Homeowners 3—Special Form (HO-3) policy provisions in Section II—Exclusions.
- Summarize each of these 2011 Homeowners 3—Special Form (HO-3) policy provisions:
  - Conditions applicable to Section II
  - Conditions applicable to Sections I and II
- Given a case describing a homeowners liability claim, determine whether the Homeowners Section II—Liability Coverages would cover the claim and, if so, the amount the insurer would pay for the claim.
- Compare the coverage provided by each of the following 2011 homeowners forms to the coverage provided by the 2011 Homeowners 3—Special Form (HO-3):
  - HO-2 Broad Form
  - HO-4 Contents Broad Form
  - HO-5 Comprehensive Form
  - HO-6 Unit-Owners Form
  - HO-8 Modified Coverage Form

Outline

HO-3 Section II—Liability Coverages

HO-3 Section II—Exclusions

HO-3 Section II—Conditions

Determining Whether Homeowners Section II—Liability Coverages Covers a Claim

Coverage Variations in ISO Homeowners Forms

Commonly Used Endorsements that Modify the 2011 ISO Homeowners Policies

HO-3 Coverage Case

Summary

Educational Objectives, continued

- Summarize the coverages provided by various 2011 ISO Homeowners policy endorsements.

- Given a case describing a homeowners claim, determine whether a 2011 HO-3 policy that may include one or more endorsements would cover the claim and, if so, the amount the insurer would pay for the claim.

Homeowners Liability, Conditions, Coverage Forms, and Endorsements

6

HO-3 SECTION II—LIABILITY COVERAGES

Individuals and families are exposed to liability through the property they own and use and through their personal activities. Section II—Liability Coverages in the Insurance Services Office, Inc. (ISO) Homeowners 3—Special Form (HO-3) form addresses this and other personal liability loss exposures.

Homeowners forms are not all alike. Some insurers draft their own homeowners forms and endorsements. Also, state-by-state variations on all forms are common. ISO homeowners policy forms combine property and liability coverages (Section I and Section II) to meet the common loss exposures faced by individuals and families. Of the ISO homeowners forms, the HO-3 is used most frequently. The forms can be endorsed to meet certain uncommon loss exposures. Section I of the ISO homeowners policy forms provides coverage for an insured's first-party loss exposures. Section II provides coverage for an insured's **third-party** loss exposures.

The HO-3's Section II contains the same coverage provisions found in the other ISO Homeowners program policy forms (HO-2, HO-4, HO-5, HO-6, and HO-8). The basic coverage provided by the HO-3 Section II—Liability Coverages applies to losses related to an insured's premises (dwelling location); personal activities (for example, pet ownership); and other incidental sources of personal liability, such as residence employees.

Section II of the ISO HO-3 contains two primary coverages and an additional coverages section:

- Coverage E—Personal Liability
- Coverage F—Medical Payments to Others
- Section II—Additional Coverages

Coverage E—Personal Liability

The Coverage E—Personal Liability Coverage provisions provide coverage if a claim is made or a suit is brought against an insured because of **bodily injury** or **property damage** arising from a covered **occurrence**. If the claim or suit brought by the third party does not allege bodily injury or property damage as defined in the policy, or if the bodily injury or property damage occurs before or after the policy period, the insurer is not obligated to pay any damages under Coverage E or to defend the insured.

Third party
A person or business who is not a party to the insurance contract but who asserts a claim against the insured.

Bodily injury
Physical injury to a person, including sickness, disease, and death.

Property damage
Physical injury to, destruction of, or loss of use of tangible property.

Occurrence
An accident, including continuous or repeated exposure to substantially the same general harmful conditions.

The term "occurrence" is particularly important in the homeowners insuring agreement. Liability coverage applies only to bodily injury and property damage that result from an occurrence during the policy period. One accident is an occurrence, even if it involves injury to more than one person or damage to more than one piece of property. Also, an occurrence can be a sudden event, a gradual series of incidents, or a continuous condition, as long as it is fortuitous. An example of a nonsudden occurrence is the gradual yet accidental seepage of pollutants from an insured's defective septic system into a neighbor's supply of drinking water.

The insurer pays up to the limit of liability for the damages for which an insured is legally liable. Liability coverage, which applies worldwide, applies to bodily injury and property damage arising from the insured's activities or premises. In most instances, such liability arises from the insured's negligence. Basic personal liability limits are $100,000 per occurrence, with higher limits available for an additional premium.

The circumstances under which personal liability can arise may be illustrated by examining the circumstances surrounding a loss. For example, if a policyholder's poodle bites and seriously injures a neighbor's one-year-old child in the child's own yard, the insured will likely be held liable for the resulting injuries and damages. In this example, a claim notice to the insurer is sufficient for the insurer to investigate and settle the loss. However, if the insured's dog bites a trespasser who enters the insured's fenced yard and mistreats the animal, the insured's liability might be questionable. In such a case, the insurer might deny the claim on the grounds that the insured does not appear to be liable for the injury. However, if the injured trespasser brings a suit against the insured, the insurer would be obligated to provide for the insured's defense and pay damages if the insured is found liable.

Defense costs coverage, which is supplemental to the liability limit, is provided even if a suit is groundless, false, or fraudulent. For example, if an individual falsely claims he tripped on an insured's sidewalk and sustained a back injury, the insurer would have to respond to the suit. The insurer provides for defense costs in addition to any coverage. If the insured is found liable, the insurer also covers the damages, up to the personal liability limit, that might apply to the trip-and-fall claim.

The insurer's obligation to defend ends only when the liability limit for the occurrence is exhausted by payment of a settlement or judgment (even if policy limits are exhausted by the costs of the claim). For example, in the trip-and-fall occurrence, assume the claimant's injuries are legitimately caused by the insured. If the individual claims $200,000 in damages and the insured's homeowners coverage has a $100,000 personal liability limit, the insurer cannot simply pay $100,000 and avoid further litigation. Rather, the insurer must defend the insured until a settlement is reached. If a settlement can be reached for $150,000, the insurer's obligations end when it pays defense costs and pays the claimant's $100,000 in damages (the policy limit). See the exhibit "Policy Definitions and How They Apply to Section II."

Policy Definitions and How They Apply to Section II

Who is an insured for liability coverage?

- The policyholder (the named insured) shown on the Declarations page and the named insured's spouse if a resident of the same household. The policyholder and resident spouse are identified as "you" in the policy.
- Residents of the household who are relatives of the named insured or spouse.
- Residents of the household who are under the age of twenty-one and in the care of the named insured or resident relatives.
- A full-time student who resided in the household before moving out to attend school. This person must be either under the age of twenty-one and in the care of the named insured or resident relatives, or a relative of the named insured under the age of twenty-four. The policyholder's twenty-two-year-old daughter who is a full-time college student would therefore qualify as an insured.
- Any person or organization legally responsible for animals or watercraft that are covered by the policy and owned by a person defined in the first three bulleted items. For example, a neighbor who walks the named insured's dog while the insured is on vacation is protected as an insured for liability coverage under the named insured's homeowners policy if the dog causes an injury while in the neighbor's care.
- Anyone employed by a person defined in the first three bulleted items, with respect to any motor vehicle covered by the policy. For example, a gardener who accidentally hits a neighbor's car while using the named insured's riding lawn mower to mow the named insured's lawn is an insured for liability coverage under the named insured's homeowners policy.
- Other persons using any vehicle covered by the policy on an insured location, with the consent of the named insured or spouse, are insureds for liability coverage. For example, if a neighbor takes the named insured's all-terrain vehicle for a test drive in the named insured's yard and accidentally strikes and injures a child, the neighbor becomes an insured for liability coverage under the named insured's homeowners policy.

Who is a residence employee versus other employees?

Coverage F—Medical Payments to Others applies to insured "residence employees," but not to other "employees." The policy defines both terms. Residence employees include domestic workers whose duties relate to maintaining or using the household premises or performing domestic or household services. Four Section II exclusions—an insured's premises that are not an insured location, motor vehicles, watercraft, and aircraft—do not apply to bodily injury sustained by a "residence employee" in the course of employment by an insured. Therefore, Coverages E and F will cover a residence employee's injuries in some situations.

An employee, as defined by the policy, is an employee of an insured who is not a residence employee.

[DA07776]

Coverage F—Medical Payments to Others

Coverage F—Medical Payments to Others covers medical payments incurred by others (not insureds or regular household residents) within three years of an injury. These medical expenses include reasonable charges for medical, surgical, x-ray, dental, ambulance, hospital, professional nursing, and funeral services, and prosthetic devices. Medical Payments to Others coverage is automatically included in all homeowners policies for a limit generally set at $1,000 per person for a single accident. This limit can be increased for an additional premium. The limit for Coverage F is shown on the declarations page.

Medical Payments to Others coverage (sometimes simply called "medical payments") may be considered to overlap with bodily injury liability coverage. However, liability coverage applies only when an insured is legally responsible for damages. Claims for medical payments are often paid when the insured feels a moral obligation to another person, even though the insured is not negligent or legally responsible. When a bodily injury claim involves a relatively small amount of money, paying it as a Medical Payments to Others claim simplifies matters by eliminating any need to determine whether an insured was legally responsible for the injuries. For example, an invited guest falls and breaks his wrist in a well-lit and properly maintained hallway in the insured's home, requiring a trip to the emergency room that costs $850. Even though the insured is not liable for the injury, the Medical Payments to Others coverage will provide reimbursement of the $850.

Coverage F—Medical Payments to Others coverage applies under these conditions:

- The injury occurs to a person who has the insured's permission to be at the insured location. For example, medical payments coverage applies if an insured's dog bites a party guest at the insured's home. Coverage does not apply if the insured's dog bites a burglar.
- The injured person is away from the insured location, and bodily injury arises out of a condition at the insured location or on property immediately adjoining the insured location. For example, if an insured is draining water from a pool into a gutter that empties at the bottom of his street and a neighbor slips in the water and breaks his wrist, the insured's medical payments coverage applies.
- A person is injured while away from the insured location by an activity performed by an insured. For example if an insured plays soccer on weekends and accidentally breaks a teammate's nose, the insured's medical payments coverage applies.

Section II—Additional Coverages

The Section II—Additional Coverages provisions supplement the protection provided by Coverages E and F. Amounts payable under this portion of the policy are in addition to the Coverage E—Personal Liability and Coverage F—Medical Payments to Others limits of liability. Section II—Additional Coverages claims are usually incidental in nature or related to claims already made by an insured under Coverages E and F.

Section II—Additional Coverages includes four additional coverages:

- Claim Expenses
- First Aid Expenses
- Damage to Property of Others
- Loss Assessment

Claims Expenses

The Claim Expenses additional coverage specifies expenses the insurer will pay when handling a claim. In addition to any judgment or settlement an insurer pays (subject to the Coverage E liability limit) on behalf of an insured, an insurer covers these claims expenses:

- "Expenses we incur"—For example, the insurer pays for the insured's legal representation when a claim or suit occurs.
- Premiums on bonds—For example, if any bonds are required in the defense of a suit, the insurer pays the bond premiums. However, the insurer will not pay the premium on bonds that exceed the policy's Coverage E limit.
- Reasonable expenses—For example, if an insurer requests an insured's assistance in the investigation or defense of a claim or suit, the insurer pays for any reasonable expenses incurred by the insured, including loss of earnings, up to $250 per day. Reasonable expenses can include parking costs, meals, and mileage.
- Postjudgment interest—For example, after a judgment has been made against an insured, interest can accrue on the amount owed to a plaintiff until the insurer actually makes that payment. Postjudgment interest amounts can be substantial if the insurer appeals the judgment to a higher court. Postjudgment interest pays for any interest expense that accrues.

First Aid Expenses

The First Aid Expenses additional coverage states that an insurer will reimburse an insured for expenses the insured has incurred when rendering first aid to others as a result of any bodily injury covered under the policy. For example, if a guest is injured in an insured's home and the insured uses supplies from her first aid kit to bandage the wound, the insured can collect reimbursement from her insurer for the first aid supplies used. The insurer will not reimburse expenses for first aid to an injured insured.

Damage to Property of Others

The Damage to Property of Others additional coverage, sometimes called "voluntary property damage" coverage, pays up to $1,000 for damage to property of others caused by an insured, regardless of fault or legal liability.

For example, an insured borrows a friend's digital camcorder to record his daughter's piano recital. During the event, he drops the camcorder and breaks it. The insured will have coverage for up to $1,000 to replace the device without having to prove that he was responsible for the loss. This coverage allows an insured to maintain goodwill by paying for relatively minor losses to another person's property, and it allows the insurer to avoid litigation expenses on small property damage claims to determine whether the insured was at fault.

An insurer will not pay under this additional coverage for property damage to the extent of any amount recoverable under Section I of the policy. For example, if the camcorder had been damaged by fire, a peril covered under Section I, the insurer would pay only the deductible amount under the Damage to the Property of Others coverage; the remaining amount would be payable under Section I.

The insurer will not pay for any property damage in these circumstances:

- The damage is caused intentionally by an insured thirteen years of age or older. (Intentional damage caused by children under thirteen is covered.)
- Property owned by an insured is damaged.
- Property owned by or rented to a tenant of an insured or a resident of the named insured's household is damaged.
- The damage arises out of a business engaged in by an insured.
- The damage is a result of an act or omission in connection with premises (other than an insured location) that the insured owns, rents, or controls.
- The damage arises out of the ownership, maintenance, or use of any motor vehicle, watercraft, aircraft, or hovercraft (other than a recreational vehicle designed for use off public roads that is not subject to motor vehicle registration and not owned by an insured).

Loss Assessment

Homeowners are sometimes billed with an assessment by their homeowners associations or other similar organizations when the organization sustains a loss for which their officers failed to secure a sufficient amount of insurance. The Loss Assessment additional coverage provides up to $1,000 for an insured's share of a loss assessment charged to the insured by a corporation or an association of property owners for these types of losses:

- Bodily injury or property damage that is not excluded under Section II of the homeowners policy
- Liability that results from an act of an elected and unpaid director, officer, or trustee

As an example, the recreation center of a condominium association (jointly owned by the individual homeowners) might sustain severe damage to its roof in an ice storm or snowstorm. If the officers are found liable for not adequately insuring the building, the association's bylaws may permit it to assess each owner for a share of the uninsured loss. The Loss Assessment additional coverage will cover that assessment for up to $1,000.

Apply Your Knowledge

Ralph is mowing the grass in his front yard when the blade on his mower strikes a rock, causing it to fly toward Sam, his next door neighbor. Sam was in Ralph's front yard walking toward him to return a hedge trimmer he had borrowed from Ralph. Sam immediately fell down, grabbed his chest, and called out for an ambulance. Upon investigation, it was determined the rock bounced off the hedge trimmer, never striking Sam. Sam sued Ralph for bodily injury. Ralph is insured by an HO-3 policy, which was in effect at the time of the accident.

Will Coverage E—Personal Liability Coverage of Ralph's HO-3 policy respond to Sam's claim?

Feedback: Yes, Coverage E—Personal Liability Coverage provisions provide coverage if a claim is made or a suit is brought against an insured because of bodily injury arising from a covered occurrence. Mowing the yard is a covered activity, and the accident occurred during the policy period. There is no indication that the occurrence was not accidental.

How will the fact that the rock never struck Sam affect the defense Ralph's insurer provides him?

Feedback: Defense costs coverage, which is supplemental to the liability limit, is provided even if a suit is groundless, false, or fraudulent. The fact that Sam is, at best, exaggerating any injury does not relieve Ralph's insurer of the cost of defending him.

HO-3 SECTION II—EXCLUSIONS

Individuals and families commonly use homeowners insurance policies to address real and personal property loss exposures and liability loss exposures that may arise as a consequence of property ownership or activities. Exclusions help limit the scope of the personal liability coverage these policies provide.

HO-3 Section II—Exclusions contains exclusions common to all of the homeowners forms used in the Insurance Services Office, Inc. (ISO) Homeowners program. Exclusions are designed to limit or preclude coverage, but because of how some exclusion provisions are worded, limited personal liability coverage may, in fact, be provided by a particular provision. Therefore, the provisions contained in Section II—Exclusions should be carefully considered with the general terms of coverage provided by Coverage E—Personal Liability and Coverage F—Medical Payments to Others, as well as Section II—Additional Coverages and Section II—Conditions, to determine the full scope of Section II coverage.

HO-3 Section II contains twenty-two exclusions that are divided into sets. Some sets apply to all of Section II, and some apply only to Coverage E or Coverage F.

Motor Vehicle and Other Motorized Craft—Exclusions

The first four exclusions of Section II apply to losses arising out of motor vehicles, watercraft, aircraft, and hovercraft. These exclusions are defined in the Definitions section of the homeowners policy and apply to both Coverages E and F. With respect to these vehicles or craft, coverage does not apply for claims arising out of these conditions:

- The ownership, maintenance, occupancy, operation, use, loading, or unloading of a motor vehicle or craft by any person unless it appears in a specific exception to the exclusion
- Negligent entrustment, by an insured, of an excluded motor vehicle or craft
- An insured's failure to supervise, or negligently supervising, a person
- An insured's "vicarious liability" for the actions of a child or minor

Motor Vehicle Liability

The homeowners policy defines a motor vehicle as any self-propelled vehicle, including an attached trailer. The Section II Motor Vehicle Liability exclusion, which applies to both Coverages E and F, is designed to limit the majority of personal motor vehicle loss exposures that would typically be insured under a Personal Auto Policy (PAP). Coverage does not apply to a motor vehicle that meets any of these criteria:

- It is required by law to be registered for use on public roads or property.
- It is involved in an organized race.
- It is rented to others.
- It is used to carry persons or cargo for a charge.
- It is used for any business purpose, except for motorized golf carts used on a golf course.

Although the motor vehicle exclusion is intended to allow the auto policy to provide virtually all motor vehicle liability coverage, the homeowners policy provides some Section II—Liability coverages for certain motor vehicles. These are examples of motor vehicles covered under Section II—Liability coverages:

- Motor vehicle designed as a toy vehicle for use by children under seven years of age that is powered by one or more batteries and has not been modified after being manufactured to exceed five miles per hour on level ground.
- Motor vehicle in dead storage on an insured location.
- Motor vehicle used solely to service a residence. (Note that with the 2011 revision, this is expanded to include not only the insured's residence but also any residence.)
- Motor vehicle designed for assisting people who are handicapped.
- Motor vehicle designed for recreational use off public roads and not owned by an insured or owned only while on an insured location.
- Motorized golf carts not capable of exceeding twenty-five miles per hour, owned by an insured, and used to play golf or used legally within a private residential association.
- Trailers currently not towed by, hitched to, or carried on another motor vehicle.

Watercraft Liability

The watercraft exclusions, which apply to both Coverages E and F, are similar to the motor vehicle exclusions. However, watercraft might be covered under one of the exceptions to the watercraft exclusions. In general, small, low-powered watercraft, or watercraft the insured uses but does not own, are included for Section II coverage. See the exhibit "Watercraft Exposures Covered by Section II of the Homeowners Policy Forms."

Watercraft not covered by the insured's homeowners policy can be properly covered by a separate watercraft policy.

Watercraft Exposures Covered by Section II of the Homeowners Policy Forms

Covered Watercraft Liability Loss Exposures	Examples
Watercraft that are stored	A 30-foot sailboat stored out of the water at a marina for the winter
Sailboats (with or without auxiliary power) shorter than 26 feet	A 17-foot catamaran owned by the insured
Sailboats (with or without auxiliary power) longer than 26 feet *not owned* by or *rented* to an insured	A 32-foot sailboat the insured borrowed from her brother for a vacation
Inboard or inboard-outdrive watercraft with engines of 50 horsepower or less that are *not owned* by an insured	A 50-horsepower jet ski rented by an insured
Inboard or inboard-outdrive watercraft of more than 50 horsepower *not owned* by or rented to an insured	A 150-horsepower inboard motor boat borrowed from a neighbor
Watercraft with one or more outboard engines or motors with 25 total horsepower or less	A fishing boat with a 15-horsepower motor, owned by the insured
Watercraft with one or more outboard engines or motors with more than 25 total horsepower that are *not owned* by an insured	A boat with a 75-horsepower outboard motor, borrowed from a friend

Includes copyrighted material of Insurance Services Office, Inc., with its permission. Copyright, ISO Properties, Inc., 2010. [DA00180]

Aircraft and Hovercraft Liability

The homeowners policy excludes all aircraft liability under Coverages E and F. However, because model airplanes or hobby aircraft that do not carry people or cargo are excluded from the policy's aircraft definition, they are covered.

As with aircraft, hovercraft liability is excluded under Coverages E and F. Hovercraft are self-propelled motorized ground-effect air-cushion vehicles. No exceptions to this exclusion are available in the homeowners policy.

Coverage E—Personal Liability and Coverage F—Medical Payments to Others

Some bodily injury and property damage loss exposures are beyond the scope of a homeowners policy or are effectively covered under other policies. Eight exclusions apply to both Coverages E and F.

Expected or Intended Injury

The Expected or Intended Injury exclusion applies to any bodily injury or property damage caused by an insured when the bodily injury or property damage is intentional or expected, even if the actual injury or damage resulting from the action was unintended when the intentional action took place. For example, assume an insured detects someone in her home late at night whom she believes to be a burglar, and, because of the darkness, she grabs a gun and shoots the burglar. The "burglar" is, in fact, a neighbor who is suffering from dementia and has accidentally wandered through the insured's open back door. Although the insured had no intention of shooting her neighbor, she undoubtedly intended to cause bodily injury when she shot him. Therefore, coverage is excluded. However, the insured may rely on an exception to the exclusion that stipulates that the exclusion does not apply to bodily injury or property damage resulting from the use of reasonable force to protect persons or property.

Business

The Business exclusion is designed to exclude coverage for bodily injury or property damage arising out of the business activities of an insured while providing coverage for occasional or part-time activities, such as insureds under the age of twenty-one selling lemonade, delivering newspapers, maintaining lawns, or babysitting. The exclusion states that the policy provides no coverage for bodily injury or property damage relating to a business operated from the residence premises or another insured location.

Business is broadly defined in the Definitions section of the policy to include a full-time, a part-time, or an occasional trade, profession, occupation, home-sharing host activity, or any other activity engaged in for money or other compensation, with these exceptions:

- Activities for which the insured received $2,000 or less during the year preceding the policy period
- Volunteer activities
- Home daycare services not involving compensation but possibly involving an exchange of services
- Home daycare services rendered to a relative

Renting property to others and home-share hosting qualify as a business, as defined by the policy. However, these three exceptions to this exclusion allow for some common rental situations:

- Rental of an insured location on an occasional basis is a covered loss exposure if the location is used only as a residence. For example, a homeowner lives in a town that hosts a popular annual arts festival. During the festival, the homeowner leaves on vacation and rents her home to festival attendees. Section II coverage would be provided to the insured during the time the home is rented.

- Rental of part of an insured location as a residence is a covered loss exposure as long as the occupying family takes no more than two roomers or boarders in a single-family unit. For example, a homeowner renting out an apartment in the residence (perhaps an apartment over an attached garage) would have Section II coverage arising out of the normal rental of that apartment.
- Rental of part of an insured location is a covered loss exposure if it is used only as an office or a school, studio, or private garage. For example, an insured could rent out a room or an apartment in the residence for use as an office, and Section II coverage would apply.

Several endorsements related to home business insurance, business pursuits, and incidental occupancies are available to provide limited liability coverage for certain business activities of the insured.

Other Coverage E and Coverage F Exclusions

These are the remaining exclusions applicable to Section II—Coverages E and F:

- Professional Services—Coverages E and F exclude coverage for the insured's rendering of or failure to render professional services. For example, an architect might be liable for a loss resulting from providing improper drawings to a client. This business loss exposure should be addressed by a professional liability policy.
- Insured's Premises Not an Insured Location—Coverages E and F are excluded for bodily injury or property damage arising out of any premises that is owned by or rented to an insured, or is owned and rented to others by an insured, but is not an insured location.
- War—Section II of the HO-3 excludes any bodily injury or property damage that results from war.
- Communicable Disease—Coverages E and F exclude coverage for any bodily injury or property damage that arises from the transmission of a communicable disease by an insured.
- Sexual Molestation, Corporal Punishment or Physical or Mental Abuse—Coverages E and F exclude coverage for any loss that arises out of sexual molestation, corporal punishment, or physical or mental abuse by an insured.
- Controlled Substance—Coverages E and F exclude any loss that results from the use, sale, manufacture, delivery, transfer, or possession of controlled substances as defined by the Federal Food and Drug Law (such as cocaine, marijuana, and other narcotic drugs, or steroids).

Exclusions That Apply Only to Coverage E

Six exclusions apply only to Coverage E—Personal Liability and not to Medical Payments to Others:

- Loss Assessment and Contractual Liability—Coverage E does not provide coverage for liability arising from any **loss assessment** charged against an insured as a member of a homeowners or condominium association or corporation. Additionally, the policy excludes liability assumed under contract or agreement. However, exceptions apply, and liability coverage is provided for two types of written contracts. The first are contracts relating to the ownership, maintenance, or use of an insured location. The second is liability of others assumed by the named insured before an accident occurs.

- Damage to the Insured's Property—Personal liability coverage is intended to address third-party liability loss exposures. An insured cannot collect payment under Section II—Liability Coverages for damage to his or her own property, even if the property repairs might serve to prevent a liability claim. For example, an insured cannot expect his homeowners policy to pay the cost of repairing a cracked and damaged sidewalk, even if the sidewalk repairs might help avoid a personal liability claim.

- Damage to Property in the Insured's Care—Coverage E does not apply to property rented to, occupied by, or in the care of an insured. However, an exception to this exclusion applies to property damage caused by fire, smoke, or explosion. If the insured rents a beach cottage for a summer vacation, Coverage E would apply if the insured accidentally starts a fire in the kitchen that results in smoke and fire damage to the cottage. However, Coverage E would not apply if the insured strikes the cottage with a vehicle, because vehicle damage to the cottage is not a result of fire, smoke, or explosion, and the cottage is in the insured's care.

- Bodily Injury to Persons Eligible for Workers Compensation Benefits— Coverage is excluded under Coverage E for bodily injury to any person who is eligible to receive or who is provided benefits by an insured under a state's workers compensation law.

- Nuclear Liability—Coverage E excludes bodily injury or property damage liability that would normally be covered under a nuclear energy liability policy.

- Bodily Injury to an Insured—Coverage E does not apply to the named insured, resident relatives, and other residents under the age of twenty-one in the insured's care for their own bodily injury, even if the injury is caused by another insured.

> **Loss assessment**
> A charge by the condominium association against the unit owners for the cost of uninsured losses.

Exclusions That Apply Only to Coverage F

Four exclusions apply only to Coverage F—Medical Payments to Others. These exclusions are in addition to the exclusions common to both personal liability and the medical payments coverage exclusions:

- Residence Employee Off Premises—Coverage F excludes bodily injury to a residence employee if an injury occurs off the insured's location and the injury does not arise out of the employee's work. Not excluded under Coverage F, and therefore included, is coverage for residence employees while they are working away from the insured location or on the insured location whether working or not.
- Bodily Injury Eligible for Workers Compensation Benefits—Any person eligible to receive payment under any workers compensation law, non-occupational disability law, or occupational disease law will not receive compensation for bodily injury under Coverage F. This exclusion applies regardless of whether the benefits are to be provided by an insured.
- Nuclear Reaction—Coverage F excludes bodily injury from any nuclear reaction, nuclear radiation, or radioactive contamination, regardless of the cause.
- Injury to a Home-Sharing Occupant—Coverage F excludes bodily injury to any home-sharing occupant.
- Injury to Residents—Coverage F excludes bodily injury to any person who regularly resides at the insured location (other than a residence employee).

HO-3 SECTION II—CONDITIONS

A homeowners insurance policy contains various sections describing what the policy covers and what it doesn't cover and in what amounts. Conditions applicable to Section II and conditions applicable to both Sections I and II provide a framework for the rest of the policy sections by describing the rights and duties of the insured and the insurer in order to maintain the policy in good standing and to facilitate prompt claim settlement.

The Homeowners 3—Special Form (HO-3) policy contains conditions also found in the other forms in the Insurance Services Office, Inc. (ISO) Homeowners program. Conditions applicable to Section II apply to liability coverage, specifically to the policy provisions described in Coverage E—Personal Liability and Coverage F—Medical Payments to Others. Conditions applicable to Sections I and II apply to both property and liability coverage and are related to policy period, cancellation, nonrenewal, and other matters.

Conditions Applicable to Section II

Section II—Conditions establishes the duties and responsibilities of the insurer and the insured. Additional requirements are described for third parties making a claim under Section II. The duties and responsibilities described for the insurer, insured, and third parties include how Section II claims will be handled. HO-3 Section II—Conditions contains ten conditions. See the exhibit "General Functions of Section II Conditions in Homeowners Policy Forms."

Limit of Liability

The Section II Limit of Liability provision stipulates that the limit of Coverage E—Personal Liability appearing on the Declarations page is the total limit of coverage for any one occurrence. This limit does not increase, regardless of the number of insureds, claims made, or people injured.

The Limit of Liability condition also states that all bodily injury and property damage that result from continuous or repeated exposure to the same harmful conditions are considered to be one occurrence. For example, assume the insured's gardener becomes ill over a period of weeks after using an insecticide the insured purchased. Even though the occurrence that caused the injury was not a single event and took place over several months, the injury is considered the result of a single occurrence. Therefore, the insurer is exposed to one limit of liability.

This condition further states that the limit of liability applicable to Coverage F—Medical Payments to Others for all medical expenses for bodily injury to one person as the result of an accident cannot exceed the Coverage F limit shown on the Declarations page. For example, an insured with a $1,000 limit for Coverage F would have $1,000 in coverage available for each guest injured in an accident in the insured's home. The limit can apply to more than one person per accident.

Severability of Insurance

For some occurrences, a claim can involve several insureds. Under the **Severability of Insurance condition**, each insured seeking protection is treated as if he or she has separate coverage under the policy. So the policy will cover a claim brought by one insured against another insured. However, the insurer's limit of liability stated in the policy is not increased for any one occurrence if more than one insured is involved.

> **Severability of Insurance condition**
>
> Policy condition that applies insurance separately to each insured; does not increase the insurer's limit of liability for any one occurrence.

Duties After "Occurrence"

The Duties After "Occurrence" condition describes several requirements the insured must fulfill if an occurrence occurs under Section II. If the insured does not fully perform the required duties following an occurrence and the insurer is therefore hindered in performing its duties, the insurer is not obligated to pay the claim.

General Functions of Section II Conditions in Homeowners Policy Forms

Section II Condition	General Function
Limit of Liability	Describes maximum limitations of and conditions for payment under Coverage E—Personal Liability and Coverage F—Medical Payments to Others.
Severability of Insurance	Stipulates that for any covered occurrence, each insured covered under the policy is treated as if he or she had separate coverage; however, the insurer's limit of liability is not increased, regardless of the number of insureds involved.
Duties After "Occurrence"	Describes requirements an insured must fulfill after an occurrence or else an insurer may deny coverage.
Duties of an Injured Person—Coverage F—Medical Payments to Others	Describes requirements an injured person must fulfill after an occurrence or else an insurer may deny coverage.
Payment of Claim—Coverage F—Medical Payments to Others	Stipulates that if an insurer pays a claim under Coverage F, the payment is not an admission of either the insurer's or insured's liability.
Suit Against Us	Describes the conditions that must be met and terms under which a suit can be filed against the insurer.
Bankruptcy of an Insured	Stipulates that the bankruptcy of an insured does not release the insurer from responsibility under the homeowners policy.
Other Insurance	Stipulates that any limits applicable to a Coverage E occurrence are paid in excess over any collectible insurance unless the other insurance is written specifically as an excess policy.
Policy Period	States that the bodily injury and property damage coverage limits apply only within the policy period covered by the policy.
Concealment or Fraud	Stipulates that Section II coverage is excluded only for an insured who is proven to have made false or fraudulent statements. Innocent insureds not involved in the fraud are not barred from protection.

Includes copyrighted material of Insurance Services Office, Inc., with its permission. Copyright, ISO Properties, Inc., 2010. [DA00218]

Duties after an occurrence include these requirements:

- Give written notice to the insurer as soon as practical.
- Cooperate with the insurer's investigation, settlement, and defense activities.
- Forward legal documents promptly to the insurer.
- Provide claims assistance to the insurer in making a settlement, enforcing any right of contribution against another party, attending hearings and trials, securing and giving evidence, and obtaining the attendance of witnesses.
- Submit evidence for damage to property of others when a claim is made under the additional coverage for damage to property of others; the insured must submit to the insurer a sworn statement of loss and show the damaged property to the insurer.
- Do not make voluntary payment; if the insured does so, it will be at the insured's own expense.

Duties of an Injured Person—Coverage F—Medical Payments to Others

This Section II—Coverage F condition stipulates that if an individual makes a claim for an occurrence under Medical Payments to Others coverage, the injured person must fulfill these requirements:

- Give the insurer written proof of the claim as soon as possible.
- Authorize the insurer to obtain copies of medical reports and records.
- Submit (the injured person) to a physical exam by a doctor chosen by the insurer as often as the insurer requires such examinations.

Note that it is the injured third party, not the insured, who must perform these duties to receive payment under Coverage F.

Payment of Claim—Coverage F—Medical Payments to Others

This Coverage F condition stipulates that the insurer's payment of a Medical Payments to Others claim is not an admission of liability by the insured or the insurer. The purpose of Section II medical payments coverage is to prevent suits or to reduce the possible damages resulting from claims by providing prompt payment for injured parties' medical expenses without the need to determine fault.

Suit Against Us

The Suit Against Us condition states that an insurer cannot be sued under the homeowners policy until certain provisions and terms have been met:

- The insured has met all of its obligations under Section II of the policy.
- The insurer cannot be joined as a party to any action against an insured.
- The obligation of the insured has been determined by a final judgment or agreement signed by the insurer.

Additional Section II Conditions

The Bankruptcy of an Insured condition stipulates that if the insured becomes bankrupt or insolvent, the insurer is still obligated to handle the occurrence as it normally would. The insurer is not relieved of any obligations under the policy by the insured's financial status. The Other Insurance condition causes Section II—Coverage E limits to be paid as excess over any other collectible insurance unless the other insurance is written specifically to provide excess coverage (such as a personal umbrella liability policy).

The Policy Period condition stipulates that coverage applies only to bodily injury and property damage that occurs during the policy period, which is indicated in the Declarations page. The claim may be filed at any time, even after the policy has expired.

The Concealment or Fraud condition excludes coverage only for the insured(s) involved in the concealment or fraud, or those making false statements. Other innocent insureds would not be excluded from liability coverage. Under Section I, concealment or fraud by any insured bars property coverage for all insureds.

Conditions Applicable to Sections I and II

The final section of the HO-3 policy includes seven conditions that apply to both Sections I and II. See the exhibit "General Functions of Sections I and II Conditions in Homeowners Policy Forms."

Liberalization Clause

The Liberalization Clause specifies how broadened coverage applies to the policy. Only homeowners with the same edition of a policy that is subsequently changed by the insurer are affected by this condition.

As an example of the application of the Liberalization Clause, suppose that in order to attract new customers, an insurer provides replacement cost coverage on contents to all insureds at no additional charge by attaching a personal property replacement cost endorsement to all new and renewal homeowners policies. On the date the additional coverage becomes effective, all existing homeowners policies issued by the insurer automatically include the additional coverage, even if the insureds are unaware of the change.

General Functions of Sections I and II Conditions in Homeowners Policy Forms

Sections I and II Condition	General Function
Liberalization Clause	Stipulates that when an insurer broadens coverage on new and renewal policies, the current policies of the insurer also receive the broader coverage
Waiver or Change of Policy Provisions	States that an insurer's representative cannot modify the policy and relinquish a right unless the insurer does so in writing
Cancellation	Describes the procedures required for the insured or the insurer to terminate a policy
Nonrenewal	Describes the procedures required for the insurer to not renew a policy
Assignment	States that the insured cannot assign the policy to another party without the written consent of the insurer
Subrogation	Stipulates that an insured can waive all rights of recovery against another party but must do so in writing and before the loss occurs
Death	Stipulates that if the named insured dies, the insurer will cover the decedent's representative as an insured

Includes copyrighted material of Insurance Services Office, Inc., with its permission. Copyright, ISO Properties, Inc., 2010. [DA07788]

Waiver or Change of Policy Provisions

A waiver or change of provision condition states that a **waiver** of a right or change of a policy provision is valid only if the insurer makes it in writing. Despite this condition, courts have permitted use of oral waivers by claims representatives made during the adjustment of a loss and after the written policy was issued, because claims representatives are the insurer's representatives and have **apparent authority** to modify policy conditions. As the insurer's agents, insurance agents with **binding authority** also are authorized to make policy changes through an oral binder that is effective until a written policy change endorsement is produced.

Cancellation

The Cancellation condition specifies the requirements for a valid termination of the policy by either the insured or the insurer. It states that the policyholder may cancel the policy at any time by returning it to the insurer or by

Waiver
The intentional relinquishment of a known right.

Apparent authority
A third party's reasonable belief that an agent has authority to act on the principal's behalf.

Binding authority
An insurance agent's authority to effect coverage on behalf of the insurer.

contacting the insurer in writing and advising the insurer of the date when cancellation is to take effect. The insurer, conversely, can cancel the policy only for certain stated reasons (determined by state regulation) by delivering a written notice of cancellation to the insured within the stipulated number of days (also determined by state regulation).

Nonrenewal

The insurer has the right to decide not to renew a policy when it expires. The Nonrenewal condition requires the insurer to provide at least thirty days' written notice to the insured if it does not plan to renew the policy. Some states require a longer period of notification. The nonrenewal notice is mailed to the address on the declarations. This constitutes sufficient proof that the insurer mailed the notice, even if the insured does not receive it.

Assignment

An insurance policy is a personal contract between the insurer and the policyholder. Therefore, the insurer must be able to choose whom it will insure. The Assignment condition states that any assignment of the policy without the insurer's written consent is invalid.

Subrogation

Subrogation refers to the insurer's right to recover its claim payment to an insured from the party responsible for the loss. Under the Subrogation condition, the insured can waive all rights to recovery against any person, provided the waiver is in writing and is made before a loss. Tenants, for example, often sign lease agreements that waive their rights against landlords for loss caused by the landlord. In the absence of any pre-loss waiver, an insurer can require the insured to assign all rights of recovery against another person to the insurer to the extent of the insurer's payment of a loss.

Death

The Death condition stipulates that if the named insured or his or her spouse should die, the insurer agrees to cover the decedent's legal representative (usually the executor or administrator of the estate) as an insured, but only to the extent that the decedent had an interest in the property covered in the policy. The term "insured" also includes resident relatives and custodians of the deceased's property as identified in the Death condition.

DETERMINING WHETHER HOMEOWNERS SECTION II—LIABILITY COVERAGES COVERS A CLAIM

Section II—Liability Coverages of any homeowners policy provides coverage for liability exposures arising from the ownership and use of the covered property and from personal activities. The application of coverage depends on the circumstances of the loss.

Knowing how to apply the liability coverages of a homeowners policy to the facts of a case is an important skill. This case study will help you make the transition from knowing policy language to determining whether policy language provides coverage for specific claims. As you progress through this case study, you can check your understanding of the coverage provided by answering the Knowledge to Action questions.

Case Facts

Sally and Jeff live in a single-family home with their five-year-old son, Matthew. Sally and Jeff maintain a homeowners policy covering their home. They do not maintain an umbrella policy or any concurrent policies.

Sally and Jeff's neighborhood regularly gathers to celebrate the Fourth of July. This year, Sally and Jeff agreed to host dinner. Their neighbor, Jean, agreed to provide dessert and host the fireworks display. On July 3, Jeff had dental surgery. Despite being under the influence of prescribed narcotics on July 4, Jeff prepared, grilled, and served hamburger patties to ten of his neighbors.

After dinner, the party moved to Jean's house. Matthew rode his battery-powered toy truck, specifically designed for children under the age of seven. The vehicle's top speed is four mph. While Matthew was driving his truck around the adults on Jean's patio, Linda, a guest, stepped backward into his path. Matthew hit Linda with his truck, causing her to lose her balance and fall against Jean's kitchen window. The window glass broke and cut Linda's hand. The party quickly ended, as Linda had to go to the emergency room for medical attention.

In the weeks following, Sally and Jeff received notice of several claims:

Claim 1: Six dinner guests became seriously ill several hours after the party. The guests allege that Jeff served them contaminated meat and that the contamination resulted from Jeff's negligent preparation. Based on a review of hamburger-meat recalls and illnesses reported by the United States Food and Drug Administration, there is no indication that the meat was contaminated before Jeff handled it. The six individuals collectively hire an attorney and file suit against Jeff, seeking compensation for medical expenses, lost wages, pain, and suffering. They demand $180,000, or $30,000 per individual.

Claim 2: Linda seeks reimbursement for $5,250 in medical expenses, including stitches and pain medication. Linda recovered without complication and foresees no additional treatment. Linda realizes it is not feasible to sue a five-year-old for negligence. To preserve her relationship with her neighbors, she does not want to file suit against Sally and Jeff for negligent parental supervision of Matthew.

Claim 3: Jean, citing Matthew's actions, demands reimbursement from Sally and Jeff for replacement of her kitchen window. The replacement cost was $200.

To meet their duty following a loss, Sally and Jeff provide prompt written notice to their insurer of the three claims and cooperate in the investigation. To confirm that the facts of these incidents are accurate, Sally and Jeff's insurer relies on recorded statements from claimants and witnesses, medical records, and inspections of the premises where the loss occurred. For the first claim, the insurer assumes Jeff's defense in the bodily injury liability lawsuit. For Linda's injury, the insurer helps her file a claim under Sally and Jeff's Medical Payments coverage. For Jean's window damage, the insurer opens a liability claim for Damage to Property of Others.

Given the facts presented in the case, will Section II—Liability Coverages of the homeowners policy cover the three claims? If so, what amount will the insurer pay for each claim? When answering the questions in this case-based activity, consider only the information provided as part of this case. See the exhibit "Case Facts."

Case Facts

Insureds	Sally and Jeff Jones
Types of policies and coverage limits	E—Personal Liability—$500,000 Each Occurrence
	F—Medical Payments to Others—$5,000 Each Person
Endorsements that affect the case	None
Other policy information	No other relevant information
Background	The insureds have complied with the policy conditions.

[DA00330]

Necessary Reference Materials

To determine whether Sally and Jeff's homeowners policy provides coverage for the three claims, you should have copies of the policy form, which is available in the *The Institutes' Handbook of Insurance Policies*; any applicable endorsements indicated on the Declarations page of the policy; and the Declarations page itself. See the exhibit "Excerpt of Homeowners Policy Declarations."

Excerpt of Homeowners Policy Declarations

Homeowners Policy Declarations

POLICYHOLDER (Named Insured)	Jeff and Sally Jones 2 Oak Lane Anytown, USA 12345	**POLICY NUMBER:** 456-7890
POLICY PERIOD	Inception: January 7, 20X1	
	Expiration: January 7, 20X2	
	Policy period begins 12:01 A.M. standard time at the residence premises.	

We will provide the insurance described in this policy in return for the premium and compliance with all applicable policy provisions.

SECTION II COVERAGES	LIMIT
E—Personal Liability	$500,000 **Each Occurrence**
F—Medical Payments to Others	$ 5,000 **Each Person**

Copyright, ISO Properties, Inc. [DA07789]

Overview of Steps

To determine whether the losses are covered and the amount the insurer would pay, you can apply the four steps of the DICE method, which stands for Declarations, Insuring Agreement, Conditions, and Exclusions. This involves analyzing the policy declarations, insuring agreement, conditions, and exclusions to determine whether any information found at each step precludes coverage at the time of the losses. Next, you determine the amounts payable for the losses by analyzing the limits of insurance.

Determination of Coverage

Apply the DICE method to the case facts for each of the three losses.

DICE Analysis Step 1: Declarations

The first step in the DICE method is to review the Declarations page to determine whether the individuals are covered and whether the incidents occurred during the policy period. In this case, the policy lists Jeff and Sally as named insureds, and the party occurred during the policy period.

DICE Analysis Step 2: Insuring Agreement

The second DICE step is to determine whether each event triggers coverage under an insuring agreement.

Knowledge to Action

Action Task: Refer to the policy to review the Coverage E and Coverage F insuring agreements and the definition of "insured," which is used in both agreements.

In Claim 3, Jean demands reimbursement from Sally and Jeff for the replacement of her kitchen window, citing the actions of their minor child, Matthew. Under Sally and Jeff's homeowners policy, who fits the policy definition of insured?

a. Only Jeff
b. Only Jeff and Sally
c. Jeff, Sally, and Matthew
d. Only Sally

Feedback: c. The insureds that are defined in the policy as "you" are the named insureds as shown in the declarations, in this case Jeff and Sally. The policy definition of "insured" also includes residents of the named insureds' household who are their relatives. Therefore, their son, Matthew, also qualifies as an insured.

Claim 1: Coverage E—Personal Liability provides coverage if a claim is made or a suit is brought against an insured for bodily injury or property damage. Illness caused by contaminated food meets the definition of bodily injury. The resulting lawsuit against Jeff is sufficient to trigger coverage under Section II.

Claim 2: With respect to Linda's injuries, Coverage F—Medical Payments to Others covers medical expenses incurred within three years of the date of an accident. The coverage also applies to a person who is off the insured location and whose bodily injury is caused by the activities of an insured. Because Matthew's driving of the toy truck on Jean's patio caused the injury, Linda can seek coverage under Coverage F.

Claim 3: The damage to Jean's window is covered under Section II—Additional Coverages, which includes Damage to Property of Others caused by an insured. This coverage does not include damage caused intentionally by an insured age thirteen or older. However, the damage was not intentional, and Matthew is only five years old. The property also is not owned by the insured or a tenant of the insured. Therefore, the coverage applies.

DICE Analysis Step 3: Conditions

The third DICE step is to determine whether all policy conditions have been met. Sally and Jeff followed policy conditions outlining their duties after an occurrence, including providing written notice to the insurer as soon as practical and cooperating in the investigation and defense of any claim or suit.

Knowledge to Action

Action Task: Refer to the policy and review Section II—Conditions.

Linda may have to comply with which of the following conditions to be paid for her injuries? Select all answers that are correct:

a. Provide the insurer with written proof of loss
b. Authorize the insurer to obtain copies of any medical reports
c. Submit to a physical exam if requested by the insurer
d. Provide the insurer with the opportunity to direct care

Feedback: a, b, and c. In Section II—Conditions, Duties of an Injured Person—Coverage F—Medical Payments to Others, the injured person may be required to perform each of these tasks to be paid.

DICE Analysis Step 4: Exclusions

The fourth DICE step is to determine whether one or more exclusions preclude coverage the insuring agreements have granted.

Knowledge to Action

Action Task: Refer to the policy and review Section II—Exclusions.

Does the Controlled Substances exclusion apply to the neighbors' claim against Jeff, given that he was under the influence of prescribed narcotics on July 4?

Feedback: No. The Controlled Substances exclusion eliminates coverage for bodily injury or property damage arising out of a person's use of a controlled substance. However, the exclusion contains an exception for the use of prescription drugs at the direction of a licensed medical provider. Therefore, the exclusion does not apply to this case.

Determination of Amounts Payable

Now that you have completed the DICE analysis, you can determine the amounts payable. This involves analyzing the limits of insurance available to pay for the loss.

Claim 1: At the direction of the insurer, defense counsel successfully negotiates a settlement with the plaintiffs through their attorney. The agreed settlement is $120,000 in total, apportioned as $20,000 to each of the six guests who became ill. Because Sally and Jeff's policy has a limit of $500,000 for each occurrence under Coverage E, the full $120,000 is covered.

Claim 2: Linda's final medical bills totaled $5,250. Because the limit for Coverage F under Sally and Jeff's policy is $5,000 per person, Linda's recovery would be limited to $5,000. That means $250 of the submitted medical bills would not be covered.

Claim 3: The Additional Coverage for Damage to Property of Others in Section II of the policy provides limits of up to $1,000 per occurrence. Therefore, the $200 cost to replace the glass in Jean's kitchen window would be fully covered. See the exhibit "Determination of Amounts Payable."

Determination of Amounts Payable

Claim	Coverage Available	Amount Payable
Guests who became ill	Coverage E—$500,000	$120,000
Linda's claim for medical expenses	Coverage F—$5,000	$5,000
Replace the broken glass in neighbor's kitchen window	Additional Coverage for Property of Others—$1,000	$200

[DA07790]

COVERAGE VARIATIONS IN ISO HOMEOWNERS FORMS

The homeowners insurance program developed by Insurance Services Office, Inc. (ISO) includes five coverage forms in addition to the widely used HO-3 form. To meet customers' needs and preferences, an insurance professional must understand the differences between these forms.

The ISO homeowners insurance program includes six coverage forms:

- Homeowners 2—Broad Form, or HO-2
- Homeowners 3—Special Form, or HO-3
- Homeowners 4—Contents Broad Form, or HO-4
- Homeowners 5—Comprehensive Form, or HO-5
- Homeowners 6—Unit-Owners Form, or HO-6
- Homeowners 8—Modified Coverage Form, or HO-8

While HO-3 is the most widely used, the other forms address different coverage needs or preferences:

- Apartment dwellers and condominium unit owners do not need full insurance on the buildings in which they live.
- Some customers will accept more restricted coverage than the HO-3 provides in exchange for lower premiums.
- Some customers are willing to pay for broader coverage than the HO-3 provides.
- Some older homes that have depreciated substantially are not well-suited for the replacement cost coverage provided by the HO-3.

An ISO homeowners form exists to address each of these situations. The primary differences between the HO-3 form and the other homeowners forms are in each form's Section I—Property Coverages. The Agreement, Section II—Liability Coverages, and Section II—Conditions are identical in all ISO homeowners forms. See the exhibit "Homeowners Forms Comparison."

HO-2 Broad Form Compared With HO-3

Like the HO-3, the HO-2 is designed for the owner-occupant of a house. An HO-2 has a slightly lower premium than an HO-3, while covering the same property for the same limits. The lower premium results from the fact that the HO-2 covers the dwelling and other structures against fewer causes of loss.

The HO-3 provides open perils coverage (also known as special form coverage) for Coverage A—Dwelling and Coverage B—Other Structures and provides named perils coverage for Coverage C—Personal Property. In contrast, the HO-2 provides named perils coverage for Coverages A, B, and C. In

Homeowners Forms Comparison

Form	Used for Insuring	Coverage A—Dwelling	Coverage B—Other Structures	Coverage C—Personal Property	Section II—Liability Coverages
HO-2 Broad Form	Owner-occupied dwellings	Named perils	Named perils	Named perils	Same in all forms
HO-3 Special Form	Owner-occupied dwellings	Open perils	Open perils	Named perils	Same in all forms
HO-4 Contents Broad Form	Tenants in residential buildings	N/A	N/A	Named perils	Same in all forms
HO-5 Comprehensive Form	Owner-occupied dwellings	Open perils	Open perils	Open perils	Same in all forms
HO-6 Unit-Owners Form	Owners of condominium or cooperative units	Named perils	N/A Included in Coverage A	Named perils	Same in all forms
HO-8 Modified Coverage Form	Owner-occupied dwellings	Modified named perils	Modified named perils	Modified named perils	Same in all forms

[DA09181]

both forms, Coverage D—Loss of Use is triggered by any loss covered under Coverage A, B, or C that makes the building unusable.

In addition to insuring against more causes of loss than named perils coverage, open perils coverage has another advantage, which involves the burden of proof:

- With named perils coverage, such as the HO-2, the insured must prove the loss was caused by a covered cause of loss for coverage to apply. The burden of proof is on the insured.
- With open perils coverage, if a loss to covered property occurs, the initial assumption is that it is covered. To deny coverage, the insurer must prove the loss was caused by an excluded cause of loss. In this case, the burden of proof is on the insurer.

By shifting the burden of proof, open perils coverage can provide an important advantage to an insured who suffers a property loss as a result of an unknown cause.

The list of named perils in the HO-2 encompasses most common insurable perils faced by homeowners. It closely resembles the list of named perils applicable to Coverage C in the HO-3 with a few minor differences. These are two examples:

- The vehicles peril is found in both policies, but the HO-2 policy has an exclusion for loss to a fence, driveway, or walk caused by a vehicle owned or operated by a resident of the premises.
- For accidental discharge or overflow of water or steam, the HO-2 excludes coverage if the building is vacant for more than sixty consecutive days. The HO-3 does not mention vacancy under this peril.

HO-4 Contents Broad Form Compared With HO-3

The HO-4 is designed specifically for people who live in rented houses or apartments. The HO-4 is essentially the same as an HO-3 without Coverages A and B. The HO-4 differs from the HO-3 in other ways, including these:

- HO-4 Coverage C is written at a limit the insured selects as adequate to cover personal property. In the HO-3, HO-2, and HO-5, the Coverage C limit is typically 50 percent of the Coverage A limit.
- Coverage D in the HO-4 is provided automatically at 30 percent of the Coverage C limit, rather than as 30 percent of the Coverage A limit, as in the HO-2 and HO-3.
- The HO-4 provides an additional coverage for building additions and alterations, with a limit equal to 10 percent of the Coverage C limit.
- The HO-4 does not include an additional coverage for furnishings provided by a landlord, because the occupant-insured of the apartment does not have an insurable interest in such property.

- Both the HO-3 and the HO-4 provide an additional coverage for increased costs imposed by a building ordinance or law. The HO-3 limit is 10 percent of the Coverage A limit, while the HO-4 limit is 10 percent of the building additions and alterations limit.
- Trees, shrubs, and other plants are covered for 10 percent of the Coverage C limit in the HO-4 policy, while the HO-3 provides coverage for up to 5 percent of the Coverage A limit.

HO-5 Comprehensive Form Compared With HO-3

The HO-5 provides the broadest property coverage of any ISO homeowners form. The HO-5 is essentially an HO-3 modified to provide open perils coverage, not only for the dwelling and other structures, but also for Coverage C—Personal Property.

The HO-5 broadens personal property coverage in some areas simply by not excluding an exposure that has been excluded by the HO-3 policy:

- The HO-5 covers water damage, including flood damage, for personal property away from a location owned, rented, occupied, or controlled by an insured.
- The HO-5 covers personal property damaged by rain through an open window, door, or roof opening, even if the building itself is not damaged.

The HO-5 special limits of $1,500 for jewelry and furs, $2,500 for firearms, and $2,500 for silverware apply not only to items that are stolen, but also to items that are misplaced or lost. The HO-3 does not cover, for any amount, items that are misplaced or lost.

HO-6 Unit-Owners Form Compared With HO-3

Condominium
A real estate development consisting of a group of units, in which the air space within the boundaries of each unit is owned by the unit owner, and all remaining real and personal property is owned jointly by all the unit owners.

Cooperative corporation
A form of real property ownership in which the real property is owned by a corporation whose shareholders are the tenants of the property.

The HO-6 is closely related to the HO-4. This form is tailored to cover the exposures faced by unit owners in a **condominium** or a **cooperative corporation**. The HO-6 provides coverage for unit owners' property and liability exposures. It differs from the HO-3 in these ways:

- The HO-6 with a mandatory Residence Premises Definition Endorsement defines residence premises as the unit where the insured resides on the inception date of the policy. The HO-3 mandatory endorsement definition includes a one- to four-family dwelling where the insured resides on the inception date of the policy.
- The HO-6 description of Coverage A—Dwelling under Section I—Property Coverages includes: (1) alterations, appliances, fixtures, and improvements that are part of the building contained within the insured unit; (2) items of real property that pertain exclusively to the insured unit; (3) property that is the unit owner's responsibility under a condominium or cooperative association's property owners' agreement; and (4)

structures owned solely by the insured at the residence location (such as a storage shed or garage).

- Coverage A—Dwelling in the HO-6 provides a basic limit of $5,000, which can be increased if needed.
- Coverage B—Other Structures coverage is eliminated from the HO-6 because Coverage A of the HO-6 includes other structures owned solely by the insured.
- Coverage C—Personal Property is subject to a limit the insured selects.
- Coverage D—Loss of Use is provided automatically at a limit that is 50 percent of the Coverage C limit, rather than 30 percent of the Coverage A limit.
- Section I—Perils Insured Against in the HO-6 provides named perils coverage for Coverages A and C, similar to the coverage provided in the HO-2.
- Loss Assessments coverage is identical in the HO-3 and the HO-6, although it is more applicable to a condominium or cooperative corporation than a private dwelling. Condominiums and cooperatives have many elements, such as driveways, outdoor lighting, and swimming pools, that belong to all unit owners collectively. Damage to any of these commonly owned elements could result in an assessment against each individual unit owner.
- Trees, shrubs, and other plants are covered for up to 10 percent of the Coverage C limit, in contrast to the HO-3 limit of 5 percent of the Coverage A limit. In the HO-6, this coverage applies to plants solely owned by the named insured on grounds at the insured unit (such as those in the yard of a townhouse-style condominium).
- The additional coverage for landlord's furnishings is not included in the HO-6 policy.
- In the HO-6 policy, coverage for debris removal does not cover the cost to remove trees that damage a covered structure or block a driveway or ramp. This cost would be the condominium corporation's responsibility.

HO-8 Modified Coverage Form Compared With HO-3

The HO-8 is designed for use when the replacement cost of an owner-occupied dwelling significantly exceeds its market value.

An example of a dwelling that might be covered under the HO-8 is an older house with obsolete construction or features that would be expensive to replace, such as hand-carved wooden moldings. Such a house could have a market value of $100,000, but the cost to rebuild might be $200,000. A homeowner may be unwilling to pay the high premium necessary to buy $200,000 of insurance on a house purchased for $100,000. In addition, the homeowner could receive more money by collecting the insurance proceeds than by selling the house, which creates an obvious moral hazard. As a result, many insurers are unwilling to write an HO-3 on such a house.

The HO-8 provision addresses this problem under Section I—Conditions. A provision in this section specifies that if the insured makes repairs after a loss, the insurer will not pay more than the cost of "common construction materials and methods" that are "functionally equivalent to and less costly than obsolete, antique, or custom construction."

The HO-8 policy covers only ten named perils, and it limits or eliminates other coverages found in the HO-3 policy. The additional coverages for collapse, landlord's furnishings, ordinance or law, and grave markers are not included in the HO-8 policy. The HO-8 policy provides limited coverage for property not on the insured premises. There are no special limits for jewelry, firearms, silverware, and similar items because the theft peril provides coverage only up to $1,000.

These are other limitations in an HO-8 policy:

- Smoke from a fireplace is an exclusion in the HO-8 that is not found in the HO-3.
- Glass or safety glazing material is limited to $100.
- Under debris removal coverage, the amount available is included in the policy limit with no additional insurance available if the policy limit is exhausted. The HO-3 provides for an additional 5 percent if policy limits are exhausted.
- Windstorm is the only peril covered for trees, shrubs, and plants and only up to a limit of $250 per item ($500 in the HO-3). The occurrence limit is the same as the limit in the HO-3 policy, which is 5 percent of the dwelling limit.
- There is no coverage for personal property owned by a guest or residence employee while the property is in any residence occupied by an insured.
- The theft peril provides off-premises coverage limited to property in banks, trust companies, self-storage facilities, and similar locations.

COMMONLY USED ENDORSEMENTS THAT MODIFY THE 2011 ISO HOMEOWNERS POLICIES

In many cases, a homeowners policy's coverage may be modified through endorsements to fit the insured's needs.

These common endorsements amend Insurance Services Office, Inc. (ISO) homeowners policies:

- Personal Property Replacement Cost Loss Settlement
- Scheduled Personal Property
- Inflation Guard

- Earthquake
- Assisted Living Care Coverage
- Credit Card, Electronic Fund Transfer Card or Access Device, Forgery and Counterfeit Money Coverage—Increased Limit
- Home Business Insurance Coverage
- Ordinance or Law—Increased Amount of Coverage
- Limited Water Back-Up and Sump Discharge or Overflow Coverage
- Supplemental Loss Assessment Coverage
- Broadened Residence Premises Definition Endorsement
- Home-Sharing Host Activities Amendatory Endorsement
- Broadened Home-Sharing Host Activities Coverage Endorsement
- Additional Residence Rented to Others—1, 2, 3, or 4 Families
- Personal Injury Coverage
- Aircraft Liability Definition Revised to Remove Exception for Model and Hobby Aircraft
- Personal Injury for Aircraft Liability Excluded

ISO homeowners policies meet homeowners' common insurance coverage needs for both property and liability losses. However, insureds can have individual needs that basic ISO policies do not cover. For example, some homeowners operate businesses out of their homes. Others have valuable personal property that requires special attention. Endorsements individualize policies to meet these needs.

Personal Property Replacement Cost Loss Settlement

On all homeowners forms, losses to items covered under Coverage C—Personal Property are settled on an actual cash value (ACV) basis. The Personal Property Replacement Cost Loss Settlement endorsement (HO 04 90) provides replacement cost coverage on personal property. Dwellings and other structures are usually covered for their replacement cost value on homeowners policies. This endorsement lists certain types of personal property, such as antiques and fine art, ineligible for replacement cost coverage.

For losses with a replacement value of more than $500, the insured must repair or replace the lost or damaged items before the insurer will pay the replacement cost. (ACV is paid until repair or replacement is made.) The insured can make an ACV claim at the time of loss and later make a claim for the additional replacement cost. To do so, the insured must notify the insurer within 180 days after the loss of his or her intent to repair or replace the damaged property.

The value of personal property based on replacement cost is usually higher than the value of personal property based on ACV. Accordingly, when this endorsement is used, many insurers require a Coverage C—Personal Property limit that is higher than the usual Coverage C limit of 50 percent of the Coverage A limit (used with actual cash value coverage).

Scheduled Personal Property

An unendorsed homeowners policy (except for the HO-5) covers personal property against only named perils. Additionally, all homeowners policies impose special sublimits on coverage for certain types of property, such as stamps and coins, regardless of the cause of loss, and they include special sublimits on coverage for theft of jewelry and other types of property.

Scheduled coverage

Insurance for property specifically listed (scheduled) on a policy, with a limit of liability for each item.

The Scheduled Personal Property Endorsement (HO 04 61) provides **scheduled coverage** for specific items, such as jewelry, furs, musical instruments, silverware, fine arts, and rare coins.

The Scheduled Personal Property Endorsement covers more causes of loss than the HO-3 and other homeowners forms. The special limits and Coverage C deductible do not apply to the endorsement.

Inflation Guard

The Inflation Guard endorsement (HO 04 46) is designed to help prevent underinsurance caused by economic inflation and rising replacement costs. Rather than increasing coverage by a fixed amount, the endorsement gradually and automatically increases limits for Coverages A, B, C, and D throughout the policy period by a percentage mutually agreed upon by the insured and insurer.

Earthquake

All unendorsed homeowners forms exclude damage resulting from any kind of earth movement—including earthquake and landslide. The Earthquake endorsement (HO 04 54) provides a means to buy coverage for this cause of loss. The mandatory deductible is usually 5 percent of the limit that applies to either Coverage A or Coverage C, whichever is greater, but not less than $500.

Assisted Living Care Coverage

Assisted Living Care Coverage (HO 04 59) provides Section I—Coverage C—Personal Property and Section II—Coverage E—Personal Liability Coverage to a relative of the insured who is a resident of a facility that provides assisted living services, such as meals, medical supervision, housekeeping, and social activities. This scheduled person must not be a resident of the insured's household. Special limits of liability apply to certain types of property, such as $250 for hearing aids and $500 for medical alert devices.

Section II coverage excludes liability assumed by the facility before an occurrence and bodily injury to a staff member of the facility.

Credit Card, Electronic Fund Transfer Card or Access Device, Forgery and Counterfeit Money Coverage—Increased Limit

Section I of the homeowners policies provides coverage up to a limit of $500 for losses resulting from the unauthorized use of an insured's credit card, bank transfer card, check forgery, or acceptance of counterfeit money. The Credit Card, Fund Transfer Card or Access Device, Forgery and Counterfeit Money Coverage (HO 04 53) provides a higher limit of coverage to as much as $10,000.

Home Business Insurance Coverage (HOMEBIZ)

For insureds who operate an office or business from their homes, the Home Business Insurance Coverage, or HOMEBIZ, endorsement (HO 07 01) provides a comprehensive business package policy when attached to a homeowners form. The endorsement, which specifically excludes professional liability coverage, also lists many examples of professional activities that are excluded, ranging from legal, insurance, or accounting services to body piercing services.

There are minimum requirements for a home business to be covered under this endorsement, such as ownership by an insured, operation from the residence premises, and a maximum of three employees.

For eligible businesses, this endorsement provides valuable commercial coverages:

- Section I—Property Coverage provides full Coverage C—Personal Property limits for business property, accounts receivable, loss of business income, extra expense, and increased Coverage C limits for other property.
- Section II—Liability Coverages provides products-completed operations coverage up to an annual aggregate limit equal to the Coverage E—Personal Liability limit; provides all other business liability coverage (including personal and advertising injury).

Ordinance or Law—Increased Amount of Coverage

Any individual who owns a house could discover after a loss that repairs or upgrades must be made in order to comply with current ordinances or laws. The Ordinance or Law—Increased Amount of Coverage endorsement (HO 04 77) increases the coverage that is provided by an HO-3 policy of 10 percent of Coverage A by increments of 25 percent.

Limited Water Back-Up and Sump Discharge or Overflow Coverage

Unendorsed homeowners policies exclude property coverage for water or waterborne materials that originate from within the insured's dwelling and back up through sewers or drains, or that overflow from a sump, sump pump, or related equipment. The Limited Water Back-Up and Sump Discharge or Overflow Coverage endorsement (HO 04 95) adds this coverage back into the policy.

Supplemental Loss Assessment Coverage

Insureds living in communities with a neighborhood association are charged a monthly fee to cover the cost of the maintenance and upkeep of the common areas of the neighborhood. An association might assess homeowners for major expenses, such as the installation of a new roof on a club house or damages paid to a person injured on the association's property.

The unendorsed homeowners policy provides some limited coverage under the Additional Coverages of Section I—Property Coverages and Section II—Liability Coverages. The Loss Assessment Coverage endorsement (HO 04 35) supplements those additional coverages with an additional amount of insurance for the premises named in the endorsement. The insured can also list additional locations and schedule an amount of insurance for them (for example, if an insured owns a secondary residence with a neighborhood association).

Broadened Residence Premises Definition Endorsement

The Broadened Residence Premises Definition Endorsement (HO 06 49) indicates a starting date and an ending date within the policy period when the residency requirement will be removed from the definition of residence premises in a homeowners policy. This definition requires that the insured reside in the premises on the inception date of the policy period. This endorsement can be used when an insured may not be planning to reside in the premises on the inception date of the policy due to, for example, extensive renovations being made to the property prior to occupancy.

Home-Sharing Host Activities Amendatory Endorsement

The intent of the Home-Sharing Host Activities Amendatory Endorsement (HO 06 53) is to clarify that the HO-3 policy does not provide any property or liability coverage for home-sharing exposures. Similar endorsements are available for each of the homeowners coverage forms. The endorsement adds new definitions for home-sharing activities and revises the existing definition of "business" to specifically address home-sharing host activities. Property such as personal property of home-sharing occupants or property used primarily for home-sharing host activities is not included in the property coverage. Liability coverage is not provided for insureds engaging in home-sharing host activities and personal injury arising out of home-sharing host activities is also excluded.

Broadened Home-Sharing Host Activities Coverage Endorsement

The Broadened Home-Sharing Host Activities Coverage Endorsement (HO 06 63) can be used to provide property and liability coverage for home-sharing host activities. This endorsement provides coverage for loss or damage to the premises and liability to others, subject to policy provisions, for insureds who engage in home-sharing host activities. Although ISO has made this coverage form available, some insurers may choose not to include such operations within their personal lines underwriting guidelines.

Additional Residence Rented to Others—1, 2, 3, or 4 Families

The Additional Residence Rented to Others—1, 2, 3, or 4 Families endorsement (HO 24 70) is designed for insureds who own rental property not at the insured location. It extends Coverage E—Personal Liability and Coverage F—Medical Payments to Others to one- to four-family residences that are owned by the insured and rented to others. The location of any additional residence must be listed on the endorsement, and the number of families that occupy each must be specified.

Personal Injury Coverage

The Personal Injury Coverage endorsement (HO 24 82) expands the liability coverage of a homeowners policy by adding the definition of personal injury and then adding coverage for personal injury. Personal injuries are defined in this endorsement as injuries arising out of one or more of these offenses:

- False arrest, detention, or imprisonment
- Malicious prosecution
- Invasion of privacy, wrongful eviction, or wrongful entry
- Publication, in any manner, of material that slanders or libels another party or disparages the other party's goods, products, or services
- Publication, in any manner, of material that violates a person's right to privacy

> ### ✓ Reality Check
>
> **Effect of Dog Bites on Liability Coverage in Homeowners Policies**
>
> Dog bites are a significant source of homeowners liability claims. ISO has introduced a canine liability exclusion endorsement that insurers can use to shield themselves from this type of claim. Insurers may ask insureds if they have a dog and, if so, what breed it is. However, several states have passed laws that prohibit insurers from discriminating against dog owners based only on breed. This endorsement could become a significant errors and omissions exposure for a producer who fails to notify an insured of its application to a policy. Therefore, an ISO rules filing requires the insured to acknowledge the endorsement in writing for it to be effective. The wording of this endorsement may cause another problem. The endorsement excludes coverage for bodily injury arising out of direct physical contact with the canine. Therefore, if a visitor tripped over a dog and was injured in the fall, coverage would be excluded.

[DA07796]

Exclusions to this coverage relate to intentional acts, criminal acts, contractual liability, employment, business activities, bodily injury to an insured, civic or public duties performed for pay, and pollutants.

Aircraft Liability Definition Revised to Remove Exception for Model and Hobby Aircraft

The increasing personal use of drones, a type of unmanned aircraft, has created additional loss exposures and loss potential for homeowners policies. These include the potential for collision with manned aircraft or possible invasion of privacy concerns. The Aircraft Liability Definition Revised to Remove Exception for Model and Hobby Aircraft (HO 34 02) endorsement can be used to manage this loss exposure. This optional endorsement amends the definition of "aircraft liability" to include unmanned aircraft, "whether or not model or hobby." The endorsement excludes liability for bodily injury or property damage arising from the operation of unmanned aircraft.

Personal Injury for Aircraft Liability Excluded

The Personal Injury for Aircraft Liability Excluded (HO 34 03) excludes "aircraft liability" from personal injury coverage provided by endorsement to homeowners policies. This aircraft exclusion is extended to include any unmanned aircraft, whether or not model or hobby. This optional endorsement can be used to manage loss exposures arising from the operation of such aircraft, including drones. See the exhibit "Summary of Endorsements."

Summary of Endorsements

Endorsement	Summary
Personal Property Replacement Cost Loss Settlement (HO 04 90)	Provides replacement cost (instead of actual cash value) coverage on personal property, awnings, carpeting, household appliances, and outdoor equipment.
Scheduled Personal Property (HO 04 61)	Provides coverage for insureds who own jewelry, furs, or other eligible property for which an unendorsed homeowners policy does not provide adequate protection.
Inflation Guard (HO 04 46)	Helps prevent underinsurance caused by economic inflation and rising replacement costs by gradually and automatically increasing limits throughout the policy period for Coverages A, B, C, and D.
Earthquake (HO 04 54)	Covers damage caused by earthquake and land shock waves caused by volcanic eruption.
Assisted Living Care Coverage (HO 04 59)	Provides personal property and liability coverage for a relative of an insured living in an assisted living facility.
Credit Card, Electronic Fund Transfer Card or Access Device, Forgery and Counterfeit Money Coverage—Increased Limit (HO 04 53)	Increases the $500 coverage provided by the unendorsed HO policy to as much as a $10,000 limit for losses resulting from the unauthorized use of an insured's credit card, bank transfer card, check forgery, or acceptance of counterfeit money; the insurance limit can be increased for this additional coverage
Home Business Insurance Coverage (HO 07 01)	Provides a comprehensive business package policy for home business when attached to a homeowners form and a wider range of coverages normally found only in a commercial insurance policy; excludes professional liability coverage and many professional activities.
Ordinance or Law—Increased Amount of Coverage (HO 04 77)	Covers repairs that must be made in compliance with current ordinances or laws.
Limited Water Back Up and Sump Discharge or Overflow Coverage (HO 04 95)	Covers direct losses from water or water-borne material that (1) backs up sewers or drains or (2) overflows or is discharged from a sump, sump pump, or related equipment even if such overflow results from mechanical breakdown or power failure.
Supplemental Loss Assessment Coverage (HO 04 35)	Supplements additional coverages for insureds in communities where monthly fees are charged to cover the maintenance and upkeep costs of the common areas; also allows the insured to list additional locations and schedule an amount of insurance for them.
Broadened Residence Premises Definition Endorsement (HO 06 49)	Used when an insured will not be residing in the residence on the inception date of the policy period. Designates a starting date and an ending date within the policy period during which the residency requirement will be temporarily removed from the residence premises definition in the policy.
Home-Sharing Host Activities Amendatory Endorsement (HO 06 53)	Mandatory endorsement that reinforces the exclusion of coverage for home-sharing activities for property and liability coverages.

Broadened Home-Sharing Host Activities Coverage Endorsement (HO 06 63)	Optional endorsement providing property and liability coverages for certain home-sharing host activities.
Additional Residence Rented to Others—1, 2, 3, or 4 Families (HO 24 70)	Designed for insureds who own rental property not at the insured location; extends Coverage E—Personal Liability and Coverage F—Medical Payments to Others to one- to four-family residences owned by the insured and rented to others.
Personal Injury Coverage (HO 24 82)	Expands liability coverage by adding definition of personal injury and coverage for it. Personal injuries arise out of false arrest, detention, or imprisonment; malicious prosecution; invasion of privacy, wrongful eviction, or wrongful entry; libel or slander against a person or organization or disparaging acts against a person's or organization's goods, products, or services; libel or slander that violates a person's right of privacy.
Aircraft Liability Definition Revised to Remove Exception for Model and Hobby Aircraft (HO 34 02)	Amends the existing aircraft exclusion under Section II of the homeowners policy forms to remove the exception for model or hobby aircraft not used or designed to carry people or cargo and exclude liability arising from the operation of unmanned aircraft, such as a drone.
Personal Injury for Aircraft Liability Excluded (HO 34 03)	Adds exclusion to personal injury coverage for "aircraft liability," meaning liability for personal injury arising out of the ownership, maintenance, occupancy, or operation of any contrivance used for flight including unmanned aircraft, whether or not model or hobby.

[DA12647]

Apply Your Knowledge

Mark and Heather's neighbor's house caught fire and sustained serious property damage. Concerned that the same type of loss could occur to them, they called their insurance agent the next day to discuss ways to strengthen the fire protection coverage of their homeowners policy. If their policy was unendorsed, what endorsements would the agent likely suggest?

Feedback: Without the Personal Property Replacement Cost Loss Settlement endorsement, their personal property that is damaged by a fire is replaced at its actual cash value. Replacement cost coverage would indemnify Mark and Heather for the current replacement cost of property with similar features.

The agent may suggest Mark and Heather consider adding an Inflation Guard endorsement, which automatically increases the homeowners coverage amount annually. The endorsement is designed to help prevent underinsurance caused by economic inflation and rising replacement costs.

The agent may also suggest the Ordinance or Law—Increased Amount of Coverage endorsement. This endorsement would cover any additional repairs or upgrades that may have to be made after a fire in order to comply with current ordinances or laws.

HO-3 COVERAGE CASE

Knowing how to apply homeowners policy language to the facts of a case is an important skill. This case study will help you make the transition from knowing policy language to applying policy language to losses to determine whether coverage applies. As you progress through this case study, you can check your understanding of the coverage provided by answering the Knowledge to Action questions.

Case Facts

Tom and Debbie live in a single-family dwelling. When they left their house to go shopping, their clothes were being dried in the clothes dryer. Unfortunately, lint in the dryer's exhaust hose caught fire. Tom and Debbie returned in time to keep the fire from spreading beyond the utility room. After notifying their insurer of the loss, they hired a contractor to repair the damage. The contractor charged $20,000 for repairs and an additional $1,000 to remove the debris. The cost to replace their damaged personal property with new property is $2,000.

The contractor warned Tom and Debbie he would have several workers carrying heavy equipment and materials in and out of their house. To avoid water damage caused by damaged water pipes, Tom and Debbie decided to store an antique dining room table and chairs in a self-storage unit. Tom had rented the unit earlier to store office furniture from his business. Unfortunately, the self-storage facility was next to a drainage ditch that overflowed during a heavy rain. The dining room table, valued at $10,000, and Tom's office furniture, valued at $2,000, were destroyed by the flood waters. Tom promptly reported the flood loss to their insurer.

When the contractor finished the repair to Tom and Debbie's home, Tom and Debbie were unsatisfied with the quality of workmanship. The contractor refused to resolve their concerns. Frustrated, Tom made several disparaging remarks that he published as reviews at several websites. The contractor discovered the remarks and threatened to sue Tom for libel. Tom promptly reported the liability claim to their insurer.

Tom and Debbie are insured with a 2011 HO-3 policy, in which Coverage A is $200,000 and Coverage C is $140,000. They have two endorsements on their policy, with the first being Personal Property Replacement Cost Loss Settlement (HO 04 90) and the second being Personal Injury Coverage (HO 24 82). Tom purchased the second endorsement on his agent's recommendation. The agent was concerned about Tom's exposure to defamation claims arising out of his role as a volunteer editor of the local homeowners' association newsletter.

Given the facts presented in the case, will the homeowners claims be covered? If so, what amount will the insurer pay for each claim? When answering the questions in this case-based activity, consider only the information provided as part of this case.

Necessary Reference Materials

To determine whether Tom and Debbie's HO-3 policy provides coverage for the fire loss, flood loss, and liability claim, you need copies of the policy forms, the two applicable endorsements indicated on the Declarations page of the policy, and the Declarations page itself.

Determination of Coverage

When examining the policy forms to determine whether coverage applies to the losses, you can apply the four steps of the DICE method. Doing this involves analyzing the policy declarations, insuring agreement, conditions, and exclusions, as well as determining whether any information found at each step precludes coverage at the time of the losses. You should also examine other categories of policy provisions, such as the insured's duties; general provisions; endorsements; and terms defined in the policy in relation to the declarations, insuring agreement, conditions, and exclusions.

Next, determine the amounts payable for the losses under the applicable policy or policies. Doing this involves analyzing the limit(s) of insurance and any deductibles that apply. It also involves determining whether more than one policy provides coverage for the same loss.

DICE Analysis Step 1: Declarations

The first DICE step is to review the declarations page to determine whether it covers the person or the property at the time of the losses.

Action Task: Review the declarations in Tom and Debbie's HO-3 policy. See the exhibit "Case Coverages Applicable."

Knowledge to Action

What questions, if any, should be asked about the Declarations page to determine whether Tom and Debbie's policy will respond to these three claims?

a. Are Tom and Debbie listed as insureds under the policy?
b. Is the location where the losses occurred insured under the policy?
c. Did the claims occur during the policy period?
d. All of the above

Feedback: d. All of these questions need to be asked to determine whether coverage is triggered. The party who suffered the losses must be an insured. Where the losses occurred will help determine whether coverage applies and, if so, how much coverage is available. Finally, the losses must occur during the

> **Case Coverages Applicable**
>
> Tom and Debbie's Coverages
>
> Tom and Debbie Smith
> 10 Hometown Street
> Yourtown, USA
>
> Policy Period: From 12:01 AM February 14, 20X1, to 12:01 PM February 14, 20X2
>
> HO-3 Policy Form with $500 deductible
>
> | Cov. A—Dwelling | $200,000 | Cov. B—Other Structures | $20,000 | Cov. C—Personal Property | $140,000 | Cov. E—Personal Liability | $300,000 |
> |---|---|---|---|---|---|---|---|
>
> Endorsements:
> - Personal Property Replacement Cost Loss Settlement (HO 04 90)
> - Personal Injury Coverage (HO 24 82)

[DA07798]

policy period in which the policy is in effect. If a loss occurs before or after the policy is in effect, there is no coverage.

The Declarations page shows both Tom and Debbie as named insureds. Their home address is shown on the Declarations page and is the residence premises. The case facts provide no indication that any of the three losses occurred outside the policy period.

DICE Analysis Step 2: Insuring Agreement

The second DICE step is to review the insuring agreement to determine whether it is applicable to the described loss.

The $20,000 cost of repair is covered under Section I of Tom and Debbie's HO-3 policy:

"SECTION I—PROPERTY COVERAGES

Coverage A—Dwelling

We cover:

The dwelling on the "residence premises" shown in the Declarations, …"[1]

The $1,000 charged by the contractor to remove the debris is also covered under Section I of Tom and Debbie's HO-3 policy:

"SECTION I—PROPERTY COVERAGES

Additional Coverages

Debris Removal

We will pay your reasonable expense for removal of:

Debris of covered property if a Peril Insured Against that applies to the damaged property causes the loss; or …"[2]

The personal property damaged while at the residence or stored at the self-storage facility is also covered under Section I of Tom and Debbie's HO-3 policy:

"SECTION I—PROPERTY COVERAGES

Coverage C—Personal Property

Covered Property

We cover personal property owned or used by an "insured" while it is anywhere in the world."[3]

The libel liability claim against Tom is also covered under the Personal Injury Coverage endorsement (HO 24 82) that is part of Section II of Tom and Debbie's HO-3 policy:

"DEFINITIONS

The following definitions are added:

'Personal Injury' means …

4. Oral or written publication, in any manner, of material that slanders or libels a … person's … services; …

SECTION II—LIABILITY COVERAGES

Coverage E—Personal Liability

…

We will:

Pay up to our limit of liability for the damages for which an insured is legally liable. …

Provide a defense at our expense, …"[4]

Knowledge to Action

Other than the end of the policy period, is there a time limit for Tom and Debbie's coverage to be in effect?

a. No, only the policy period is relevant to when coverage will expire.
b. Yes, the antique table and chairs have only thirty days of coverage while at the self-storage unit.
c. Yes, the debris must be removed within thirty days of the loss or coverage for that expense will expire.
d. Yes, Tom has only thirty days to report the libel claim against him to their insurer to avoid voiding their coverage.

Feedback: b. The personal property in the self-storage unit has coverage for only thirty days, as it is covered by Section I—E. Additional Coverages—Property Removed:

> "Section I—E. Additional Coverages
>
> ...
>
> 5. Property Removed
>
> We insure covered property against direct loss from any cause while being removed from a premises endangered by a Peril Insured Against and for no more than 30 days while removed."[5]

DICE Analysis Step 3: Conditions

The third DICE step is to review the policy conditions to determine whether they preclude coverage at the time of the loss.

Tom and Debbie have complied with all policy conditions, including timely reporting and cooperating in the investigation and resolution of each claim.

DICE Analysis Step 4: Exclusions

The fourth DICE step is to review the policy exclusions to determine whether they exclude or limit coverage of the loss.

Knowledge to Action

Explain why each of the exclusions would not apply to one of Tom and Debbie's losses.

- Neglect in Section I for the fire loss
- Water, specifically flood waters at the self-storage unit, in Section I for the fire claim

Feedback: For the Neglect exclusion to apply, an insured would have to be negligent after the loss, of which there is no indication in the facts provided. Arguably, Tom should not have selected a self-storage facility so close to a drainage ditch, but flooding may not have been readily foreseeable. The Water exclusion does not apply to the removed property, because the Property Removed additional coverage states that this property is covered against direct loss from any cause, which would include flood.

Determination of Amounts Payable

Determining the amounts payable involves analyzing the limits of insurance available to pay for the loss and considering any deductibles that may apply. It also involves determining whether more than one policy provides coverage for the same loss.

These are the amounts payable for each of the damages mentioned in the case facts (not considering the deductible):

- Contractor's bill to repair the fire damage—$20,000. The amount is well below the policy limit for Coverage A of $200,000 and is paid in full minus the $500 deductible, which is $19,500.
- Contractor's bill to remove the debris to be able to effect repairs—$1,000. This amount, combined with the $19,500 for the contractor's repair bill, is well below the limit of Coverage A and paid in full.
- Personal property damaged by the fire—$2,000. This amount is well below the policy limit for Coverage C of $140,000 and paid in full. Also, Tom and Debbie's HO-3 policy was endorsed at the time of the loss with the Personal Property Replacement Cost Loss Settlement (HO 04 90), which allows for the cost to be paid in full without deduction for depreciation.
- The antique dining room table and chairs damaged by flood waters while at the self-storage unit—$10,000. The furniture was not damaged by the fire but was taken to the storage unit for protection. The Personal Property Replacement Cost Loss Settlement (HO 04 90) endorsement does not apply to the full value of the table and chairs because they are antique. Antiques are an unusual class of property in that their advanced age makes them more valuable, not less. Consequently, antiques are ineligible for replacement cost loss settlement and the claim representative will have to determine the appropriate depreciation to apply when adjusting this loss.
- Tom's office furniture at the self-storage unit also damaged by flood waters—$2,000. The property was in the storage unit before the fire loss and was not removed from the premises because it was endangered by a Peril Insured Against. Therefore the Water exclusion should apply and no amount is payable for this damage.
- The value of the contractor's libel claim against Tom is unknown. However, the Personal Injury Coverage endorsement (HO 24 82) does apply, and this claim is payable up to the Section II—Coverage E—Personal Liability limit of $300,000. The defense costs are also payable in addition to the $300,000 limit.

SUMMARY

The HO-3's Section II—Liability Coverages is designed to meet the common liability loss exposure needs of individuals and families. Section II includes two of the primary coverages listed in the homeowners policy declarations: Personal Liability and Medical Payments to Others. Section II also contains some additional coverages that apply to first aid expenses and damage to property of others, as well as other incidental personal loss exposures.

Section II—Exclusions of the HO-3 contains twenty-two exclusions, some of which apply to Section II and some of which apply to Coverage E or Coverage F. Because of how some of the exclusion provisions are worded, limited coverage may, in fact, be provided by a specific provision. Therefore, exclusion provisions should be carefully considered with the rest of the Section II terms and conditions to determine the full scope of personal liability coverage.

These are the ten conditions that apply to Section II of the HO-3 and establish the duties and responsibilities of the insured, the insurer, and third-party claimants in a liability claim: Limit of Liability, Severability of Insurance, Duties After "Occurrence," Duties of an Injured Person—Coverage F—Medical Payments to Others, Payment of Claim—Coverage F—Medical Payments to Others, Suit Against Us, Bankruptcy of an Insured, Other Insurance, Policy Period, and Concealment or Fraud. These seven conditions apply to both Sections I and II of the HO-3: Liberalization Clause, Waiver or Change of Policy Provisions, Cancellation, Nonrenewal, Assignment, Subrogation, and Death.

The DICE method can be used to determine whether, and for what amount, a claim is covered under Section II—Liability Coverages of a homeowners policy.

In addition to form HO-3, the ISO homeowners program includes five forms—HO-2 (Broad Form), HO-4 (Contents Broad Form), HO-5 (Comprehensive Form), HO-6 (Unit-Owners Form), and HO-8 (Modified Coverage Form)—that meet coverage needs or preferences that the HO-3 does not address.

Endorsements add or delete coverage, change definitions, or clarify the intent of insurance policies. These are common ISO endorsements for homeowners policies: Personal Property Replacement Cost Loss Settlement; Scheduled Personal Property; Inflation Guard; Earthquake; Assisted Living Care Coverage; Credit Card, Electronic Fund Transfer Card or Access Device, Forgery and Counterfeit Money Coverage—Increased Limit; Home Business Insurance (HOMEBIZ); Ordinance or Law—Increased Amount of Coverage; Limited Water Back-Up and Sump Discharge or Overflow Coverage; Supplemental Loss Assessment Coverage; Broadened Residence Premises Definition Endorsement; Home-Sharing Host Activities Amendatory Endorsement; Broadened Home-Sharing Host Activities Coverage Endorsement; Additional Residence Rented to Others—1, 2, 3, or 4 Families;

Personal Injury Coverage; Aircraft Liability Definition Revised to Remove Exception for Model and Hobby Aircraft; and Personal Injury for Aircraft Liability Excluded.

You should now be able to apply policy language to homeowners losses to determine whether the losses are covered and the amount for which they are covered.

ASSIGNMENT NOTES

1. Copyright, Insurance Services Office, Inc., 2011
2. Copyright, Insurance Services Office, Inc., 2011
3. Copyright, Insurance Services Office, Inc., 2011
4. Copyright, Insurance Services Office, Inc., 2011
5. Copyright, Insurance Services Office, Inc., 2011

Direct Your Learning

7

Other Residential Insurance

Educational Objectives

After learning the content of this assignment, you should be able to:

▸ Contrast the DP-3 policy with the HO-3 policy in regard to each of the following:
- Types of property covered
- Other coverages
- Perils insured against
- Exclusions and conditions
- Coverage for liability and theft losses

▸ Given a case describing a dwelling claim, determine whether the Dwelling Property—Special Form (DP-3) policy would cover the claim and, if so, the amount the insurer would pay for the claim.

▸ Explain how the coverages under the HO-3 policy are modified by the Mobilehome Endorsement (MH 04 01) and other ISO endorsements unique to mobilehome coverage.

▸ Describe the operation of the National Flood Insurance Program and the coverage it provides.

▸ Describe the operation of FAIR plans and beachfront and windstorm plans and the coverage they provide.

Outline

Dwelling Policies

Dwelling Coverage Case Study

Mobilehome Coverage

The National Flood Insurance Program

FAIR and Beachfront and Windstorm Plans

Summary

Other Residential Insurance

DWELLING POLICIES

Because dwelling policies are used widely, particularly to insure rental dwellings, an understanding of the coverages provided by the DP-3 policy and how they differ from the HO-3 policy is important.

Some residences are not eligible for homeowners coverage for various reasons. Here are some of those reasons:

- The residence is not owner-occupied.
- The value of the dwelling is below the minimum limit for a homeowners policy.
- The residence does not otherwise meet an insurer's underwriting guidelines.

An insured might not want a homeowners policy for either or both of two reasons: The insured might not want or need the full range of homeowners coverages, and a homeowners policy might cost more than the insured is willing to pay.

A dwelling policy can be used to cover owner- and nonowner-occupied residences or to meet the needs of customers who do not want or need a homeowners policy. Although many differences exist between the dwelling and homeowners policies, among the most important differences is the fact that the unendorsed Insurance Services Office, Inc. (ISO) Dwelling Property 3—Special Form DP 00 03 (DP-3) does not provide any theft coverage for personal property or any liability coverages. However, both of these coverages can be added to the dwelling policy by an endorsement or a supplement.

Structures Eligible for Dwelling Policies

The HO-3 policy covers owner-occupied one- to four-family dwellings. Dwelling policies are designed principally for insuring one- to four-family dwellings, whether owner-occupied or tenant-occupied. However, dwelling policies may also be used for four other kinds of property and activities:

- A dwelling in the course of construction
- Mobile homes at a permanent location
- Houseboats, in some states
- Certain incidental business occupancies, if the businesses are operated by the owner-insured or by a tenant of the insured location

Coverages

The DP-3 offers property coverages on a dwelling and its contents that are similar to the coverages under Section I (property) of the HO-3 and other homeowners forms.

The dwelling form includes five coverages:

- Coverage A—Dwelling
- Coverage B—Other Structures
- Coverage C—Personal Property
- Coverage D—Fair Rental Value
- Coverage E—Additional Living Expense

Unlike the HO-3 policy, the dwelling policy does not automatically include all the property coverages. A limit for each desired coverage (dwelling, other structures, and personal property) must be shown on the Declarations page (with appropriate premium charges). Loss of use coverages (fair rental value and additional living expense), however, are automatically included in the DP-3.

Although a dwelling policy can be used for insuring only personal property with no dwelling or structures coverage, this is rarely done. The DP-3 form is more commonly used to cover only the dwelling and other structures (for example, to insure a house rented unfurnished to tenants) or to cover the dwelling, other structures, and personal property.

Coverage A—Dwelling

The DP-3 form provides coverage for the dwelling on the described location shown in the declarations and specifies that it must be used principally for dwelling purposes. The HO-3 form refers to the dwelling on the residence premises, including attached structures. The dwelling form also specifically states that, if not covered elsewhere in the policy, building equipment and outdoor equipment used for the service of the premises and located on the described location are covered. For example, if the insured owns a lawn mower kept in the garage of the insured dwelling and uses it to cut the grass at the insured location, the lawn mower would be included under Coverage A (if the insured did not purchase Coverage C—Personal Property). The remainder of the Coverage A language is similar in the dwelling and homeowners forms.

Coverage B—Other Structures

Although the dwelling and homeowners forms have some minor differences in their wording, their coverage for other structures is essentially the same. Structures set apart from the dwelling by clear space or connected to the dwelling by only a fence, utility line, or similar connection are defined as included under Coverage B. As in the HO-3 policy, Coverage B includes detached structures, such as garages and storage sheds, on the insured premises. Gravemarkers and mausoleums are specifically excluded under Other Structures in the DP-3 form, whereas the HO-3 policy provides up to $5,000 for gravemarkers as an additional coverage.

Coverage C—Personal Property

If Coverage C is selected, coverage under the dwelling form applies to personal property usual to the occupancy of a dwelling that is owned or used by the insured or resident family members. Coverage applies while the property is on the described location.

Unlike the homeowners form, the dwelling form has no special limits that apply to any specific type of personal property. For example, the homeowners form has special limits on theft losses to jewelry, furs, firearms, silverware, and similar types of property; the dwelling form has no such limits. Because the unendorsed dwelling form has no theft coverage, such theft limitations are not necessary. The homeowners policy has a special sublimit on money and related items, but the dwelling form excludes coverage for money altogether. The homeowners policy provides a special sublimit on watercraft (including their furnishings, equipment, and outboard motors), but the dwelling form excludes boats other than rowboats and canoes.

To cover personal property, the insured chooses a Coverage C limit in the dwelling form. If an insured is a landlord and has no personal property in the insured dwelling (or chooses not to insure personal property), he or she can choose to purchase only Coverage A under the DP-3. The HO-3 policy has no such option.

Coverage D—Fair Rental Value and Coverage E—Additional Living Expense

Coverages D and E in the DP-3 form correspond roughly to Coverage D—Loss of Use in the HO-3 form, which includes both fair rental value and additional living expense coverages. Coverage D covers the fair rental value of a property rented to others when it becomes unfit for its normal use because of a loss by a covered peril. Coverage E covers the increase in living expenses for the insured if the described property becomes unfit for its normal use because of a loss by a covered peril.

Other Coverages

Many of the other coverages provided in the dwelling policy correspond to the additional coverages in the homeowners policy, but there are some differences. Loss assessment coverage, which is included automatically (up to $1,000) in the homeowners policy, can be added to the dwelling policy by endorsement for an additional premium. The additional coverages in the homeowners policy for landlord's furnishings and for credit cards, transfer cards, forgery, and counterfeit money are not available in the dwelling policy.

Other Structures

The DP-3 form provides up to 10 percent of the Coverage A limit for Coverage B—Other Structures as outlined in the Other Coverages provision. This coverage is additional insurance and does not reduce the Coverage A limit for the same loss.

Debris Removal

The debris removal coverage of the DP-3 form is included in the limit that applies to the damaged property. In contrast, the HO-3 provides an additional 5 percent of the applicable coverage limit for debris removal if the amount to be paid for the damage to the property plus the debris removal expense exceeds the coverage limit for the damaged property. The debris removal coverage under the HO-3 also provides coverage for trees, shrubs, and plants, subject to sublimits. There is no debris removal coverage for trees, shrubs, and plants in the DP-3 form.

Improvements, Alterations, and Additions

The DP-3 form provides 10 percent of the Coverage C limit as additional insurance to cover a tenant's improvements, alterations, and additions for loss by a covered peril. No comparable coverage exists in the HO-3 form.

Worldwide Coverage

The DP-3 form provides up to 10 percent of the Coverage C limit for loss to the property covered under Coverage C, except rowboats and canoes, while that property is anywhere in the world. The HO-3 form provides worldwide coverage for personal property owned or used by an insured, with no limitation except that a 10 percent limitation applies to property usually located at a secondary residence of the insured.

Fair Rental Value and Additional Living Expense

The DP-3 form provides up to 20 percent of the Coverage A limit for losses under both Coverage D—Fair Rental Value and Coverage E—Additional Living Expense as outlined in the Other Coverages provision. This coverage is additional insurance and does not reduce the Coverage A limit for the same loss. Under the HO-3 form, the corresponding additional limit for loss of use is 30 percent of the Coverage A limit.

Reasonable Repairs

The DP-3 form, like the HO-3 form, provides coverage for the cost of reasonable repairs made after the occurrence of a covered loss solely to protect covered property from further damage. This coverage does not increase the limit of liability that applies to the covered property.

Property Removed

Under both the DP-3 and HO-3, covered property is protected if it is removed from the premises because it is endangered by an insured peril. Under both policies, this coverage applies to direct loss from any cause (as long as an insured peril necessitated the removal) for thirty days. In the dwelling form, as in the homeowners form, the limit for this coverage is the same as the limit for the property being moved.

Trees, Shrubs, and Other Plants

In both the HO-3 and the DP-3 forms, the maximum limit that can be applied (as an additional amount of insurance) to trees, shrubs, other plants, or lawns is 5 percent of the Coverage A limit. The limit for any one tree, plant, or shrub is $500, and only specified perils are covered. This coverage can be expanded by endorsement to include the perils of wind and hail.

Fire Department Service Charge

The DP-3 form, like the HO-3 form, will pay up to $500 for fire department service charges. Coverage is not provided if the property is located within the limits of the city, municipality, or protection district furnishing the fire department response. This coverage is additional insurance, and no deductible applies.

Collapse

The DP-3 form offers coverage for building collapse due to specified perils. As in the HO-3 form, coverage is for direct physical loss to covered property resulting from collapse caused by any of six perils:

- Coverage C—Personal Property perils
- Decay that is hidden from view
- Hidden insect or vermin damage, unless the insured is aware of the damage prior to the collapse
- Weight of contents, equipment, animals, or people
- Weight of rain collecting on a roof
- Use of defective materials or methods of construction

Collapse coverage does not increase the limit of liability that applies to the damaged covered property.

Glass or Safety Glazing Material

The DP-3 form provides coverage for breakage of glass or safety glazing material that is part of a building, storm door, or storm window, and for damage to covered property caused by breakage of such glass or safety glazing material. The coverage does not apply if the dwelling has been vacant for more than sixty consecutive days before the loss. This coverage does not increase the limit of liability that applies to the damaged property. Similar coverage is included in the HO-3 form.

Ordinance or Law

The DP-3 form provides coverage for increased costs the insured incurs because of the enforcement of any ordinance or law. If the insured has purchased Coverage A, ordinance or law coverage is provided up to 10 percent of the Coverage A limit. If there is no Coverage A limit, up to 10 percent of the Coverage B limit is provided for ordinance or law coverage. This coverage is additional insurance. Coverage under the HO-3 form is similar and provides up to 10 percent of Coverage A for ordinance or law coverage as additional insurance.

If the insured is a tenant at the described location, the limit applying to ordinance or law coverage is up to 10 percent of the limit that applies to improvements, alterations, and additions.

Perils Insured Against

Coverage A—Dwelling and Coverage B—Other Structures

The DP-3, like the HO-3, uses the special form approach and insures against "risk of direct loss to property" (as opposed to named perils coverage) under Coverage A—Dwelling and Coverage B—Other Structures. In both the DP-3 and the HO-3 forms, the coverage for direct physical loss to real property is determined by the causes of loss that are excluded. Those causes of loss that are not excluded are covered. For example, the DP-3 form excludes coverage for theft of any property that is not part of a covered building or structure. It also excludes loss caused by wind, hail, ice, snow, or sleet to outdoor radio and television antennas and aerials, and to trees, shrubs, other plants, or lawns. Other exclusions in the DP-3 are essentially the same as those in the HO-3.

Coverage C—Personal Property

Although the Coverage C named perils under the DP-3 form are similar to the named perils coverage in the HO-3 form, there are some differences. Theft of personal property is not covered under the DP-3, but coverage is provided for damage to covered property caused by burglars, unless the dwelling has been vacant for more than sixty days. For example, if burglars break down a door, damage a table, and steal a television, the damage to the door and the table would be covered, but the loss of the stolen TV would not be covered. The DP-3 specifically excludes pilferage, theft, burglary, and larceny under the peril of vandalism or malicious mischief.

The windstorm or hail coverage in the DP-3 also differs slightly from the HO-3. The DP-3 specifically excludes wind or hail damage to canoes and rowboats; the HO-3 covers such damage to watercraft and their trailers, furnishings, equipment, and outboard motors, but only while the items are inside a fully enclosed building.

Dwelling Policy General Exclusions

The general exclusions in the DP-3 track closely with the Section I exclusions in the HO-3. These exclusions include loss caused directly or indirectly by several perils or events:

- Ordinance or law, except as provided in the Other Coverages section
- Earth movement, such as an earthquake
- Water damage, such as flood and backup of sewers and drains
- Power failure that occurs off the described location
- Neglect on the part of the insured
- War
- Nuclear hazard
- Intentional loss
- Weather conditions that contribute to any of the preceding excluded causes of loss
- Acts or decisions of other persons, groups, organizations, or governmental bodies
- Faulty construction, planning, materials, or maintenance

Dwelling Policy Conditions

The DP-3 form contains a single section of conditions. Similar conditions are found in the HO-3 policy, but some HO-3 conditions apply only to Section I, while others apply to both Section I and Section II (liability). Because the DP-3 form has no Section II (liability) coverage, there is no need to specify the section to which the conditions apply. These conditions include the insured's duties after a loss, loss to a pair or set, other insurance, mortgage clause, and other similar conditions regarding the coverage. See the exhibit "Comparison of the HO-3 and the DP-3 Forms."

Coverage for Liability and Theft Losses

Although the ISO dwelling forms do not provide coverage for liability or theft losses, such coverages are available by adding a personal liability supplement and a theft endorsement.

Personal Liability Supplement

Liability coverage may be written as an addendum to the dwelling policy or as a separate policy using the personal liability supplement (DL 24 01). An

Comparison of the HO-3 and the DP-3 Forms

Coverage	HO-3	DP-3
A—Dwelling	Limit selected by insured	Same
	Replacement cost coverage if limit is at least 80% of replacement cost	Same
	Automatically included	Included only if limit selected and shown on Declarations page
B—Other Structures	10% of Coverage A	10% of Coverage A
	Automatically included	Provided in the Other Coverages section
	Replacement cost coverage if limit is at least 80% of replacement cost	Same
C—Personal Property	50% of Coverage A automatically included	Included only if limit selected and shown on Declarations page
	Worldwide coverage up to Coverage C limit	Worldwide coverage only up to 10% of Coverage C
	ACV (actual cash value) coverage	Same
D—Loss of Use	30% of Coverage A	Coverage D—Fair Rental Value and Coverage E—Additional Living Expense
	Automatically included	20% of Coverage A Provided in the Other Coverages section for both Coverage D and Coverage E
Additional/Other Coverages		
• Loss assessment	$1,000	None (can be added by endorsement)
• Credit card, electronic fund transfer card or access device, forgery and counterfeit money	$500	None
• Landlord's furnishings	$2,500 at residence	None included in the Other Coverages section, but if the dwelling is rented, the owner/landlord's furnishings are covered up to the Coverage C limit
• Debris removal	Additional 5% of limit of liability available	Included in limit of coverage
	Includes coverage for trees, shrubs, and plants, subject to a sublimit	No coverage for trees, shrubs, and plants
• Improvements, alterations, and additions	None	Tenant may use up to 10% of Coverage C (additional insurance)

• Reasonable repairs	Included in limit	Same
• Property removed	Covered up to 30 days from date of loss	Same
• Trees, shrubs, plants	5% of Coverage A, up to $500 per item for limited perils (not including wind or hail)	Same
	Additional insurance	Additional insurance
• Fire dept. service charge	$500	Same
• Collapse	Covered for limited perils	Same
• Glass or safety glazing material	Covered	Covered
• Ordinance or law	10% of Coverage A	10% of Coverage A. If no Coverage A, 10% of Coverage B. If insured is tenant, 10% of improvements, alterations, and additions limit
Personal Property—Special Limits/Exclusions	$200 for money	Money excluded
	$1,500 for securities and other documents	Securities and documents excluded
	$1,500 for watercraft	Watercraft excluded (except rowboats and canoes)
Perils Insured Against		
• Coverages A & B	Special-form coverage (risk of direct loss, subject to exclusions)	Same
• Coverage C	Named perils (broad form)	Same
	Theft coverage included by endorsement	No theft coverage (theft can be added)
Section II—Liability		
• E—Personal Liability	Automatically included	None
• F—Medical Payments to Others	Automatically included	None
		Liability and medical payments can be added by purchase of personal liability supplement

This comparison is based on Insurance Services Office (ISO) forms. It can be used as a quick reference and as an easy method to compare the HO-3 and DP-3 policies. However, only the actual policy forms contain complete coverage information, and those forms should be used to determine coverage wording.

[DA05619]

insured who has both a homeowners policy on his or her residence and a dwelling policy on a rental dwelling also has the option of obtaining liability coverage for the rental dwelling by purchasing the homeowners additional residence rented to others endorsement (HO 24 70) for an additional premium.

The personal liability supplement provides Coverage L—Personal Liability and Coverage M—Medical Payments to Others. These coverages are similar in format and language to Coverage E—Personal Liability and Coverage F—Medical Payments to Others in Section II of the homeowners policy.

The exclusions and additional coverages in the personal liability supplement attached to the DP-3 are virtually the same as those applicable to Section II of the homeowners policy. The main difference is that the additional liability coverage for loss assessment provided (up to a limit of $1,000) in the HO-3 form is not provided in the personal liability supplement.

Residential Theft Coverage

An insured may choose between two endorsements to the dwelling form to provide theft coverage similar to that provided in the homeowners policy.

The first endorsement, the Broad Theft Coverage (DP 04 72) endorsement, provides coverage against the perils of theft, including attempted theft, and vandalism or malicious mischief as a result of theft or attempted theft on-premises and off-premises. Off-premises coverage is available only if the insured purchases on-premises coverage. The endorsement includes special limits similar to the sublimits included in the HO-3 form, such as those for money, jewelry, and firearms. See the exhibit "Broad Theft Coverage—Special Limits of Liability."

Broad Theft Coverage—Special Limits of Liability

Category	Limit
Money, bank notes, bullion, gold	$200
Securities, accounts, deeds	$1,500
Watercraft of all types, including their trailers	$1,500
Trailers or semitrailers, other than those used with watercraft	$1,500
Jewelry, watches, furs	$1,500
Firearms and related equipment	$2,500
Silverware, goldware, platinumware, and pewterware	$2,500

[DA05620]

The second endorsement, the Limited Theft Coverage (DP 04 73) endorsement, covers only on-premises theft, attempted theft, and vandalism or malicious mischief as a result of theft or attempted theft. The endorsement includes special limits only for watercraft and their trailers, trailers not used for watercraft, and firearms and related equipment. It does not cover off-premises theft.

DWELLING COVERAGE CASE STUDY

Knowing how to apply the Dwelling Property—Special Form (DP-3) dwelling policy to the facts of a case is an important skill. This case study can help the student begin to make the transition from knowing policy language to knowing how to apply policy language to losses.

This case helps the student to apply the Insurance Services Office, Inc. (ISO) DP-3 dwelling policy to a given set of facts. The unendorsed DP-3 policy covers the dwelling but does not include liability coverage.

Case Facts

Based on the facts presented in this case, will the property claim be covered? If so, what amount would the insurer pay for the claim?

Wally and Dawn are a young married couple who have just purchased their first home. They had been saving money for over a year so that they could make this purchase, and now their funds are limited. The three-bedroom home was a bargain but will require a lot of work over the next few years. Before obtaining insurance coverage for the home, Wally and Dawn received several quotes from different insurers. They discovered that the cost of an HO-3 homeowners policy was much higher than that of a DP-3 dwelling policy. Although the homeowners policy provided broader coverage, the couple decided to purchase the dwelling policy to save money. The policy does not include any endorsements.

About six months after Wally and Dawn obtained the policy, the home was damaged as a result of an electrical fire in the basement. Most of the fire damage was restricted to the basement, but there was smoke damage throughout the home. The total cost of home repairs was $35,000. The washer and dryer also needed to be replaced, and there was damage to some personal property stored in the basement, which amounted to a total actual cash value (ACV) of $2,350. Wally and Dawn could not live in the house for one month after the fire and rented an apartment for $725 for the month. Also, while the house was being repaired, a burglary occurred. During the night, someone broke in through the back door, and a television and some stereo equipment valued at $2,800 were stolen. The cost to repair the damage to the door and its framing was $3,150.

To confirm that the facts about an accident are accurate, insurers frequently rely on police reports, recorded statements from claimants and witnesses, and inspections of the premises where the loss occurred. See the exhibit "Case Facts."

Case Facts

Insureds	Wally and Dawn Jones
Types of policies and coverage limits	DP-3 Policy • Coverage A—Dwelling ($145,000 limit) • Coverage B—Other Structures (10 percent of Coverage A limit) • Coverage C—Personal Property ($25,000 limit) • Coverage E—Additional Living Expenses (20 percent of Coverage A limit) $500 deductible applies
Endorsements that affect the case	None
Other policy information	No other relevant information
Background	The insureds have complied with the policy conditions.

[DA05621]

Case Analysis Tools

To determine whether Wally and Dawn's DP-3 provides coverage for the damage to the home, the insurance or risk management professional should have copies of the applicable policy forms. See the exhibit "Dwelling Fire Policy."

To determine whether a policy covers a loss, many insurance professionals apply the DICE method. ("DICE" is an acronym for categories of policy provisions: declarations, insuring agreement, conditions, and exclusions.) The DICE method has four steps:

1. Review of the declarations page to determine whether it covers the person or the property at the time of the loss
2. Review of the insuring agreement to determine whether it covers the loss
3. Review of policy conditions to determine compliance
4. Review of policy exclusions to determine whether they preclude coverage of the loss

Each of these four steps is used in every case. Other categories of policy provisions should be examined. For example, endorsements and terms defined in the policy should be reviewed in relation to the declarations, insuring agreement, exclusions, and conditions.

Dwelling Fire Policy

DWELLING FIRE POLICY

POLICYHOLDER (Named Insured): Wallace & Dawn Jones
32 Happy Lane
Anytown, USA 123456

POLICY NUMBER: ABC-DEF

POLICY PERIOD

Inception: March 5, 20XX

Expiration: March 5, 20XX

Policy period begins 12:01 A.M. standard time at the described location.

FIRST MORTGAGEE AND MAILING ADDRESS:

Anytown Bank & Trust
Main Street
Anytown, USA 12345

We will provide the insurance described in this policy in return for the premium and compliance with all applicable policy provisions.

COVERAGES	LIMIT
A—Dwelling	$145,000
B—Other Structures	Included
C—Personal Property	$ 25,000
D—Rental Value	Included
E—Additional Expense	Included

Deductible: $500.

CONSTRUCTION: Frame **NO. FAMILIES:** One **TYPE ROOF:** Approved

YEAR BUILT: 1948 **PROTECTION CLASS:** 6

POLICY PREMIUM: $ 987.00 **COUNTERSIGNATURE DATE:** March 1, 20XX

AGENT: J. Smith

Copyright, ISO Properties, Inc. [DA05622]

Determination of Coverage

To examine the policy forms and determine whether coverage applies to the losses, the insurance professional can apply the DICE method, which involves four steps.

The first DICE step is to review the Declarations page to determine whether the individuals are covered and whether the incidents occurred during the policy period. In this case, Wally and Dawn are listed as named insureds on the Declarations page, and the losses occurred during the policy period.

The second DICE step is to determine whether the loss triggers coverage under the DP-3 dwelling policy. Coverage for the fire damage is triggered under the DP-3 policy for both Coverage A and Coverage C. For Coverage A, the perils insured against cover risk of direct physical loss to property, subject to exclusions. Because neither fire nor smoke is specifically excluded, the damage to the home is covered. See the exhibit "Perils Insured Against."

Perils Insured Against

PERILS INSURED AGAINST

A. Coverage A – Dwelling And Coverage B – Other Structures

1. We insure against direct physical loss to property described in Coverages A and B.
2. We do not insure, however, for loss:
   a. Excluded under General Exclusions

Includes copyrighted material of Insurance Services Office, Inc., with its permission. Copyright, Insurance Services Office, Inc., 2013. [DA05623]

For Coverage C—Personal Property, the perils of fire or lightning and the peril of smoke are both listed as covered perils, so the damaged washer, dryer, and other personal property are covered. See the exhibit "Coverage C—Personal Property."

The cost to rent an apartment would also be covered under Coverage E—Additional Living Expense. This coverage provides for "any necessary increase in living expenses" incurred to maintain a normal standard of living, as long as the loss is covered under the Coverage A or C perils. The peril must also cause the premises to be unfit for its normal use; in this case, the insurer has agreed that this is so. See the exhibit "Coverage E—Additional Living Expense."

The burglary loss of the television and stereo equipment is not covered because theft is not listed as one of the covered perils under Coverage C. The damage to the door, however, is covered under the "Damage by Burglars" peril, which covers damage to covered property that is caused by burglars. The

Coverage C—Personal Property

B. Coverage C – Personal Property

We insure for direct physical loss to the property described in Coverage C caused by a peril listed below unless the loss is excluded in the General Exclusions.

1. Fire Or Lightning …
7. Smoke

This peril means sudden and accidental damage from smoke, including the emission or puffback of smoke, soot, fumes or vapors from a boiler, furnace or related equipment.

This peril does not include loss caused by smoke from agricultural smudging or industrial operations.

Includes copyrighted material of Insurance Services Office, Inc., with its permission. Copyright, Insurance Services Office, Inc., 2013. [DA05624]

Coverage E—Additional Living Expense

E. Coverage E – Additional Living Expense

1. If a loss to property described in Coverage A, B or C by a Peril Insured Against under this Policy makes the Described Location unfit for its normal use, we cover any necessary increase in living expenses incurred by you so that your household can maintain its normal standard of living.

   Payment will be for the shortest time required to repair or replace the Described Location or, if you permanently relocate, the shortest time required for your household to settle elsewhere.

Includes copyrighted material of Insurance Services Office, Inc., with its permission. Copyright, Insurance Services Office, Inc., 2013. [DA05625]

wording of this peril specifically emphasizes that theft of property is not covered. Also, there is no coverage if the dwelling has been vacant for more than sixty days (however, a dwelling under construction is not considered vacant). In this case, the home was vacant, but only for thirty days. Furthermore, the home was under construction at the time of the loss, so coverage for the damage to the door will be covered. See the exhibit "Damage By Burglars."

The third DICE step is to determine whether all policy conditions have been met. Wally and Dawn have complied with all policy conditions, including promptly notifying the insurer of the loss. Also, the policy limits meet all insurance-to-value requirements as outlined in the DP-3 policy.

The fourth DICE step is to determine whether one or more exclusions preclude coverage that the insuring agreements have granted. In this case, none of the exclusions applies.

> **Damage By Burglars**
>
> 9. Damage By Burglars
>   a. This peril means damage to covered property caused by burglars.
>   b. This peril does not include:
>   (1) Theft of property; or
>   (2) Damage caused by burglars to property on the Described Location if the dwelling has been vacant for more than 60 consecutive days immediately before the damage occurs. A dwelling being constructed is not considered vacant.

Includes copyrighted material of Insurance Services Office, Inc., with its permission. Copyright, Insurance Services Office, Inc., 2013. [DA05626]

Determination of Amounts Payable

Determining the amount payable for a loss under the DP-3 policy involves analyzing the limit of liability available to pay losses.

Because fire and smoke are covered under the DP-3 policy and the insurance-to-value requirements have been met, the $35,000 damage to the home is covered in full. The cost of replacing the washer, dryer, and other personal property are also covered in full for the ACV of $2,350. Wally and Dawn will pay the $500 deductible for these losses one time unless the insurer determines that the fire loss and the burglary loss are two separate events. In that case, Wally and Dawn may have to pay a single $500 deductible for all losses related to the fire and then another $500 deductible for the burglary damage. The cost of renting an apartment for one month while the home was unfit for normal use will also be covered for $725 under Coverage E—Additional Living Expenses because this is less than the limit of 20 percent of the Coverage A limit. The cost to repair the damage caused by burglars will be paid in the amount of $3,150. The theft loss is not covered, so the $2,800 for the television and stereo equipment will not be paid. See the exhibit "Determination of Amounts Payable."

> **Determination of Amounts Payable**
>
> $35,000 damage to the home—Covered in full because the Coverage A limit is $145,000 and the insurance-to-value requirements have been met.
>
> $2,350 actual cash value of replacing the washer, dryer, and other personal property—Covered in full because the Coverage C limit is $25,000.
>
> $725 cost of renting an apartment for one month while the home was unfit for normal use—Covered in full under Coverage E—Additional Living Expenses because the amount is less than the limit of 20 percent of the Coverage A limit.
>
> $3,150 cost to repair the damage caused by burglars—Covered in full under "Damage by Burglars" peril.
>
> $2,800 cost of stolen television and stereo equipment—Not covered because theft is not listed as a covered peril for Coverage C.
>
> Deductible—Wally and Dawn will pay the $500 deductible for these losses one time unless the insurer determines that the fire loss and the burglary loss are two separate events. In that case, Wally and Dawn may have to pay a single $500 deductible for all losses related to the fire and another $500 deductible for the burglary damage.

[DA05627]

MOBILEHOME COVERAGE

Mobile homes are generally less expensive than homes built on permanent foundations, making them a popular choice for seasonal or vacation homes and also providing a less costly option for home buyers.

Mobilehome owners often lease the land on which they place their home. Many mobilehome owners lease or own other structures as well. These factors and others create special needs to be addressed in mobilehome coverages.

Mobilehome coverage is provided through an endorsement that modifies provisions of the HO-3 policy (or similar policies). Additional mobilehome endorsements can be added to the policy to customize the coverage according to policyholders' needs.

Examining the provisions of ISO mobilehome endorsements illustrates how these coverages modify the HO-3 policy to meet mobilehome owners' unique needs. Mobilehome exposures and coverages are examined here.

Mobilehome Exposures

The owners of mobile homes face the same exposures to loss that owners of conventional homes face, as well as vulnerability to additional exposures. A mobilehome owner might experience loss from one or more of several typical exposures:

- Damage to or destruction of the mobile home
- Damage to or destruction of other structures on the residence premises
- Damage to or destruction of personal property in the mobile home or in other structures
- Loss of use of the mobile home
- Liability loss because of bodily injury to others or damage to the property of others

For example, if a tornado struck a mobile home, the mobile home would likely be damaged or destroyed. Other structures on the premises, such as a garage or shed, might also sustain damage or be demolished. Personal property, such as clothing, detached furniture, dishes, tools, and toys from the mobile home and other structures might be destroyed or lost. Finally, the homeowner could suffer loss of use of the mobile home if the damage is extensive enough that the homeowner requires alternate housing until the mobile home is repaired or replaced.

Vulnerability to Additional Exposures

By definition, a mobile home is not permanently affixed to the land on which it is located. Most states consider mobile homes to be moveable property and not real estate. The exposure of mobile homes to some types of losses is greater than the exposure of homes built on permanent foundations.

Mobile homes are assembled in a factory and transported to their location in a complete or semicomplete condition. They are constructed of lighter materials than those used for homes built on permanent foundations, and special construction techniques are used. Because of their construction materials and loose foundation, mobile homes are particularly vulnerable to damage from windstorm, tornado, and earthquake.

Mobile homes' wheels are generally removed when the structure is set on blocks, piers, or masonry footings. When the mobile home is set in place, it should be tied down to anchors buried in the ground to prevent the unit from moving. Doing this helps protect it from being moved sideways or lifted off the ground in a windstorm, a vulnerability that results from the lightweight design. Some state codes require that mobile homes be tied down, and many insurers provide mobilehome coverage only if the structure is properly tied down.

Skirting material is often attached to the bottom of a mobile home to conceal the wheels, blocks or piers, and tie-downs and give the appearance of a permanent structure. The skirting also reduces the buildup of debris underneath the mobile home and helps prevent damage that might subsequently result from this inherent vulnerability. For example, the skirting would prevent burning brush or leaves from blowing under the mobile home and causing fire damage.

Because mobile homes are frequently used as vacation homes, they may be located in recreational areas subject to greater loss exposure, such as in the mountains, beside a lake or river, or in heavily wooded areas. Compared with year-round residential mobile homes, the loss exposure of vacation mobile homes may be increased by the absence of services. For example, vacation areas often do not have full-time fire departments, and cellular and land-based telephone services may be limited in remote areas. Moreover, in these locations, the absence of nearby neighbors who could report a fire when the owner is away presents an increased exposure to fire and the possibility of greater severity when a loss occurs.

Other Property Exposure Considerations

The contents of mobile homes and other structures on the premises are usually similar to those in conventional dwellings, and they are subject to the same exposures. However, mobile homes often have built-in cabinets, appliances, and furniture, which are considered part of the mobile home rather than personal property. Additionally, an owner of a mobile home is subject to the same liability exposures as an owner of a conventional home.

Mobilehome Coverages

Many specialty insurers have developed policies for mobile homes, and the policies may also insure prefabricated, manufactured, or modular houses that are manufactured in one location and moved to their permanent location. ISO has developed special endorsements for insuring mobile homes. ISO has designed an endorsement specifically for mobile homes to be used with an HO-3 policy. According to ISO rules, mobilehome endorsements can also be used with an HO-2 policy. Mobilehome tenants may use the HO-4 policy without adding the mobilehome endorsement.

A mobile home is eligible for coverage if it is designed for portability and year-round living. Typically, a mobile home must be at least ten feet wide and have an area of at least 400 square feet to qualify for the mobilehome endorsement.

A mobilehome policy is created by attaching the Mobilehome Endorsement (MH 04 01) to a homeowners form and a declarations page. As with all homeowners policies, other endorsements may be attached to modify the coverage. The mobilehome endorsement states that the insurance is subject to all applicable provisions of the homeowners form except as revised by the endorsement. The mobilehome policy modifies the HO-3 policy in several ways:

- Definitions—The definition of "residence premises" is changed in the mobilehome endorsement to mean the mobile home and other structures located on land owned or leased by the insured where the insured resides on the inception date of the policy period. This location must be shown as the residence premises on the declarations page.

- Section I—Property Coverages, Coverage A—Dwelling—This coverage applies to a mobile home used primarily as a private residence and to structures and utility tanks attached to the mobile home. It also applies to floor coverings, appliances, dressers, cabinets, and similar items that are permanently installed. In addition, coverage is provided for materials and supplies (located on or next to the residence premises) for construction, alteration, or repair of the mobile home or other structures on that premises.

- Section I—Property Coverages, Coverage B—Other Structures—The liability coverage limit for other structures on the premises is a maximum of 10 percent of the limit that applies to Coverage A, with a minimum limit of $2,000.

- Section I—Property Coverages, Additional Coverages—An extra additional coverage provided in the mobilehome endorsement is unique to mobile homes. This "property removed" coverage applies if the mobile home is endangered by an insured peril, requiring removal to avoid damage, and provides up to $500 (with no deductible) for reasonable expenses incurred by the policyholder for removal and return of the entire mobile home. The mobilehome endorsement removes the ordinance or law additional coverage that is provided by the HO-3; however, it may be restored by another endorsement.

- Section I—Conditions, Loss Settlement—According to the loss settlement condition in the mobilehome endorsement, carpeting and appliances are not included as property to be valued on the basis of actual cash value (ACV). Therefore, such property is included in Coverage A, and—if the required amount of insurance is met—replacement cost coverage applies.

- Section I—Conditions, Loss to a Pair or Set—Additional coverage is added to repair or replace damaged parts of a series of panels to match the remainder of the panels as closely as possible or to provide an acceptable decorative effect. However, the coverage does not guarantee that replacements will be available, and the insurer is not required to pay for repair or replacement of the entire series of pieces or panels.

- Section I—Conditions, Mortgage Clause—This provision modifies the word "mortgagee" in the policy to include a lienholder (a lending institution that holds title to the mobile home).

The mobilehome endorsement amends the homeowners policy in regard to Section I—Property Coverages. The endorsement does not amend Section II—Liability Coverages. Therefore, the liability coverage under a mobilehome policy is the same as the liability coverage under a homeowners policy. However, because the endorsement changes the definition of "residence premises," any reference to the insured location in Section II would apply to the mobile home and other structures at the location shown on the declarations page.

A mobilehome policy can be endorsed with many of the typical homeowners endorsements. These endorsements are available only with the mobilehome policy:

- Actual Cash Value Mobilehome endorsement (MH 04 02)—This endorsement changes the loss settlement terms on the mobile home and other structures to apply an ACV basis rather than a replacement cost basis. Because carpeting and appliances are included as part of the mobile home (Coverage A), losses to such property would also be settled on an ACV basis. This endorsement is typically used by an insurer that prefers not to provide replacement cost coverage on the mobile home—for example, because the mobile home is old.
- Transportation/Permission to Move endorsement (MH 04 03)—This endorsement provides coverage for perils of transportation (collision, upset, stranding, or sinking) and coverage for the mobile home and other structures at the new location anywhere in the United States or Canada for a period of thirty days from the effective date of the endorsement. Losses are subject to a transportation peril deductible specified in the endorsement or elsewhere in the policy.
- Mobilehome Lienholder's Single Interest endorsement (MH 04 04)—This endorsement may be required by a lienholder. It provides coverage only to the lienholder for collision and upset transportation exposures, subject to numerous recovery conditions. It also provides coverage to the lienholder for any loss resulting from the owner's conversion, embezzlement, or secretion (concealment) of the mobile home.
- Property Removed Increased Limit endorsement (MH 04 06)—This endorsement allows the policyholder to increase the $500 limit, provided as an additional coverage under the ISO Mobilehome Endorsement (MH 04 01), for removing a mobile home that is endangered by an insured peril. Removal costs for a mobile home could easily exceed $500. This endorsement enables the policyholder to recover a greater share of the removal cost and encourages the policyholder to remove the property when necessary to avoid damage.
- Ordinance or Law Coverage endorsement (MH 04 08)—This endorsement enables the mobilehome policyholder to add ordinance or law coverage for an amount equal to a specified percentage of the Coverage A limit. The provisions of this endorsement are virtually identical to those in the Ordinance or Law additional coverage provision in the homeowners policy.
- Actual Cash Value Loss Settlement for Windstorm or Hail Losses to Mobilehome Roof Surfacing endorsement (MH 04 25)—This endorsement defines roof surfacing as shingles or tiles, cladding, materials covering the roof, roof flashing, and other material used for moisture protection. When roof surfacing is damaged by windstorm or hail, the

property loss settlement for the roof surfacing is made on an ACV basis. However, other buildings, such as those insured under Coverage A or B, may be settled at replacement cost (as stipulated by the policy conditions) except for the roof surfacing itself (as defined by the endorsement).
- Broadened Residence Premises Definition endorsement (MH 04 27)—This endorsement indicates a starting date and an ending date within the policy period during which the residency requirement will be temporarily removed. It is used when the insured will not be residing on the premises on the inception date of the policy period.

THE NATIONAL FLOOD INSURANCE PROGRAM

Both homeowners and dwelling policies exclude flood losses. To make flood insurance available to property owners, the federal government provides it through the National Flood Insurance Program (NFIP) at subsidized rates for both dwellings and commercial buildings, as well as for the contents of both.

Because of the catastrophic loss potential of a flood, the cost to insure against flooding would raise property insurance rates significantly. The National Flood Insurance Act of 1968 (42 U.S.C. §§4001 et seq.) established the NFIP. Administered by the Federal Emergency Management Agency (FEMA), this program makes federal flood insurance available in all states, the District of Columbia, Puerto Rico, Guam, and the United States Virgin Islands.

NFIP flood insurance cannot be written everywhere in the U.S., nor can coverage be placed on every type of building or contents. Such insurance can be written only on an eligible building, or on eligible contents within an eligible building, located within an eligible community.

Community Eligibility

Flood insurance may be written only in communities that FEMA has designated as participating communities in the NFIP. A community's residents become eligible for flood insurance in one of two ways:

- The community applies to the Federal Insurance Administration (FIA) to be included in the NFIP.
- FEMA determines that an area is flood-prone and notifies the community that it has one year to decide whether to join the NFIP. The FIA notifies those communities and offers to help deal with their flood problems should they elect to join the NFIP. A community that chooses not to join the NFIP is not eligible for federal flood assistance. A community must participate in the flood program within one year of notification or risk denial of federal or federal-related construction, acquisition, and other assistance.

If a community identified as flood-prone does not wish to participate in the NFIP, it has two options: contest the designation or simply choose not to participate. A community that successfully contests the flood-prone designation is still eligible for federal aid if a flood occurs. If a community chooses not to participate in the NFIP, its access to federal funds is limited.

Community participation in the NFIP is voluntary, although some states require NFIP participation as part of their floodplain management program. Each identified flood-prone community must assess its flood hazard and determine whether flood insurance and floodplain management would benefit its residents and economy.

Incentives and Programs

A community has many incentives for participating in the NFIP. A community that includes a **special flood hazard area (SFHA)** must participate in the NFIP program for NFIP flood insurance to be available within that community. Furthermore, the law restricts development by prohibiting any form of federal financial assistance for acquisition or construction purposes in an SFHA. For example, only NFIP participating communities are eligible for loans guaranteed by the Department of Veterans Affairs, insured by the Federal Housing Administration, or secured by the Rural Housing Service.

If a disaster occurs as a result of flooding in a nonparticipating community, no federal financial assistance can be provided for the permanent repair or reconstruction of insurable buildings in SFHAs. Eligible applicants for disaster assistance may, however, receive forms of disaster assistance that are not related to permanent repair and reconstruction of buildings. If a community is accepted into the NFIP within six months of a disaster, these limitations on federal disaster assistance are lifted.

Emergency Program

Once a community has submitted an application for flood insurance and all other necessary information to the FIA, the FIA prepares a **flood hazard boundary map** if one does not exist. A flood hazard boundary map is based on approximate data and identifies, in general, the SFHAs within a community. These maps not only identify flood hazard areas, but also define areas where people in SFHAs can buy coverages. They also are used in the NFIP's emergency program for floodplain management and insurance purposes. The FIA sends the community's map to the state coordinating agency, the state insurance commissioner, the regional FEMA flood specialist, and other federal agencies.

When a community first joins the NFIP, property owners in special flood hazard areas can purchase limited amounts of insurance at subsidized rates under the **emergency program**. Although the community is eligible under the emergency program, the FIA arranges for a detailed study of the community and its susceptibility to flood. The study results in the publication of a **Flood**

Special flood hazard area (SFHA)
Area that the NFIP has classified as being expected to experience flooding at least once in 100 years.

Flood hazard boundary map
A temporary map designed to identify flood-prone areas in the community.

Emergency program
Initial phase of a community's participation in the National Flood Insurance Program in which property owners in flood areas can purchase limited amounts of insurance at subsidized rates.

Flood Insurance Rate Map (FIRM)
A map that shows exact boundaries for special flood hazard areas, the various flood zones, and base flood elevations.

Insurance Rate Map (FIRM) that divides the community into specific zones to identify the probability of flooding in each zone.

The amount of coverage is based on the type of building or contents, and only four emergency premium rates apply:

- For residential buildings
- For residential contents
- For nonresidential buildings
- For nonresidential contents

These rates, which apply per $100 of insurance, are uniform in all eligible communities. The maximum limits are $35,000 for a single- or two- to four-family dwelling and $10,000 for its contents. Limits vary for states and territories that are not in the lower forty-eight states and for other types of residential and nonresidential buildings.

As an example of how emergency program coverage applies, consider Helen, who owns a home in a flood-prone area. Helen's home is valued at $60,000, and the contents of her home are worth $19,000. The community in which Helen lives has qualified under the emergency flood insurance program. Therefore, Helen can insure her house for $35,000 and the contents for $10,000, the maximum limits available.

Once the first layer of insurance coverage has been made available to individuals in a flood-prone area through the emergency program, they cannot obtain federal or federally insured loans for new construction unless they purchase flood insurance. New construction includes not only new buildings but also building repair, reconstruction, or improvement costs that amount to 50 percent or more of the building's market value before the project's start or, if the project is necessary to restore a damaged building, the building's market value at the time of the damage.

Regular Program

Under the emergency program, federally subsidized rates in limited amounts are available before completion of a community's Flood Insurance Study (FIS). After FEMA completes its assessment of a community's flood-prone area, establishes an accurate FIRM, and calculates actuarial rates, the community is promoted from the emergency program to the second and final NFIP phase, the **regular program**.

Full limits of coverage are available to communities in the regular program. The maximum limits are $250,000 for a single- or two- to four-family dwelling and $100,000 for its contents, with variations for nonresidential buildings. The conversion from the emergency program to the regular program depends on the community's enacting and enforcing floodplain management regulations. A community that fails to convert to the regular program is suspended from the program and is ineligible for any flood insurance.

Regular program
Second phase of the National Flood Insurance Program in which the community agrees to adopt flood-control and land-use restrictions and in which property owners purchase higher amounts of flood insurance than under the emergency program.

The example involving Helen demonstrates how the coverage limits of the regular program function. Helen's home is valued at $60,000, and her contents are worth $19,000. Under the emergency program, she has $35,000 of insurance on her home and $10,000 worth of coverage for its contents. Once her community is under the regular program, Helen can apply for and pay premiums for full coverage (maximum available limits of $250,000 for a single-family home and $100,000 for contents). The coverage is subject to deductibles, which apply separately to building and to contents. See the exhibit "NFIP Flood Insurance Coverage Limits."

NFIP Flood Insurance Coverage Limits

Coverage Type	Emergency Program Limit	Regular Program Limit
One- to four-family structure	$ 35,000*	$250,000
One- to four-family home contents	$ 10,000	$100,000
Other residential structures	$100,000**	$250,000
Other residential contents	$ 10,000	$100,000
Business structure	$100,000**	$500,000
Business contents	$100,000	$500,000
Renter contents	$ 10,000	$100,000

* In Alaska, Guam, Hawaii, and U.S. Virgin Islands, the amount available is $50,000.

** In Alaska, Guam, Hawaii, and U.S. Virgin Islands, the amount available is $150,000.

Adapted from the National Flood Insurance Program, Producer Manual, "Rating: I. Amount of Insurance Available," www.fema.gov/pdf/nfip/prodmanual200510/05rate.pdf (accessed January 1, 2018). [DA05801]

Flood Insurance Coverage

Three flood insurance policies are available:

- The dwelling form is used for any dwelling having an occupancy of no more than four families, such as single-family homes, townhouses, row houses, and individual condominium units.
- The general property form is used for all other occupancies—that is, multi-residential and nonresidential, except for residential condominium building associations.
- Residential condominium building associations are eligible for coverage under the residential condominium building association form.

All three policies protect insureds against direct losses to real and personal property from the flood peril. These policies do not cover indirect losses, such as additional living expenses; rent; rental value; and enforcement of any ordinance or law regulating the construction, repair, or demolition of buildings. See the exhibit "Standard Flood Insurance Policy Forms."

Waiting Period

To avoid adverse selection, the NFIP generally requires a thirty-day waiting period for new flood insurance policies and for endorsements that increase coverage on existing policies. Coverage does not become effective until thirty days after the date of the application or, in certain cases, thirty days after receipt of the application by the NFIP or its representative.

Absent the waiting period, property owners might delay purchase of flood insurance until an impending flood endangered their property. An exception to the waiting period is made for flood insurance that is purchased initially in connection with a new or an increased mortgage on a property. In such cases, the policy becomes effective at the time the mortgage becomes effective, provided that the policy is applied for at or before the transfer of ownership or date of mortgage.

For example, Alan purchases a home on riverfront property. The property settlement is scheduled for July 25 at noon, and the mortgage becomes effective at the same time. Alan submits an application and pays the appropriate premium to NFIP on July 24 for flood insurance on his new home. Alan's flood policy will become effective at noon on July 25 when the property is transferred to him. Because a new mortgage is involved, Alan's flood policy is not subject to the thirty-day waiting period.

Write-Your-Own (WYO) Program

The NFIP provides government-underwritten flood insurance through two mechanisms:

- A producer may write the business directly through the servicing representative designated by the FIA. FIA has elected to have state-licensed insurers' agents and brokers sell flood insurance to consumers. State regulators hold the insurers' agents and brokers accountable for providing NFIP customers with the same standards and level of service required of them in selling other lines of insurance. FIA underwrites the applications submitted by the servicing representatives and directly processes claims for losses under the policies. The servicing representatives receive a commission for the policies they write.

- A producer may place the business with an insurer participating in FIA's **Write-Your-Own (WYO) program**.

Write-Your-Own (WYO) program
A program allowing private insurers to write flood insurance under the National Flood Insurance Program (NFIP).

The WYO program is a cooperative undertaking of the insurance industry and the FIA. Insurers participating in the WYO program issue the majority of NFIP policies in force. WYO allows private insurers participating in the program to sell and service flood insurance under their own names.

Standard Flood Insurance Policy Forms

Policy Form	Description
Dwelling Policy Form	The Dwelling Policy Form may be issued to homeowners, residential renters, condominium unit owners, and owners of residential buildings containing two to four units. The policy provides building and/or contents coverage for: • A detached, single-family, non-condominium residence with incidental occupancy limited to less than 50 percent of the total floor area • A two- to four-family, non-condominium building with incidental occupancy limited to less than 25 percent of the total floor area • A dwelling unit in a residential condominium building • A residential townhouse/rowhouse • Manufactured mobile homes
General Property Policy Form	The General Property Policy Form may be issued to owners or lessees of non-residential buildings or units, or residential condominium buildings that are uninsurable under the Residential Condominium Building Association Policy (RCBAP). The policy provides building and/or contents coverage for these and similar "other residential" risks: • Hotel or motel with normal guest occupancy of six months or more • Apartment building • Residential cooperative building • Dormitory • Assisted-living facility It also can be used to cover these types of non-residential risks, among others: • Shop, restaurant, or other business • Mercantile building • Factory or warehouse • Nursing home
Residential Condominium Building Association Policy (RCBAP) Form	The Residential Condominium Building Association Policy Form may be issued to condominium associations to insure eligible residential condominium buildings.

Adapted from www.fema.gov/national-flood-insurance-program/standard-flood-insurance-policy-forms (accessed January 1, 2018). [DA05802]

Regardless of whether the NFIP or a WYO insurer issues a policy, the coverage provided is identical, and WYO insurers use exactly the same language used in policies that the NFIP issues directly. In the WYO program, the FIA determines rates, coverage limitations, and eligibility. The NFIP totally reinsures the coverage. Insurers receive an expense allowance for policies written and claims processed, while the federal government retains responsibility for losses. Insurers collect premiums, retain commissions, and use the remainder of the premiums to pay claims.

If flood losses exceed the amounts an insurer holds to pay flood claims, the federal government makes up the difference. However, if flood insurance premiums exceed losses, the insurer pays the excess to the federal government. Participating insurers issue and service flood insurance policies through their own operations and can retain approximately 30 percent of the premium to cover expenses.

The goals of the WYO program are to increase the number of flood policies written, to improve services, and to involve private insurers in the sale of flood insurance. More than 90 percent of all NFIP policies are written through private insurers under the WYO program.

Flood Insurance Reform

The Flood Insurance Reform Act of 2004 (Pub.L. 108-264) reformed the NFIP and the terms of the National Flood Insurance Act. It created a five-year pilot program to reduce losses to properties experiencing repetitive flood insurance claims. "Repetitively flooded" homes are those that have received four or more flood insurance claim payments of more than $5,000 each, with the cumulative amount exceeding $20,000, or two or more claim payments that cumulatively exceed the value of the property.

The reform act's preamble included congressional findings that quantify the motivation behind the act:

- The NFIP insured more than 4 million policyholders.
- About 48,000 properties in the program had experienced, within a ten-year period, two or more flood losses in which each loss was more than $1,000.
- About 10,000 repetitive-loss properties experienced two or three losses that cumulatively exceeded building value.
- These repetitive-loss properties cost taxpayers about $200 million annually.
- About 1 percent of insured properties accounted for 25 to 30 percent of claims.
- The majority of repetitive-loss properties were built before the 1974 implementation of floodplain management standards created under the original program and were eligible for subsidized flood insurance.

In an average year, fewer than 1 percent of all NFIP-insured properties represent 25 percent of all loss payments. This act provided a disincentive to property owners to live in repetitively flooded areas. Rather than encouraging rebuilding, the program provides repeatedly flooded homeowners with assistance in either elevating or moving their homes away from flood waters. Most mitigation offers involve elevation assistance. Those who refuse mitigation assistance pay for choosing to live in risky areas because refusal of a mitigation offer triggers the rate increases. Previously, many individuals and communities had no incentive to elevate their properties or to move.

To illustrate, the property owner of a repeatedly flooded property who refuses a reasonable mitigation offer will experience a flood insurance premium increase to 150 percent of the chargeable rate for the property at the time of the mitigation offer. Property owners can appeal rate increases following refusal of mitigation offers.

The act helps people move away from flood-prone areas by providing a $450 million increase over five years in an existing FEMA grant assistance program. The increase is to be used by local communities to relocate or elevate properties sustaining the most flood damage, saving an estimated $65 to $70 million annually by preventing or mitigating losses and paying for itself five to six years after program completion. In cases in which a buyout is the best option, the act includes a purchase offer and an appeals process, as well as safeguards to ensure continued home ownership.

Finally, the act reduces intensive development in repeatedly flooded areas to help restore the natural functions of floodplains, such as wildlife biodiversity and wetlands that absorb flood waters.

> ### ✅ Reality Check
>
> **Spring Rains Bring Disaster**
>
> *The flooding problems that AccuWeather.com feared would ensue across the Northeast have evolved. Unfortunately, flooding will remain an issue for many communities through the next several days.*
>
> *Melting snow was a significant contributor to the flooding across the central Appalachians. The arrival of colder air will slow the melting rate the rest of this weekend. A few mountain peaks will even have snowflakes.*[1]
>
> Individuals living in low-lying areas often look forward to spring with dread. Rather than thinking about warmer temperatures and budding flowers, these families and their communities start preparing for floods. This is particularly true when spring rains follow a winter season with heavy snow amounts. Thawing snow causes the ground to become saturated, and even minor downpours can cause significant flooding. A major storm system with many days of rain can only lead to disaster.
>
> In 2008, floods in large areas of the Midwest caused billions of dollars in property damage and loss of life. Cedar Rapids, Iowa, suffered significant effects from this storm. In 2009 and 2010, heavy rains combined with melting snow caused flooding in the Red River Valley and particularly in Fargo, North Dakota, resulting in substantial property damage losses. Similar weather patterns also caused spring flooding and property damage in states along the East Coast and into New England in 2007.
>
> Such events underscore the importance of flood insurance to individuals and businesses as well as the fact that the flood loss exposure is not limited to coastal locations.

[DA05803]

FAIR AND BEACHFRONT AND WINDSTORM PLANS

Urban riots in the 1960s and windstorms affecting increasingly popular coastal communities have resulted in excessive property damage and, consequently, restricted insurance availability. State governments have therefore been prompted to develop programs that enable homeowners to purchase insurance for urban and coastal properties that are not insurable in the voluntary insurance market.

Most residences are insured under either a homeowners or a dwelling policy provided by a private insurer in the voluntary market, through which organizations willingly insure properties with average and below-average exposure to losses. However, insurers are reluctant to insure some residential dwellings that have greater-than-average exposure to losses. Examples of such homes include those in urban and coastal areas that are exposed to windstorm losses. Several government plans are available to insure such homes, which previously were uninsurable or were insurable only through the nonstandard market at very high premiums. (The nonstandard market is composed of organizations that insure properties with above-average exposure to losses.)

Examining two types of insurance plans, Fair Access to Insurance Requirements (FAIR) plans and beachfront and windstorm plans, illustrates how state governments have responded to the needs of homeowners who have difficulty insuring properties that face greater-than-average exposure to losses. A review of each of these plans focuses on the purposes and operations of the plan as well as the property that is eligible and the coverages available under the plan.

FAIR Plans

FAIR plans make standard lines of property insurance available for exposures located in areas underserved by the voluntary market. Participating private insurers and state insurance authorities coordinate efforts to provide such coverage. Each state with a FAIR plan has enacted its own legislation in response to local market needs, so the coverage provided and the methods of operation vary considerably.

Purpose and Operation

Lenders usually will not extend credit for the purchase of property unless the owner can obtain adequate property insurance coverages. FAIR plans make insurance coverage available when insurers in the voluntary market cannot profitably provide coverage at a rate that is reasonable for policyholders and provide the needed support for credit. Urban areas that are susceptible to damage caused by riots and civil commotion pose greater-than-average risk of loss for insurers in the voluntary market and are candidates for state-run FAIR plans. Some FAIR plans provide certain coverages for owners of coastal properties that pose greater-than-average exposure to windstorm damage. The potential hazard of brush fires in some wooded, suburban areas may also pose greater-than-average risk for insurers; consequently, some FAIR plans provide coverage for homes located in hazardous brush areas.

A property owner who is unable to obtain basic property insurance in the voluntary market can apply for insurance to the state's FAIR plan through an authorized insurance agent or broker. The FAIR plan might operate as a policy-issuing **syndicate**, in which the plan issues the policies and the plan's staff handles underwriting, processing, and possibly claim handling. In several states, the FAIR plan contracts with one or more voluntary insurers to act as servicing organizations. For a percentage of premium, these insurers perform underwriting, policyholder service, and claim handling functions. In the majority of plans, all licensed property insurers are required to share payment for plan losses in proportion to their share of property insurance premiums collected within the state.

Syndicate
A group of insurers or reinsurers involved in joint underwriting to insure major risks that are beyond the capacity of a single insurer or reinsurer; each syndicate member accepts predetermined shares of premiums, losses, expenses, and profits.

Eligible Property

To be eligible for FAIR plan coverage, a property must be ineligible for coverage in the voluntary market, and the policyholder must have the property inspected by the FAIR plan administrator. Only property that meets the FAIR plan inspection criteria can be insured through the program. If the property fails to meet the basic safety levels (such as older houses in poor repair), owners can be required to make improvements as a condition for obtaining insurance. If the problems are not corrected, the state can deny insurance, provided the exposures are not related to the neighborhood location or to hazardous environmental conditions that are beyond the owner's control (such as a location next to a fireworks factory).

Under most FAIR plans, five types of exposures are considered uninsurable:

- Property that is vacant or open to trespass
- Property that is poorly maintained or that has unrepaired fire damage
- Property that is subject to unacceptable physical hazards, such as poor housekeeping or storage of flammable materials
- Property that violates a law or public policy, such as a condemned building (one that is considered unfit for human habitation)
- In some states, property that was not built in accordance with building and safety codes

Coverages

Some state FAIR plans provide limited homeowners coverage; however, most plans provide coverage only for fire and a limited number of perils, which often include vandalism, riot, and windstorm. Available limits of insurance and mandatory deductibles vary widely among plans.

When a policyholder wants greater coverage than that offered by the FAIR plan (such as when an expensive suburban home is written in the FAIR plan because it is located in a wooded area), a specialty insurer can write a **difference in conditions (DIC) policy**. This additional policy can cover risks of direct loss while excluding fire and the other perils covered under the FAIR plan policy. Because fire is the primary loss exposure for these suburban properties and FAIR plans provide coverage for that exposure, private insurers are willing to provide coverage for other perils.

Difference in conditions (DIC) policy, or DIC insurance
Policy that covers on an "all-risks" basis to fill gaps in the insured's commercial property coverage, especially gaps in flood and earthquake coverage.

Beachfront and Windstorm Plans

Properties located along the Atlantic and Gulf Coasts are especially vulnerable to windstorm loss. Serious winter storms can strike from the mid-Atlantic states northward, and the southern Atlantic and Gulf Coast states are subject to damage from hurricanes. Hurricanes in Florida and Hawaii have resulted in costly wind damage. Beginning in the late 1960s and beyond, insurers in the voluntary market withdrew from writing property coverage in coastal areas.

Because these properties were uninsurable, numerous coastal states responded by developing beachfront and windstorm plans. Use of these plans and FAIR plans providing windstorm coverages has increased with the popularity and value of coastal properties.

Purpose and Operation

Beachfront and windstorm plans are similar to FAIR plans in that they make insurance coverage available for properties with greater-than-average exposure to loss and provide the needed support for credit. Most beachfront and windstorm plans provide insurance coverage for windstorm and hail losses that cannot be obtained in the voluntary market. Under these plans, losses from tidal water are generally excluded and should be covered under a flood insurance policy.

The operation of beachfront and windstorm plans is similar to that of FAIR plans. Some states that offer beachfront and windstorm plans operate using a single servicing organization that provides the underwriting, policyholder services, and claim handling services. Others operate as policy-issuing syndicates in which the plan issues the policies and the plan's staff provides services. In all plans, insurers that write property coverages in that state are required to share in plan losses in proportion to their share of state property insurance premiums.

Eligible Property

Properties eligible for coverage under beachfront and windstorm plans must be ineligible for coverage in the voluntary market and must be located in designated coastal areas. Furthermore, in some states, they must be located within a certain distance of the shoreline. Owners of property in coastal areas can obtain coverage for most real and personal property through these plans. Eligibility for coverage under each plan requires that buildings constructed or rebuilt after a specified date conform to an applicable building code. In addition to dwellings and other residential buildings, mobilehomes may be eligible if they meet certain construction and tie-down requirements.

As with FAIR plans, beachfront and windstorm plans will not insure certain types of property:

- Property that is poorly maintained or that has unrepaired damage
- Property that is subject to poor housekeeping
- Property that violates a law or public policy

Coverages

The perils insured against in beachfront and windstorm plans vary by state, but many such plans provide only windstorm and hail coverage. In those states, policyholders must obtain other property coverages through the voluntary insurance market or other nonstandard markets. A few states offer broader property coverages through the plans. The maximum limits of insurance available, as well as deductibles, vary among states. State plans generally contain a provision that no application for new coverage or increase in limits will be accepted when a hurricane has formed within a certain distance of the beach area where the property is located.

In recent years, some states have merged their FAIR and beachfront and windstorm plans as the popularity of coastal properties and these plans has grown. Florida and Louisiana have merged their FAIR and windstorm plans to create state-run property insurance companies: Florida Citizens Property Insurance Company (CPIC) and Louisiana Citizens Property Insurance Corporation (Louisiana Citizens), respectively. These state plans provide coverage for a range of exposures throughout the state; however, the primary loss exposure is beachfront windstorms.

SUMMARY

Homeowners policies are a common type of residential insurance. Not all residences, however, are eligible for homeowners coverage, and not all insureds want or need a homeowners policy. For these residences and customers, a dwelling policy may be more appropriate. Dwelling policies may be written for one- to four-family owner- or tenant-occupied dwellings, dwellings under construction, or mobile homes at a permanent location.

Knowing how to apply the dwelling policy to the facts of a case is a critical skill. The first stage in this process is determining whether a loss is covered, and, if so, the second stage involves determining how much an insurer should pay for the loss.

ISO provides a mobilehome endorsement for homeowners policies to create a policy that covers typical homeowners exposures along with unique exposures and considerations associated with mobile homes. The mobilehome endorsement replaces definitions; modifies some coverages; and adds coverages, conditions, and a clause that meet the needs of mobilehome owners and their insurers. Additional ISO mobilehome endorsements may be used to further modify the policy.

The National Flood Insurance Act of 1968 established the National Flood Insurance Program (NFIP), administered by the Federal Emergency Management Agency (FEMA). Flood insurance may be written only in communities that FEMA has designated as participating communities in the NFIP. A community joins the NFIP by participation in two sequential programs: the emergency program and the regular program.

Amounts of insurance are limited for each program, and a waiting period applies. The Write-Your-Own (WYO) program is a cooperative undertaking between the NFIP and private insurers. In 2004, Congress passed the Flood Insurance Reform Act to create a five-year pilot program to reduce losses to properties experiencing repetitive flood insurance claims.

Fair Access to Insurance Requirements (FAIR) plans and beachfront and windstorm plans are provided by private insurers coordinating with state insurance authorities to provide insurance for properties with greater-than-average exposures to loss in areas underserved by the voluntary market. Property under both types of plans must meet state-specified eligibility requirements, and coverages under the plans usually correlate with the plan's purpose. FAIR plans for urban properties cover fire and a limited number of other perils, whereas beachfront and windstorm plans typically cover windstorm and hail. However, in recent years, the distinction has blurred, and some states have merged their plans.

ASSIGNMENT NOTE

1. "Latest on the Northeast Flooding," www.accuweather.com/blogs/news/story/26118/flood-situation-update-for-nor.asp (accessed March 14, 2010).

Direct Your Learning

8

Other Personal Property and Liability Insurance

Educational Objectives

After learning the content of this assignment, you should be able to:

▹ Summarize the coverages provided by personal inland marine policies.

▹ Compare the coverages typically provided for watercraft under each of the following:
- HO-3
- Personal Auto Policy
- Small boat policies
- Boatowners and yacht policies

▹ Summarize the coverage provided by the typical personal umbrella policy.

▹ Given a case describing a liability claim, determine the following:
- Whether the loss would be covered by a personal umbrella policy
- The dollar amount, if any, payable under the umbrella policy
- The dollar amount, if any, payable under the underlying insurance policies
- The dollar amount, if any, payable by the insured

Outline

Inland Marine Floaters

Personal Watercraft Insurance

Personal Umbrella Liability Insurance

Umbrella Coverage Case Study

Summary

Other Personal Property and Liability Insurance

INLAND MARINE FLOATERS

A homeowners policy may not provide adequate insurance for some types of personal property. Often, such coverage needs can be met with a personal inland marine policy.

Inland marine insurance is designed to cover property that has special value or that frequently moves ("floats") from one location to another. Although these types of personal property are covered under a homeowners policy, they are usually subject to certain limitations. Examples of such property include jewelry, furs, fine arts, silverware, cameras, stamp and coin collections, clothes and luggage, sports equipment, and musical instruments.

Characteristics and Components

The restrictive nature of some personal property coverages under a homeowners policy creates the need for personal inland marine policies, which can provide higher limits of insurance for losses of a particular type or that occur at a particular location. For example, homeowners coverage for theft of jewelry is frequently limited to $1,500 or less, homeowners coverage for coins and medals is limited to $200, and homeowners coverage is limited to $1,000 or less for personal property that is usually located at an insured's premises other than the **residence premises**.

Often, individuals who own these types of property insure them by adding an endorsement to the homeowners policy. Examples can illustrate some of the reasons people may prefer to obtain coverage under a separate personal inland marine policy:

- A couple owns highly valued paintings and sculptures, and their insurer is reluctant to provide the requested amount of coverage by endorsement to their homeowners policy.
- To insure his collection of costly cameras and lenses, an amateur photographer needs customized coverage that his homeowners policy cannot offer.
- A retired person owns valuable jewelry or golf equipment but lives in a retirement home and has no homeowners policy.
- A couple want to keep their homeowners premium separate from the premium on jewelry or collectibles because the homeowners premium is paid together with their mortgage payment.

Inland marine insurance
Insurance that covers many different classes of property that typically involve an element of transportation.

Residence premises
The place where the insured resides as identified in the policy declarations.

Although personal inland marine insurance can be customized to meet a variety of coverage needs, personal inland marine policies share these general characteristics:

- The coverage is tailored to the specific type of property to be insured, such as jewelry, cameras, or musical instruments.
- The insured may select the appropriate policy limits.
- Policies are often written without a deductible.
- Most policies insure property worldwide with special form coverage (open perils), subject to exclusions.

> **Open Perils Coverage**
> Special form (open perils) coverage was formerly known as "all risks of physical loss or damage," but as a result of expansive court decisions, the word "all" was dropped.

[DA00845]

In addition to the shared characteristics, personal inland marine policies have a shared structure consisting of three components:

- Declarations page
- Common Policy Provisions
- Coverage form

The Declarations page lists the named insured, the policy period, the premium, any deductible, any forms attached, and other options. Together with the Declarations page, the Common Policy Provisions and a coverage form complete the policy.

Common Policy Provisions

The Common Policy Provisions of the Insurance Services Office, Inc. (ISO) personal inland marine policy include an insuring agreement, definitions, exclusions, and conditions. (Each personal inland marine policy also contains other conditions and exclusions that are listed in the particular coverage form selected.)

The insuring agreement states that the insurer is providing the insurance described in the policy in return for the premium paid by the insured and the insured's compliance with policy provisions.

The Definitions section describes which terms in the policy refer to the insured and which refer to the insurer.

The Common Policy Provisions exclude coverage for losses caused directly or indirectly by several perils:

- War
- Nuclear hazard
- Governmental action (such as property seized by a public authority)
- Intentional loss
- Neglect

The Conditions section of the Common Policy Provisions specifies that insured property may have scheduled coverage by which articles or items are specifically listed. With certain exceptions, the amount paid for a covered loss is the least of four amounts:

- The actual cash value of the insured property at the time of loss or damage
- The amount for which the insured could reasonably be expected to have the property repaired to its condition immediately before loss
- The amount for which the insured could reasonably be expected to replace the property with property substantially identical to the lost or damaged article
- The amount of insurance stated in the policy

The Conditions section of the Common Policy Provisions also specifies that insured property may have unscheduled coverage by which articles are covered on a **blanket basis**, such as stamps or coins in a collection. Separate loss settlement conditions apply to unscheduled property, with limitations on an absolute dollar amount (such as $250 per any one stamp or coin) and limitations determined by the proportion of the loss amount to the amount of blanket insurance provided.

Blanket basis
A basis for insuring all items within a single amount of insurance without specifically identifying each item.

A personal inland marine policy generally extends coverage to the named insured and members of the insured's family living in the same household.

Coverages

In the ISO personal inland marine program, two types of coverage forms are available: specialized and general.

Specialized forms are used to cover a single category of personal property, such as outboard motors and boats, fine arts, cameras, or motorized golf carts. In addition to the wide variety of specialized ISO forms, insurers often offer their own versions of these forms, making personal inland marine a highly customized line of business.

General forms are broader and generic in nature. These three general forms are commonly used to provide coverage on a single form for many kinds of personal property:

- Personal Articles Standard Loss Settlement Form
- Personal Property Form
- Personal Effects Form

Personal Articles Standard Loss Settlement Form

The Personal Articles Standard Loss Settlement Form provides special form coverage for any of several classes of personal property, including jewelry, furs, cameras, musical instruments, silverware, golfer's equipment, fine arts, and stamp and coin collections. A specific amount of insurance is shown in the policy for each class of property or for each specific article. (An agreed value version of the endorsement is also available.)

In addition to the exclusions listed in the Common Policy Provisions, the Personal Articles Standard Loss Settlement Form excludes losses caused by wear and tear, deterioration, **inherent vice**, or insects or vermin.

Inherent vice
A quality of or condition within a particular type of property that tends to make the property destroy itself.

Additional exclusions apply to fine arts. The Personal Articles Standard Loss Settlement Form excludes coverage for breakage of fragile articles unless the breakage is caused by fire or lightning; explosion, aircraft, or collision; windstorm, earthquake, or flood; malicious damage or theft; or derailment or overturn of a conveyance.

Personal Property Form

The Personal Property Form provides special form coverage on unscheduled personal property owned or used by the insured and normally kept at the insured's residence. The form also provides worldwide coverage on the same property when it is temporarily away from the residence premises. The Personal Property Form can be used to insure thirteen classes of unscheduled personal property. Coverage applies when a separate amount of insurance is shown for any of these classes:

- Silverware
- Clothing
- Draperies and rugs
- Electronic equipment and musical instruments
- Objects of art
- China and glassware
- Cameras
- Sports equipment and supplies
- Major appliances
- Bedding and linen

- Furniture
- Professional personal property and all other personal property
- Building additions and alterations

The total amount of insurance in each category is the maximum limit of recovery for any single loss to property in that category. The total amount for the thirteen categories is the total policy limit. Many of the exclusions that apply in the Personal Articles Standard Loss Settlement Form also apply to the Personal Property Form.

Personal Effects Form

The Personal Effects Form is designed for frequent travelers. It provides special form coverage on personal property such as luggage, clothes, cameras, and sports equipment normally worn or carried by tourists and travelers. The form covers property worldwide, but only while the property is away from the insured's permanent residence. **Personal effects** are not covered when in storage. Many of the exclusions that apply in the Personal Articles Standard Loss Settlement Form and the Personal Property Form also apply to the Personal Effects Form.

Personal effects
Personal property items owned by individuals that are personal in nature, such as jewelry, clothes, wallets, or purses.

The Personal Effects Form specifically excludes these types of property:

- Accounts, bills, currency, deeds, securities, passports
- Animals
- Artificial teeth or limbs
- Contact lenses
- Bicycles, hovercraft, motors, motor vehicles, watercraft
- Household furniture
- Merchandise for sale or exhibition
- Physicians and surgeons instruments
- Salesperson's samples
- Theatrical property
- Contraband property in the course of illegal transport or trade

Because the homeowners policy covers personal property worldwide, most homeowners do not see any need to purchase coverage under an inland marine Personal Effects Form. Coverage is occasionally sold to those who are ineligible for homeowners policies or to travelers who want the broadest possible protection on their luggage and other personal effects.

PERSONAL WATERCRAFT INSURANCE

Many individuals and families own personal watercraft. Personal watercraft can vary from a small rowboat to a houseboat to a large ocean-going yacht. A variety of insurance policies are available to meet an insured's specific personal watercraft coverage needs.

The loss exposures associated with the ownership and operation of watercraft are many and varied. For example, one individual might own a small flat-bottomed fishing boat with a low horsepower motor and trailer, used only on inland lakes, while another family owns a large boat with twin outboard motors that they use on coastal waters. One individual may believe that the watercraft coverage provided by his homeowners policy and Personal Auto Policy (PAP) is adequate; another may believe that a small boat policy or boatowners or yacht policy is required.

Personal watercraft insurance, found under a variety of policies and coverage forms, is available to meet the insuring requirements of these individuals and families.

Personal watercraft includes small rowboats, canoes, outboard and inboard motorboats, sailboats, houseboats, and power yachts. The types of loss exposures and hazards arising from the ownership and operation of personal watercraft can help determine the appropriate type of insurance contract to treat the loss exposures.

Because watercraft are used on bodies of water for recreational purposes and few restrictions apply to their operation, certain personal insurance policies limit or restrict coverage. Watercraft property and liability loss exposures are not intended to be covered by homeowners and auto policies; therefore, other coverage forms are designed specifically to address watercraft loss exposures.

These personal insurance policies provide watercraft or watercraft-related coverage:

- HO-3
- PAP
- Small boat policies
- Boatowners and yacht policies

HO-3 Watercraft Coverage

Property and liability coverage for watercraft and related equipment is available under the HO-3. However, this coverage is limited by exclusions. Insurance professionals and insureds should be aware of these exclusions and policy limitations to ensure that the scope of the coverage provided adequately meets the insured's risk management requirements. If the homeowners watercraft coverage does not suffice, boatowners insurance or yacht insurance may be an appropriate alternative.

The HO-3 Section I—Property Coverages provides limited physical damage coverage under the homeowners policy that may be adequate for rowboats, canoes, and small outboard boats. Section I watercraft physical damage coverage includes these provisions:

- A $1,500 limit applies to watercraft, including trailers, furnishings, equipment. (For example, an insured's $800 kayak is fully covered for physical damage loss.)
- Coverage is provided on a named-perils-only basis. (The insured's kayak is covered only for the HO-3 Section I perils, not for **perils of the sea**.)
- Windstorm coverage applies (up to the $1,500 limit) only when the craft is inside a fully enclosed building.
- Theft coverage does not apply to the boat and motor when away from the residence premises; accessories, trailers, and other boating personal property are excluded from this coverage. (For example, the insured's kayak would not be covered if it is stolen from the roof of the insureds' car while the insureds are traveling.)

Perils of the sea
Accidental causes of loss that are peculiar to the sea and other bodies of water.

The liability section of the homeowners policy includes a detailed watercraft exclusion focusing on craft of certain size and length. HO-3 Section II watercraft liability coverage, by virtue of the scope of the exclusion, covers only certain limited watercraft loss exposures:

- All watercraft not powered, except sailing vessels twenty-six feet or more in length. Therefore, catamarans, sailboards, canoes, rowboats, and smaller sailboats (without auxiliary power) are covered.
- All inboard, inboard-outdrive, and sailing vessels not owned or rented by an insured. Therefore, any boat borrowed or operated on behalf of an insured is covered. For example, a forty-two-foot-long sailboat, if borrowed by the insured, would be covered for liability under the homeowners policy. The same boat, if rented or owned, would be excluded.
- All inboard and inboard-outdrive boats of fifty horsepower or less, rented to an insured.
- All sailing vessels with auxiliary power, if less than twenty-six feet long.
- All boats powered by an outboard motor or motors, unless the motor both exceeds twenty-five horsepower and was owned by an insured at policy inception. For example, a boat powered by a fifty-horsepower outboard motor and purchased by the insured during the homeowners policy period would be covered for liability until the renewal date.

The homeowners forms limit the watercraft covered under Section II—Liability coverages according to the type and length of the watercraft and the horsepower of the motor or motors. However, liability coverage for an otherwise excluded watercraft can be covered under Section II by attaching a Watercraft endorsement (HO 24 75) specifically scheduling the watercraft (boat and motor) for liability coverage.

Personal Auto Policy Watercraft Coverage

The PAP does not provide physical damage or liability coverage for watercraft, motors, or watercraft-related equipment. However, physical damage loss to a boat trailer is covered if the trailer is described on the PAP declarations page. For example, if the insured has other than collision coverage on a boat trailer and the trailer is stolen, the PAP provides coverage. Also, a boat trailer the insured owns is covered for liability (regardless of whether it is described on the declarations page) if it is designed to be pulled by a private passenger auto, pickup, or van. The PAP also covers nonowned trailers under Part D—Coverage for Damage to Your Auto to a limit of $1,500. Therefore, any boat trailer the insured may rent or borrow could be covered under the PAP for auto-related loss exposures.

If an insured has the use of any nonowned watercraft trailers that exceed $1,500 in value, or if the insured has any watercraft (which are excluded under the PAP), the appropriate coverage for such loss exposures can be provided under a small boat policy or boatowners or yacht policy.

Small Boat Policies

Because of the watercraft coverage limitations and exclusions in the homeowners and personal auto policies, boat owners usually opt to address the property and liability loss exposures related to their ownership and operation of watercraft by obtaining more comprehensive and appropriate coverage.

Small boat policies are designed to cover boats up to a certain size (such as twenty-six feet in length). Many insurers have developed such policies, which have various names (often with a nautical theme). Although small boat policies are not standard, they have certain common features regarding covered property, covered perils, and policy exclusions. See the exhibit "Personal Watercraft Coverage."

A small boat policy may cover the boat, motor, equipment, and trailer. Most small boat policies are written on an actual cash value (ACV) basis and contain a deductible, such as $100, $250, or more.

A small boat policy can be written to provide named perils or special form ("all-risks") coverage. Most small boat policies are of the special form type and cover all direct physical losses to covered watercraft except losses that are specifically excluded. Typical property loss exposures covered under a small boat policy could include damage to the boat as a result of a collision with another object, theft of the boat's motor or equipment, lightning damage to the boat's electrical and navigational equipment, and wind damage to a sail.

Generally, a small boat policy includes liability insurance for bodily injury, loss of life, illness, and property damage to third parties arising out of the ownership, maintenance, or use of the boat. Medical payments coverage is typically included for any insured person who sustains bodily injury while in, upon,

> **Personal Watercraft Coverage**
>
> Some types of small watercraft may not be classified as small boats and thus are not covered (on a minimal basis) under a homeowners policy or PAP or eligible for standard small boat insurance. Personal watercraft include high-speed, single-engine inboard-powered craft, such as Jet Skis, WaveRunners, and Sea-Doos. They are no more than sixteen feet in length and use a water-jet pump as their primary propulsion source. Specialty insurers provide personal watercraft coverage to insure these types of risks.
>
> Loss exposures related to these personal watercraft result from high performance and handling characteristics associated with their speed, power, and size, as well as from minimal operator and passenger protection because of the exposed nature of carriage. Additionally, operators and owners increasingly use personal watercraft for passenger float-towing or waterskiing, which pose additional loss exposures. For example, an individual with a Jet Ski may use a tow rope to tow several of his friends through the water on an inflated inner tube. He can be held liable for any injuries his friends suffer while being towed.
>
> Coverages commonly provided by personal watercraft coverage include these:
>
> - Physical damage coverage
> - Liability coverage
> - Medical payments coverage
> - Trailer coverage
> - Additional coverage options—uninsured boater, nonowned watercraft liability, and emergency towing

[DA00846]

boarding, or leaving the boat. Liability loss exposures covered under a small boat policy can include bodily injury liability for injuries sustained by passengers when a boat collides with a dock, property damage liability for damage to the dock resulting from the collision, and liability for medical payments to a patron on the dock who sustains a minor leg injury as a result of the collision.

These major exclusions are commonly found in small boat policies:

- General risks of direct loss—There is no coverage for loss caused by wear and tear, gradual deterioration, vermin and marine life, rust and corrosion, inherent vice, latent defect, mechanical breakdown, or extremes of temperature.
- Repair or service—Loss or damage from refinishing, renovating, or repair is not covered.
- Business pursuits—Coverage is excluded if the boat is used to carry passengers for compensation, if the boat or insured property is rented to others, or if the covered property is being operated in any official race or speed contest. For example, if an insured owns a small motorboat, coverage is excluded for the boat if he engages in official motorboat racing contests.

Boatowners and Yacht Policies

Many insurers have developed special boatowners package policies for boats up to a certain length, such as twenty-six feet. Larger boats are usually written under yacht policies. Both types of policies combine physical damage, liability, and medical payments coverage in one policy and typically include perils of the sea coverage. Other coverages are also frequently added to the policy, either by automatic inclusion or by endorsement. Although boatowners and yacht policies have no standard rules or forms, they contain certain common features, including warranties, persons insured, physical damage coverage, liability coverage, medical payments coverage, and other coverages.

Personal watercraft insurance generally contains several **warranties**. If a warranty is violated, higher premiums may be required, or the coverages may not apply, depending on the warranty. These are the major personal watercraft insurance warranties:

- Pleasure use—The insured warrants that the boat will be used only for private, pleasure purposes and will not be hired or chartered unless the insurer approves. For example, an insured with a boatowners policy could jeopardize his coverage if he routinely charters his boat for deep-sea fishing trips.

- Seaworthiness—The insured warrants that the boat is in a seaworthy condition. For example, an insured who fails to properly maintain his boat in order to maintain its seaworthiness could jeopardize his coverage.

- Lay-up period—The insured warrants that the boat will not be in operation during certain periods, such as during the winter months. The lay-up period is usually shown on the declarations page. For example, an insured may have a lay-up period from November 1 to April 1 of each policy year.

- Navigational limits—These warranties limit the use of the vessel to a certain geographical area (for example, inland waterways, and coastal areas only). Navigation limits are stated on the declarations page of the policy. For example, if an insured wishes to operate outside the stated navigational limits, permission must be obtained from the insurer (and an additional premium may be charged) for coverage to apply.

The insured includes those named on the declarations page, resident relatives of the household, and persons under the age of twenty-one in the insured's care. The insured's paid captain and crew are also considered insureds. Other persons or organizations using the boat without a charge are covered provided the named insured gives permission. For example, an insured may lend her boat to a local youth organization for a day on the water. The organization would be considered insureds under a typical boatowners or yacht policy.

Boatowners and yacht policies contain physical damage coverage (also called **hull insurance**) on either a named perils or a special form basis covering the boat or "hull," equipment, accessories, motor, and trailer. Because a special form policy covering risks of direct physical loss or damage is broader than a

Warranty
A promise made by an insured that guarantees compliance with the insurer's conditions.

Hull insurance
Insurance that covers physical damage to vessels, including their machinery and fuel but not their cargo.

named perils policy, the coverages provided by insurers for watercraft hull coverage can vary greatly.

Certain property damage exclusions are commonly found in boatowners and yacht policies:

- Wear and tear, gradual deterioration, rust, corrosion, mold, wet or dry rot, marring, denting, scratching, inherent vice, latent or physical defect, insects, animal or marine life, weathering, and dampness of atmosphere. For example, the coverage is not designed to protect against lack of routine maintenance and the products of age and weathering.
- Mechanical breakdown or faulty manufacturing, unless the loss was caused by fire or explosion.
- Freezing and thawing of ice, unless the insured has taken reasonable care to protect the property. For example, an insured could install a circulating water system to keep the water from freezing around the boat in icy conditions.
- Loss that occurs while the boat is used in any official race or speed contest. However, most watercraft policies do not exclude sailboat racing.
- Intentional loss caused by an insured.
- War, nuclear hazard, and radioactive contamination.

Boatowners and yacht policies can be written on either a replacement cost basis or an ACV basis. Because replacement cost coverage offers better protection for the insured than coverage on an ACV basis, this difference in valuation is important in any comparison of boat policies. Yachts are typically insured on an agreed value basis. Agreed value means that in the event of a total loss, the insurer pays the insured the full amount stated in the policy declarations as the total, or agreed, value of the hull. Small boats are usually written with a $100 to $250 deductible. Medium to large boats often carry a deductible equal to 1 percent to 10 percent of the insured value of the watercraft.

Basic watercraft liability policies typically cover only bodily injury and property damage perils related to the operation of watercraft. In addition, boatowners and yacht policies typically include a form of liability coverage called **protection and indemnity (P&I) insurance**. P&I is a broader form of bodily injury and property damage coverage that protects an insured against bodily injury and property damage liability arising from the ownership, maintenance, or use of the boat, and also against crew injuries, wreck removal, and negligence for an unseaworthy vessel. Defense costs arising from any claim, including suits from third parties, are also covered.

Protection and indemnity (P&I) insurance

Insurance that covers shipowners against various liability claims due to operating the insured vessel.

This list represents most of the exclusions that insurers include in boatowners and yacht policies:

- Intentional injury or illegal activities.
- Renting the watercraft to others or carrying persons or property for a fee without the insurer's permission.
- Liability arising out of water-skiing, parasailing (a sport using a type of parachute to sail through the air while being towed by a powerboat), or other airborne or experimental devices.
- Using watercraft (except sailboats in some policies) in any official race or speed test.
- Losses covered by a workers compensation or similar law. (For example, any of the insured's employees who are injured in the course of their duties—such as a captain injured while preparing a boat for a sail—and who should otherwise be covered by workers compensation or a similar law are excluded from coverage.)
- Bodily injury or property damage arising out of transportation of the boat on land. (Coverage can be included with the payment of an additional premium.)
- Liability assumed under a contract.
- Injury to an employee if the employee's work involves operation or maintenance of the watercraft (unless otherwise covered by the P&I coverage).
- Business use.
- Discharge or escape of pollutants unless sudden or accidental. (For example, coverage would not apply to a yacht that is slowly leaking diesel fuel into the water where it is docked, causing possible pollution damage.)
- War, insurrection, rebellion, and nuclear perils.

Medical payments coverage under boatowners and yacht insurance policies includes coverage for such bodily-injury related expenses as medical, surgical, x-ray, dental, ambulance, hospital, professional nursing, and funeral services; and for first aid rendered at the time of the accident. An insured does not have to be at fault for the coverage to apply. Coverage is usually limited to a maximum of $1,000 to $5,000 per person per occurrence, although this can be increased for an additional premium.

Covered persons include the insured, family members, or any other person (except employees of the insured, trespassers, and racing participants) while in, upon, boarding, or leaving the covered watercraft. Therefore, medical payments coverage in boat policies is similar to that provided in personal auto policies because it covers the insured and family members. In contrast, medical payments coverage in homeowners policies does not cover the insured or resident family members (and is thus named "medical payments to others").

Additional coverages may be added to or provided in boatowners and yacht policies:

- **Uninsured boaters coverage** may be offered by endorsement or as a coverage option by insurers to boatowners. Coverage is structured similarly to the uninsured motorists coverage found in the PAP, with certain limitations and restrictions specific to the scope of watercraft loss exposures. For example, uninsured boaters coverage typically excludes bodily injury caused by an individual's occupying or being struck by any watercraft owned by the insured or by any family member insured under the policy.
- The insured's liability for injury to maritime workers (except crew members) injured in the course of employment who are covered under the **United States Longshore and Harbor Workers' Compensation Act** and for which the insured might be held responsible may be included under watercraft liability coverage.
- The legal obligation of the insured to remove a wrecked or sunken vessel following a loss may be included in a boatowners or yacht policy.
- Bodily injury or property damage arising out of transportation of the boat on land can usually be included in a boatowners or yacht policy for an additional premium.
- Damage to or loss of the insured's personal effects, for a limited amount, may be included in a boatowners or yacht policy. Personal effects coverage applies to property not intended for the normal operation of the boat, such as an insured's portable television, stereo, camera, or other personal items.
- The cost of commercial towing and assistance, for a limited amount, may be included in or added to the policy.
- Hurricane protection coverage may be available by endorsement to reimburse boatowners for the costs of removing their watercraft from the water if a hurricane is approaching or to cover the costs of moving the boat to a safe harbor because of an approaching storm. For example, if a hurricane is approaching the marina area where an insured's boat is docked, hurricane protection coverage would reimburse the insured the costs of hiring a professional to move the boat to a safe location, on the basis that the cost of doing so would be significantly less than the potential total loss of the boat in the hurricane.

Uninsured boaters coverage
Coverage for the insured's bodily injury incurred in a boating accident caused by another boat's owner or operator who is uninsured and who is legally responsible for the injury; similar to the PAP's uninsured motorists coverage.

United States Longshore and Harbor Workers' Compensation Act (LHWCA)
A federal statute that eliminates the right of most maritime workers (other than crew members of vessels) to sue their employers and, in return, requires such employers to provide injured or ill workers with benefits like those provided by state workers compensation statutes.

PERSONAL UMBRELLA LIABILITY INSURANCE

Most personal umbrella policies provide not only higher limits but also broader coverage than underlying personal insurance policies.

A personal umbrella policy provides liability protection to insureds for amounts over the liability limits on existing homeowners, personal auto, and watercraft policies. Lawsuits arising from personal liability exposures can result in catastrophically high settlements that may exceed the liability limits of these existing policies. Once the liability limits under these policies are exhausted, the insured might be forced to pay a substantial amount from personal assets. Therefore, most individuals and families may benefit from having a personal umbrella policy.

Purposes of Personal Umbrella Coverage

A personal umbrella policy is designed to provide bodily injury, personal injury, and property damage liability coverage in case of a catastrophic claim, lawsuit, or judgment. Umbrella coverage provides additional liability limits over any underlying insurance policies, such as homeowners Section II—Liability Coverages, personal auto liability, and personal watercraft liability policies. A condition of umbrella coverage is that the insured must maintain certain underlying policies with specified limits. If the loss is covered by one of these underlying policies, the umbrella insurer pays only after these limits are exhausted. See the exhibit "Relationship of Personal Umbrella Policy to Typical Underlying Coverages."

The personal umbrella policy also typically provides drop-down coverage, which is broader than the underlying coverage. When the underlying insurance does not apply to a particular loss and the loss is not excluded by the umbrella coverage, the umbrella coverage "drops down" to cover the entire loss, less a self-insured retention (SIR). Usually the retention (which is similar to a deductible) is $250, but it can be as high as $10,000. The SIR applies only when the loss is not covered by an existing underlying policy.

The amount of personal umbrella coverage purchased typically ranges from $1 million to $10 million. The policy covers the named insured, resident relatives, and usually persons using (with the insured's permission) cars, motorcycles, recreational vehicles, or watercraft owned by or rented to the named insured. Also, persons younger than twenty-one who are in the care of the named insured or of a resident relative generally are covered.

Personal Umbrella Coverages

Because each insurance company has its own forms and rules, there is no single standard umbrella policy; however, most insurers' umbrella policy provisions are similar. The Insurance Services Office, Inc. (ISO) Personal Umbrella Liability Policy is a widely used form and includes a listing of definitions, the Insuring Agreement, Exclusions, and General Provisions.

Insuring Agreement

The ISO Personal Umbrella Liability Policy Insuring Agreement states that the policy covers bodily injury and property damage as well as personal injury for which an insured becomes legally liable. The definitions of these coverages are similar to those contained in other liability policies. Bodily injury is defined as bodily harm, sickness, or disease, including required care, loss

Relationship of Personal Umbrella Policy to Typical Underlying Coverages

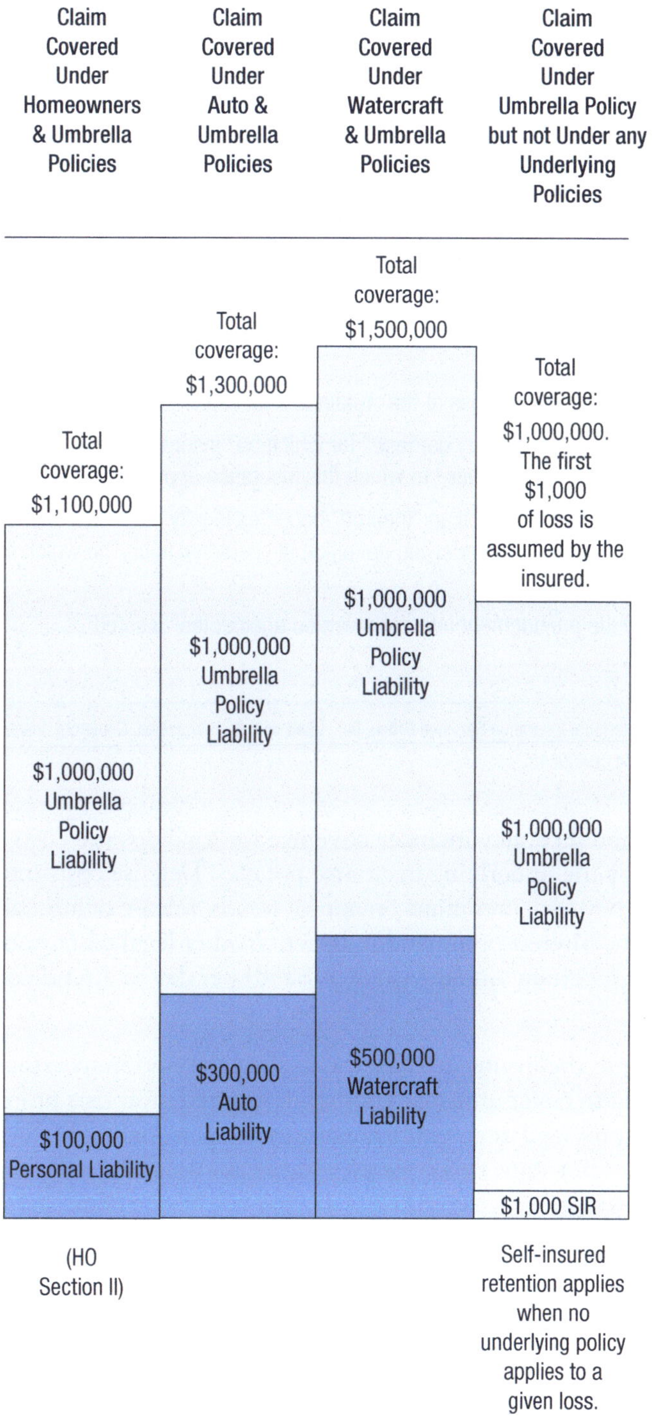

Claim Covered Under Homeowners & Umbrella Policies	Claim Covered Under Auto & Umbrella Policies	Claim Covered Under Watercraft & Umbrella Policies	Claim Covered Under Umbrella Policy but not Under any Underlying Policies
Total coverage: $1,100,000	Total coverage: $1,300,000	Total coverage: $1,500,000	Total coverage: $1,000,000. The first $1,000 of loss is assumed by the insured.
$1,000,000 Umbrella Policy Liability	$1,000,000 Umbrella Policy Liability	$1,000,000 Umbrella Policy Liability	$1,000,000 Umbrella Policy Liability
$100,000 Personal Liability	$300,000 Auto Liability	$500,000 Watercraft Liability	$1,000 SIR
(HO Section II)			Self-insured retention applies when no underlying policy applies to a given loss.

of services, and death. Property damage is defined as physical injury to or destruction of tangible property and includes loss of use of the property. In addition to bodily injury and property damage, the definition of personal injury in the umbrella policy includes false arrest, false imprisonment, wrongful entry or eviction, malicious prosecution or humiliation, libel, slander, defamation of character, invasion of privacy, and assault and battery not intentionally committed or directed by a covered person. See the exhibit "Personal Umbrella Liability Policy."

Personal Umbrella Liability Policy

PERSONAL UMBRELLA LIABILITY POLICY

II. Coverages

A. Insuring Agreement

We will pay damages, in excess of the "retained limit", for:

1. "Bodily injury" or "property damage" for which an "insured" becomes legally liable due to an "occurrence" to which this insurance applies; and

2. "Personal injury" for which an "insured" becomes legally liable due to one or more offenses listed under the definition of "personal injury" to which this insurance applies.

Damages include prejudgment interest awarded against the "insured".

Includes copyrighted material of Insurance Services Office, Inc., used with its permission. Copyright, Insurance Services Office, Inc., 2014. [DA00848]

The personal umbrella policy includes coverage for legal defense costs that are not payable by the underlying insurance policies. Defense costs include payment of attorney fees, premiums on appeal bonds, release of attachment bonds, court costs, interest on unpaid judgments, other legal costs, and loss of earnings up to a certain amount (such as $250) per day to attend court hearings.

Some states require the insurer to offer the insured the option to extend the personal umbrella to cover uninsured and underinsured motorists protection. This coverage is provided as an endorsement to the personal umbrella policy. If the insured does not want this coverage, state laws usually require that he or she reject it in writing.

Exclusions

Because personal umbrella policies provide broad coverage, certain important exclusions usually are included:

- Intentional injury—An act committed or directed by a covered person with intent to cause personal injury or property damage.
- Business property and pursuits—Liability arising out of a business activity or business property, other than claims involving an insured's use of a private passenger automobile.
- Public or livery conveyance—Liability arising out of the operation of an auto while being used as a public or livery conveyance, including any period while logged into a transportation network (TNC) platform.
- Professional liability—Rendering or failure to render professional services.
- Aircraft—All liability arising out of the ownership, maintenance, use, loading, or unloading of aircraft.
- Watercraft—Coverage for large watercraft is excluded except for the insured's liability for smaller boats that are normally covered by the underlying homeowners policy or for watercraft covered by underlying insurance.
- Recreational vehicles—Liability arising out of the ownership, maintenance, or use of recreational vehicles, such as golf carts and snowmobiles, unless there is underlying insurance.
- Transmission of any communicable diseases—Liability that results from the insured's transmission of a communicable disease.
- Directors and officers—Liability coverage for acts of directors or officers of a corporation except for officers and directors of a not-for-profit organization.
- Damage to the insured's property—Damage to property an insured owns.
- Workers compensation—Any obligation for which the insured is legally liable under a workers compensation, disability benefits, or similar law.
- Nuclear energy—Applies to insureds who are or should be insured under nuclear energy policies.

Conditions

These are among the most important conditions in the personal umbrella policy:

- The insured must maintain the underlying insurance coverages and limits shown in the declarations. If underlying coverage is not maintained, the policy will pay no more than would have been covered if the underlying insurance was in effect.
- The insured must give the insurer written notice of loss as soon as practicable.

- The umbrella policy is excess over any other insurance, whether collectible or not.
- The policy territory is worldwide.

UMBRELLA COVERAGE CASE STUDY

Individuals and families use insurance to mitigate risk of financial loss. A sound plan for personal risk management will include knowledge of what potential loss circumstances are covered by a personal umbrella policy and applicable underlying policies.

Many individuals and families typically purchase several insurance policies, such as personal auto insurance and homeowners insurance. However, they may encounter loss circumstances for which they are held liable and for which their underlying policies provide no coverage. They might also face a claim whose value exceeds the limits of the underlying policy. Such losses may be covered by an umbrella policy.

Case Facts

How does an umbrella policy, in concert with underlying coverages like personal auto and homeowners policies, respond to high-value claims?

Matt and Zoey are married and own a single-family home. They also own three cars: a new minivan driven mainly by Matt, a hybrid subcompact driven to work by Zoey, and a ten-year-old pickup truck they use mostly on weekends.

On a Saturday afternoon, Matt was driving the pickup truck to take bulky household items to donate to a charity-sponsored thrift store. In the store parking lot, Matt mistakenly stepped on the gas pedal when he meant to use the brake. He lost control of the truck and crashed into a group of customers who had just exited the store. Matt called 911 and his insurance agent immediately and complied with all other policy conditions.

No one was killed in the accident, but five persons sustained serious injuries. Matt was found to be completely liable for the $1.8 million in medical bills incurred by those injured.

Shortly after the accident, television and newspaper reporters came to Matt and Zoey's house for interviews about the incident. Zoey fielded their questions and angrily suggested that the police officer responding to the accident had advised the injured persons to exaggerate their injuries in order to extract a bigger liability award. The police officer denied having done so and sued Zoey for slander. A jury found Zoey liable and awarded $1 million to the police officer for slander.

Matt and Zoey's home is insured under a Homeowners 3—Special Form (HO-3) policy for $370,000. Their homeowners policy includes liability coverage with a $500,000 per occurrence limit and lists Zoey and Matt as named insureds.

Like the homeowners policy, their personal auto policy (PAP) carries a $500,000 per occurrence liability limit. Both Zoey and Matt are listed as named insureds.

Matt and Zoey were concerned about the risk of financial loss that could result from bodily injury, personal injury, or property damage liability in case of a catastrophic claim, lawsuit, or judgment. To address their concern, they purchased a personal umbrella policy with both Zoey and Matt listed as named insureds. Their umbrella policy provides $2 million of liability coverage, with a $500,000 deductible that applies to exposures retained under the PAP or homeowners policies. A $2,000 deductible applies to events covered by the umbrella policy but not covered by the PAP or homeowners policy.

An umbrella policy's coverage generally begins where the primary policies' coverage ends. A well-designed insurance plan will coordinate the umbrella coverage with the policy limits of the underlying primary policies. For instance, if the PAP and HO-3 policies each have $300,000 limits of liability, the umbrella policy should have a $300,000 deductible. Some umbrella policies use the term "deductible." Others (such as the ISO umbrella form) use the term "retained limit." The terms have the same meaning in umbrella insurance.

All three of Matt and Zoey's policies—PAP, HO-3, and personal umbrella—were paid up and in force at the time of the accident. See the exhibit "Case Facts."

Case Facts

Insureds	Matt and Zoey
Types of policies and coverage limits	• HO-3 $500,000 per occurrence • PAP $500,000 per occurrence • Umbrella $2 million per occurrence
Endorsements that affect this case	None
Other policy information	• Umbrella—$500,000 deductible for exposures retained under the PAP or HO-3 • Umbrella—$2,000 for events not covered by the PAP or HO-3
Background	• The insureds have complied with the policy conditions. • The auto accident resulted in a $1.8 million liability loss. • The slander suit resulted in a $1 million liability loss.

[DA05629]

Case Analysis Tools

To determine whether Matt and Zoey's insurance policies provide coverage for the auto accident or the slander suit, the insurance or risk management professional should have copies of the policy forms and any applicable endorsements indicated on the Declarations pages of the policies. See the exhibit "Homeowners Policy Declarations."

To determine whether a policy covers a loss, many insurance professionals apply the DICE method. ("DICE" is an acronym for categories of policy provisions: declarations, insuring agreement, conditions, and exclusions.) The DICE method has four steps:

1. Review of the declarations page to determine whether it covers the person or the property at the time of the loss
2. Review of the insuring agreement to determine whether it covers the loss
3. Review of policy conditions to determine compliance
4. Review of policy exclusions to determine whether they preclude coverage of the loss

Each of these four steps is used in every case. Other categories of policy provisions should be examined. For example, endorsements and terms defined in the policy should be reviewed in relation to the declarations, insuring agreement, exclusions, and conditions.

Determination of Coverage

To determine whether the PAP, the HO-3, and/or the umbrella policy provide coverage for Matt's $1.8 million liability from the accident and for Zoey's $1 million liability from the slander suit, the insurance professional can apply the four steps of the DICE method. See the exhibit "Umbrella Policy Declarations."

Auto Accident

The first DICE step includes determination of whether the driver or vehicle is described on an insured's Declarations page and whether the accident occurred during the policy period. In this case, Matt and Zoey's PAP includes the pickup truck as a covered auto, and both Matt and Zoey are insureds under the policy. The umbrella policy Declarations page shows Matt and Zoey as insureds and notes the number of eligible automobiles. The HO-3 shows Matt and Zoey as insureds for liability coverage, but does not list any vehicles.

The second DICE step is to determine whether the events have triggered coverage under the insuring agreement of one or more of their three insurance policies. In the PAP insuring agreement, the insurer agrees to pay damages for bodily injury and property damage for which an insured is legally responsible because of an auto accident. Accidentally driving the truck into the pedestrians qualifies as an auto accident, and the resultant injuries qualify as bodily injury. See the exhibit "Part A—Liability Coverage Insuring Agreement."

Homeowners Policy Declarations

Homeowners Policy Declarations

POLICYHOLDER: Matt and Zoey
(Named Insured) 216 Brookside Drive
Anytown, USA 40000

POLICY NUMBER: 296 H 578661

POLICY PERIOD: **Inception:** March 30, 20X1
Expiration: March 30, 20X2

Policy period begins 12:01 A.M. standard time at the residence premises.

FIRST MORTGAGEE AND MAILING ADDRESS:

Federal National Mortgage Assn.
C/O Mortgagee, Inc.
P.O. Box 5000
Businesstown, USA 55000

We will provide the insurance described in this policy in return for the premium and compliance with all applicable policy provisions.

SECTION I COVERAGES	LIMIT	
A—Dwelling	$ 370,000	**SECTION I DEDUCTIBLE:** $ 250
B—Other Structures	$ 37,000	(In case of loss under Section I, we cover
C—Personal Property	$ 185,000	only that part of the loss over the
D—Loss of Use	$ 111,000	deductible amount shown above.)

SECTION II COVERAGES	LIMIT	
E—Personal Liability	$ 500,000	Each Occurrence
F—Medical Payments to Others	$ 1,000	Each Person

CONSTRUCTION: Masonry Veneer **NO. FAMILIES:** One **TYPE ROOF:** Approved

YEAR BUILT: 1990 **PROTECTION CLASS:** 7 **FIRE DISTRICT:** Cook Township

NOT MORE THAN 1000 FEET FROM HYDRANT

NOT MORE THAN 5 MILES FROM FIRE DEPT.

FORMS AND ENDORSEMENTS IN POLICY: HO 00 03, HO 04 61

POLICY PREMIUM: $ 350.00 **COUNTERSIGNATURE DATE:** March 1, 20X1 **AGENT:** A.M. Abel

Copyright, ISO Properties, Inc. [DA05630]

Umbrella Policy Declarations

COVERGOOD MUTUAL INSURANCE COMPANY
UMBRELLA POLICY DECLARATIONS
(excerpts)

Named Insured and Address
Matt and Zoey
216 Brookside Drive
Anytown, USA 40000

Policy Period
03/30/20X1 to 03/30/20X2
12:01 A.M. Standard Time

This policy covers the residence premises at the location shown above.

Umbrella Policy Limit of Liability
$2,000,000 per occurrence

Deductibles
The deductible amounts shown herein remain applicable in the event that the underlying insurer is unable to pay for any reason, such as insolvency:

Retained Exposure Type	*Deductible*
Auto Liability	$500,000 per occurrence
Personal or Homeowners Liability	$500,000 per occurrence
Watercraft Liability	$500,000 per occurrence

A $2,000 deductible will apply to any occurrence that is covered by this umbrella policy AND is not covered by any underlying insurance. The $2,000 deductible applies only if the named insured maintains the underlying insurance for the loss exposures listed below under "Eligible Loss Exposures" and has complied with the conditions of the underlying policies.

Eligible Loss Exposures
The named insured declares that, as of the effective date of this personal umbrella policy, all eligible loss exposures are listed herein:

Eligible Loss Exposure	*Number*
Automobiles	3
Residences	1
Watercraft	0

Underlying Insurance Policies
The named insured declares that, as of the effective date of this personal umbrella policy, these underlying insurance policies are in force:

Policy Type	*Insurance Company*	*Policy Number*
Personal Auto Liability	Roadworthy Risk Co.	RRC-658213
Homeowners	Covergood Mutual	CM45671

[DA05631]

Part A—Liability Coverage Insuring Agreement

PART A – LIABILITY COVERAGE

INSURING AGREEMENT

A. We will pay damages for "bodily injury" or "property damage" for which any "insured" becomes legally responsible because of an auto accident. Damages include prejudgment interest awarded against the "insured". We will settle or defend, as we consider appropriate, any claim or suit asking for these damages. In addition to our limit of liability, we will pay all defense costs we incur. Our duty to settle or defend ends when our limit of liability for this coverage has been exhausted by payment of judgments or settlements. We have no duty to defend any suit or settle any claim for "bodily injury" or "property damage" not covered under this policy.

B. "Insured" as used in this Part means:

1. You or any "family member" for the ownership, maintenance or use of any auto or "trailer".

2. Any person using "your covered auto".

3. For "your covered auto", any person or organization but only with respect to legal responsibility for acts or omissions of a person for whom coverage is afforded under this Part.

4. For any auto or "trailer", other than "your covered auto", any other person or organization but only with respect to legal responsibility for acts or omissions of you or any "family member" for whom coverage is afforded under this Part. This Provision (B.4.) applies only if the person or organization does not own or hire the auto or "trailer".

Includes copyrighted material of Insurance Services Office, Inc., with its permission. Copyright, ISO Properties, Inc., 2003. [DA05632]

In the HO-3 Section II insuring agreement, the insurer agrees to pay damages for bodily injury and property damage for which an insured is legally responsible because of a covered occurrence. The insuring agreement in the personal umbrella liability policy covers bodily injury and property damage for which an insured becomes legally liable. For the second DICE step, the auto accident appears to trigger coverage under the PAP, HO-3, and umbrella policies. See the exhibit "Personal Umbrella Liability Policy."

The third DICE step is to determine whether all policy conditions, such as timely reporting of the loss to the insurer, have been met. For the purposes of this case study, assume that they have been.

The fourth DICE step is to determine whether one or more exclusions preclude coverage that the insuring agreements have granted. Section II exclusions of the HO-3 note that liability coverage does not apply to bodily injury or property damage arising out the ownership, maintenance, or use of motor vehicles owned by the insured. Therefore, there is no coverage under the HO-3 for the auto accident.

> **Personal Umbrella Liability Policy**
>
> PERSONAL UMBRELLA LIABILITY POLICY
>
> II. Coverages
>
> A. Insuring Agreement
>
> We will pay damages, in excess of the "retained limit", for:
>
> 1. "Bodily injury" or "property damage" for which an "insured" becomes legally liable due to an "occurrence" to which this insurance applies; and
>
> 2. "Personal injury" for which an "insured" becomes legally liable due to one or more offenses listed under the definition of "personal injury" to which this insurance applies.
>
> Damages include prejudgment interest awarded against the "insured".

Includes copyrighted material of Insurance Services Office, Inc., used with its permission. Copyright, Insurance Services Office, Inc., 2014. [DA00848]

Slander Lawsuit

To determine whether the PAP, the HO-3, and/or the umbrella policy provide coverage for Zoey's $1 million liability from the slander suit, the insurance professional can again apply the four steps of the DICE method.

The first DICE step includes determination of whether the party involved is described on an insured's PAP, HO-3, or umbrella Declarations page and whether the accident occurred during the policy period. In this case, Zoey is an insured under all three policies, and the incident occurred during the policy period of all three policies.

The second DICE step is to determine whether the event has triggered coverage under the insuring agreement of one or more of the three insurance policies. In the PAP insuring agreement, the insurer agrees to pay damages for bodily injury and property damage for which an insured is legally responsible because of an auto accident. Zoey's alleged slander does not qualify as an auto accident.

In the HO-3 Section II insuring agreement, the insurer agrees to pay damages for bodily injury and property damage for which an insured is legally responsible because of a covered occurrence. Importantly, the HO-3 definition of "bodily injury" does not include slander. Zoey's alleged slander does not qualify as a covered event under the HO-3.

The insuring agreement in the personal umbrella liability policy covers bodily injury and property damage as well as personal injury for which an insured becomes legally liable. Bodily injury is defined as bodily harm, sickness, or disease, including required care, loss of services (such as the inability to perform household chores after an injury), and death. Property damage is defined as physical injury to or destruction of tangible property and includes loss of use of the property. The definition of personal injury in the umbrella policy includes false arrest, false imprisonment, wrongful entry or eviction, malicious prosecution or humiliation, libel, slander, defamation of character, invasion of privacy, and assault and battery not intentionally committed or directed by a covered person. Zoey's alleged slander does qualify as personal injury under the umbrella policy.

The third DICE step is to determine whether all policy conditions, such as timely reporting of the loss to the insurer, have been met. Once again, assume that they have been.

The fourth DICE step is to determine whether one or more exclusions preclude coverage that the insuring agreements have granted. There are no umbrella exclusions that would take away the coverage for Zoey's alleged slander.

Determination of Amounts Payable

Regarding the auto accident, the $1.8 million liability exceeds Matt and Zoey's PAP liability limit of $500,000 per occurrence. The PAP will pay the full policy limits of $500,000 for this event. Because the loss amount exceeds the umbrella deductible, the personal umbrella liability policy will respond. The $500,000 deductible shown on the umbrella Declarations page (the limit payable under the PAP) will be applied, and the umbrella policy will pay $1.3 million for this occurrence. The HO-3 policy, because of the exclusion noted, will not respond to the loss from the auto accident. Because the PAP and the umbrella have covered the full $1.8 million ($500,000 by PAP and $1.3 million by the umbrella), nothing is payable by Matt.

Regarding the $1 million slander lawsuit award, the HO-3 policy provides no liability coverage because its definition of bodily injury does not include slander. The PAP provides no coverage because the insuring agreement promises to pay only for liability for which an insured becomes legally liable because of an auto accident. The personal umbrella policy will provide coverage; the $2,000 deductible applies because the event is covered by the umbrella and is not covered by the underlying PAP and HO-3 policies. Therefore, the personal umbrella policy will pay $998,000 for this occurrence. The balance of $2,000 is payable by Zoey for the slander award. See the exhibit "Relationship of a $2,000,000 Umbrella Policy to Typical Underlying Coverages."

Although the umbrella policy limit is $2 million, two claims were paid—$1.3 million and $998,000—totaling more than $2 million. The policy limits apply per occurrence; there is no limit on the number of claims that can be covered, up to $2 million each. See the exhibit "Determination of Amounts Payable."

Relationship of a $2,000,000 Umbrella Policy to Typical Underlying Coverages

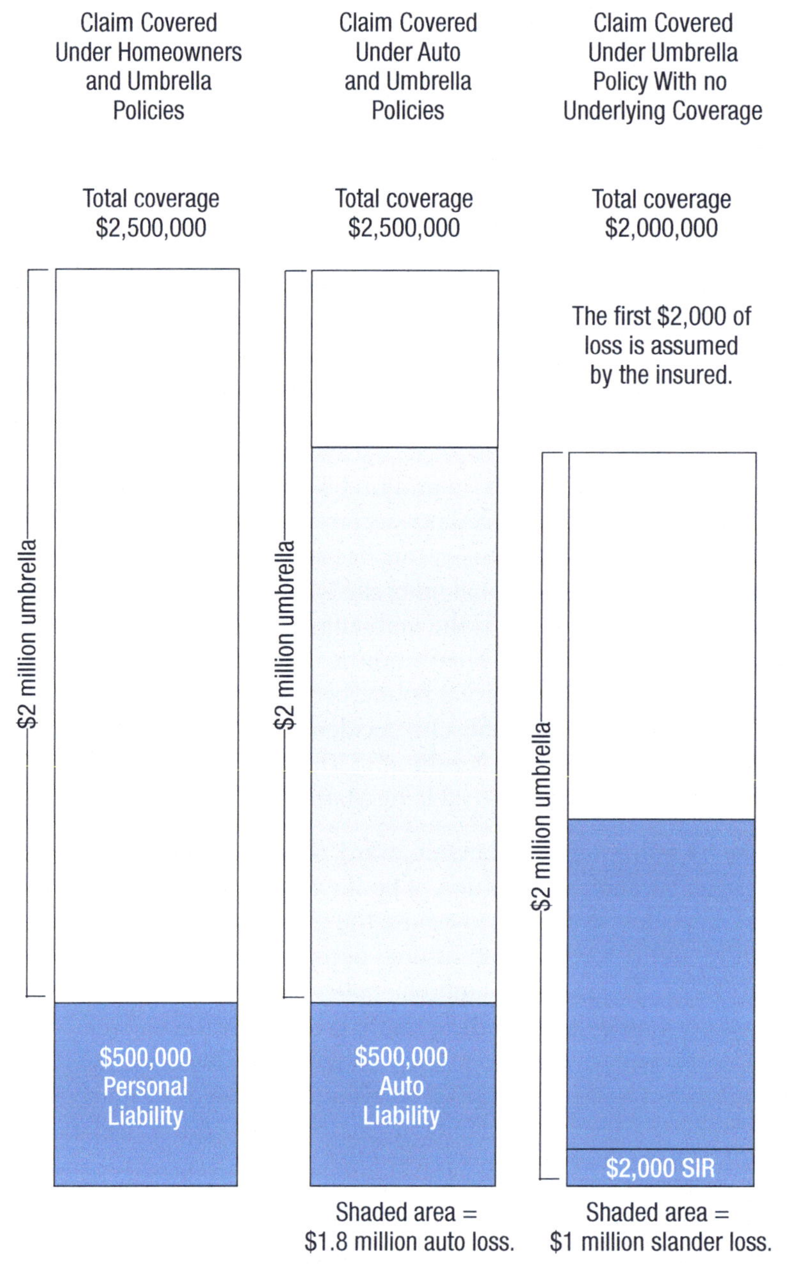

Claim Covered Under Homeowners and Umbrella Policies	Claim Covered Under Auto and Umbrella Policies	Claim Covered Under Umbrella Policy With no Underlying Coverage
Total coverage $2,500,000	Total coverage $2,500,000	Total coverage $2,000,000

The first $2,000 of loss is assumed by the insured.

- $2 million umbrella / $500,000 Personal Liability
- $2 million umbrella / $500,000 Auto Liability — Shaded area = $1.8 million auto loss.
- $2 million umbrella / $2,000 SIR — Shaded area = $1 million slander loss.

[DA05633]

> **Determination of Amounts Payable**
>
> Of the $1.8 million in damages resulting from the auto accident:
>
> - Matt and Zoey's PAP will pay its policy limit of $500,000.
> - Matt and Zoey's umbrella policy will pay the remaining $1.3 million.
> - Matt and Zoey's HO-3 policy pays nothing.
> - Matt and Zoey pay nothing.
>
> Of the $1 million in damages resulting from the slander lawsuit:
>
> - Matt and Zoey are responsible for the first $2,000.
> - Matt and Zoey's umbrella policy will pay the remaining $998,000.
> - Matt and Zoey's PAP policy pays nothing.
> - Matt and Zoey's HO-3 policy pays nothing.

[DA05634]

SUMMARY

Inland marine insurance is designed to cover property that has special value or that frequently moves ("floats") from one location to another. Commonly used personal inland marine forms include the Personal Articles Standard Loss Settlement Form, the Personal Property Form, and the Personal Effects Form. Personal inland marine insurance can be used to provide coverage for personal property in circumstances when homeowners policy coverage is not available or is too restrictive.

Personal watercraft insurance covers a variety of watercraft, from small rowboats and canoes to houseboats and large yachts. Loss exposures for such watercraft vary and can help insurance professionals determine the appropriate insurance policy or policies for a specific watercraft, whether an HO-3, a PAP, a small boat policy, or a boatowners or yacht policy.

The purpose of the personal umbrella policy is to provide excess liability coverage over underlying policies, such as homeowners and personal auto policies, and to provide broader coverage than basic policies. A personal umbrella policy protects the insured against catastrophic claims, lawsuits, or judgments.

To determine how coverage applies under a personal umbrella policy and any underlying insurance, one must establish facts about the umbrella policy and underlying policies and apply the DICE method to those facts.

- Are the persons or vehicles covered under the policies, and did the event take place during the policy period?
- Is the loss event covered by the underlying policies and/or the umbrella policy?

- Have the policy conditions been met?
- Are there exclusions that may apply to deny coverage?

Answering these questions will allow determination of how much is payable by the umbrella insurer, by the underlying insurer(s), and by the insured.

Direct Your Learning

Life Insurance Planning

Educational Objectives

After learning the content of this assignment, you should be able to:

▸ Describe the financial impact of the premature death personal loss exposure on the following types of family structures:
- Singles without children
- Single-parent families
- Two-income families
- Traditional families
- Blended families
- Sandwiched families

▸ Describe the needs approach and the human life value approach for determining the appropriate amount of life insurance.

▸ Summarize the various types of life insurance.

▸ Summarize the distinguishing characteristics of life insurance provided by each of the following sources: individual life insurance, group life insurance, and government-provided life insurance.

▸ Summarize the common life insurance contractual provisions and riders.

▸ Given a scenario regarding a particular family structure with its associated financial and family obligations, recommend an appropriate life insurance product, considering the following factors:
- Need for life insurance
- Types of life insurance
- Sources of life insurance
- Life insurance contractual provisions and riders

9

Outline

Premature Death Loss Exposures

Determining the Amount of Life Insurance to Own

Types of Life Insurance

Sources of Life Insurance

Common Life Insurance Contractual Provisions and Riders

Life Insurance Case Study

Summary

Life Insurance Planning

PREMATURE DEATH LOSS EXPOSURES

An individual's premature death can have devastating financial consequences when his or her future earnings or the value of the services he or she performs to maintain a home and family is lost.

Unexpected death can occur at any age. However, most life insurers statistically consider a premature death to be any death that occurs before age sixty-five. The premature death loss exposure can affect the ability of potential survivors to make mortgage payments, provide for children's education, meet daily living expenses, generate retirement income, meet tax obligations, and designate financial gifts to others.

Life insurance is a means by which individuals and families can reduce or eliminate the financial impact of the premature death loss exposure. Several types of individuals and families can benefit from having life insurance:

- Singles without children
- Single-parent families
- Two-income families
- Traditional families
- Blended families
- Sandwiched families

Costs Associated With Premature Death

An individual's premature death can leave a variety of unfulfilled financial and emotional obligations, such as an unpaid mortgage, college tuitions, and support for young children. Premature death can occur because of a variety of factors, including family history, personal lifestyle, accident, or environmental factors.

The costs required to support one's family over a lifetime are significant and can vary depending on the specific type of family structure. When a family's key wage earner dies prematurely, replacement income is not always readily available. Life insurance is a key financial planning tool that is often used to provide for these costs associated with premature death:

- Lost income—Deceased wage earner's income is lost.
- Final costs—Funeral costs, medical expenses, and so forth.

- Outstanding debts—Credit card debts, mortgage, and so forth.
- Unpaid long-term obligations—To supplement retirement savings and fund college tuitions, child-care expenses, home maintenance expenses, and so forth.
- Estate planning costs—Estate taxes, probate costs, lost charitable contributions, and so forth.
- Unfulfilled family obligations—Both economic and noneconomic; for example, the family's standard of living may be adversely affected or a child may grieve over the loss of a parent.

Singles Without Children

Singles without children are individuals who are not married or in a long-term, committed relationship and who do not have dependent children. The Internal Revenue Service (IRS) recently reported that more than two-thirds of today's middle-income taxpayers are single or members of single-headed households. Over the past four decades, demographic and economic changes have significantly altered the societal view of family and relationships. For example, a single person without children could be an unmarried individual in his or her late twenties or thirties, a divorced person, or a person over age sixty-five whose spouse has died.

A single person may not need life insurance to reduce the financial impact of the premature death loss exposure if no one financially depends on him or her; perhaps just a small amount of life insurance may be required to cover funeral expenses and any uninsured medical expenses. However, younger singles may want to provide financial support for elderly parents or dependent siblings and other family members. Others may require life insurance to cover any significant debt that might pass on to surviving family members. Still others may require life insurance proceeds to allocate toward any estate taxes payable or to fund gifts or trusts for designated survivors.

Single-Parent Families

Singles with children include single parents, single grandparents caring for a child, or other relatives or guardians who fulfill parental responsibilities related to a dependent child or children. Singles with children have many responsibilities, including those related to generating income, managing the household, and providing emotional support to children or other dependents.

The financial impact of the loss of a single person with a child or children can be significant. Frequently, singles with children have little or no life insurance, relying instead on government insurance resources such as Social Security survivors benefits. Additionally, they may consider the cost of life insurance an unnecessary expense at a time when they are already shouldering greater financial and emotional demands. While the emotional impact of the premature death of a loved one is not lessened by life insurance, singles with children can use life insurance as a tool to ensure that their loved ones will be cared for properly in terms of housing, education, and other expenses, and they can use the process of obtaining life insurance (which can include drafting a will) to appoint guardians of their choice for their dependent children.

Two-Income Families With Children

Two-income families with children can include unmarried couples (including relatives or guardians) who care for dependent children. However, this category is primarily populated with individuals who are married and employed and who have children. Increasingly, both spouses in a relationship must work in order to maintain the family's customary economic standard of living or to attain a higher standard of living.

The financial impact of the premature death of either spouse in a two-income family can be devastating when dependent children are involved. The loss of one spouse's earnings can affect the surviving spouse's ability to properly maintain the household, provide for related expenses, fund future retirement, and ensure the financial well-being of the children beyond any governmental benefits they may receive. Life insurance can enable the family to maintain its "two-income" standard of living.

Two-Income Families Without Children

Two-income families without children can include individuals who are married or are in a long-term, committed relationship but who do not care for dependent children. While this category is primarily populated with couples without children or couples whose children have grown out of any dependency, it can also include working grandparents or other relatives who no longer have dependent-child responsibilities.

Married working couples without children or other two-income family arrangements that do not involve children may not be severely affected by the premature death of one wage earner. For example, the surviving individual is employed, and the surviving individual has no costs related to dependent children (any children have already been educated and live independently). However, the surviving wage earner may face financial implications that modest amounts of life insurance can address, such as satisfying outstanding indebtedness, supporting aging parents or other financially dependent relatives, making mortgage payments, supplying funds for retirement, or maintaining his or her current lifestyle.

"Traditional" Families

"Traditional" families are those that consist of a mother, a father, and their children. In the traditional family category, only one parent is employed, while the other partner manages the household and takes care of the dependent children. The number of traditional families has declined in recent years because of economic pressures and changing lifestyles.

The premature death of one of the parents in this category can generate significant financial uncertainty. For example, if the deceased parent was the working spouse, the loss of earnings can severely affect the family's standard of living. Household expenses must still be met, mortgages paid, retirement funded, and allocations provided for children's education costs. The surviving spouse may need to return to the workforce, thus possibly generating child-care costs. Life insurance benefits, in addition to Social Security survivors benefits, can greatly mitigate this significant uncertainty.

If the deceased parent was the spouse managing the household and taking care of dependent children, the death of that individual can have a financial impact just as great as that from the death of the wage earner. For example, the household must still be maintained and managed, and child-care costs may be incurred or may increase. These expenses reduce the surviving wage earner's income and can adversely affect the family's standard of living.

Blended Families

A blended family is a family unit in which one or both partners bring with them dependent children from a prior relationship. One or both partners in the blended family may be employed.

The financial impact of the premature death loss exposure on blended families primarily relates to the dependent children's needs and can be significant. As with other individual and family types, the death of a wage earner relates to financial implications, while the death of a nonworking spouse relates to additional household management and child-care costs. Other unique financial needs of the blended family relate to the dependent children; children from a previous relationship may be older and reaching the ages at which education costs and the costs of supporting them escalate. Children may be born into the blended relationship, extending the timeline for child-care costs. Life insurance can offset the uncertainty of such expenses, particularly when other contractual resources for these expenses, such as alimony and child support, may be limited.

"Sandwiched" Families

Members of the sandwiched generation include baby boomers, now middle-aged, who are providing financial support to both younger and older family members. A typical sandwiched family could consist of an aging parent or dependent family member who receives financial assistance or other types of support from his or her adult child or another younger relative. This same adult child or younger relative, in turn, supports his or her own dependent children; therefore, this is a generation "sandwiched" between an older and a younger generation that both require financial support and care.

The premature death of a member of the sandwiched generation can have an extensive financial impact. The death of a wage earner can dramatically reduce the funds available to support not only dependent children but also dependent aging parents or other relatives. Additionally, funds may no longer be available to help maintain the current standard of living or manage the household. Death of a nonworking member of the sandwiched generation can generate an increase in child-care costs and also other costs related to the nonfinancial support (such as physical care) and support of aging parents or other dependent relatives. Life insurance can be used to offset these increased costs as well as to fund retirement income; a deceased working spouse can no longer contribute to any retirement programs.

DETERMINING THE AMOUNT OF LIFE INSURANCE TO OWN

An individual's premature death can leave loved ones, including a surviving spouse, children, other family members, and other dependents, in a state of financial uncertainty. For this reason, among many others, it is vital to properly determine an appropriate amount of life insurance that will meet survivors' financial needs.

The amount of life insurance individuals require usually changes over time, based on their age and needs related to their family structure. For example, young couples with children and a mortgage usually require more life insurance than middle-aged couples without dependents.

Several methods exist for estimating the amount of life insurance an individual requires in order to reduce or eliminate the financial uncertainty of a premature death. Some life insurers suggest that an arbitrary approach to determining life insurance requirements is sufficient, such as calculating an amount based on a simple multiple (for example, six to eight times) of earnings of the insured individual. Such an approach, while simple, is imprecise and can lead to a shortfall. Two basic methods—the **needs approach** and the **human life value approach**—are more precise ways to estimate life insurance amounts.

Needs Approach

The needs approach is used to identify an adequate amount of life insurance based on survivors' needs, including those of the decedent's family or other dependents. It is based on identifying a family's economic needs after considering its Social Security survivors benefits or other available existing life insurance benefits. An insurance professional using the needs approach would gather facts about a family's financial needs by asking questions about its economic needs and available resources. See the exhibit "Fact-Gathering for the Needs Approach: Key Questions."

Needs approach
Method used to determine an adequate amount of life insurance based on the survivors' needs and the amount of existing life insurance, financial assets, and expected Social Security benefits.

Human life value approach
A mathematical computation used to determine how much life insurance is needed by valuing a human life.

> **Fact-Gathering for the Needs Approach: Key Questions**
>
> - How much is your home mortgage payment?
> - What are your other annual living expenses?
> - Do you have funds reserved for your children's college education?
> - How large is your emergency fund?
> - What is your total credit card debt?
> - Is anyone relying on your contributions to a retirement fund as support for their own retirement?
> - Have you estimated your final expenses (for example, funeral, burial, probate)?
> - How large are any outstanding loans you have?
> - Do you want to leave money to a charity or another not-for-profit organization?
> - Do you want to leave money to a friend or relative?
> - What is the potential tax bill on your property or estate?

[DA05664]

The objective of the needs approach is to determine the total financial requirements of the insured's surviving dependent family. From that amount, assets such as any existing life insurance benefits, governmental benefits, or other available liquid assets are applied against the family's total financial requirements, generating the amount of life insurance or additional life insurance the individual should own.

A needs and benefits/assets review typically generates results that fall into one or more of these financial categories:

- Final expenses needs
- Debt elimination needs
- Family living expense needs
- Special needs
- Retirement income needs
- Life insurance and other assets

Final Expenses Needs

Final expenses are incurred immediately before death and immediately thereafter. They can include a decedent's uninsured medical bills, funeral and burial costs, federal estate taxes and state inheritance (estate) taxes, and any probate costs. (Probate is the legal process of validating a will and settling an estate.)

Debt Elimination Needs

Debt elimination relates to a decedent's outstanding debt or financial obligations. These expenses can include satisfying a mortgage balance owed, eliminating outstanding consumer and/or credit card debts, and funding children's education.

Family Living Expense Needs

A family's living expenses include any expense required to maintain the household, provide for child care, or fund any other expenses related to daily living. When determining the family's living expenses, consideration is given to any income that might be generated by a surviving spouse (or that might be lost if that spouse leaves the workforce to support children at home). Also, financial requirements that exceed the surviving spouse's income, such as the funds required to sustain the family's current standard of living, are calculated per year and multiplied by the projected total number of years of need (for example, the number of years remaining until a worker's estimated retirement date or the number of years remaining until children are financially independent).

Special Needs

Special needs expenses are expenses that remain or financial obligations that must be funded after an individual's death. Special needs can include monetary gifts to family members or charitable institutions, a trust, or an emergency fund for unanticipated expenses.

Retirement Income Needs

Retirement income needs relate to the income needed to support a surviving spouse during his or her retirement. A surviving spouse may have been relying on the decedent's ability to fund retirement for the couple. A needs and benefits/assets review should consider the impact of a premature death on sources of retirement benefits other than the Social Security benefits the survivor will receive when he or she becomes eligible for them.

Life Insurance and Other Assets

Existing life insurance and any other income-producing assets that can be used to fund survivors' well-being and to help them maintain their previous standard of living are totaled and applied to their financial requirements to determine an appropriate amount of life insurance. Assets can include the proceeds from current life insurance, whether from an individually held policy or a group policy provided by an employer; Social Security survivors benefits; retirement accounts; or pension death benefits. See the exhibit "Needs Approach Illustration."

Needs Approach Illustration

Most life insurers provide software programs or online tools that are used to precisely determine an estimate of an individual's life insurance needs. In a simplified view, however, a basic illustration using a needs approach case offers examples of the types of expenses and assets that develop the total amount of life insurance required.

The needs approach can be illustrated by analyzing the insurance needs of a member of the sandwiched generation, Dave, age forty, who is married and has two children. Dave's wife, Kathy, age thirty-five, does not currently work. Dave provides financial support to his widowed mother, assisting her with her daily living expenses.

Dave earns $90,000 annually as an advertising executive. Both Dave and Kathy want their children, as well as Dave's mother, to be financially secure if Dave dies prematurely. Dave and Kathy understand that some needs, like debt elimination, ongoing family living expenses, and special needs, could increase because of inflation. However, Dave assumes that, should he die, the life insurance benefit could be invested at an interest rate equal to the inflation rate.

Note that the worksheet includes estimates for final expenses needs; debt elimination (including mortgage payments and tuition funding); family living expenses, including household maintenance, other cost of living expenses, and support of Dave's mother; emergency funding; and retirement income needs. The family's needs are offset by assets including existing checking and savings accounts, group life insurance, Dave's pension, and Social Security survivors benefits.

Needs Approach—Dave

Final Expenses Needs		
Funeral costs	$ 8,000	
Uninsured medical expenses	5,000	
Probate costs	3,000	
Federal taxes	0	
State taxes	0	
Total Final Expenses		$ 16,000
Debt Elimination Needs		
Satisfy outstanding mortgage(s)	$180,000	
Fund children's education	200,000	
Eliminate outstanding credit card debt	2,500	
Eliminate outstanding consumer debt	0	
Total Debt Elimination Needs		$382,500
Family's Living Expenses Needs		
Household maintenance expenses	$100,000	
Other living expenses	$250,000	
Child-care expenses	$ 0	
Dave's mother's living expenses	$120,000	
Total Family Living Expenses Needs		$470,000
Special Needs		
Gifts to family members	$ 0	
Gifts to charity	$ 0	
Fund a trust	$ 0	
Establish an emergency fund	$ 50,000	
Total Special Needs		$ 50,000

Retirement Income Needs		
Funds for Kathy's retirement needs (Social Security supplement)	$ 400,000	
Total Retirement Income Needs		$400,000
Total Needs:		$1,318,500
Life Insurance and Other Assets		
Checking and savings accounts	$ 15,000	
Group (employer-provided) life insurance	90,000	
Personal life insurance	0	
Social Security survivors benefits	$ 250,000	
Retirement account/pension fund benefits	$ 50,000	
Total Life Insurance and Other Assets		$ 405,000
Total Assets:		$ 405,000
Total Life Insurance Needs		
Total needs		$1,318,500
Minus total assets		$ 405,000
Additional Life Insurance Needed	$ 913,500	

> Dave's total recommended life insurance amount is approximately $900,000. Although this amount may appear significant, it will enable Dave's wife, Kathy, to continue caring for their dependent children without having to obtain a job (and assume related child-care costs) to replace Dave's lost lifetime of income. Additionally, it will enable Dave's wife and dependent children to continue living in accordance with their current standard of living by supplying benefits for home and living expenses, as well as other financial needs, and it will also allow Dave's mother to continue to receive financial support.

[DA05677]

Human Life Value Approach

The human life value approach estimates an individual's income for his or her remaining working life and factors in other items such as the individual's age in relation to retirement and the cost of self-maintenance. Cost of self-maintenance means that portion of total wages that the wage earner consumes in the course of daily living; the surplus amount is the remaining wages that go to the family to meet its needs. This surplus is the human life value, which would require replacement in the event of the wage earner's death.

A present value factor is applied to the total amount of income requiring replacement—the human life value. Because a human life has economic value only in relation to others, such as children or a spouse, this approach is typically used for families with principal wage earners.

A separate calculation is made to estimate the total of any existing life insurance, savings and investments, and Social Security benefits. A present value factor is applied to any additional income item that is received over time, such as Social Security benefits. This sum is then subtracted from the human life value to determine the total amount of new or additional life insurance required.

The objective of the human life value approach is to determine the total amount of income that is lost when a primary wage earner dies. To develop an accurate estimate, one would consider the individual's net pay rather than gross pay; include the other economic factors noted; and supply an estimate of the interest rate that could be earned, on average, over the individual's expected working period. These items are then applied to a present value computation. See the exhibit "Human Life Value Approach."

The human life value approach, which focuses on replacing a primary wage earner's lost income, typically develops a lower appropriate insurance amount than does the needs approach, which also considers any unusual expenses (such as the desire to make charitable bequests) and recurring expenses (such as for additional child care required).

> **Human Life Value Approach**
>
> Consider these human life value assumptions applicable to Jiao, age thirty-seven, a working mother with two children:
>
> Average expected net income per year: $75,000
>
> Cost of self-maintenance: 40 percent (or $30,000)
>
> Jiao's income that must be replaced: $45,000
>
> Time to retirement: Thirty years
>
> Interest rate: 6 percent
>
> This information is used to calculate "A"—Human life value
>
> Jiao's existing life insurance (through her employer): $40,000
>
> Savings: $10,000
>
> Social Security benefits: $24,000 per year for six years (interest rate: 6 percent)
>
> This information is used to calculate "B"—Other income available
>
> A minus B equals "C"—Jiao's total life insurance requirement
>
> Present value tables help an individual calculate what an amount of money, invested today, would accumulate to at a specified interest rate for a specified number of years. Software can also quickly perform the same calculation. For example, to develop Jiao's human life value, $45,000 of annual lost income must be projected at 6 percent interest over the remaining thirty years of her working life. In Jiao's case, the present value of the lost income over the next thirty years is $619,417.40.
>
> To develop the amount of other income available to Jiao's survivors, the insurance representative should add her existing life insurance ($40,000), savings ($10,000), and present value of projected Social Security benefits over twenty-four years ($58,015.78) to arrive at a total of $108,015.78.
>
> Jiao's total additional life insurance need is thus $511,401.62 (or $619,417.40 - $108,015.78). Jiao might decide to purchase a life insurance policy with a face amount of $500,000 or $550,000 to satisfy her insurance requirements.

[DA05685]

TYPES OF LIFE INSURANCE

Life insurers sell a variety of insurance contracts, many of which are designed for specific needs of individuals and their families. Some policies provide a savings mechanism that increases the value of the policy over time and that may be used even while the insured is living.

Common types of life insurance that meet the needs of most insureds include these:

- Term life
- Whole life
- Universal life

- Variable life
- Variable universal life
- Specialty products, such as second-to-die insurance

These common types of insurance meet the needs of most insureds, but specialty products offer benefits that are tailored to meet the specific needs of particular insureds.

Term Life

Term life insurance is often called term, term life, or term insurance. As its name implies, term insurance is life insurance that provides coverage for a specified period, such as ten or twenty years, with no cash value. If the insured dies during the policy term, the policy value is paid to the beneficiary.

Term insurance is regarded as temporary protection. Other types of life insurance, such as whole life and variable life, are regarded as permanent products. Term is an uncomplicated life insurance product. It is life insurance only; it has no savings, investment, or cash value/loan value aspect.

Term life is useful to someone whose current need for life insurance will diminish after a number of years. Consider a household with two working parents and one infant child. Each income is necessary to maintain the family's lifestyle and to provide for the dependent child. Should one parent die, life insurance can replace that parent's earning power. However, that income may be essential only until the child has completed college. Similarly, term insurance may be purchased to match the duration of a home mortgage.

With most life insurance products, the annual premium escalates rapidly as the insured ages. The parents of young children might choose, for example, a twenty-year term life insurance policy. They can protect the income of the insured person for that time span and avoid the high annual premiums that would apply in later years.

Term is often a low-cost way to obtain life insurance to protect income during critical times. For some term policies, premiums increase with the insured's age and are based on mortality rates. Because mortality rates increase with age, term insurance premiums also increase. However, a popular form of term (level term) has a fixed annual premium for a fixed number of years. Insureds with level term pay a higher rate in the early years in exchange for a flat, affordable rate in the later years of the term.

Most term policies carry some guarantee of renewability, so that the insured can continue the insurance beyond a fixed number of years (although doing so may require a higher rate). Most term insurance policies are renewable for a specific period or to a specific age. Insurers typically do not allow renewal after a certain age, such as sixty-five, seventy, or seventy-five. However, some insurers guarantee renewability to an older age, such as ninety-five or ninety-nine.

Convertible
Characteristic of a term insurance policy that allows the policy to be exchanged for some type of permanent life insurance policy with no evidence of insurability.

Whole life insurance
Life insurance that provides lifetime protection, accrues cash value, and has premiums that remain unchanged during the insured's lifetime.

Many policies are also **convertible**, so that the insured may exchange the term policy for a whole life policy without meeting any new insurability requirements such as a physical examination.

Whole Life

Whole life insurance is a hybrid combination of life insurance and an investment vehicle. Unlike term, its coverage is not limited to a fixed period. Whole life is permanent life insurance designed to provide coverage for a lifetime.

For a given amount of coverage, the annual premium for whole life is higher than for term life. The selling point for whole life, given that it costs more than term for the same amount of coverage, is that whole life is a savings vehicle that develops a cash value as time passes. In the early years of a whole life policy, insureds pay an annual premium that covers more than the projected mortality costs for insureds at that age. In effect, the extra money is used to build the cash value.

The cash value, with some limitations, is available to the insured during the life of the policy, either as a loan or as a cash payment upon surrender of the policy. Whole life is suitable for someone who wants permanent protection and who needs the discipline of paying insurance premiums to enforce savings. To determine the suitability of a whole life policy, a prospective insured might compare the annual premiums to those of a term policy for the same coverage amount and then calculate the savings that might accumulate for the term insurance buyer by investing the difference in premiums.

Compared with term life insurance, the higher cost of whole life insurance could prompt an insured who has limited disposable income to underinsure. For example, an insured who is attracted to the savings feature of the ordinary life policy to provide for her children's future needs might purchase a $100,000 ordinary life policy with a premium that matches her disposable income. Instead, that disposable income might be used to purchase a $500,000 twenty-year term life policy, which would better meet her family's needs in the event of her untimely death.

Unlike term, whole life is available to meet financial obligations that continue for a lifetime, such as the expense of a last illness and a funeral. Also, whole life can be useful for estate planning; for example, a policy may be used specifically to reduce estate shrinkage by taxes.

Universal Life

Universal life insurance
Flexible premium permanent life insurance that separates the protection, savings, and expense components.

Universal life insurance policies have more in common with whole life than with term life. Like whole life, universal life is a permanent product that combines life insurance protection with an investment or a savings aspect. Universal life can be considered a modern twist on the traditional whole life product.

The basic premise of universal life is like that of whole life: the insured makes premium payments that exceed the amount needed to cover the mortality risk (cost of insurance). The policyholder accumulates cash value from the amount of premiums paid in excess of the cost of the insurance protection and expenses.

The unbundling of the insurance protection, savings, and expense components is the distinguishing characteristic of universal life. Policyholders receive an annual disclosure that shows the amount of premiums paid, the amount of insurance (death benefit), expenses, and interest earned and credited on the cash value.

Another hallmark of universal life is that two interest rates are stipulated in the policy. One is a guaranteed minimum rate, such as 2.5 percent. The cash value of the policy is guaranteed to earn interest at that rate or higher. The other rate is the current market interest rate; if that rate is higher than the guaranteed minimum rate, the cash value will earn that higher rate.

For most universal life policies, the insured's premium payments are flexible, provided that there is enough cash value in the policy to cover the cost of insurance and expenses. The insured may increase, decrease, or even miss a premium payment. While the insurer may establish maximum premium payments, the insured can pay higher premiums in order to grow the cash value. The appeal to the insured is that the growth in cash value is tax-deferred.

Flexibility is a fundamental characteristic of universal life. In addition to the flexibility with premium payments, the insured has options to increase the death benefit, borrow against the cash value, withdraw from (and thereby reduce) the cash value, or add insureds to the policy.

Universal life appeals to insureds who want to combine life insurance protection with an investment. As noted, the tax-deferred accumulation of cash value adds to the appeal, as does the flexibility with premium payments. For example, an insured might make higher premium payments when children are young, then decrease or even skip premium payments when paying for the children's college tuition.

There are risks to universal life. The flexibility allows insureds to be less than fully committed to a premium payment discipline, and policies can lapse when premiums are not paid and the cash value is insufficient to cover the cost of insurance and expenses. Also, insureds may expect a certain level of earnings on the cash value, based on current interest rates. In an environment of falling rates, the cash value may grow more slowly than hoped and require larger premium payments to maintain the coverage.

Variable Life

A **variable life insurance** policy is similar to a whole life policy in that it provides cash value over time and permanent insurance protection, but it enables policyholders to choose among investment accounts (mutual funds made up

Variable life insurance

A form of life insurance providing a death benefit that may change with time due to its variable cash value.

of common stocks, bonds, or other investments) offered by the insurer and to move cash values among these accounts. The investment performance results of the accounts affect the amount of the policy cash values and sometimes the death benefit.

Variable life insurance offers level premiums and is appropriate for persons who want the benefit of using competitive investment strategies and some protection against inflation over the life of their insurance program. However, investment performance of stocks and bonds can vary considerably, and the policy should be held for several years, such as five, ten, fifteen, or twenty, to take full advantage of the flexible investment benefit. A significant advantage of variable life insurance over many other investments is that the policyholder can move the policy cash value amount among investments without incurring any current income tax liability for capital gains.

Variable Universal Life

Variable universal life insurance combines the features of universal life insurance and variable life insurance. The cash values in variable universal life insurance are not guaranteed, nor is any minimum interest rate. The cash value of the policy is determined by the investment experience of a separate account that is maintained by the insurer. However, the policyholder can select the separate account in which the flexible premiums are invested.

Under variable universal life insurance, insurers impose significant initial expense charges and sometimes surrender charges (based on potential sales charges) for managing policyholder investment accounts. The latter charges decline after the policy ages ten to fifteen years and usually reach zero. Insurers may charge annual (or periodic) investment management fees, expense charges, and sometimes other administration fees. In addition to all of these "expense loadings" of variable universal life insurance policies, insurers charge for the mortality cost of insurance protection provided by the policy. This charge varies with the insured's attained age to reflect the insurer's exposure for the policy.

Other Types of Life Insurance

Term, whole, universal, and variable are the most popular types of life insurance. Other specialized types of life insurance include these:

- Current assumption whole life
- Second-to-die (survivorship) life insurance
- First-to-die (joint) life insurance

> **Variable universal life insurance**
> A form of universal life insurance that allows the policyholder to make fund choices for the investment component but that has no guaranteed cash value and no guaranteed interest rate.

Current Assumption Whole Life

Current assumption whole life insurance (also called interest-sensitive life insurance) includes features of a traditional whole life policy and a universal life policy. Under the current assumption policy, the premium and the cash value can be periodically recalculated by the insurer, based on new actuarial assumptions (drawn from the insurer's investment results and loss experience). The insurer guarantees a minimum interest rate, and some insurers offer maximum mortality and expense charges. These policies can have appeal at a time when interest rates are rising because higher investment earnings for the insurer can result in reduced premiums and/or increased cash value for the policyholder.

Second-to-Die (Survivorship) Life Insurance

Traditionally, life insurance policies pay the death benefit at the death of the insured person. In a second-to-die policy, two lives are insured in a single policy, with death benefits payable to the beneficiary when both insureds have died. The two lives insured are frequently those of a married couple, with the death benefit contemplated to pay for the federal estate taxes due in larger estates.

These survivorship policies can be traditional fixed-premium whole life policies, current assumption policies, universal life, or even a combination of permanent and term life insurance. Premiums for such policies are typically lower than those of a comparable policy on an individual life because benefits are not payable until both lives have ended.

First-to-Die (Joint) Life Insurance

Like second-to-die life insurance, first-to-die policies cover two individuals. The difference is that the death benefit is payable upon the first death. Typically, the buyers are a married couple, often with two incomes. The appeal of such a policy is that when the first person dies, the death benefit can provide the survivor with funds to cover a home mortgage, other personal or business debt obligations, and dependent care. Although premiums are typically higher than for second-to-die policies, this option is less costly than taking separate policies on each life. See the exhibit "Life Insurance Feature Comparison."

Life Insurance Feature Comparison

	Term Life Insurance	Whole Life Insurance	Universal Life Insurance	Variable Life Insurance	Variable Universal Life Insurance	Current Assumption Whole Life	Second-to-Die Life Insurance	First-to-Die Life Insurance
Time Period	Temporary	Permanent	Permanent	Permanent	Permanent	Permanent	Varies	Varies
Death Benefit	Yes	Yes	Yes	Yes	Yes	Yes	Yes	Yes
Investment or Savings Component	No	Yes	Yes	Yes	Yes	Yes	Varies	Varies
Low Cost	Yes	No	No	No	No	No	Yes	Yes
Flexible Premiums	No	No	Yes	No	Yes	Yes	Varies	Varies
Investment Choices	N/A	No	No	Yes	Yes	No	No	No

[DA05724]

SOURCES OF LIFE INSURANCE

The source from which an individual should obtain life insurance depends on his or her coverage needs and budget. Life insurance may be purchased individually, be group-based, or government provided. These three sources are distinguished by cost, the payer, and the standards applied to providing coverage.

When consumers purchase their own life insurance, they may choose from a wide variety of products, such as **term life insurance**, whole life insurance, universal life insurance, and variable life insurance. Unlike group life insurance, individual life insurance coverage is not tethered to the insured's employment status or subject to the kinds of changes that might be made to a group insurance plan. This stability and the ability to choose, however, entail a trade-off. As opposed to the other sources of life insurance, which limit the insured's coverage options, the cost of individual life insurance does not include a group or volume discount. When a consumer buys an individual life insurance policy, he or she bears its entire cost, which varies based on his or her age, gender, health, and habits. Additionally, each application for individual life insurance must be evaluated by the insurer, increasing its cost. Therefore, individual life insurance is an ideal choice for younger individuals who are in good health, as they may find that their positive age- and health-related attributes present premiums that are more attractive than those from other sources of life insurance.

Term life insurance

Life insurance that provides coverage for a specified period, such as ten or twenty years, with no cash value.

In contrast with individual life insurance, group life insurance provides coverage to a number of individuals under one master contract issued to a sponsoring organization. The insured members are not parties to the contract and receive certificates of insurance as evidence of their protection, as opposed to individual policies. Employers represent the largest category covered by group insurance. Employer groups can consist of individual employees or can be multi-employer arrangements. Group life insurance plans can be financed solely by employers (noncontributory plans) or might require contributions from employees (contributory plans). See the exhibit "Group Life Insurance at a Glance."

The third primary source of life insurance coverage is through the federal government as part of Social Security benefits. Social Security benefits include monthly death benefits for surviving spouses, dependent children, and dependent parents. These benefits accrue during an individual's years of employment in the same manner as other Social Security benefits. A maximum amount applies to the benefits that can be paid to surviving spouses and other surviving family members. In most cases, this limit ranges from 150 to 180 percent of what would have been the decedent's primary insurance amount if they were retiring at that time. See the exhibit "Government-Provided Life Insurance: Beneficiaries."

Apply Your Knowledge

Anton, 26, has had no serious medical problems and maintains a healthy diet and exercise regimen. His new employer offers life insurance through a contributory plan. However, Anton is concerned that his contribution may overtax his budget. Should Anton explore another source of life insurance? If so, which one?

Feedback: Yes, Anton should explore purchasing his own individual life insurance policy. He should explore the open market and obtain several competitive, comparable quotes that allow him to make an informed choice between an individual plan—which, despite its lack of group discount, could offer a lower premium because of Anton's age and health—and the contributory plan, whose premium may be more affordable because its group discount outweighs the potential increased cost associated with supplementing the cost of insuring older workers.

Group Life Insurance at a Glance

Characteristic	Description
Eligible Groups	Major types of groups eligible for group life insurance include employers; unions; debtors of a common creditor; and a variety of groups affiliated by profession, school, religion, or even hobby. Insurers often require that the group exist for some purpose other than the purchase of insurance. Many states also restrict the types of groups that are eligible for group insurance.
Eligible Employees or Members	Employee eligibility for coverage is determined by state law and company underwriting standards. Generally, employees, directors, partners, sole proprietors, retired employees, and even independent contractors and dependents of employees can be covered in a group life plan. Coverage for new employees generally is subject to a probationary period. Group insurance is generally provided without a medical examination or other evidence of insurability. A person in poor health who is unable to buy individual life insurance might obtain group life insurance if he or she is a member of an eligible group. Therefore, mortality experience is slightly higher in group life insurance than with individually written coverage.
Benefits	The amount of life insurance may be determined automatically, through a formula or schedule, to minimize adverse selection. Otherwise, those in poor health are likely to choose large amounts of insurance. However, in some plans (known as flexible benefits or cafeteria-style plans), employees can choose from among a number of kinds and amounts of employee benefits, and thus tailor their own benefit plans that include group life insurance. Although many formulas and schedules are available for relating the amount of insurance to earnings, popular practice is to provide life insurance equal to some multiple of the employee's annual salary, often one, two, or three times rounded to the nearest $1,000. Many insurers stipulate a minimum and maximum amount of insurance that can be issued on any one life within the group.
Typical Coverage	Group life insurance can take the form of group whole life or group universal life, but the majority of employer-sponsored group life insurance is yearly renewable term insurance. This coverage is pure protection and does not develop a cash value. The premium charged to the employer usually changes annually to reflect the experience of the group being insured. The employer often pays all or part of the premium, but it is common for employees to contribute to the cost, especially at higher amounts of coverage. The cost of the group life, if paid by the employer, can be considered as income to an employee covered in a group life plan. However, the Internal Revenue Service (IRS) allows employees to exclude from their gross wages the amount paid by the employer on their behalf to purchase the group term life insurance. The favorable tax treatment is limited; only the premiums for the first $50,000 of coverage are excluded from taxable income.

[DA07738]

Government-Provided Life Insurance: Beneficiaries

Beneficiary	Benefits
Surviving Spouses	Widows or widowers of an individual eligible to receive Social Security benefits can receive full benefits when they reach retirement age. As with Social Security benefits, this age varies based on the survivor's date of birth but is generally over the age of sixty-six. Reduced benefits are paid to surviving spouses starting at age sixty. If a surviving spouse is disabled, benefits may start as early as age fifty. Full benefits are generally 100 percent of the deceased spouse's basic benefit amount.
	Divorced spouses are also eligible for survivors benefits if the marriage lasted for ten years or longer. Benefits paid to divorced spouses do not affect any payments made to others who are eligible for survivors benefits. The age requirements are similar to those paid to existing spouses.
	Surviving spouses of any age who are caring for dependent children younger than sixteen years are also eligible for reduced benefits, generally a percentage of the decedent's primary insurance amount (PIA).
Dependent Children and Parents	Unmarried children are also eligible to receive Social Security survivors benefits if they are less than eighteen years of age. Benefits will be paid up to age eighteen or nineteen if the child is attending secondary or high school full time. Benefits are also payable to disabled surviving children if the disability occurred before the age of twenty-two. In most cases, dependent children receive 75 percent of the deceased parent's PIA.
	In addition to dependent children, parents who are dependent on the deceased individual can receive survivors benefits. For parents to be considered dependent, they must have relied on the decedent for at least half of their living support. Dependent parents must be at least sixty-two years old to receive dependent parent benefits.

[DA07739]

COMMON LIFE INSURANCE CONTRACTUAL PROVISIONS AND RIDERS

Life insurance policies contain several common contractual provisions and riders that apply to the coverage and benefits provided.

Common contractual provisions in life insurance policies stipulate how coverage will be provided and specify the conditions under which benefits will be paid. Riders are additions to life insurance contracts that customize the policies to better meet the insureds' needs.

Common Life Insurance Contractual Provisions

Policyholders and insureds should understand how common life insurance contractual provisions apply, along with the options that may be available under a life insurance policy.

Assignment Clause Provision

A life insurance policyowner can assign the policy to another person (typically contingent upon insurer notification). An absolute assignment transfers all ownership rights to another party. A collateral assignment assigns the policy to another as collateral for a loan. A collateral assignment transfers only certain policy rights to a creditor.

Beneficiary Designations

Various types of **beneficiaries** can be designated in a life insurance policy. Most policies indicate a primary beneficiary, the first one to collect benefits under the policy. Some policies name a contingent beneficiary to receive benefits if the primary beneficiary is not alive at the time of the insured's death. The policyowner may also designate beneficiaries as either revocable or irrevocable. A revocable beneficiary designation denotes that the policyowner can make beneficiary changes without the beneficiary's consent. An irrevocable beneficiary designation means beneficiary changes must have the beneficiary's consent. Beneficiary designations can also be specific, such as "Mary Smith, wife of the insured," or designated as a class, such as "surviving children of the insured."

Beneficiary
Person(s) designated in a life insurance policy to receive the death benefit.

Dividend Options

Life insurance policies that pay dividends are called participating policies. An insurer may pay dividends based on its favorable loss, expenses, or investment results. Dividends, however, are not guaranteed. Several dividend options are available under a participating life insurance policy. See the exhibit "Life Insurance Dividend Options."

Excluded Risks

Some life insurance policies specify types of losses that are not covered. Such exclusions usually involve hazardous occupations or recreational activities of the insured. Some life insurance policies exclude coverage for death during active military service or while in an aircraft other than a commercial airliner. For example, some life insurers would decline to provide coverage, or provide only modified coverage, for a sports car enthusiast who regularly takes part in weekend auto racing events.

Life Insurance Dividend Options

Option	Description
Cash option	Dividends are paid in cash, usually at the policy anniversary date.
Accumulated option	Dividend amounts remain with the insurer and accumulate interest. Dividends and accumulated interest can subsequently be withdrawn at any time or can be paid in addition to death benefit amounts.
Premium reduction option	Dividend amounts can be applied to pay for future premium payments due.
Paid-up additions	Dividends may be used to buy increments of paid-up whole life insurance, which would increase the amount of the death benefit paid under the policy.
One-year term insurance	Dividends may also be used to purchase term, rather than whole, life insurance for one year. If the insured dies within that time, the term life amount is added to the death benefit payable under the policy.

[DA07741]

Grace Period

For most policies, the **grace period** is thirty-one days. If an insured dies during the grace period, death benefits would still be paid. Generally, the death benefit is reduced by the overdue premium amount that is due the insurer.

Incontestable Clause

The **incontestable clause** designates a period, usually two years, after which the insurer cannot deny a claim because of any misrepresentation on the part of the policyowner. In life insurance policies, the application is considered part of the life insurance contract. Therefore, any fraudulent or misrepresented information provided by the policyowner on the application can serve as the basis for the insurer's contesting a claim during the contestable period. Not all losses will be paid even after the contestable period has passed; exclusions, such as death as the result of engaging in an excluded hazardous activity, would still apply.

Misstatement of Age or Sex

The misstatement of age or sex provision allows the insurer to adjust the death benefit on a life insurance policy to reflect the true age and sex of the insured based on the amount of the premium paid if it is determined that a misstatement of age or sex occurred. Life insurance policy premiums are based substantially on actuarial tables that estimate the likelihood of an individual's

Grace period
A provision that continues a life insurance policy in force for a certain number of days (usually thirty or thirty-one) after the premium due date, during which time the policyowner can pay the overdue premium without penalty.

Incontestable clause
A clause that states that the insurer cannot contest the policy after it has been in force for a specified period, such as two years, during the insured's lifetime.

death based on his or her age at the date the policy is issued and the individual's sex. If a misstatement is discovered—either during the policy period or at the time of death—there could be an adjustment in the face value of the policy or in the amount of premiums owed. For example, a policyholder may be issued a refund if the misstatement was of an older age at the time of policy issuance; or charged more if the misstatement was of a younger age at the time of policy issuance. A misstatement of sex is also treated by adjusting the face amount of the policy (when different premiums apply for males and females). Usually, such a misstatement results from a clerical error in the completion of the application or in the preparation of the life insurance contract.

Nonforfeiture Options

Policyowners have three **nonforfeiture options**:

- Cash surrender value—The policyowner would surrender the policy for cash, and all of the insurer's future obligations under the policy would cease. Any outstanding loan amounts would be deducted from the cash surrender amount.
- Reduced paid-up insurance—The policyowner may elect to use the accumulated cash value in the policy to purchase paid-up insurance at a reduced face amount. The type of coverage provided is the same as that provided under the original contract that was surrendered.
- Extended term insurance—The policyowner may choose to continue the full death benefit of the original policy, but for a shorter period, under a term policy.

> **Nonforfeiture options**
> Provisions in a life insurance policy that give the policyowner a choice of ways to use the cash value if the policy is terminated and that protect the policyowner from forfeiting the cash value.

Policy Loan Provisions

Life insurance policies that accumulate cash value contain a policy loan provision. Under this provision, policyowners can borrow an amount up to the cash value of the policy, subject to interest. If a policy loan is not repaid at the time of the insured's death, outstanding loan amounts (including interest) are deducted from the death benefit amount. Because no repayment schedule is set for life insurance policy loans, the policyowner has flexibility in repaying the loan.

Reinstatement Clause

A reinstatement clause allows a policyowner to reinstate a life insurance policy that has lapsed for nonpayment of premium. Most insurers allow reinstatement within a specified period, such as three or five years after the policy has lapsed. Most reinstatement clauses require the policyowner to provide evidence of insurability, pay all outstanding premiums with interest, and repay any outstanding policy loans, including interest. Most insurers do not allow policies that have been surrendered for cash value to be reinstated.

Settlement Options

Death benefits under a life insurance policy can be paid to the beneficiary in a single lump sum. The policyowner or beneficiary, however, may select from additional **settlement options**. See the exhibit "Life Insurance Settlement Options."

Settlement options
Various ways of paying life insurance policy proceeds to the beneficiary.

Life Insurance Settlement Options

Option	Description
Interest option	The life insurer retains the death benefits and pays only the interest to the beneficiary at periodic intervals—generally used on an interim basis until the lump-sum payment or another settlement option is made.
Fixed-period option	The death benefits are paid over a specified period of time. The amount of the periodic payment is a function of the amount of the death benefit, the rate of interest paid on the balance of the death benefit held by the insurer, the frequency of benefit payments, and the period selected by the beneficiary.
Fixed-amount option	Death benefits are paid in fixed amounts at predetermined intervals, usually monthly. Interest payments are included in the fixed amount, which may extend the time period during which payments will be made.
Life income option	The beneficiary receives the death benefit over his or her life. Life income options may include a no-refund option, which will pay benefits only until the death of the beneficiary. Other life income options would allow for payments remaining after the primary beneficiary's death to be paid to a contingent beneficiary. Life income amounts are based on actuarial tables using the beneficiary's age and sex.

[DA07742]

Suicide Clause

All life insurance policies contain a **suicide clause** that protects life insurers from adverse selection that could occur if a person planning to commit suicide purchases a large amount of life insurance shortly before ending his or her life. Most policies will refund the policy premium to the beneficiary if a suicide occurs within the first two years of the policy.

Suicide clause
A clause that states the insurer will not pay the death benefit if the insured commits suicide within a certain period (usually two years) after policy inception.

Common Life Insurance Riders

Rider
Similar to an endorsement; modifies a life insurance policy.

Life insurance **riders** or policy "add-ons" provide additional types of benefits or benefit extensions to the basic life insurance policy. Additional premiums are generally charged for these coverage extensions.

Accelerated Death Benefits

Traditionally, life insurance was a means to pay for final death expenses after an insured died. In the case of a catastrophic or terminal illness, however, the insured may need to access life insurance benefits to finance medical expenses before death. Some life insurers offer riders that provide for the discounted value, or a portion of such value (such as 50 percent), of the policy death benefit to be paid to the policyowner in the event of certain contingencies, such as a terminal illness (an illness that would result in death within about one year). Other riders may cover a catastrophic illness (such as cancer), or the need for long-term care in a nursing home or similar facility. Accelerated death benefits resemble viatical life settlements, in which the life insurance policy is sold to a third party, who becomes the beneficiary in the event of the original insured's death. The insured receives an amount, generally less than the face value of the policy but more than the accumulated cash value, and relinquishes his or her interest and that of any beneficiaries.

Additional Life Insurance Riders

Accidental death benefit
Provision in a life insurance policy that doubles (or triples) the face amount of insurance payable if the insured dies as a result of an accident.

Accidental death benefits—The **accidental death benefit** (often referred to as "double indemnity") provides an additional death benefit when death results from accidental bodily injury, or accidental means, as defined in the rider. In most cases, the amount of the accidental death benefit is equal to the face amount of the basic policy (for example, a $100,000 life insurance policy would pay $200,000 to the beneficiary if the provisions of this rider were met).

Disability income rider—A disability income rider may be added to a life insurance policy to provide a regular monthly income if the insured becomes permanently disabled. Most riders specify a level of income for a determined period of time.

Guaranteed insurability rider (guaranteed purchase option)
Rider that permits the policyowner to buy additional amounts of life insurance at standard rates without evidence of insurability.

Guaranteed insurability rider—A **guaranteed insurability rider** is added to many policies, particularly those issued to younger insureds, and can guarantee access to coverage if a policyholder becomes uninsurable due to poor health in the future. It must normally be purchased before a certain age, often forty. The type of insurance that can be purchased under this option is usually limited to a form of whole life insurance.

Waiver of premium rider—Under the waiver of premium rider, the insurer agrees to waive the payment of any premium falling due while the policyowner or insured is disabled, as defined in the waiver of premium provision. To be eligible for the benefit, the policyowner must have incurred a disability (as defined by the waiver of premium benefit) before the age stipulated in the contract (usually age sixty or sixty-five).

Apply Your Knowledge

Larry neglects to indicate a heart condition in his application for life insurance. If Larry were to die five years after the policy went into effect, the insurer would nevertheless be obligated to pay benefits based on which one of the following life insurance contractual provisions?

a. Excluded risks
b. Reinstatement clause
c. Incontestable clause
d. Suicide clause

Feedback: c. The incontestable clause, which designates a period, usually two years, after which an insurer cannot deny a claim because of any misrepresentation on the part of the policyowner.

LIFE INSURANCE CASE STUDY

Based on the facts presented in this case, what is the impact of premature death on this family? What are the family's life insurance needs? What amount and what type of policies, if any, should be purchased?

Kevin, age forty-three, and Patricia, age forty-one, are a married couple with two children, ages eight and eleven. Kevin earns $120,000 annually as a marketing and sales manager for a local firm. Patricia earns $32,000 annually as an administrative assistant with the local school district. She works only during the school term so she can be home with the children when they are on summer break.

Kevin and Patricia purchased their home ten years ago. It is currently valued at $309,000, with an outstanding mortgage of $142,500. They have one family car, valued at $27,500, which has an outstanding loan amount of $2,600. Kevin's employer supplies him with a company car for which all expenses are paid.

Kevin is contributing to a 401(k) plan sponsored by his employer, who matches his contributions up to 5 percent. The current value of his tax-deferred contributions, employer contributions, and investment earnings is $232,000. This amount includes a rollover of proceeds from a 401(k) plan at a previous employer. Kevin also has a group universal life (GUL) policy through his employer in an amount equal to his salary ($120,000) and has purchased additional coverage up to two times his salary for a total of $240,000.

Patricia has a defined benefit retirement plan with the school district and has the option to contribute to a non-matching 403(b) plan, but she does not participate in it. Based on a retirement age of sixty-five, she would receive $392 monthly. If Patricia predeceases Kevin, he would be entitled to 50 percent of her monthly benefits starting at age sixty-five. The school district provides $15,000 in group insurance coverage to Patricia, and she has no other life insurance coverage. Kevin and Patricia are also both eligible to receive Social Security benefits in retirement.

The needs approach or the human life value approach can be used to determine whether Kevin and Patricia have sufficient life insurance in the event of their premature death. The agent has decided to use the needs approach for Kevin and Patricia. To accomplish this, the agent evaluates the family's current financial situation, economic needs, and available resources, such as existing life insurance and retirement plans. If additional coverage is needed, types and sources of life insurance as well as additional provisions or riders would also be discussed.

Needs Analysis Steps

Calculating Kevin and Patricia's life-insurance needs entails several steps of analysis to determine cash needs in the event of Kevin's premature death as well as the assets the couple has available to meet those needs.

Expense Needs

Although both Kevin and Patricia are employed, the first step in determining life insurance needs would focus on Kevin as the primary wage earner in the family. This process entails review of the family's cash needs, such as ongoing living expenses, outstanding debt, and funding for the children's education, as well as final expenses that would arise in the event of Kevin's premature death. The same process would then be used to determine the family's cash needs in the event of Patricia's premature death.

The goal of this review is to determine how much money will be required to maintain the family's current standard of living should Kevin die prematurely. In this case, it is assumed that Patricia would continue to work in her current job with the same retirement benefits and that she would also receive Social Security benefits at retirement age. If Patricia planned to change jobs in the event of Kevin's premature death, the expense need projections would be adjusted. For example, the new job may have a higher salary or different retirement benefits. Patricia's current employment allows the family to avoid child-care expenses because her hours match those of the children's school hours and she is home during summer vacation. If she were to change to a job that had longer hours and required her to work during the summer, the needs calculation would have to reflect additional child-care expenses. See the exhibit "Expense Needs—Kevin and Patricia."

Expense Needs—Kevin and Patricia

Final Expenses Needs

Funeral costs	$ 9,500
Estate settlement	7,500
Federal taxes	0
State taxes	0
Total Final Expenses	$17,000

Debt Elimination Needs

Satisfy outstanding mortgage(s)	$142,500
Fund children's education	175,000
Eliminate outstanding credit card debt	3,750
Eliminate outstanding car loan	2,600
Total Debt Elimination Needs	$323,850

Family's Living Expenses Needs

Household maintenance expenses	$150,000
Other living expenses	200,000
Child-care expenses	0
Total Family Living Expenses Needs	$350,000

[DA05700]

Special Needs

The next step would involve considering whether the family has any expenses related to special needs in addition to maintaining its current standard of living. Such expenses could include gifts to charitable institutions or establishment of a trust. Kevin and Patricia's only special need is establishing an emergency fund that would cover any unanticipated expenses following Kevin's premature death. See the exhibit "Special Needs Expenses—Kevin and Patricia."

Retirement Income Needs

After the family's living expense needs are calculated, it is necessary to consider how much income Patricia would need in retirement. This calculation is based on her age at Kevin's death and other sources of retirement income, including her defined benefit pension plan and Social Security benefits. Much of Kevin and Patricia's current funding for retirement is based on Kevin's 401(k) proceeds. In the event of his premature death, Patricia would need to supplement her retirement income to cover all of her living expenses. See the exhibit "Retirement Needs—Kevin and Patricia."

Special Needs Expenses—Kevin and Patricia

Special Needs

Gifts to family members	$ 0
Gifts to charity	0
Fund a trust	0
Establish an emergency fund	$ 25,000
Total Special Needs	$ 25,000

[DA05701]

Retirement Needs—Kevin and Patricia

Retirement Income Needs

Patricia's supplemental retirement income	$350,000
Total Retirement Income Needs	$350,000

[DA05702]

Total Needs

The final step of the needs approach is adding all of the calculated expense needs to determine the total dollar amount required to meet monthly, ongoing, special, and retirement income needs. This amount will form the basis for determining whether Kevin is carrying a sufficient amount of life insurance or whether additional life insurance should be purchased. See the exhibit "Total Needs—Kevin and Patricia."

Total Needs—Kevin and Patricia

Total Needs

Final expense needs	$ 17,000
Debt elimination needs	$ 323,850
Family living expenses needs	$ 350,000
Special needs	$ 25,000
Retirement income needs	$ 350,000
Total Needs	$1,065,850

[DA05703]

Assets Available

After all of Kevin and Patricia's needs have been reviewed and calculated, the next step is to determine the dollar amount of assets that are available to meet these needs. These available assets include Kevin's group life coverage, his retirement account, and benefits that would be paid by Social Security. Patricia would not receive survivors benefits under Kevin's Social Security until she reaches retirement age. Social Security will, however, pay monthly survivors benefits to the children until they turn eighteen (in most cases). See the exhibit "Assets Available—Kevin and Patricia."

Assets Available—Kevin and Patricia

Life Insurance and Other Assets

Group life insurance	$ 240,000
Checking and savings accounts	$ 11,000
Social Security survivors benefits	$ 335,000
Retirement account	$ 232,000
Total Assets	$ 818,000

[DA05704]

Total Life Insurance Needs

After all of the family's expense needs have been identified and compared to the available assets, the insurance professional would be ready to advise Kevin and Patricia regarding the adequacy of their current life insurance program. Based on the total needs of $1,065,000 and available assets to meet those needs of $818,000, there is a shortfall of $247,000. See the exhibit "Total Life Insurance Needs—Kevin and Patricia."

Total Life Insurance Needs—Kevin and Patricia

Total Life Insurance Needs

Total needs	$ 1,065,000
Minus total assets	$ 818,000
Additional Life Insurance Needed	$ 247,000

[DA05706]

Recommendations

Based on this review, it is recommended that Kevin should purchase an additional $247,000 of life insurance. The insurance professional would explain several options available to the family.

Types and Sources of Life Insurance

One option would be for the family to purchase an individual term life policy for $250,000 from a private life insurer. This would be a cost-effective method to close the current gap in assets required to meet the family's needs in the event of Kevin's premature death.

Another option may be a combination of group universal life and individual term life. If his employer-sponsored group life plan allows it, Kevin could purchase an additional $120,000 increment under that plan and purchase the remaining amount from a life insurer under an individual term policy. The advantage of purchasing additional universal life insurance is that it provides permanent coverage (as long as Kevin is employed) and builds cash value. Term coverage is temporary but generally less costly than a universal policy. A $250,000 ten-year term policy would also cover the majority of the family's temporary needs, such as the children's future education and the mortgage elimination needs.

Because these needs will change over time, it is important to periodically conduct a needs approach review as the family's situation changes. This review would also include an evaluation of the family's needs in the event of Patricia's premature death.

Life Insurance Contractual Provisions and Riders

As part of purchasing additional coverage, Kevin and Patricia would need to designate beneficiaries in the policies. Kevin would designate Patricia as the primary beneficiary and then name the children as contingent beneficiaries. This would allow the children to collect the death benefits if Patricia predeceases Kevin.

It is also important to consider the settlement options available to Patricia in the event of Kevin's death. Death benefits are often paid in a lump-sum amount to the primary beneficiary. Patricia would need to consider her employment situation, the children's ages, and the family's needs at the time of Kevin's death. Patricia may decide that a fixed-period option would be more appropriate than a lump-sum payment; it would provide periodic payments for a specified period while the children are still in school and she continues to collect a salary from her job.

Kevin may consider adding a disability income rider to the life insurance policy if he does not already have disability coverage in place. This rider would provide a regular monthly income to the family for a specified period if

Kevin were to become permanently disabled. An additional premium would be charged for this rider. See the exhibit "Suggested Correct Answers."

Suggested Correct Answers

Need for life insurance:

Additional $247,000 (Total need of $1,065,000 minus total assets of $818,000)

Types of life insurance:

1. Purchase an individual ten-year term life insurance policy from a private insurer in the amount of $250,000

or

2. If available, increase current group universal life insurance policy by one $120,000 increment and purchase an individual ten-year term life insurance policy from a private insurer in the amount of $130,000

Contractual provisions:

Designate spouse as primary beneficiary and children as contingent beneficiaries in the event spouse prececeases children.

Riders:

Consider adding a disability income rider to provide continuing income in the event of a permanent disability.

[DA05707]

SUMMARY

The premature death loss exposure can have a significant financial impact on individuals, their dependents, and families of all types. This impact can be reduced or eliminated with life insurance. Benefits of life insurance can vary based on various individual and family needs.

Two primary methods are used to determine the appropriate amount of life insurance for an individual: the needs approach and the human life value approach. Both methods yield precise amounts; however, the needs approach considers all recurring and unusual expenses, whereas the human life value approach focuses on replacing a primary wage earner's income.

Term life insurance is a popular, low-cost option to provide life insurance protection for a specified time period. Permanent types of life insurance that include some investment or savings aspect include whole life, universal life, variable life, and variable universal life. Other specialized types of life insurance are current assumption whole life, second-to-die life insurance, and first-to-die life insurance.

Life insurance can be purchased individually or may be available through group/employer-based programs or government-based programs. Each of these channels presents advantages and limitations, which individuals must consider as part of their life insurance planning.

Several common life insurance provisions stipulate how coverage will be provided. These provisions may also affect how death benefits will be paid. Riders are attached to life insurance policies to provide additional benefits and generally require payment of additional premiums.

It is important for individuals and families to review their financial and family obligations to determine the need for life insurance. This review should also include consideration of the types and sources of life insurance, contractual provisions, and additional riders that could be used to tailor coverage for specific needs.

Direct Your Learning

10

Retirement Planning

Educational Objectives

After learning the content of this assignment, you should be able to:

- Describe these aspects of retirement:
  - Factors that influence the retirement loss exposure
  - Investing to achieve financial goals
- Compare the characteristics of traditional IRAs and Roth IRAs.
- Summarize the following types of tax-deferred retirement plans:
  - 401(k) plan
  - Profit-sharing plan
  - Thrift plan
  - Keogh plan
  - 403(b) plan
  - SIMPLE (Savings Incentive Match Plan for Employees)
  - ESOP (Employee Stock Ownership Plan)
  - SEP (Simplified Employee Pension) plan
- Describe the following types of employer-sponsored retirement plans:
  - Defined benefit
  - Defined contribution
  - Defined benefit 401(k) plans
- Summarize the various types of individual annuities.
- Describe the following with regard to the United States Social Security program:
  - The basic characteristics of OASDHI
  - Covered occupations

Outline

The Retirement Loss Exposure and Achieving Financial Goals

Individual Retirement Accounts

Types of Tax-Deferred Retirement Plans

Employer-Sponsored Retirement Plans

Individual Annuities

Social Security Program (OASDHI)

Summary

10.1

10

Educational Objectives, continued

- The eligibility requirements for insured status
- The types of benefits provided

Retirement Planning

THE RETIREMENT LOSS EXPOSURE AND ACHIEVING FINANCIAL GOALS

When planning for retirement, individuals and families should calculate the financial resources needed to pay expenses once income from full-time employment ends. Investing is one way to achieve this and other financial goals.

Many individuals look forward to retiring from the active workforce. Retirement, however, means that regular earnings cease while living expenses continue. This gap forms the basis of the retirement loss exposure. Increased costs for age-related expenses such as healthcare, long-term care, and inflation—along with finite financial resources—can create potentially ruinous effects. Prudent financial planning throughout one's earning years is an effective way to limit exposure to this risk.

Factors That Influence the Retirement Loss Exposure

The essence of the retirement loss exposure is reduced or eliminated regular income, which makes retirees vulnerable to economic peril. The objective of retirement planning is to accumulate sufficient funds to meet expenses and maintain an acceptable standard of living.

This planning involves estimating the living expenses that will arise after income from full-time employment ceases, along with the anticipated length of retirement. Planning should consider the potential costs of healthcare, long-term care, and expenses related to spending more time on a hobby, recreational activity, or travel. Failure to carefully plan for needs such as these can result in a lower standard of living in retirement and the need to continue working past a planned retirement age.

Social Security is one source of retirement income. However, individuals should supplement the minimal retirement income Social Security provides with additional sources, such as employer-sponsored retirement and pension plans. Some employer plans are funded exclusively by employees, while others are funded by employees and employers. In addition to Social Security benefits and qualified employer-based retirement plans, individuals may use personal savings and investments, annuities, individual retirement accounts

(IRAs), and cash value from life insurance policies to supplement their retirement savings. See the exhibit "Planning for Retirement—A Defined Contribution Plan Example."

> ### Planning for Retirement—A Defined Contribution Plan Example
>
> William contributes 9 percent of his salary annually to a defined contribution plan, a tax-deferred 401(k) plan. His employer matches up to 4 percent of all contributions; therefore, William's annual defined contribution is 13 percent. Under this plan, William is responsible for making decisions on allocating funds among different investment options. Unlike a defined benefit plan, William's actual payout at retirement is not predetermined and will depend on how long the plan is funded, the investment returns earned, and the age at which William decides to retire.

[DA07765]

As the baby boom generation (those born between 1946 and 1964) continues to age, the proportion of the United States population over age sixty-five will increase dramatically. This growth in the number of older individuals threatens to place a strain on the Social Security and healthcare systems. Furthermore, members of this generation are expected to live longer than previous generations and, therefore, spend more years in retirement. Because Social Security benefits provide only a minimum level of income, and retirement funds must sustain individuals longer than previous generations, retirees must use other methods to accumulate the savings required to meet retirement expense needs.

The ability of baby boomers to increase their retirement savings is also affected by what is sometimes referred to as the "sandwich generation" effect. Many baby boomers have expenses related to the care of elderly parents, and, at the same time, support or pay college tuitions for adult children. This effect further constrains individuals from increasing contributions to retirement plans or personal savings.

It is important to consider the effect of inflation in planning for retirement and estimating future expenses. Inflation is an increase in the prices of goods and services. Rising prices are especially problematic for retirees whose income is fixed. Goods and services such as healthcare, assisted living, long-term care, and prescription drugs are particularly affected by higher inflation. During inflationary periods, interest rates tend to rise, which can negatively affect the overall economy. The effect of inflation on the future value of the dollar must be considered from the current planning period through the retirement age period. See the exhibit "Three-Legged Stool of Retirement Savings."

Three-Legged Stool of Retirement Savings

Individuals cannot rely on only one source, such as Social Security, to fully fund retirement needs. When planning for retirement, individuals must take advantage of employer-sponsored retirement plans or establish traditional or Roth IRAs, as well as build personal savings accounts, certificates of deposit, or money market accounts. An effective mix of these three sources can establish sufficient funds to meet retirement income needs and maintain a desired standard of living.

[DA07766]

Investing to Achieve Financial Goals

Investors have various objectives. What may be a primary objective for one investor may be a secondary or nonexistent objective for another. Each investor must decide what he or she most wants to accomplish when investing for retirement. Such decisions depend, in part, on the age of the investor and how many years remain until retirement. Some investment objectives work best when implemented over a span of several years. See the exhibit "Investment Goals."

Investment Goals

Investment Goal	Description
Capital Appreciation	The increase in value of investments over a relatively long period is often intended to help investors pay for long-term goals such as retirement.
Preservation of Capital	Preservation of capital is a conservative objective that focuses on maintaining the value of investments, rather than on increasing their value. This often entails selecting investments that have low risk of losing value but result in a low rate of return. Even when the economy is growing, investors with a short-term investment horizon, such as saving for a down payment on a house, may choose this strategy. Investors who are close to or already in retirement may also select this objective. To preserve the purchasing power of invested funds, investors pursuing this objective should select investments with a rate of return that at least matches the rate of inflation.
Current Income	Some investors prefer to place a higher priority on generating income from their investments than on long-term capital appreciation. This objective is especially attractive to investors who are retired and may need to supplement Social Security benefits or a former employer's pension plan to pay living expenses.
Growth and Income	Some investors seek both capital appreciation (growth) and current income (income). This combination can result in a high total rate of return but comes with a higher level of risk that the investment will lose value.
Liquidity	The ability to quickly sell an investment with minimal loss of principle can allow an investor to meet sudden obligations that require cash, such as a health condition requiring expensive medical care. An example of a highly liquid investment is a savings account.
Minimizing Taxes	Minimizing taxes is often an objective for high-income investors. Such investors will place a priority on investments whose earnings are not taxed even though the rate of return may be lower than that of comparable investments. The purpose is to obtain a tax savings large enough to offset the lower rate of return, which would result in a higher net rate of return, after taxes.

[DA07767]

All investments entail risk. It's possible to earn substantial income, or lose some or all of the original investment. Certain investments offer a guaranteed investment outcome. Such investments have little investment risk and a correspondingly low rate of return. Other investments, such as the purchase of stock in a new company, can be speculative because the company does not have an established track record. The financial reward to the investor can be high if the company's performance exceeds expectations, but there is also a high probability the company may not perform as expected. Some of the common risks that affect investors include these:

- Purchasing power (or inflation) risk—the risk associated with the purchasing power of an investment's proceeds
- Market risk—the risk associated with fluctuations in prices of financial securities, such as stocks and bonds
- Interest-rate risk—the risk associated with price changes of existing investments due to changes in the general level of interest rates in the capital markets
- Maturity risk—the risk associated with securities that may mature at a time when interest rates in the capital markets are lower than those provided by the maturing investments, causing the investor to reinvest at a lower rate of interest
- Financial (or credit) risk—the risk that issuers of investments may have financial difficulties and, as a result, may not pay investors as expected
- Business risk—the risk associated with the nature of the industry in which the issuer of an investment operates and the management of the issuer itself
- Liquidity risk—the risk that an asset may not be easily or quickly convertible into cash at a reasonable price
- Investment manager risk—the risk associated with the variability in performance of persons responsible for managing an investor's assets

Many types of investments are available for retirement planning. An investor chooses a strategy based on his or her retirement objectives, financial goals, and the time horizon over which the investment will accumulate. See the exhibit "Types of Investments."

Types of Investments

Savings Instruments

Commercial banks and other financial institutions offer a variety of savings instruments that are free of market risk; interest-rate risk; and, when insured by the Federal Deposit Insurance Corporation (FDIC), financial (or credit) risk. The main advantage of savings instruments is their high liquidity, which makes them a safe haven for funds that are readily available for emergencies and short-term financial goals. However, purchasing power (or inflation) risk must be considered because the rate of return at times has been too low to keep pace with the cost of inflation.

Four commonly used forms of this type of investment are savings accounts, certificates of deposit (CDs), money market mutual funds, and money market deposit accounts.

Stocks

Investors who purchase stock in a corporation hold an ownership interest in the corporation and share a portion of its profits and losses. Because stock prices can go up or down dramatically in a relatively short period, stocks are the most risky of the commonly used types of investment. However, investors expect that they will be compensated for this higher risk with a higher rate of return than they would receive on a more conservative investment. Because of the high risk inherent in stock investment, many investors nearing retirement will reduce the portion of stocks in their individual retirement portfolios and increase the portion of bonds.

Bonds

Governments and corporations sell bonds to raise funds to finance projects. Bonds are certificates of debt that include the seller's promise to pay investors a fixed amount on a fixed maturity date. The promise typically includes interest payments at fixed intervals at a fixed (coupon) rate of interest. Corporate bonds are more risky than savings accounts because of the risk that corporations may run into financial difficulty and default on their promise; however, bonds retain less risk than stocks. As a result, the expected rate of return earned on a bond is higher than that of a savings account but lower than that of stock. The rate of return earned on a government-issued bond is typically lower than that earned on a corporate-issued bond. Investors in bonds enjoy low liquidity risk because bonds can be sold before their maturity date. However, the sales price is subject to the current market conditions and interest rate and could, therefore, be lower than the original price.

Mutual Funds

Normally, a mutual fund is an actively managed pool of funds from a group of investors. Because a mutual fund owns a variety of investments, the risks associated with any one investment are diluted. This dilution, referred to as diversification, is a major advantage of mutual funds. Some mutual funds, such as index funds and lifecycle (or target date) funds, are passively managed. The managers of these funds do not invest in individual securities in an attempt to outperform the market. Index funds are considered to be passively managed because the fund manager tries only to follow an index such as the Standard & Poor's 500 or Wilshire 5000 rather than individual stocks. Lifecycle funds typically invest in a combination of stocks and bonds that gradually shifts more toward bonds as the investor approaches retirement, thus pursuing a more conservative investment objective.

> **Annuities**
>
> Because average life span continues to increase, retired persons have a higher likelihood of exhausting their financial assets to pay expenses. Annuities, which are contracts sold by insurance companies, address this problem with their promise of lifetime income. In return for a lump sum payment or a series of payments to the insurance company, the investor receives lifelong income through regular payments, usually after retirement.
>
> **Real Estate**
>
> Despite the variations and uncertainty of the housing market, an investor will benefit from shelter and security provided by a house. However, those benefits typically are not provided by other real estate investments such as commercial office buildings, shopping centers, residential rental property, mortgages, and real estate investment trusts (REITS). In fact, such investments can create burdens beyond the initial investment, such as dealing with complex tax issues and difficult tenants.

[DA07768]

INDIVIDUAL RETIREMENT ACCOUNTS

Traditional and Roth individual retirement accounts (IRAs) provide alternative investment options when an employer's retirement plan does not fit an individual's needs, and when an individual is seeking a tax deduction or wants to reduce his or her tax burden in retirement.

The Employee Retirement Income Security Act (ERISA) of 1974 created the **traditional IRA** so individuals without employer-sponsored pension plans could save for retirement. The Taxpayer Relief Act of 1997 created the **Roth IRA**, which boasts many of the same advantages of a traditional IRA and fewer disadvantages. Many individuals choose to invest in an IRA in addition to other retirement investment plans.

In order to contribute to either traditional or Roth IRAs, an investor must have earned taxable income during the year. Taxable compensation includes wages, salaries, tips, commissions, fees, bonuses, self-employment income, taxable alimony, and separate maintenance payments. Investment income, pension, annuity income, and rental income do not qualify. A traditional IRA restricts eligibility based on the investor's age; a Roth IRA does not. However, unlike a traditional IRA, a Roth IRA limits contributions based on the investor's modified adjusted gross income. This income limitation is periodically increased to account for inflation.[1] See the exhibit "IRAs: Investor Eligibility."

Annual contribution limits for a Roth IRA are the same as those for a traditional IRA. However, unlike a traditional IRA, contributions to a Roth IRA are made with funds that have already been taxed. See the exhibit "IRAs: Annual Contribution Limitations (as of 2011)."

Traditional individual retirement account (IRA)
A retirement savings plan by which an individual can use tax-deductible and tax-deferred methods for accumulating funds.

Roth IRA
A retirement savings plan by which an individual can accumulate investment income on a tax-free basis (subject to certain limitations).

IRAs: Investor Eligibility

Traditional IRA	Roth IRA
• Earned taxable compensation	• Earned taxable compensation
• Under 70.5 years of age	• Eligible at any age
	• Eligibility may be phased out or lost as income increases

[DA07777]

IRAs: Annual Contribution Limitations (as of 2011)

Traditional IRA	Roth IRA
• $5,000 limit per individual under 50 years of age	• Same limits as traditional IRA
• $6,000 limit per individual 50 years of age or older	• Invest with after-tax funds
• Invest with before-tax funds	

[DA07778]

Contributions to a traditional IRA can be deducted from federal income tax under two circumstances. First, an individual who is not currently a participant in an employer-sponsored retirement plan can make an IRA contribution that is deductible up to the maximum annual limit. Second, an individual who is a participant in an employer's retirement plan can deduct up to the maximum annual limit for an IRA contribution if his or her modified adjusted gross income is below a certain limit, which, like the Roth IRA's income limitation, is periodically adjusted to account for inflation. If an individual has income above the phase-out limits, he or she can still contribute to a traditional IRA, but will not be able to deduct his or her contributions when calculating the amount owed in federal income taxes. By contrast, annual contributions to a Roth IRA are not income-tax deductible, regardless of participation in an employer-sponsored retirement plan or the individual's level of income. See the exhibit "IRAs: Tax Treatment of Contributions."

IRAs are intended to be retirement investment plans. Therefore, owners of IRAs are penalized if they withdraw funds (receive distributions) from the account before they are fifty-nine-and-one-half. Conversely, to avoid other penalties, an owner must start receiving distributions at no later than seventy-and-one-half years. As with a traditional IRA, Roth IRAs are intended to be retirement investment plans. Therefore, penalty-free distributions of earnings

IRAs: Tax Treatment of Contributions

Traditional IRA	Roth IRA
• Tax deductable	• Not tax deductible
• Tax deductibility may be phased out or lost as income increases	

[DA07779]

cannot be made before the owner is fifty-nine-and-one-half. However, unlike a traditional IRA, Roth IRAs impose no penalty if the owner does not start receiving distributions before reaching age seventy-and-one-half. In fact, during the lifetime of a Roth IRA owner, there are no required distributions. This unique feature of a Roth IRA allows the owner's funds to accumulate tax-free. See the exhibit "IRAs: Distributions."

IRAs: Distributions

Traditional IRA	Roth IRA
• Subject to penalty if withdrawn before owner of IRA is 59.5 years of age	• Earnings subject to penalty if withdrawn before owner of IRA is 59.5 years of age or the IRA is less than 5 years old
• Subject to penalty if withdrawals start after owner of IRA is 70.5 years of age	• Not subject to penalty if withdrawals start after owner of IRA is 70.5 years of age

[DA07780]

The funds in a traditional IRA appreciate and earn interest on a tax-deferred, not tax-free, basis. As such, distributions are taxed as ordinary income if no penalty applies. If a distribution is made before the owner of the IRA has reached age fifty-nine-and-one-half, a 10 percent tax penalty will be applied. However, this penalty may be waived if one of several, primarily health-related, exceptions applies.

Because the contributions, but not earnings, to a Roth IRA consist of after-tax dollars, they can be withdrawn without subjecting the investor to any additional federal income tax or penalty, even if he or she has not reached fifty-nine-and-one-half. The earnings made on the contributions can also be withdrawn tax free and without a penalty, but only if the IRA has been in existence for five years or more and the owner is at least fifty-nine-and-one-half years of age. If these conditions are not met, the earnings withdrawn will be taxed as ordinary income and a 10 percent penalty will be applied. However, the tax and penalty may be waived if the IRA owner becomes disabled or dies. They also may be waived if the withdrawn funds are used to purchase the IRA owner's first home (subject to a $10,000 limit). See the exhibit "IRAs: Tax Treatment of Distributions."

IRAs: Tax Treatment of Distributions

Traditional IRA	Roth IRA
• Taxed as ordinary income	• Not taxed if conditions met
• Several exceptions to premature withdrawal penalty	• Few exceptions to premature withdrawal penalty

[DA07781]

Apply Your Knowledge

Sally, forty-eight, has had her current job for twenty years, during which she has contributed to an employer-sponsored retirement plan that she believes will sufficiently provide for her early retirement years. However, because she is concerned that her healthcare and long-term care expenses will increase substantially if she lives into her eighties and beyond, Sally would like to establish a retirement savings account that will allow her investment to accrue until she reaches that age range and potentially needs to withdraw from the fund. Which kind of IRA would most effectively meet Sally's needs?

Feedback: Sally should invest in a Roth IRA, because, unlike a traditional IRA, Roth IRAs impose no penalty if the owner does not start receiving distributions before reaching age seventy-and-one-half. In fact, during the lifetime of a Roth IRA owner, there are no required distributions. This unique feature of a Roth IRA allows the funds of the owner to continue to accumulate tax-free.

TYPES OF TAX-DEFERRED RETIREMENT PLANS

The federal government has created multiple qualified (tax-deferred) retirement plans with unique characteristics to meet the different needs of employees or employers.

Qualified, or tax-deferred, retirement plans are those plans described in the Internal Revenue Code that are given special tax advantages if they comply with certain legal requirements.

401(k) Plan

Section 401(k) of the Internal Revenue Code allows employees to contribute a portion of their pretax salary to a qualified retirement plan. Employers often match their employees' contributions. Payment of income tax on contributions, and the earnings from those contributions, is deferred until withdrawals are made, which usually occurs during retirement. Employee contributions are automatically deducted from their salary.

An inflation-adjusted limit applies to annual contributions.[2] However, employees over fifty can make an additional catch-up contribution (also limited to an inflation-adjusted maximum). Like most tax-favored retirement plans, 401(k) plans restrict the withdrawal of funds. Withdrawal of funds without penalty is allowed only for one of these reasons:

- Attainment of age fifty-nine-and-one-half or older
- Separation from employment
- Death or disability
- Hardship for the employee as defined by the Internal Revenue Service (IRS)

The government enforces these withdrawal restrictions on retirement savings to encourage individuals to save money to provide personal financial resources during their retirement.

Profit-Sharing Plan

The purpose of a profit-sharing plan is to distribute a percentage of an employer's profit among participating employees. An employer's annual contributions are discretionary and are allocated to individual employees' accounts according to a preestablished formula, often based on a participant's compensation. In such a case, each participating employee would receive a uniform proportionate share. Alternatively, the formula could be based on the amount of compensation and the age of each participant. Whichever basis is used, total contributions cannot exceed 25 percent of the employee's total covered compensation. Because of their discretionary and unpredictable nature, profit-sharing plans are often used in conjunction with other retirement plans.

Thrift Plan

A thrift (or savings) plan allows an employee to contribute a certain percentage of his or her salary, which the employer will then match with a percentage of what the employee contributed. If the employer limits the amount it will match, employees may be allowed to make an additional contribution that is unmatched by the employer. Thrift plans can be partially funded with before-tax or after-tax contributions, which are usually deducted from the employee's salary. If the plan is funded with before-tax contributions, it is subject to the same withdrawal restrictions as a 401(k) plan.

Keogh Plan

Keogh plans were developed to give owners of unincorporated businesses and other self-employed individuals the same tax advantages as their employees when investing for retirement. The employees of such employers can also participate in a Keogh plan. To be eligible to participate, a self-employed individual must have earned income in the current year (earned income is essentially the net earnings—or net profit—for a business, determined by subtracting business expenses from net revenues). The resulting amount, if positive, can be inserted into a formula provided by the IRS to calculate the amount that may be contributed to each employee's and self-employed individual's plan. The contributed amount is deducted from the individual's gross income on his or her individual tax return. Self-employed individuals who establish Keogh plans may use the rules of another plan, such as a profit-sharing or 401(k) plan, to determine the plan's administration and the contributions and withdrawal restrictions.

403(b) Plan

Section 403(b) of the Internal Revenue Code allows an employee of a tax-exempt organization that operates solely for charitable, religious, scientific, or educational purposes to invest in a tax-sheltered annuity. The annuity is tax-sheltered because the contributions are made with before-tax compensation. Further, the contributions and the earnings on the contributions are not taxed until withdrawal, which is usually during retirement. Contributions are treated much the same as in a 401(k) plan: they are subject to the same annual limit on their amounts and are typically made through payroll deductions.

SIMPLE

Savings Incentive Match Plan for Employees (SIMPLE) is intended to encourage employers with 100 or fewer employees to establish qualified retirement plans. These employers are exempt from administrative requirements that other plans impose. Employees contribute before-tax compensation through payroll deductions, and the employer makes matching contributions for its eligible employees. Employee eligibility is subject to a minimum salary requirement, and, as with 401(k) plans, annual contributions are limited, with a provision for catch-up contributions for those fifty and older.[3] When offering a SIMPLE plan, employers may not sponsor another qualified retirement plan. Withdrawals are taxed as ordinary income and subject to a penalty if withdrawn before the employee reaches fifty-nine-and-one-half.

ESOP

Employee Stock Ownership Plans (ESOPs) are qualified retirement plans that operate much like profit-sharing plans, with two primary differences:

- In an ESOP, the employer's contributions are not dependent on whether it has made a profit.
- ESOP employer contributions may be in the form of cash or employer's stock, and the value of either form of contribution is limited to 25 percent of payroll. If the contribution is in the form of stock and it cannot be easily sold on an established market, the employee must be allowed to sell it back to the employer at its fair market value.

SEP Plan

A Simplified Employee Pension (SEP) plan is essentially a form of a traditional individual retirement account (IRA) that enables employers to contribute to their employees' retirement accounts or allows the self-employed to fund their own retirement accounts. SEPs differ from traditional IRAs in several ways. First, the annual contribution limit is much higher for a SEP than for an IRA. Also, unlike for an IRA, an employer must contribute to the employee's SEP if the employee is at least twenty-one and has worked for the employer in the current year and in three of the last five years. Similar to an IRA, the income tax on an employer's contributions and the earnings on those contributions is deferred until withdrawal, at which time they are taxed as ordinary income (withdrawals are subject to the same restrictions as traditional IRAs).

Apply Your Knowledge

Which one of the following retirement plans' unpredictability often causes investors to couple it with another retirement savings plan?

a. 401(k) plan
b. Thrift plan
c. Profit-sharing plan
d. Employee stock ownership plans

Feedback: c. Profit-sharing plans are often used in conjunction with other retirement savings plans because an employer's annual contributions are discretionary. An employer's contribution to a 401(k) plan and a thrift plan, by contrast, is based on the employee's contribution. In an employee stock ownership plan, the employer's contributions are not dependent on whether it has made a profit.

EMPLOYER-SPONSORED RETIREMENT PLANS

The global financial crisis starting in 2008 decimated many previously sound retirement accounts. Employees should carefully examine the characteristics of the retirement plans offered by their employer to minimize the impact of such events on their retirement plans.

Defined benefit plan
A pension plan that is based on the monthly retirement benefit rather than on the contribution rate.

Defined contribution plan
A pension plan in which the contribution is a percentage of the participating employee's earnings or a flat dollar amount.

The two main types of employer-sponsored retirement plans are the **defined benefit plan** and the **defined contribution plan**. A third type is a combination of those two. It is referred to as a defined benefit 401(k) plan. Each of these types of plans has distinguishing characteristics in terms of what is contributed, the benefits paid, and the risks and advantages to the employee and employer.

Defined Benefit Plans

A defined benefit plan is sponsored by an employer, who is responsible for providing a fixed monthly benefit at the time of an employee's retirement. The amount the employer must contribute varies depending on the investment earnings on the contributions. Typically the employee makes no contributions to the plan.

The amount of the benefit is usually based on a formula that takes into account the number of years an employee has worked for the employer. For example, an employee may receive 1 percent of his or her salary for every year of service, up to a total of twenty years. The amount of salary used in the formula varies from employer to employer; one approach is to average the most recent five years of the employee's pay. Payment of benefits starts when the employee retires and continues for as long as he or she lives. Ancillary benefits may also be provided. These include funds for early retirement, termination, death, disability, or another event that ends employment before the normal retirement age of sixty-five years.

There are risks that an employee will not receive the full benefit amount promised by the employer. For example, the employee might not remain employed by the employer until retirement age, the plan could be terminated by the employer, or the employer might not contribute sufficient funds. Many of these risks are outside the employee's control but can be at least partially mitigated through ancillary benefits, placing contributions in a pension trust, or having terminated plan benefits guaranteed by the Pension Benefit Guaranty Corporation. Overall, the employee risks involved with a defined benefit plan are much lower than those of most other qualified employer-sponsored retirement plans.

Defined Contribution Plans

In a defined contribution plan, the sponsoring employer is responsible for contributing a fixed matching percentage of the contributions an employee makes. A common example of a defined contribution plan is a 401(k) plan, in which an employer might match up to 50 percent of an employee's 4 percent salary contribution.

The employer does not promise that a fixed monthly benefit will be available upon the employee's retirement. The employer's contribution remains the same, and it is the benefits received by the employee that vary. If an employee wants a benefit that is high enough to replace a certain percentage of his or her earnings decrease on retirement, the employee, not the employer, will have to increase contributions to make up the difference. For example, if an employee in his mid-twenties has a retirement goal of replacing 60 percent of his pre-retirement income and his contributions earn 7.5 percent interest, he will need to contribute 10 percent of his salary to the plan. However, if his earnings decrease to 5.5 percent, he will have to increase his contributions to 15 percent of his salary.

Defined contribution plans force employees to assume the investment risk of earnings volatility. When the economy and investment markets are down, as they were during the global financial crisis that began in 2008, it tends to affect older workers more because they have less time to recover before they retire.

Defined contribution plans do not provide the ancillary benefits found in many defined benefit plans. No additional funds are payable by the employer if an employee dies, becomes disabled, or is terminated before retirement age. The risk of mortality, disability, or another event that causes early termination is transferred to the employee.

It is often easier for employers to administer and explain the benefits of a defined contribution plan than of a defined benefit plan. For this reason, among others, defined contributions plans are becoming more common than defined benefit plans. The global financial crisis that began in 2008 has accelerated the trend. Even before the crisis, however, Congress found the trend disturbing because it had created defined contribution plans to supplement, not replace, defined benefit plans. To reverse the trend toward defined contribution plans, Congress passed the 2006 Pension Protection Act to create the defined benefit 401(k) plan.

Defined Benefit 401(k) Plans

A defined benefit 401(k) plan, also called the DB (k), is a combination of a defined benefit plan and a defined contribution plan that offers the benefits of a 401(k) savings plan along with a guaranteed flow of income. To be eligible, the employer must have between two employees and five hundred employees. The plan must have a defined benefit portion of 1 percent of an employee's average salary per year of service, up to twenty years of the employee's final average pay. On the defined contribution or 401(k) side, the plan must have a provision that automatically enrolls employees with a 4 percent employee contribution unless they decline to participate. The employer must match at least 50 percent of the employee's 401(k) contribution, up to 4 percent of the employee's compensation (or a total of a 2 percent match of the employee's salary). It must also have a defined contribution portion that automatically enrolls employees in a 401(k) plan with a 4 percent contribution unless they decline to participate.

Vesting for the defined benefit portion occurs after three years of service. As a result, the funds stay with the employer if an employee is terminated before three years. For the defined contribution 401(k) portion, vesting occurs immediately. Withdrawals at retirement are made as monthly checks similar to a traditional pension plan.

Some of the advantages for employers are less paperwork, fewer regulations, and less cost compared to operating a defined benefit plan and a 401(k) separately. This plan also does not have a top-heavy rule meant to prevent highly paid employees from receiving a larger percentage of benefits or contributions than other employees. These advantages are meant to encourage employers to offer these plans to their employees. Employers can offer a defined benefit 401(k) plan as an incentive to attract and retain workers in a "scarce resource" (employee) environment—an additional reason for employers to adopt the plan.

INDIVIDUAL ANNUITIES

Annuities have become popular vehicles for retirement investing. They can be purchased individually or on a group basis from a life insurance company, and, regardless of the source, they generally provide periodic payments to the recipient for as long as he or she lives.

Annuity
A type of life insurance policy or contract that makes periodic payments to the recipient for a fixed period or for life in exchange for a specified premium.

The owner of an **annuity** (who can be an individual or an entity) pays a specified premium to an insurer in exchange for a promise that the insurer will make payments at a specified interval to return the principal, plus interest, to the individual insured (annuitant). These annuity payments are typically guaranteed to continue throughout the life of the annuitant; consequently, they are often called life annuities. The beneficiary of an annuity is the individual or entity designated to receive the death benefit if the annuity owner or annuitant dies.

The period during which the benefits are paid is called the payout period. The payout amount, or cash value, is made up of the premium (principal) and the interest earned over the life of the annuity. Each periodic payment (benefit) includes a portion of both principal and interest, and it might include a survivor benefits amount as provided by the annuity contract. When the annuitant dies, the premium is entirely liquidated and nothing or very little remains for the heirs. This is called the mortality risk of life annuities.

Annuities can be classified by the starting date of the annuity, the party that determines the investment and bears the investment risks, or the premium payment method. See the exhibit "Types of Annuities."

Types of Annuities

Annuity Types Based on the Date Benefits Begin	Deferred Annuity: Benefits paid at specified future point
	Immediate Annuity: Benefits typically paid within thirty days of premium payment
Annuity Types Based on the Party Bearing the Investment Risk	Fixed-Dollar Annuity: Insurer bears risk
	Variable Annuity: Investor bears risk
	Combination Plan: Investor bears risk
	Equity Indexed Annuity: Insurer bears risk
Annuity Types Based on Premium Payment Method	Flexible-Premium Annuity: Premium amount and frequency determined by investor
	Single-Premium Annuity: Premium is one lump-sum payment

[DA07754]

Annuity Types Based on the Date Benefits Begin

The period between the annuity owner's purchase of the annuity and the annuitant's age at which benefit payments begin is called the accumulation period. **Deferred annuity** benefits are not payable until a specified time in the future (such as when the annuitant reaches a certain age, or after a specified number of years). Under an **immediate annuity**, benefit payments begin soon after the annuity owner purchases the annuity. Because the accumulation period for immediate annuities is shortened for early payouts, immediate annuities typically do not earn as much interest as the earnings from deferred annuities. See the exhibit "Deferred Annuities Versus Immediate Annuities."

Deferred annuity
An annuity with an accumulation period that usually lasts a number of years.

Immediate annuity
An annuity contract bought with a single payment and with a specified payout plan that starts right away.

Annuity Types Based on the Party Bearing the Investment Risk

Generally, the party that bears an annuity's investment risk can be either the annuity owner or the insurer that provides the annuity. Annuities classified in this fashion fall into four general categories. See the exhibit "Annuity Types Based on the Party Bearing the Investment Risk."

Deferred Annuities Versus Immediate Annuities

Deferred Annuity	Immediate Annuity
Primary advantage is that it is a more effective instrument for retirement planning, as it enables the annuity owner to make premium payments during the accumulation period—which accumulate tax-deferred interest—for periodic payout over the annuitant's lifetime. If the annuitant dies before any payout is made on the contract, the annuitant's beneficiaries pay ordinary income taxes on the earnings, as opposed to paying inheritance taxes on the distribution.	Primary advantage is that it enables an individual to receive periodic payments while also investing for future earnings and payouts. It provides fewer tax-deferred interest earnings, but the annuitant pays less ordinary income tax on the early payouts when they are received. Additionally, for individual/nonqualified annuity policies issued after January 18, 1985, any taxable amount received or withdrawn before age fifty-nine-and-one-half is generally subject to a 10 percent federal early-withdrawal penalty.

[DA07755]

Annuity Types Based on Premium Payment Method

Two types of annuities are classified based on the premium payment method:

- Flexible-premium annuities
- Single-premium annuities

Flexible-premium annuities enable the annuity owner to decide when to pay periodic premiums. Most flexible-premium annuities require a minimum payment amount, if a payment is made during a given period (such as monthly or annually).

The owner of a single-premium annuity purchases the annuity using one lump-sum payment. This single premium may be paid well in advance of the payout period (called a single-premium deferred annuity, or SPDA), or it may be paid shortly before the payout begins (called a single-premium immediate annuity). A single-premium immediate annuity might be purchased by an individual at retirement to enable him or her to begin receiving the lifetime benefits available through the annuity. For example, the heir to a large estate or a lottery winner might purchase an immediate annuity to provide tax-deferred safekeeping of the assets while still receiving periodic payouts throughout his or her lifetime.

Annuity Types Based on the Party Bearing the Investment Risk

Fixed-Dollar Annuity (Fixed Indexed Annuity)	Insurer invests its customers' annuity premiums in securities such as bonds, real estate, and mortgages in exchange for a fixed rate of return.
	Value of annuity does not fluctuate with market performance, but interest rate annuitant earnings may.
	Considered a more conservative investment than other types of annuities and, therefore, has a lower rate of return.
Equity Indexed Annuity (EIA)	Fixed-dollar annuity linked to a stock market index.
	Insurer guarantees payment of minimum principal amount and a minimum interest rate.
	Value of the return can increase with the market, based on the index values, but if the market fares poorly, the premium and interest rate will never drop below the guaranteed rates. EIAs can exceed their guaranteed value at maturity.
Variable Annuity (VA)	Owner invests annuity premiums in diversified subaccounts with various objectives (such as growth or fixed income) to optimize returns according to an investment time horizon.
	Insurer hires experts to manage subaccounts, which are separate from the insurer's general assets. Consequently, subaccounts are protected from the insurer's creditors if the insurer becomes insolvent.
	When the payout period begins, the current value of the investment fund is converted into units. The annuity guarantees that a specified number of units will be paid periodically, but the value of each unit will vary as determined by the performance of the subaccounts.
Combination Plan	Combines features of fixed-dollar and variable annuities.
	Insurer might make the investment decisions in the interests of the annuity owner, but the annuity owner bears the investment risk.

[DA07756]

SOCIAL SECURITY PROGRAM (OASDHI)

Most individuals who work a minimum time period and pay Social Security taxes are eligible for benefits through Social Security. Family members of an eligible worker may also receive certain benefits. The benefits provided by Social Security are minimal, however, and other sources of retirement income, disability income, and insurance are suggested to supplement Social Security payments.

The United States federal Social Security program, also known as OASDHI (old age, survivors, disability, and health insurance system), was designed to provide benefits to qualified individuals upon their retirement or if they become disabled and are unable to work, and to supplement medical care. Most occupations are covered; however, some are not. Eligibility for insured status under OASDHI extends not only to covered workers; benefits may also be provided to their families. Most Social Security benefits that are paid are retirement benefits; however, additional benefits can include survivors death benefits, disability benefits, and Medicare benefits.

Basic Characteristics of OASDHI

Most working individuals are covered under the Social Security program for some benefits, and most are currently paying or will pay Social Security taxes based on their earnings. Workers are entitled to Social Security retirement benefits if they were fully insured at the age at which they retired. Social Security defines "fully insured" as having earned forty quarters of coverage. A quarter of coverage is earned for each quarter of a year that an individual works. Effectively, an individual is fully insured after ten full years of work; the quarters do not have to be consecutive as long as forty quarters are earned.

Calculation of Social Security benefits is complicated; however, the Social Security Administration mails a benefit estimate statement to insured individuals every year. It also offers a website with tools to help individuals estimate their future financial needs, to identify the Social Security programs for which they might be eligible, to learn how their age at retirement and other types of earnings and pensions affect their Social Security benefits, and to answer many other questions. The website also offers planners and calculators for disability and survivors benefits, and individuals can apply for Social Security benefits through a link from the Social Security Administration website.[4]

Covered Occupations

Individuals in most occupations, including self-employed individuals who earn $400 or more in one year, pay Social Security taxes and earn Social Security benefits. Certain occupations have special rules for calculating Social Security taxes and benefits. Some types of work or workers are not covered, including federal workers; foreign agricultural workers; students performing service for a school, college, or university; nursing students; Job Corps workers; work not in the course of the employer's trade or business; newspaper delivery workers; work covered by the Railroad Retirement Act; and employment by a foreign government, an international organization, or an instrumentality of a foreign government.

Eligibility Requirements for Insured Status

Individuals must be insured under the Social Security program to receive retirement, survivors, or disability benefits. To receive any Social Security benefits, an individual must have insured status. "Fully insured status" is one requirement for particular types of benefits; however, some benefits may apply if the individual qualifies as "currently insured." To qualify for disability benefits, an individual must have "disability-insured status."

The government uses an individual's lifetime earnings record, reported under his or her Social Security number (SSN), to assign Social Security credits for a specified amount of work (a quarter) and to determine insured status. Alien workers (those who are not U.S. citizens or nationals) are subject to special rules for determining insured status.

To be fully insured, an individual must have at least six credits and meet certain age requirements based on various dates at the time of retirement; however, no more than forty credits are required, regardless of the individual's birth date. An individual may earn no more than four credits in a year. The full retirement age is currently sixty-six. However, in 2003, the full retirement age began increasing from sixty-five to sixty-seven starting with individuals born in 1938. See the exhibit "Age to Receive Full Social Security Benefits."

An individual who has currently insured status can receive certain Social Security benefits. To qualify for currently insured status, he or she must have at least six Social Security credits during the full thirteen-quarter period that ends the year he or she dies, most recently becomes entitled to disability benefits, or becomes entitled to retirement insurance benefits. Periods of disability are generally not counted when computing Social Security credits.

An individual who has disability-insured status qualifies for certain disability benefits. To qualify, the individual must have at least twenty credits during a forty-calendar-quarter period (called the 20/40 rule). The forty-calendar-quarter period ends in the quarter the individual is determined to be disabled, and he or she is fully insured in that calendar quarter. Individuals who are disabled before age thirty-one can qualify for disability insurance benefits as an option to the 20/40 rule, called "special insured status." Blind workers who are fully insured are not required to meet the 20/40 rule or the requirements for special insured status.

Age to Receive Full Social Security Benefits

Year of Birth	Full Retirement Age
1937 or earlier	65
1938	65 and 2 months
1939	65 and 4 months
1940	65 and 6 months
1941	65 and 8 months
1942	65 and 10 months
1943–1954	66
1955	66 and 2 months
1956	66 and 4 months
1957	66 and 6 months
1958	66 and 8 months
1959	66 and 10 months
1960 and later	67

Social Security Administration, "Age to Receive Full Social Security Retirement Benefits," Retirement Age, May 29, 2009, www.ssa.gov/pubs/retirechart.htm (accessed December 21, 2009). [DA05713]

Types of Benefits Provided by Social Security

Social Security provides several possible benefits to insured individuals and/or their dependents. These benefits are most often provided under the Social Security law:

- Retirement (old age) benefits are paid to insured workers and their eligible dependents.
- Survivors (death) benefits are paid to surviving dependents of insured workers.
- Disability benefits are paid to insured workers and their eligible dependents.
- Health insurance benefits (Medicare) are paid to insured persons age sixty-five or older and to certain other beneficiaries.

Except for Medicare, Social Security benefits are based on the individual's primary insurance amount (PIA). The PIA is calculated by applying a formula to the worker's average monthly earnings over a specified number of years. A family maximum benefit (FMB) is also calculated from the PIA to limit the benefit amount that may be paid to a worker and his or her eligible dependents. These calculations are complicated, but the amounts are provided on an individual's annual Social Security statement.

Retirement (Old Age) Benefits

An individual can receive retirement (old age) benefits when he or she reaches age sixty-two and has attained fully insured status. The retirement insurance benefit equals the individual's PIA. In certain cases, a special minimum benefit is provided to some individuals who have had low earnings.

For workers born in 1937 and earlier, the full-benefit retirement age is sixty-five. Starting with workers born in 1938, the full-benefit retirement age gradually increases to age sixty-seven for workers born in 1960 and later. A fully insured worker may begin receiving retirement benefits at age sixty-two, but the benefit amount would be permanently reduced. Optionally, a worker can elect to delay retirement until age seventy and receive increased benefits starting at age seventy. See the exhibit "Percentage of Social Security Benefits Gained With Delayed Retirement."

Percentage of Social Security Benefits Gained With Delayed Retirement

Year of Birth	Yearly Rate of Increase	Monthly Rate of Increase
1933–1934	5.5%	11/24 of 1%
1935–1936	6.0%	1/2 of 1%
1937–1938	6.5%	13/24 of 1%
1939–1940	7.0%	7/12 of 1%
1941–1942	7.5%	5/8 of 1%
1943 or later	8.0%	2/3 of 1%

Note: If you were born on January 1, you should refer to the rate of increase for the previous year.

Social Security Administration, "Delayed Retirement Credits," Retirement Planner, January 6, 2010, www.ssa.gov/retire2/delayret.htm (accessed January 7, 2010). [DA05714]

The spouse of a retired worker who has reached age sixty-two can receive a lifetime reduced retirement benefit that is 50 percent of the fully insured worker's PIA, up to the FMB. If the worker retires at age sixty-five, the full spousal retirement benefit can be paid to the spouse. If the spouse is entitled to a personal retirement benefit, then the spouse would receive the larger of his or her personal benefit or his or her spousal benefit.

If the spouse cares for any unmarried child, stepchild, or grandchild of the worker under age sixteen or for a disabled child, stepchild, or grandchild of the worker, additional benefits may also be provided for each qualified dependent on the worker's retirement until the FMB has been met.

Survivors (Death) Benefits

Survivors (death) benefits may be paid to the surviving spouse and other qualified dependents of a deceased worker who was fully insured at the time of his or her death.

The surviving spouse qualifies for survivors benefits if he or she is at least age sixty or is disabled and at least age fifty. The surviving spouse can receive 100 percent of the deceased worker's survivor PIA if that spouse is full-benefit retirement age. The benefit amount is reduced for younger surviving spouses.

Unmarried children and qualifying grandchildren of a deceased worker can receive a child's monthly survivors benefit. This benefit is generally 75 percent of the deceased parent's PIA. The child must be under age eighteen, or eighteen and an elementary or a secondary student, or eighteen or older but disabled before age twenty-two. Certain limitations apply.

A parent who was dependent on the insured worker before his or her death and who has reached age sixty-two can also receive a survivors benefit. If only one parent is entitled to benefits, the surviving parent's benefit is generally 82.5 percent of the deceased worker's PIA. If two parents are entitled to surviving parent's benefits, the benefit amount is generally 75 percent of the deceased worker's PIA.

Additionally, the surviving spouse who cares for an eligible child or grandchild receives a mother's or father's surviving spouse benefit. This benefit is generally 75 percent of the deceased worker's PIA. Note that all of these benefits combined are subject to the FMB.

Finally, a lump-sum death benefit may be paid to the survivors of a worker who dies having met the fully insured or currently insured status. This lump sum of $255 is paid in addition to any monthly survivors benefits. Certain restrictions can apply—for example, if the survivor was convicted for the felony homicide of the qualified worker or the qualified worker was granted tax exemption as a member of a religious group.

Disability

The Social Security disability income (SSDI) Monthly Cash Benefits are designed to replace a portion of a wage earner's income for a short period of time if the wage earner becomes disabled because of an injury or illness. A five-month waiting period applies before any benefits will be paid. Auxiliary benefits may be paid to the spouse and other dependents of the injured worker.

Establishment of a Social Security disability period is essential for determination of numerous Social Security benefits. A "period of disability" under the Social Security law is a continuous period during which an individual is disabled. The established period of disability is not counted when determining an individual's insured status under Social Security and is not counted in determining the monthly benefit amount payable to the worker and his or her dependents. This period of disability is also used in determining other types of Social Security benefits for the worker's family.

Health Insurance (Medicare)

Under Social Security, people age sixty-five or older, those under sixty-five with certain disabilities, and people of all ages with specified medical conditions can qualify to receive federal Medicare health benefits including hospital insurance, medical insurance, and prescription drug coverage. Medicare beneficiaries can also choose to take advantage of Medicare Advantage plans that offer higher benefit levels and include managed-care plans and private fee-for-service plans.

SUMMARY

Effective planning is needed to accumulate sufficient funds to meet the costs of living in retirement. An investor should be aware of the types of investment risks that an investor's funds will be exposed to and should consider these risks before investing.

Traditional and Roth IRAs allow individuals to establish their own tax-favored retirement plans, as long as the plans comply with a set of conditions unique to each plan. Individuals should compare investor eligibility, how much funding can be contributed, how the contributions will be treated for tax purposes, how an individual can withdraw or distribute funds, and how distributions will be treated for tax purposes before deciding which type of IRA meets their needs.

A variety of qualified retirement plans is available to help both employees and employers invest for retirement. Each plan has unique characteristics that meet different needs for employees and employers. Some of the more prevalent retirement plans are these:

- 401(k) plan
- Profit-sharing plan
- Thrift plan
- Keogh plan
- 403(b) plan
- SIMPLE
- ESOP
- SEP

In some cases, a combination of plans will best meet employees' retirement income needs.

The two main types of employer-sponsored retirement plans are the defined benefit plan and the defined contribution plan. A defined benefit 401(k) plan is a combination of the two.

Three fundamental classifications of annuities are based on the starting date of the annuity, the party that determines the investment and bears the investment risks, or the premium payment method. Various types of annuities are available under each of these classifications.

The United States federal Social Security program, also known as OASDHI, was designed to provide benefits to qualified individuals upon their retirement, if they become disabled and are unable to work, and to supplement medical care. Benefits may also be provided to the families of qualified individuals. Social Security benefits include retirement, survivors (death), disability, and health insurance.

ASSIGNMENT NOTES

1. The Internal Revenue Service website reports the most recent income eligibility, contribution limitations, and distribution information at www.irs.gov/retirement/article/0,,id=226255,00.html (accessed June 13, 2011).
2. The Internal Revenue Service website reports the most recent annual 401(k) contribution limitations and catch-up contribution figures at www.irs.gov/retirement/article/0,,id=120298,00.html (accessed June 13, 2011).
3. The Internal Revenue Service website reports the most recent annual SIMPLE contribution limitations and catch-up contribution figures at www.irs.gov/retirement/participant/article/0,,id=151294,00.html (accessed June 13, 2011).
4. Social Security Administration, Social Security Online, January 4, 2010, www.ssa.gov (accessed January 7, 2010).

Direct Your Learning

11

Disability and Health Insurance Planning

Educational Objectives

After learning the content of this assignment, you should be able to:

- Describe the financial impact of disability and other health-related personal loss exposures on individuals and families.

- Summarize the distinguishing characteristics of each of the following types of disability income insurance:
  - Individual disability income insurance
  - Group disability income insurance
  - Social Security disability income program

- Describe the characteristics of the following nongovernment programs for providing healthcare benefits:
  - Traditional health insurance plans
  - Managed-care plans
  - Consumer-directed health plans

- Describe each of the following government programs for providing healthcare benefits:
  - Original Medicare
  - Medicare Advantage
  - Medicare Supplement Insurance
  - Medicare Part D Prescription Drug Coverage
  - Medicaid

- Describe the considerations an individual should review when choosing a long-term care insurance policy, including typical benefits provided or excluded, coverage triggers, eligibility provisions, and other economic issues.

Outline

Disability and Health-Related Personal Loss Exposures

Disability Income Insurance

Health Insurance Plans

Government-Provided Health Insurance Plans

Long-Term Care Insurance

Summary

Disability and Health Insurance Planning

DISABILITY AND HEALTH-RELATED PERSONAL LOSS EXPOSURES

Sometimes people are injured outside the workplace or become seriously ill, rendering them unable to report to their jobs for many months. For those without disability and health insurance, such injuries and illnesses can deplete a family's savings and lead to bankruptcy filing or mortgage foreclosure.

Individuals and families are subject to numerous loss exposures. Most people understand the importance of securing property and liability insurance to protect their home, autos, and business from various loss exposures. Many individuals recognize the need for life insurance for themselves and their spouse and dependents. Most individuals, especially as they age, also understand the need for retirement planning. However, fewer individuals recognize the potential financial devastation they could face if they or their spouse were to become disabled or to suffer a serious or lengthy illness.

Each day, individuals face numerous exposures that could result in their injury, illness, or disability. In many respects, a long-term disability or health condition could be more damaging to a family's financial condition than the death of a primary wage earner. When a wage earner dies, a family loses that individual's income. However, upon the individual's death, the family no longer incurs costs of living for that individual (such as food, clothing, transportation, housing, medical care, and so forth). Adequate financial assets, life insurance, and survivors benefits can help prevent significant changes to a family's standard of living, or even financial ruin, when a death occurs.

For example, as in the case of death, when a primary wage earner becomes disabled or suffers a serious health condition, the family loses that individual's income. However, the individual continues to incur costs of living and generally incurs other expenses because of his or her disability or health condition. In both cases, an individual would likely require medical care. The costs of repeated medical visits or treatments can quickly mount into thousands of dollars, and many medical treatments can be very costly, especially for serious medical conditions. If hospitalization or skilled nursing facilities are involved, costs may increase astronomically. A disabled individual might require rehabilitation and/or further education to enable him or her to return to work, either in the same job or in a new profession that better accommodates the disability.

Disability Loss Exposures

Many people are anxious about the financial impact that death could have on their families. Ironically, the chance that an individual will become disabled is greater than the chance of an early death. Most people fail to consider how a long-term disability—for example, one that lasts six months to a year or more—would affect their family. Most families do not have savings that would sustain them for such lengthy time periods and cover the associated medical and other costs. Many families cannot maintain any savings at all or may only have savings that protect them for a month or two.

In addition to the loss of the disabled individual's wages, there are generally medical expenses to be paid (with or without health insurance), and the individual may incur costs for rehabilitation—treatment to enable him or her to regain strength and be able to return to work—or for education so that he or she could qualify for another type of job in which the disability would not be a concern.

The United States Social Security Administration survey results led to a 2007 estimate that more than 75 percent of Americans living in the U.S. are insured under the government's disability insurance program (available to much of the working population). However, there are limitations to the benefits in that program, so the need for personal disability insurance remains. See the exhibit "Disability and Health Facts."

Disability and Health Facts

According to the National Safety Council, in 2008 these were true:

- Every second, a disabling injury occurs in the U.S., and every four minutes the injury is fatal.
- Only 10 percent of disabling accidents and illnesses that occur are work-related; the other 90 percent are not covered by workers compensation.

The United States Census Bureau reports that, in 2008, 18 percent of Americans were classified as disabled.

The Social Security Administration reports the following:

- As of 2007, three out of ten Americans entering the workforce today will become disabled before they retire.
- In 2008, the average monthly benefit paid by Social Security Disability Insurance (SSDI) was only $1,004 per month (an income that would not support most families).
- In 2005, only 39 percent of claims made for SSDI benefits were approved.
- As of 2007, excluding workers in public employment, 70 percent of workers had no long-term disability insurance.

Council for Disability Awareness, "Chances of Disability: Me, Disabled?" www.disabilitycanhappen.org/chances_disability/disability_stats.asp (accessed January 6, 2010). [DA05709]

Health-Related Loss Exposures

Many Americans do not have health insurance, and young, healthy individuals often do not recognize the need for such coverage or the financial benefit it can provide. The high cost and, often, the lack of availability of health insurance is a significant reason why many lower-income, single-wage-earner families and elderly individuals do not purchase it. While private healthcare insurance is available to individuals who do not have group health insurance, some are unaware that private plans exist. Additionally, the cost of private health insurance for the benefits provided is significantly greater than the cost of group health insurance (as provided by an employer) because private plans lack the cost savings from economies of scale.

Certain individuals belong to associations that offer group healthcare insurance plans with lower premiums. Generally, under private insurance and smaller group plans, individuals or associations select fewer benefits or higher copayments to save money on premiums. Also, these plans might offer benefits only for lesser-quality medications and older treatment methods, often using outdated technology. An added overhead expense in private and small-volume health insurance plans, which is reflected in higher premiums, might be costs related to multiple administrative systems for handling enrollments and benefits.

Many lower-income individuals and families either are unable to purchase or do not have access to health insurance (private or group). The costs of medical treatment often cause uninsured individuals to avoid medical treatment for illnesses or injuries until their health has deteriorated enough that more costly medical treatment is required. Some illnesses require long-term care, and lower-income individuals are less likely to purchase long-term care insurance, as well. Additionally, a disabled individual might lose his or her job, along with any healthcare insurance and disability benefits provided by the employer. Consequently, the choice not to purchase health insurance can ultimately cost far more than the insurance premiums that are saved.

Individuals who have health insurance tend to live longer and have a better quality of life than uninsured individuals. Individuals who have insurance are more likely to visit healthcare providers for recommended medical examinations, such as regular physicals, blood tests, mammograms, prostate exams, routine gynecological and obstetric exams, colonoscopies, and other routine medical tests. When problems are discovered, insured individuals are more likely to seek the appropriate medical care as soon as possible, which decreases overall costs and increases the chance for a healthy outcome.

Long-Term Care Loss Exposures

Individuals and families who have health insurance can still suffer financial difficulty or devastation because of the costs of long-term care for certain serious medical conditions, such as cancer, dementia, Alzheimer's disease, multiple sclerosis, and many other diseases. Individuals requiring long-term healthcare might need skilled nursing care after hospitalization or might need long-term in-home healthcare to assist them with their daily activities. The costs for these services can quickly deplete savings and investments.

Insurance Treatment of Disability, Health-Related, and Long-Term Care Loss Exposures

Unexpected, high medical costs; disability costs; and long-term care costs, which continue to increase in the U.S., can easily exhaust an individual's or a family's savings and retirement funds and can drive some individuals or families into bankruptcy and/or cause them to lose their homes and other possessions. Fortunately, insurance options exist to help individuals and families better manage the financial loss exposures that they face related to disability, health conditions, and long-term care.

Various sources offer disability insurance, which replaces lost income when a wage earner becomes disabled. Disability benefits and options can be selected to best meet the needs of the individual or family. In some cases, multiple forms of disability insurance, such as private and government insurance, combine to provide the best coverage.

Health insurance is also available from various sources to pay for routine and/or major medical expenses, such as limited hospitalization, surgery, and so forth. Various levels of coverage and benefits can be selected. Health insurance premiums vary depending on the benefits selected, the level of care, and the age and health of individuals for whom the coverage is purchased. Premiums also vary depending on the source of the insurance plan, such as whether it is obtained through an employer or association (group health insurance plans) or is an individual plan. As with disability insurance, multiple forms of health insurance, such as individual and group plans and/or the government's plan (Medicare), may combine to provide the best coverage for individuals who qualify.

Long-term care insurance has emerged to pay the costs associated with treatment of a serious, long-term medical condition. It helps pay the costs of skilled nursing facilities and other care facilities, adult daycare, and home healthcare. Long-term care insurance is offered by various sources, and options can be selected based on the level of care to be provided and various features of the insurance coverage.

DISABILITY INCOME INSURANCE

A severe injury or illness that prevents a wage earner from working can destroy the financial security of the individual and his or her family and could lead to such difficulties as mortgage foreclosure or bankruptcy. Disability income insurance can provide protection against such situations when injury or illness prevents a wage earner from working.

Individuals rarely anticipate that they might become so severely ill or injured that they would be unable to work and earn their normal income. Consequently, the need for disability income insurance is often overlooked. Some employers provide disability income insurance for their employees, who may see that provision as a safety net, but a closer inspection of an employer-provided disability policy might reveal that employees still bear considerable risk of losing income because of a disability.

Disability income insurance is designed to replace a portion, often 60 percent, of an individual's income if he or she becomes disabled. An injury or illness can result in a short-term disability (described as a few days to eighty-nine days) or a long-term disability (described as ninety days up to five years, or up to a lifetime benefit limit). Disability insurance policies contain a variety of provisions that specify the length of a qualifying disability, the types and extent of disability, the time in which the policy coverage is in effect, the benefits provided, any waiting period before benefits will be paid, and many other features of the policy.

An overview of these three types of disability income insurance provides insight into the products and options available to help wage earners avoid the financial duress that is often associated with disability:

- Individual disability income insurance
- Group disability income insurance
- Social Security disability income (SSDI) program

Provisions of a Disability Income Policy

Major provisions of a disability income policy include the benefit periods, the perils insured against, the waiting period, the definition of disability that applies, the benefits that are provided, and the renewal or continuance provision.

Benefit Periods

A disability income policy specifies a benefit period and a maximum benefit period. The benefit period is the time period for which benefits will be paid to a disabled individual (the insured). As described in the policy, the benefit period ends when the insured "returns to work" or reaches the maximum benefit period. The maximum benefit period is the longest period for which benefits will be paid to the insured.

Various benefit periods can be provided. For example, a maximum benefit period may be five years, "to age 65," or a lifetime benefit. Policies with maximum benefit periods that extend many years require higher premiums; therefore, when selecting a maximum benefit period, individuals must consider their financial needs, their own age, and the ages of their dependents, as well as weigh the benefits against costs.

Perils Insured Against

A disability income policy provides specified benefits in the event that the insured individual suffers any illness, accident, or injury that causes the individual to lose income. Some disability policies pay disability income benefits for certain types of permanent injuries, such as the loss of a limb or blindness.

Waiting Period

Disability income policies do not pay benefits immediately when an individual suffers an illness or injury. Instead, they have a waiting period, often called an elimination period. The waiting period is the time that elapses after a wage earner becomes disabled, before income benefits will be paid. The waiting period may be seven days for a short-term disability policy, or it may be thirty days, sixty days, ninety days, or one year or more for a long-term disability policy. Short-term disability insurance is available as group insurance and may be called a sick leave plan.

Shorter waiting periods require higher insurance premiums to cover the insurer's costs. Consequently, individual insureds often choose the longest waiting period that they can afford to be without income. Employers who provide group disability income insurance often select a waiting period that takes effect when employees' short-term disability ends or sick leave has been exhausted.

Definition of Disability

A disability income policy's definition of "disability" describes the extent of disability that is required for income payments to begin. This definition might be based on the insured's inability to perform occupational duties, on the amount of earned income lost, or both.

When the definition is based on the insured's inability to perform job duties, the description might refer to "any occupation," "own occupation," or "split definition."

The term "any occupation" means that the individual is totally disabled and unable to perform the duties of any occupation. A policy that uses the "any occupation" definition of disability will not pay benefits if the insured can perform the duties of another occupation or can attain the necessary education or training to perform the duties of a new occupation.

The term "own occupation" means the insured is unable to return to the duties of his or her specific occupation. With an "own occupation" policy, if the insured is able to earn income from another occupation, he or she will still receive 100 percent of the disability benefits. For example, Bob has a disability policy that defines disability as "own occupation." Bob, a mail clerk with a severe knee injury, cannot deliver mail throughout an office complex, his normal duties. However, he can perform alternate duties such as operating a computer to track mail requests from various departments and requesting pickup and delivery from parcel delivery vendors. Under this "own occupation" policy, Bob would be paid full benefits while he performs his new duties. Under a disability policy that defines disability as "any occupation," Bob could not collect benefits because he could perform the duties of some other occupation. A policy that uses the "own occupation" definition requires a higher premium.

Some disability policies use a modified "own occupation" definition, which means full benefits are paid if the insured is unable to perform the duties of his or her specific occupation or any other occupation. But if this insured is able to earn income from another occupation, the benefit payments are reduced in proportion to the income earnings from the other occupation.

Under a disability policy that uses a "split definition" for disability, the "any" and "own" occupation concepts are combined. For example, the policy might use an "any occupation" definition for the first six months of disability, and then it might revert to an "own occupation" definition if the disability extends beyond six months. Using the example with Bob, the mail clerk, under a "split definition" policy that uses an "own occupation" definition for the first nine months and an "any occupation" definition for disability that extends beyond nine months, Bob would receive benefits for the first nine months while he works the alternate duties; however, if he is unable to deliver the mail after nine months, his benefits would end.

When the definition of disability is based on the amount of earned income lost, a specified percentage of earned income lost will result in the payment of benefits. For example, assume Joyce, a nurse, was injured and could not perform her nursing duties, but she could perform the duties of a desk job—with a decrease in salary of 30 percent. Under a disability policy that states that benefits will be paid if earned income is reduced by 25 percent or more as a result of the disability, Joyce would receive benefits. If Joyce's disability were such that she could not perform any duties of any job, she would receive full benefits from this policy.

Some policies combine these approaches in defining disability. For example, a policy might apply the amount of earned income lost approach to the first six months of disability and then apply an "own occupation" approach for the remaining benefit period, up to the maximum period or when the disability ends.

Benefits Provided

The benefits provided under a disability income policy vary depending on the type of disability policy: individual, group, or SSDI. The benefits provided tie together all of the policy features—such as the waiting period, the benefits periods, the perils insured against, and the definition of disability—with features such as the amount of coverage and the payment period (weekly, monthly), and any terms for coordination of benefits with other disability income policies.

Renewal or Continuance Provision

A provision in a disability income policy specifies whether it is noncancelable, guaranteed renewable, or conditionally renewable. The provision determines whether the policy can be renewed by the insured, whether the insurer can cancel the contract, whether the insurer is required to grant a renewal on request, or whether the policy terms (including the premiums) may be changed at renewal.

A noncancelable disability income policy can never be canceled by the insurer. Additionally, the insurer cannot change the benefits provided, the rates, or other policy features unless the insured requests a change. A noncancelable policy is most attractive to insureds.

A guaranteed renewable policy will continue as long as the premiums continue to be paid, up to a specified age, such as sixty-five or seventy, as long as the insured is gainfully employed (earning a reasonable salary). Even though the insurer must renew the policy at the insured's request, the insurer reserves the right to raise premiums on renewal for reasons specified in the contract. This alternative to a noncancelable policy is less attractive to insureds.

A conditionally renewable policy provides that the insurer has an option to increase the premium and change the policy terms at renewal. Also, this policy allows the insurer to cancel the contract if the conditions for renewal are not met. See the exhibit "Comparison of Disability Income Insurance Plans."

Individual Disability Income Insurance

Individual disability income insurance generally provides monthly benefits to a disabled wage earner for a selected period to reimburse the wage earner's income during a period of total or partial disability. Individual policies will usually replace 60 percent of an insured's lost income, and sometimes up to 70 or 80 percent under some plans. Individuals purchase individual disability income insurance, which is available to the public through insurance brokers and agents.

Coverages and provisions under individual disability income insurance are typically the same as those for group insurance. Individuals should seek a policy that best meets their potential disability income needs, either as primary coverage or supplemental to other disability income insurance. Some life insurance policies include riders that provide disability coverage. Individuals should consider such riders in their disability planning, as well.

Individual disability income insurance is purchased using after-tax dollars. Consequently, disability benefits that are paid from an individual policy are not taxable to the insured. This enables the insured to receive more disability income at the time it is needed most.

Comparison of Disability Income Insurance Plans

Provision	Individual Disability Insurance	Group LTD Insurance	SSDI Monthly Cash Benefit
Definition of Disability	Depends on insurer, but may be split definition such as "own occupation" or "any occupation."	Often split definition with "own occupation" at first and then conversion to "any occupation."	Very restrictive—"substantial gainful activity," similar to "any occupation."
Portability/Need for Supplementation	Entirely portable—not linked to any employment or association—insured owns policy; supplemental disability insurance may not be needed.	Not usually portable—terminates with change of employer or association, or termination of employer's or association's contract; supplemental disability insurance may be desirable.	Portable, but restrictions on qualifying disabilities and benefit periods may create need for supplemental disability insurance.
Taxation of Benefits	Nontaxable—purchased with after-tax dollars.	Usually taxable—premiums paid by employer as a taxable benefit or through employee payroll with pre-tax dollars; association policy may be nontaxable.	Usually nontaxable, but exceptions may exist.
Riders Available	Numerous riders are available depending on insurer.	Riders available only if selected by employer or association.	None.
Flexibility	Very flexible—can add or remove riders, can choose waiting periods, benefit amounts, and other options.	Not flexible—usually restricted to employer's or association's selected options.	No flexibility—defined by Social Security laws.

[DA05715]

An advantage of individual disability income insurance over group insurance is that no membership in a group is required to purchase the coverage. A job change will not affect coverage, so the insured can purchase a noncancelable policy at a young age, when premiums are lower, and continue the coverage until retirement or beyond. Additionally, some individuals do not qualify for group disability income insurance because of tenure requirements before the benefit is available; this is never the case with individual coverage. Finally, group and Social Security benefits may not be adequate to cover the insured's disability income needs. In this case, an individual disability income policy may be used to supplement other coverage provided. Some insurers limit the maximum amount of monthly benefits that an insured can receive from all disability income sources, restricting the insured to a specified percentage of his or her income. This discourages over-insurance and fraudulent disability claims.

Various options, often called riders, are available for purchase with an individual disability income insurance policy. Premiums for these riders vary based on the payout—the amount of benefits the insurer is likely to pay. See the exhibit "Common Individual Disability Income Policy Riders."

Group Disability Income Insurance

Group disability income insurance is made available through an employer or some type of association. Because an individual organization purchases many policies, economies of scale enable the insurer to offer lower premiums to the insured individuals.

Group disability income insurance generally provides weekly or monthly benefits to a disabled wage earner for a selected period to reimburse the wage earner's income during a period of total or partial disability.

An employer may offer both short-term and long-term disability income insurance plans. Short-term plans might offer weekly benefits, with a short waiting period (one to seven days), and short maximum benefit periods. A long-term disability plan (often called LTD) might have a higher maximum benefit payout, such as $3,000 or $5,000 per month or $60,000 per year. LTD policies usually replace around 60 percent of an insured's lost income. Premiums are paid by the employer in part or in full, and premiums may be deducted from the insured's payroll on a before-tax basis; consequently, benefits are taxed as ordinary income when they are paid to the insured during disability. Under an association's plan, premiums are paid by the individual with after-tax dollars, so benefits are not taxable.

The waiting period under an LTD plan might require a three-month to six-month wait for benefits to begin after a disability occurs. Most group LTD plans use a split definition of disability, with which an "own occupation" definition applies for an initial disability period, such as two years, and then an "any occupation" definition applies for the remaining benefit period, until the maximum benefit period is reached. Because group policies are purchased

Common Individual Disability Income Policy Riders

Rider	Description	Example
Waiver of premium	Excuses a disabled insured from making premium payment during a period of covered disability.	During a paid disability period, the insured pays no premium for the disability income insurance.
Guaranteed insurability	Enables an insured to purchase specified additional amounts of insurance on stated policy anniversary dates, without providing proof of insurability.	Every five years, an insured may have the option to increase his or her monthly disability benefit by a specified amount (such as $2,000), based on documented income increases.
Cost of living adjustment (COLA)	After a specified period, provides an increase in the monthly benefits to be paid during a disability. The amount of increase is usually specified in the rider, and the percentage may be applied before any disability occurs.	Each year after benefits begin, the monthly benefit amount is increased by 4 percent. Alternately, each year after a disability income policy is issued, a 3 percent increase is applied to the monthly benefit amount.
Future increase option (FIO)	Guarantees the insured's insurability for a specific period, allowing the option to increase the monthly benefit as the insured's income increases, based on documented income increases.	Until age fifty-five, the insured has the option to increase the monthly benefit based on individual income tax reports for the previous year. No exams are required.
Automatic Increase Rider (AIR)	Increases the insured's monthly benefit amount each year for a specified number of years to keep up with inflation.	A 25 percent increase in coverage is applied each year for the first five years the policy is in force.
Residual (partial) disability	Allows for partial payment of benefits, in proportion to the income lost, when the insured suffers a specified percentage of reduction in earned income. This benefit is typically paid after a period of disability. Residual disability is integrated into some individual disability income policies.	After two years of total disability, an insured returns to an alternate job for which her income is reduced by 20 percent. The residual disability rider would pay 20 percent of the total monthly disability payment to the insured.
Social Security Supplement Coverage	Provides additional benefits to an insured when Social Security disability benefits do not apply. Social Security uses a strict definition of disability, compared with individual disability income policies, so this rider helps cover any gap in coverage.	While drawing disability benefits, an insured is convicted of a felony and imprisoned for one year (which would halt Social Security disability coverage). The rider provides benefits during the year of incarceration.

[DA05716]

in bulk, options are limited compared with the options available in individual plans.

Most LTD plans have a coordination-of-benefits provision that defines how disability income benefits from other plans, such as SSDI and state disability plans, will affect benefits paid by the LTD plan. These provisions generally do not account for individual disability income insurance.

Under most LTD plans, when the individual's employment or association ends, the group disability income coverage terminates. The coverage also terminates if the employer fails to pay the premium for the employee, or if the group policy is terminated by the employer or association. Most LTDs do not have provisions to enable an insured to convert the plan to an individual disability income policy.

Social Security Disability Income Program

Rules to qualify under the Social Security disability income (SSDI) program are strict compared with other disability plans. The program provides two protections for disabled workers:

- Monthly cash benefits
- Establishment of a period of disability

The requirements for these two protections are nearly the same, so a disabled worker is generally eligible for both.

Disability Definition

To be considered "disabled" under Social Security, a worker must be unable to engage in any substantial gainful activity because of a "medically determinable" physical or mental impairment as defined in the Social Security law. A substantial gainful activity is one that requires significant activities that are physical, mental, or a combination of the two, in work that is performed for profit, even if no profit is realized. This work will qualify whether it is full-time or part-time work. This disability definition is comparable to an "any occupation" definition, as it encompasses the individual's previous work and any type of work that could be expected for the individual's age, education, and work experience.

Furthermore, for a worker to qualify as disabled, the worker's impairment must be established by objective medical evidence, and it must be expected to last for at least twelve consecutive months or to result in the individual's death. Other nonmedical criteria must be met for the individual to qualify. Special rules apply for blindness, and special circumstances related to the disability can disqualify an individual.

Monthly Cash Benefits

Payment of benefits requires a five-month waiting period. Benefits are paid to individuals who have yet to reach full retirement age under Social Security.

The monthly cash benefit is generally equal to the primary insurance amount (PIA) as described in the Social Security law. Auxiliary benefits may also be provided for a qualified disabled worker's eligible dependents. In specified cases, even if a worker is disqualified, eligible dependents can still receive auxiliary benefits.

Disabled worker benefits may be reduced, including the auxiliary benefits, to fully or partially offset any workers compensation benefit and any disability benefits received under a federal, state, or local disability plan. These benefits are subject to the Social Security Family Maximum Benefit (FMB).

Establishment of a Disability Period

Establishment of a disability period is essential for determination of numerous Social Security benefits. A "period of disability" under the Social Security law is a continuous period during which an individual is disabled. The established period of disability is not counted in determining an individual's insured status under Social Security and is not counted in determining the monthly benefit amount payable to the worker and his or her dependents. This period of disability is used in determining other types of Social Security benefits for the worker's family.

A period of disability must be established during a worker's disability or within twelve months after the disability ends, assuming the worker has met "disability insured status" and the disability lasted at least five consecutive months. Special exceptions exist to the five-month waiting period; for example, the period is not required if the worker suffers a subsequent disability.

HEALTH INSURANCE PLANS

Various types of group and individual (nongroup) healthcare plans are available in the private, nongovernmental market. Some employers offer self-insured plans for their employees.

Most American healthcare consumers participate in group healthcare plans (as opposed to individual plans). In addition to employer self-insured plans, three broad types of healthcare plans provide the majority of private healthcare resources for Americans:

- Traditional health insurance plans
- Managed-care plans
- Consumer-directed health plans (CDHPs)

These plans vary in terms of premiums, fees, benefits, out-of-pocket requirements, healthcare delivery, eligibility requirements, and regulatory authority. See the exhibit "Self-Insurance Plans."

> ### Self-Insurance Plans
>
> In addition to the availability of commercial health insurance and Blue Cross and Blue Shield plans, many employers self-insure part or all of the health insurance benefits they provide to their employees. Self-insurance, also called self-funding, means that the employer funds and pays part or all of an employee's medical expenses. Employers that self-insure either perform their own claim processing or contract with third-party administrators to manage the plans, including enrolling employees and processing claims.

[DA05661]

Traditional Health Insurance Plans

Traditional health insurance plans insure many individuals and families through the use of "fee for service" or **indemnity plan** coverage. Providers of traditional health insurance plans include commercial insurers and Blue Cross and Blue Shield plans.

Indemnity plan
A type of healthcare plan that allows patients to choose their own healthcare provider and reimburses the patient or provider at a certain percentage (usually after a deductible is paid) for services provided.

Major life and health insurers, and some property-casualty insurers, offer commercial, or private, health insurance (any nongovernmental health coverage) to the public. Commercial health insurance offers many benefits packages and premium variations, often tailored to specific needs of large or small groups, or of individuals.

Individual plan consumers include workers of all ages with no employer-sponsored health insurance coverage, young unemployed adults, and business owners with no group coverage. Purchasers of nongroup policies for family coverage tend to be over age thirty-five.

Basic medical expense coverage
Coverage for medical expenses, such as hospital and surgical expenses, physicians' visits, and miscellaneous medical services.

Major medical insurance
Insurance that covers medical expenses resulting from illness or injury that are not covered by a basic medical expense plan.

Blue Cross and Blue Shield plans historically were not-for-profit plans, although they are now often administered by for-profit organizations. Because of this not-for-profit history, Blue Cross and Blue Shield providers usually are not described as "commercial insurers" and typically are regulated by state laws separate from those regulating other insurers. Blue Cross and Blue Shield plans provide **basic medical expense coverage** and **major medical insurance** on either an individual or a group basis. Blue Cross and Blue Shield plans also sponsor managed-care plans.

Blue Cross plans usually contract with hospitals and pay them directly, rather than paying insureds (also called "subscribers"), and Blue Shield plans often pay physicians directly. Basic medical expense coverage pays for routine healthcare expenses. Major medical insurance plans provide broader coverage for medical expenses, as well as catastrophic coverage for more costly treatment. Major medical insurance plans usually have deductibles, which insureds must pay out of pocket. See the exhibit "Example Benefits of Basic and Major Medical Insurance Coverage."

Example Benefits of Basic and Major Medical Insurance Coverage

Basic Medical Insurance Coverage	Major Medical Insurance Coverage
• Hospital expenses	• Hospital room and board
• Surgical expenses	• Hospital services and supplies
• Physician visits	• X-rays
• Additional medical services, such as ambulance and mental health services	• Diagnostic tests
	• Physician and surgeon services
	• Prescription drugs
	• Home healthcare services
	• Durable medical equipment
	• Additional services, such as convalescent nursing-home care and dental services

[DA07792]

Managed-Care Plans

Managed-care plans manage the quality of their members' care and control healthcare costs. Managed-care plans often involve the same insurers that administer traditional plans; however, managed care involves an insurer negotiating benefits and fees with a network of healthcare providers. The customer receives significant premium savings and reduced out-of-pocket costs as a result, but often with reduced flexibility. Most managed-care plans cover a standard array of services including hospital care, physicians' and surgeons' services, laboratory and x-ray services, and outpatient and maternity care, among other services. Some plans provide emergency care, while others do not or only provide emergency services at a higher cost to the member.

Managed care plan
A type of healthcare plan that provides members with comprehensive services and encourages them to use providers belonging to the plan.

These are the most prevalent forms of managed-care plans:

- **Health maintenance organization (HMO)**—An HMO contracts with healthcare providers to provide comprehensive services to its members for a low, fixed, prepaid fee, with small co-payments for routine visits. A "gatekeeper physician" usually must preapprove specialists' visits. HMOs control costs by requiring preapproval for specified physicians' treatments and specialists' services, along with oversight of diagnostic tests and treatments. Members save costs through lower premiums and out-of-pocket

Health maintenance organization (HMO)
An organization that provides all the care needed by its members in exchange for a fixed fee.

expenses. For example, Courtney's HMO family plan may provide routine care for her family with small co-payments per visit, while covered visits to an emergency room—or to a specialist referred by her primary care physician—would be more than the primary care co-payment.

- **Preferred provider organization (PPO)**—PPO members may choose any provider, but preferred providers offer decreased medical service costs and lower deductibles. No primary care physician is required, and any physician may make specialist referrals. Some Blue Cross-Blue Shield plans are PPOs. PPOs are one of the more expensive forms of managed-care plans, but they are popular because they blend the advantages of both traditional indemnity plans and HMOs. For example, Jacob and his family, with school-age children, may benefit from a PPO family plan. It would enable his wife to see her out-of-network OB-GYN (though her co-payment would be more than if the OB-GYN were in-network). Their routine care with in-network providers would require minimal co-payments, while the co-payments would double for network specialists. Hospital and emergency care would require a somewhat larger co-payment.

- Exclusive provider organization (EPO)—EPOs contract with insurers to provide healthcare to plan members at a much lower premium than healthcare provided by other plans. The EPO charges insurers an access fee for use of the network, negotiates with healthcare providers to set fee schedules for guaranteed service levels, and helps resolve issues between insurers and healthcare providers. Except for emergencies, plan members must exclusively use EPO network healthcare providers. For example, Tabitha and her husband obtain healthcare strictly from EPO providers with small co-payments per visit. Out-of-network emergency care would be covered, but the co-payment would be relatively large. An EPO is similar to an HMO plan in many ways, such as the very limited out-of-network coverage. The differences between an EPO and HMO are more evident to the providers. Providers in an HMO receive payments from the insurer on a monthly basis. Providers in an EPO receive payment only for services they provide. Plus, EPO premiums are frequently lower than those for an HMO.

- **Point-of-service (POS) plan**—A POS has characteristics of both HMOs and PPOs, but more closely resembles an HMO. A POS plan controls medical costs, but the member must choose a primary care physician from within the POS network. This physician becomes the member's "point of service" and can refer a member inside or outside the network. Some services are provided by non-network providers with reduced POS payments. The POS handles all paperwork and billings for network care, whereas the member handles paperwork, bills, and record-keeping for out-of-network care. For example, Kaleb's POS family plan provides routine care from a selected primary care physician with small co-payments. If Kaleb's primary care physician referred him to a specialist outside the POS network, Kaleb's insurer would pay for a reduced portion of his covered medical

Preferred provider organization (PPO)
An administrative organization that meets the common needs of healthcare providers and clients and that identifies networks of providers and contracts for their medical services at discounted rates.

Point-of-service (POS) plan
Managed-care plan that combines the characteristics of an HMO and a PPO; has a network of preferred providers who, if used by the member, charge little or nothing for services; heathcare received out of the network is covered, but members must pay substantially higher coinsurance charges and a deductible.

care. Kaleb would be required to pay the specialist's medical bills up front and then file an insurance claim and await reimbursement.

Some private insurers extend managed-care benefits to Medicare recipients. Medicare Advantage (MA) plans, often called Medicare Part C, offer options similar to other managed-care plans. In addition to the basic benefits provided by Medicare under Part A and Part B, beneficiaries may be eligible for managed-care services and supplemental benefits and health services. Some supplemental benefits are mandatory for enrollees, and others are optional.[1] MA plans may offer these managed-care options:

- HMO
- Provider-sponsored organizations
- PPO
- Medical savings accounts (MSAs), which combine the use of a health savings account (HSA) with a high-deductible catastrophic health plan
- Private fee-for-service (PFFS) plans, which give beneficiaries more choices through the ability to obtain services from any Medicare-approved provider accepting the plan's payment
- Special needs plans (SNPs), which enroll one or more types of individuals with special needs as defined by law, including those who have been institutionalized, who are eligible for both Medicare and Medicaid, and who have severe or disabling chronic conditions

Consumer-Directed Health Plans

Consumer-directed health plans (CDHPs) provide consumers with access to high-quality care without requiring deductibles for preventive care. CDHPs can provide healthcare benefits to those who might otherwise be uninsured. CDHPs usually include three major components:

- An HSA or a health reimbursement arrangement (HRA)
- High-deductible medical coverage, with preventive care not charged against the deductible
- Access to informational tools for making informed healthcare decisions

People covered by CDHPs pay lower premiums for their health coverage because the deductibles are high. Using either an HSA or HRA, they set aside money that can be used to help satisfy the deductible. HSAs are funded by enrollees themselves, and the money in the HSA can be rolled over for future use at year's end. No taxes are withheld from the funds contributed to an HSA. The money in an HRA is contributed by the employer and is not included in the employees' income for tax purposes. The employer's distributions to the employee are tax deductible, and unused funds in HRA accounts can be rolled over from year to year for future use.

Participants set aside HSA and HRA funds at the start of a year for medical expenses before the participant begins to pay out-of-pocket costs. For example, if a consumer has an annual deductible of $2,000 and a $1,000 HSA or HRA fund, the consumer's first $1,000 of medical expenses are paid from that fund. The consumer then pays the remaining expenses out of pocket, up to $2,000, when major medical coverage applies. See the exhibit "Basic Provisions of the Affordable Care Act of 2010."

Basic Provisions of the Affordable Care Act of 2010

The Patient Protection and Affordable Care Act (PPACA) of 2010, often called the Affordable Care Act, was intended to reform the private health insurance industry and help curb rising medical-care costs. The Affordable Care Act was upheld by the United States Supreme Court in two major challenges. All of its provisions are in effect as of 2015. Provisions of the act make health insurance available to more individuals and provide improved coverage provisions. These benefits are or will be evident under the new laws:

- Insurers cannot decline insurance for children (under age nineteen) with pre-existing medical conditions; this protection will extend to individuals of all ages as of 2014.
- Adult children (up to age twenty-six) can join or remain covered under a parent's healthcare plan.
- Insurers cannot rescind benefits (retroactively cancel coverage) because an insured or the employer made an honest mistake or omission on the insurance application.
- Insurers cannot place lifetime dollar limits on essential benefits; annual dollar limits are being phased out and will not be allowed after 2014.
- Insurers may be required to pay for certain preventative services (such as screenings, flu and pneumonia vaccines, well-baby and well-child visits) without applying co-payments, coinsurance, or deductibles.
- Individuals can choose primary care physicians from within a plan's provider network, can obtain services from an OB-GYN without a referral from a physician, and can seek emergency care at a hospital outside the plan's network without prior approval.
- Insurers are required to spend set percentages of premiums received on direct medical care or improvements to the quality of care provided, and must meet annual federal reporting requirements; insurers must provide rebates to participants if the percentages are not met.

U.S. Department of Health & Human Services, "Key Features of The Affordable Care Act," June 24, 2015, www.hhs.gov/healthcare/facts/timeline/timeline-text.html (accessed August 3, 2015). [DA07793]

Apply Your Knowledge

Bonita has a ten-year-old son, Ray, who has a number of medical conditions and prefers to see certain specialists for his treatments. Bonita changed jobs, and her new employer offers two managed-care options, a PPO plan and an EPO plan. While Bonita would prefer a flexible plan with low deductibles and co-payments and minimal paperwork, Ray would like to continue treatments with his preferred specialists.

Which one of these options would best meet Bonita's and Ray's healthcare needs?

a. Her employer's PPO plan
b. Her employer's EPO plan
c. Private healthcare insurance

Feedback: a. A PPO plan offered by her new employer would best meet their healthcare needs because it would provide greater flexibility to enable Ray and Bonita to seek medical care from the physicians and specialists with whom they have been treated previously. If one of their providers is out-of-network, they could still see that provider, but they would pay higher costs, co-payments, and deductibles for such treatments.

GOVERNMENT-PROVIDED HEALTH INSURANCE PLANS

Medicare and Medicaid provide the cornerstone of America's healthcare services.

People age sixty-five or older, under sixty-five with certain disabilities, or of all ages with specified medical conditions can qualify to receive federal Medicare health benefits. Medicare provides benefits under four programs:

- Original Medicare
- Medicare Advantage (Part C)
- Medicare Supplement Insurance (Medigap)
- Medicare Part D Prescription Drug Coverage

In addition to the original Medicare Part A and Part B, the Medicare Advantage (MA) program (called Part C) became available in 1997. Some private insurers offer Medicare Supplement Insurance (Medigap) to cover costs that are not paid by Medicare. The Medicare Prescription Drug, Improvement, and Modernization Act of 2003 provided Medicare beneficiaries with assistance in paying for prescription drugs (Medicare Part D).

Medicaid, a federal-state government healthcare plan, provides a public assistance (welfare) healthcare plan for low-income persons.

Medicare
Social insurance program that covers the medical expenses of most individuals age sixty-five and older.

Original Medicare

Medicare is part of the federal Old Age and Survivors Disability Health Insurance (OASDHI) program. It is a social insurance program that covers the medical expenses of most individuals age sixty-five and older, providing them with an affordable healthcare option.

Under the original Medicare program, beneficiaries have two basic coverages: Part A (hospital insurance) and Part B (medical insurance). Beneficiaries have options when deciding how to receive Medicare-covered services. The options available can vary depending on where the beneficiary lives. Most beneficiaries are placed in the original Medicare program, but they can then review their health and prescription needs annually and switch to different plans during certain periods toward the end of each year.

Medicare Part A is largely financed through payroll taxes paid by employees and employers. Medicare Part B is largely financed through a monthly premium paid by beneficiaries and the federal government's general revenues. The premiums are adjusted each year based on plan experience.

Medicare Part A helps pay for in-hospital services, and Medicare Part B pays for medically necessary non-hospital services. See the exhibit "Medicare Benefits."

Generally, people are eligible for Medicare if they or their spouses worked for at least ten years in Medicare-covered employment, are age sixty-five or older, and are citizens or permanent residents of the United States. People who are not yet sixty-five may also qualify for coverage if they have a disability or end-stage renal disease (permanent kidney failure requiring dialysis or transplant).

Most people receive Part A coverage automatically when they reach sixty-five years of age. Enrolling in Part B is optional. A beneficiary can enroll in Part B any time during a seven-month period that begins three months before turning sixty-five. The premium is usually taken out of monthly Social Security, Railroad Retirement, or Civil Service Retirement payments, and beneficiaries who do not receive those payments must pay the Part B premium every three months. Requirements for premium-free or premium-based coverage can vary in some circumstances. People who have limited income and resources may qualify for state assistance to pay for Part A and Part B.

Medicare Advantage plans
Health insurance plan options that provide benefits in addition to basic Medicare; offered by private insurers that contract with Medicare and available to beneficiaries currently enrolled in Medicare Part A and Part B.

Medicare Advantage (Part C)

Beneficiaries who need more services than Medicare covers can choose private health insurance (Medicare-approved) plans called **Medicare Advantage (MA) plans** or Part C plans. Part C plans cover medically necessary care offered by nearly any hospital or doctor in the country, but they do not cover all healthcare costs. The benefits offered by MA plans must at least equal Medicare Part A and B benefits, but they do not have to cover every benefit in the same manner. For example, plans that pay less than Medicare for some

Medicare Benefits

Medicare Hospital Insurance (Part A)	Medicare Medical Insurance (Part B)
• Inpatient care in hospitals • Critical access hospitals (rural, small facilities that offer limited outpatient and inpatient services) • Skilled nursing facilities (not custodial or long-term care) • Hospice care • Some home healthcare	• Doctors' services • Outpatient hospital care • Some other medical services that Part A does not cover, such as physical and occupational therapy, and some home healthcare
Medicare Advantage (Part C) Plans	**Medicare Supplement Insurance (Medigap)**
• Benefits consistent with Medicare Part A and B • Medically necessary care offered by nearly any United States hospital or physician • Choices of Medicare managed-care plans, private fee-for-service (PFFS) plans, and special needs plans (SNP), if applicable • Supplemental benefits could include lower out-of-pocket costs, dental, vision, hearing, and/or health and wellness programs • Some offer replacement prescription drug program for Part D	• Medicare exclusions and limitations • Medicare cost-sharing provisions • Medicare out-of-pocket charges (deductibles, coinsurance, co-payments, and emergency healthcare out of the U.S.)
Medicare Prescription Drug Coverage (Part D)	
• Subsidizes costs of prescription drugs underwritten through private insurance carriers • Provides coverage for beneficiaries having high or unexpected prescription drug bills	

[DA07794]

benefits, like skilled nursing facility care, can balance their benefits package by offering lower co-payments for doctor visits.

The plans, services, and fees of MA plans vary by location. People participating in an MA plan may pay a monthly premium in addition to the Medicare Part B premium and generally pay a fixed co-payment (such as $20) for each doctor visit. Medicare pays the MA plan a set monthly amount for each beneficiary who participates.

MA plans can use excess Medicare subsidies to offer supplemental benefits to members. For example, some plans limit members' annual out-of-pocket spending to protect against catastrophic medical costs or to provide benefits not available through Medicare.

A Medicare beneficiary can choose between different types of MA plans:

- Medicare managed-care plans, such as health maintenance organizations (HMOs), preferred provider organization (PPO) plans, and others—Also called coordinated care, these plans may require the beneficiary to pay fixed fees and co-payments for services obtained from preferred providers. These plans may also offer prescription drug plans that replace the Medicare prescription drug program (Medicare Part D).
- Private fee-for-service (PFFS) plans—A type of Medicare Advantage plan in which a beneficiary may go to any Medicare-approved doctor or hospital that accepts the plan's payment. Medicare pays the PFFS plan a portion of the premium, and the beneficiary must pay the difference to the provider, although Medicare has strict limits on what patients can be charged. The PFFS plan provides all Medicare and additional benefits to the beneficiary.
- Special needs plans (SNP)—A special plan providing more-focused healthcare for specific groups of people, such as those who have both Medicare and Medicaid, who reside in a nursing home, or who have certain chronic medical conditions. SNP providers coordinate the services and medical care providers to meet beneficiaries' unique needs. Except in emergencies, SNP beneficiaries may be required to use services available within the plan network. SNPs are required to provide Medicare prescription drug coverage (Part D).

Beneficiaries should choose a plan that offers the benefits that will best suit their personal medical care needs.

Medicare Supplement Insurance (Medigap)

Medicare Supplement Insurance policies (also called Medigap policies) are sold by private insurers to fill the gaps in original Medicare Parts A and B coverage. Premiums for Medigap policies can be costly, but they provide coverage for a number of benefits and fill the gaps left within Medicare provisions. However, the benefits provided by Medigap policies do not include paying the costs for Medicare Parts C and D. Additionally, a person who has purchased an MA plan does not require a Medigap policy because the benefits covered are typically the same.

Medicare Prescription Drug Coverage (Part D)

Medicare Part D is a voluntary program through which the government subsidizes the costs of beneficiaries' prescription drugs underwritten through private insurance carriers. It provides coverage for beneficiaries who have very high or unexpected prescription drug bills. All Medicare beneficiaries are eligible for this coverage, except when it is provided separately under MA plans.

Beneficiaries may sign up for Part D upon first becoming eligible for Medicare (three months before the month they reach sixty-five years of age until three months after they turn sixty-five). If they receive Medicare coverage as a result of a disability, they can sign up from three months before to three months after their twenty-fifth month of receiving cash disability payments.

Medicare beneficiaries generally pay monthly premiums for Part D, which vary by plan, and a yearly deductible. They also pay a part of the prescription costs, including a deductible (co-payment) or **coinsurance**. Some plans offer more coverage and cover additional drugs for higher monthly premiums. Beneficiaries with limited income and resources may qualify for extra governmental assistance and may not have to pay a premium or deductible.

Coinsurance
Medical insurance provision that requires the insured to pay part of the covered medical expenses in excess of the deductible.

Medicaid

Medicaid is a means-tested federal-state welfare program that covers the medical expenses of low-income persons, including those who are aged, blind, or disabled; members of families with dependent children; and pregnant women and certain children. Low-income Medicare beneficiaries requiring nursing home coverage are also eligible. An investigative process determines eligibility.

Benefits and eligibility for Medicaid can vary by state because states help fund the program. The federal government pays almost 60 percent of all Medicaid expenses, so while each state administers its own program, the federal Centers for Medicare and Medicaid Services (CMS) set requirements for quality, funding, and eligibility. To receive matching funds and grants, each state must conform to federal guidelines. Each state's poverty level determines the federal matching formula. The wealthiest states receive a federal match of 50 percent, while poorer states receive a greater percentage of funding. Medicaid's costs average 22 percent of each state's budget.

The largest group of Medicaid recipients is children, composing almost half the number of total recipients. A limited income is one of the primary eligibility requirements for Medicaid, but poverty alone does not qualify applicants to receive Medicaid benefits. See the exhibit "Medicaid Provisions."

Medicaid sends benefit payments directly to healthcare providers. In some states, Medicaid beneficiaries must pay a small fee (co-payment) for medical services. While Medicaid eligibility is based on income and assets, specific requirements can vary. In some situations, any category of applicant may be denied coverage.

Special rules apply to applicants who are disabled children living at home, are living with HIV/AIDS, or are residents of a nursing home. Disabled children may be covered under Medicaid if they are U.S. citizens or permanent residents. They may be eligible even if their parents are not, or if they live with people other than their parents.

Additionally, Medicaid provides the largest portion of federal money spent on healthcare for people living with HIV/AIDS, who usually must progress from an HIV-positive diagnosis to AIDS before qualifying under the "disabled"

Medicaid Provisions

Persons Eligible for Benefits	Eligibility Requirements	State-Dependent Benefits
Low income: • Children • Pregnant women • Parents of eligible children • People with disabilities • Eligible people who have little or no medical insurance	Criteria include: • Age • Pregnancy • Disability • Blindness • Income and resources • Status as a U.S. citizen or a lawfully admitted immigrant	May provide: • Inpatient and outpatient hospital services • Physician services • Medical and surgical dental services • Some in-home care • Custodial nursing home care • Personal care • Some prescriptions

[DA07795]

category. More than half of Americans who have AIDS receive Medicaid payments.

While a living Medicaid recipient does not pay for services, once that recipient dies, Medicaid may recover costs paid for healthcare from the recipient's property, if any. Eligibility guidelines, for example, may allow a recipient to own one home, one car, and $2,000 in assets (such as savings accounts or retirement plans), but recipients' financial records are reviewed up to five years prior to an application for benefits to determine eligibility.

Retirees and other people facing high nursing home costs are subject to special Medicaid eligibility standards that attempt to prevent them from disposing of substantial assets before applying for Medicaid. As a result, any asset or financial transfers without fair market value (usually gifts) that take place during the five years preceding the Medicaid application can be subject to penalties.

Apply Your Knowledge

Harold retired at age sixty-five after working thirty-five years at a job that contributed to Medicare. Harold's retirement income and investments allow him to afford some healthcare coverage. Harold has ongoing treatments for normal hearing and vision loss. Harold believes participation in a wellness program improves his quality of life and reduces his medical costs. Harold prefers to save on premiums by paying some of his medical costs out of pocket.

Which one of these Medicare benefits would be most appropriate for Harold's preferences and needs?

a. Medicare Part A and Part B
b. Medicare Advantage (MA) (Part C) plan
c. Medicare Supplement Insurance (Medigap)
d. Medicare prescription drug coverage (Part D)

Feedback: b. A Medicare Advantage (MA) (Part C) plan would be most appropriate because it would pay benefits equal to Medicare Part A and Part B but could provide additional benefits that would meet Harold's preferences and needs. For example, such a plan might provide hearing and/or vision coverage and might provide a wellness program. An MA plan might also include limitations on high-cost medical treatments. Medicare Part A and Part B (a.) would not be needed with an MA plan, and, because Harold prefers to pay some out-of-pocket costs, neither Medicare Supplement Insurance (c.) nor Medicare prescription drug coverage (d.) would meet his needs.

LONG-TERM CARE INSURANCE

Long-term care insurance is an increasingly important coverage. Almost half of all people who have reached age sixty will require some form of long-term care during their lifetimes. The overall average length of stay in a nursing home is about two and one-half years, and the cost of long-term care is staggering.

When choosing a long-term care (LTC) policy, a consumer should bear in mind many considerations regarding benefits, coverage triggers, eligibility, and other economic issues:

- Coverage basics
- Coverage triggers
- Benefits typically provided
- Benefits typically excluded
- Inflation protection
- Guaranteed renewability
- Nonforfeiture options
- Tax treatment
- Waiver of premium
- Elimination period
- Eligibility provisions

Group and individual policy insurers take different approaches to eligibility, and age is the most important factor.

Coverage Basics

Long-term care insurance can provide for the daily custodial care as well as the long-term nursing care that an individual may need outside of a hospital. Neither Medicare nor private medical expense insurance covers long-term care for expenses associated with confinements in such facilities as nursing homes or custodial care centers for extended periods. Medicare covers skilled nursing care only up to a maximum of 100 days. Medicare excludes altogether custodial care, or nonmedical care that helps an individual with the activities of daily living (ADLs), and intermediate nursing care, which is care for a stable condition that requires daily care but not twenty-four-hour nursing supervision.

Additionally, most elderly patients in nursing homes do not initially qualify for long-term care under the strict eligibility requirements of Medicaid, a joint federal and state public assistance program that pays for healthcare for low-income individuals and families. Medicaid pays a large percentage of the nation's nursing home bills. However, many applicants do not qualify for Medicaid, and its eligibility requirements change frequently. An applicant for Medicaid may have to dispose of assets to qualify for benefits. Additionally, some nursing homes do not accept Medicaid recipients. LTC insurance provides a means to preserve the assets of individuals who require long-term care, as well as the assets of their families.

Consequently, many elderly people have purchased LTC insurance to pay for the enormous medical bills that result from extended stays in nursing homes. Individuals can purchase LTC insurance, and some employers offer group plans that enable individuals to obtain coverage at reduced rates.

No standard LTC policy exists, and a consumer should consider several basic aspects of policies when comparing them:

- Benefit period—The length of time after filing a claim that the insurer will pay for care (from one year up to lifetime coverage)
- Daily benefit—The maximum dollar or percentage amount the insurer will pay for care daily (from about $30 to $300 per day)
- Elimination period or deductible—The length of time and the amount of money an insured must pay out of pocket before the insurer starts to pay (from "first day coverage" to a one-year wait)
- Level of inflation protection—The amount by which benefits will increase over time to keep up with inflation

The consumer can choose any combination of benefits, deductibles, or inflation protection options, all of which affect premium cost.

Coverage Triggers

A critical LTC policy provision involves the conditions that determine who is eligible to receive benefits, often referred to as coverage triggers. The most common triggers are ADLs, medical necessity, and cognitive impairment, which necessitates care to protect the patient and others from threats to safety caused by the patient's condition.

Under most LTC policies, an insured qualifies for benefits when unable to perform a specified number (such as two or three) of the ADLs listed in the LTC policy. If an insured under an LTC policy with a cognitive impairment trigger is cognitively impaired, the insured qualifies for coverage. If an insured under the LTC policy meets the medical necessity trigger, coverage for the insured's LTC needs will be provided, subject to the policy limits and provisions.

Most LTC policies contain more than one of these coverage triggers, such as ADLs and cognitive impairment. An insured would, however, need to satisfy only one of the triggers to become eligible for coverage under an LTC policy.

Benefits Typically Provided

Purchasers of LTC insurance typically have a choice of benefits—such as a daily benefit of up to $80, $120, or $160—that is paid over a maximum period of two, three, or four years, or for the insured's lifetime. Some insurance allows purchasers to select a maximum lifetime benefit amount, such as $300,000. Some policies provide a maximum benefit equal to the daily dollar limit times the policy duration, subject to a daily maximum dollar limit. For example, $100 per day for five years might actually mean a maximum benefit of $182,500, which can be used no more rapidly than $100 per day. Additionally, policies can cover home healthcare, adult daycare, and respite care.

A "bed reservation benefit guarantee" holds a bed for a short hospital stay, paying for a number of days to hold a nursing-home bed in case the insured requires hospitalization. For example, if an insured is temporarily absent during a stay in a long-term care facility, the insurer might continue to pay for the insured's room and reserve the bed, for up to a stated number of days per calendar year.

The policies typically cover skilled nursing home care, intermediate nursing care, and custodial care. Many policies also cover home healthcare services. Some plans cover only skilled nursing care provided in the home by registered nurses and other skilled personnel. Other plans are broader and also cover home health aides provided by licensed agencies. However, few policies cover the cost of having someone come into the home to cook meals, clean the home, or run errands.

The majority of LTC policies sold today are comprehensive policies. They typically cover care and services in a variety of long-term care settings, for which they pay daily benefits:

- The insured's home, with benefits including skilled nursing care; occupational, speech, physical, and rehabilitation therapy; and help with personal care, such as bathing and dressing. Many policies also cover some homemaker services, such as meal preparation or housekeeping, in conjunction with the personal care services the insured receives.
- Adult day healthcare centers.
- Hospice care.
- Respite care.
- Assisted living facilities (also called residential care facilities or alternate care facilities).
- Alzheimer's special care facilities.
- Nursing homes.

Many policies may also pay for services or devices to support insureds living at home:

- Equipment such as in-home electronic monitoring systems
- Home modification, such as grab bars and ramps
- Transportation to medical appointments
- Training for a friend or relative to learn to provide personal care safely and appropriately

Some policies provide some payment for family members or friends to help care for an insured, but they may do so on a limited basis or only in relation to the costs that the family member incurs.

Many policies provide the services of a care coordinator, usually a nurse or social worker in the insured's community. The care coordinator can meet with the insured and discuss the specific personal situation and help arrange for and monitor care. The care coordinator's help is usually optional; the insured uses it if and when desired, and care is not limited to the providers that the care coordinator may recommend.

Benefits Typically Excluded

Like all insurance, LTC policies have exclusions. The outline of coverage that the consumer receives before applying for coverage and the policy itself list these exclusions, which often follow state regulations regarding what exclusions are allowed.

LTC policies have these typical exclusions:

- Care or services provided by a family member, unless the family member is a regular employee of an organization that is providing the treatment,

service, or care and the organization he or she works for receives the payment for the treatment, service, or care; and the family member receives no compensation other than the normal compensation for employees in the applicable category.
- Care or services for which no charge is made in the absence of insurance.
- Care or services provided outside the United States, its territories, or possessions. However, a growing number of policies now have an international care benefit that can provide care outside the U.S.
- Care or services resulting from a war or an act of war, whether declared or not.
- Care or services resulting from an attempt at suicide (while sane or insane) or an intentionally self-inflicted injury.
- Care or services for alcoholism or drug addiction (except for an addiction to a prescription medication when administered upon the advice of a physician).
- Treatment provided in a government facility (unless otherwise required by law).
- Services for which benefits are available under Medicare or another governmental program (except Medicaid); any state or federal workers compensation, employers liability, or occupational disease law; or any motor vehicle no-fault law.

Although most policies do not pay for care the insured receives from a family member, friend, or other individual who is not normally paid to provide care, some policies provide a cash payment for each day that the insured receives care from anyone, even if it is a family member or friend. These policies cost about 25 percent to 40 percent more but allow more flexibility in using benefit dollars. Most policies provide training and support for family and friends who provide care.

Most policies require that the facility, agency, or individual providing care meet certain minimum standards with respect to quality, safety, and training. For example, a nursing home that is not licensed but operates in a state that requires licensure would not be covered. In states that do not require long-term care facilities or programs to be licensed, the insurance policy would typically describe the staffing, safety, and other features that should be present to ensure that the insured receives appropriate care.

LTC policies focus on paying for the types of services and providers that meet the needs of insureds who cannot perform their ADLs on their own or who have cognitive-impairment needs. They do not pay for care or services unrelated to these needs, such as hospital stays or prescription medications. Some policies may pay for prescription drugs provided while the insured is in a care facility (but not at home), and some policies pay for transportation costs to help the insured get to medical appointments when physically or cognitively impaired.

Some policies provide coverage for care related to everyday household needs such as housekeeping, laundry, meals, and managing medications—so-called "instrumental activities of daily living"—but only when the insured receives that care as part of the help he or she gets from a paid care provider for assistance with ADLs. Most policies do not pay for in-home assistance if all the insured needs is help with services such as housekeeping, meals, laundry, and transportation.

Finally, LTC policies do not pay for items provided solely for the insured's comfort or convenience, such as a television in the insured's nursing-home room or a visit to the facility's hair salon.

Inflation Protection

Inflation can substantially erode the real value of LTC insurance benefits. For example, assuming an annual inflation rate of 5 percent, a current daily charge of $120 would increase to $318 in twenty years. Therefore, protection against inflation is usually available as an optional benefit.

Insurers use two major methods for providing protection against inflation:

- Some policies allow insureds to purchase additional amounts of insurance in the future with no evidence of insurability. The premium is based on the insured's current age, but evidence of insurability is not required.
- Other policies provide for an automatic benefit increase in which the daily benefit is increased by a specified percentage for a number of years, such as 5 percent annually for the next ten or twenty years. Adding an automatic benefit increase to a long-term policy is expensive and may double the annual premium in some cases, especially if an insured at an advanced age purchases the policy.

Guaranteed Renewability

Most individual LTC insurance policies have guaranteed renewability provisions. An LTC insurer cannot cancel the policy on the basis of change in the insured's health. Once the policy has been issued, it cannot be canceled. However, premiums can be increased for the underwriting class in which the insured is placed.

Nonforfeiture Options

Some LTC policies now provide nonforfeiture options. When the insured cancels an LTC policy, the premiums paid for the policy until the policy is canceled can be returned to the insured or used to purchase the same benefit for a shorter benefit period or a reduced benefit for the existing benefit period while eliminating the need for more premiums.

The nonforfeiture value is similar to a reduced paid-up amount of insurance after the premiums have been paid for a number of years. For example, an insured might have purchased a $100/day benefit twenty years ago and now chooses not to pay any future premiums. Under a nonforfeiture option, the policy is currently paid up for a reduced benefit amount, such as $65 per day.

Tax Treatment

Insureds can deduct premiums charged for LTC policies as itemized medical expenses on federal tax returns. An insured who pays more than 7.5 percent of adjusted gross income for medical expenses (including LTC insurance premiums) can deduct those expenses from federal income taxes. Some special LTC insurance policies are tax-qualified (nontaxed) policies, which makes the LTC benefits tax-free. Nonqualified policies require that the insured pay additional taxes based on the value of the benefits received.

Some states allow LTC premium deductions on state income tax returns, regardless of whether a policy is federally qualified. Employees in group plans generally can pay premiums with pretax dollars, further lowering their costs.

Waiver of Premium

Waiver of premium is an important feature in an LTC policy. It allows, for example, an incapacitated insured to stop paying premiums while receiving benefits and keeping the policy in force with full coverage. In many cases, the premiums must be paid until a time period (usually several months) has been satisfied, and then they are waived. For example, an LTC policy might have a requirement that the insured be in a nursing home for a specified period, such as sixty to ninety days, before a waiver of premium is allowed.

Elimination Period

Most LTC insurance plans are sold subject to an **elimination period** that functions like a time deductible. The LTC policy elimination period or deductible is the length of time and the amount of money an insured must pay out of pocket before the insurer starts to pay. The time span can range from first-day coverage to a one-year wait.

In other words, coverage does not begin until after a certain period has elapsed and the insured has paid up to a specified dollar threshold. A longer elimination period can substantially reduce the annual premium. Common elimination periods are 30, 60, 100, or 180 days, with the most common periods ranging from zero to 90 days.

> **Elimination period**
> Initial time period in a health insurance or disability income policy during which benefits are not paid.

Eligibility Provisions

Individual LTC insurance is medically underwritten, meaning that an insurer can refuse an application for a policy from an applicant who does not meet medical guidelines. Applicants for group policies usually face less-stringent underwriting guidelines than applicants for individual policies.

Age is the primary factor in determining the cost of an LTC policy. The younger an insured is, the less expensive the premiums. However, the younger insured will also pay premiums for a longer time. The best time for a consumer to purchase an LTC policy is between ages fifty and fifty-five because premiums will cost nearly twice as much for a policy purchased in one's sixties. However, buying LTC insurance might be desirable before age fifty if the insured has an employer-sponsored group plan.

LTC insurers have varied underwriting guidelines, and many medical conditions are not insurable under most LTC plans. In general, many conditions controlled with medications are insurable. An applicant must list on the application any current or past medical problems, as well as provide medical records from healthcare providers as part of the underwriting process.

Some insurers reject LTC applicants, and a husband and wife with different risk characteristics can each receive a different underwriting decision from the same insurer based on that insurer's medical underwriting guidelines. An applicant who is refused coverage by one insurer might be successful in applying for LTC insurance from another insurer; for example, some LTC insurers specialize in obtaining coverage for high-risk applicants. Applying for coverage while one is in reasonably good health is advisable.

All LTC insurance policies have physician certification (or gatekeeper) provisions that determine whether the insured is eligible for policy benefits. A gatekeeper provision states the requirements that the insured must meet to receive benefits.

A common type of gatekeeper provision requires that, to qualify for coverage, the insured must be unable to perform a certain number of ADLs, such as two out of five, without help from another person.

SUMMARY

Individuals face numerous exposures that could result in their injury, illness, and possible disability. In many respects, a long-term disability or health condition may be more damaging to a family's financial condition than the death of a primary wage earner. Fortunately, insurance options exist to help individuals and families better manage the financial loss exposures that they face related to disability, health conditions, and long-term care.

Disability income insurance is designed to replace a portion of an individual's income if he or she becomes disabled because of an injury or illness. Disability insurance policies contain a variety of provisions that specify when and how disability benefits are determined and paid. Three types of disability income insurance are available: individual disability income insurance, group disability income insurance, and the Social Security disability income (SSDI) program. The plans may be combined to help wage earners avoid the financial duress that is often associated with disability.

Healthcare plans can be categorized into three types of plans. The most common providers of traditional health insurance plans are commercial insurers, Blue Cross and Blue Shield plans, and employer self-insured plans. The most common managed-care plans are health maintenance organizations, preferred provider organizations, exclusive provider organizations, and point-of-service plans. Medicare Advantage plans offer managed care for Medicare beneficiaries. Consumer-directed health plans combine health savings accounts or health reimbursement arrangements with high-deductible medical coverage.

People age sixty-five or older, under sixty-five with certain disabilities, and of all ages with certain medical conditions can qualify to receive federal Medicare health benefits, which include Part A (hospital insurance), Part B (medical insurance), and Part D (prescription drug coverage). Medicare beneficiaries can choose Medicare Advantage plans (Medicare Part C) for benefit levels in addition to those provided by Medicare. Medicare Supplement Insurance (Medigap) helps cover any gaps.

Low-income people can receive healthcare benefits under the state-federal Medicaid program, a public assistance plan for low-income persons, including people with certain disabilities and low-income Medicare beneficiaries requiring nursing home coverage.

When choosing an LTC policy, a consumer should bear in mind coverage triggers, benefits typically provided or excluded, inflation protection, guaranteed renewability, taxation, nonforfeiture options, waiver of premium, and the elimination period. Age is the most important factor governing eligibility and premium costs for both group and individual policies.

ASSIGNMENT NOTE

1. Health Insurance Online, "Merritt Personal Lines Manual: Mechanics of Medicare Managed Care," 2011, www.online-health-insurance.com/health-insurance-resources/MPLM/content/mechanics-of-medicare-managed-care.htm (accessed June 17, 2011).

Index

Page numbers in boldface refer to pages where the word or phrase is defined.

SYMBOLS

401(k) Plan, 10.13
403(b) Plan, 10.14
2011 HO-3 Section I—Property Coverage Case Study, 5.29

A

Abandonment of Property, 5.27
Accelerated Death Benefits, 9.26
Accidental death benefit, **9.26**
Actual cash value (ACV), **4.9**
Additional Coverages, 5.14
Additional Duties for Physical Damage Coverage, 4.20
Additional Duties for Uninsured Motorists Coverage, 4.20
Additional Life Insurance Riders, 9.26
Additional Residence Rented to Others—1, 2, 3, or 4 Families, 6.39
Additional Section II Conditions, 6.20
Add-On Plans, **2.11**
Agreement and Definitions, 3.3, 5.8
Aircraft and Hovercraft Liability, 6.12
Aircraft Liability Definition Revised to Remove Exception for Model and Hobby Aircraft, 6.40
Annuity, **10.18**
Annuity Types Based on Premium Payment Method, 10.20
Annuity Types Based on the Date Benefits Begin, 10.19
Annuity Types Based on the Party Bearing the Investment Risk, 10.19
Apparent authority, **6.21**
Applicable Endorsements, 3.8
Appraisal, **4.11**, 5.26
Arbitration, **3.48**
Asset Exposed to Loss, 1.4
Assets Available, 9.31
Assets Exposed to Loss, 1.5, 1.9
Assignment, 6.22
Assignment Clause Provision, 9.22
Assisted Living Care Coverage, 6.36
Attachment, **3.17**
Auto Accident, 8.22
Auto Loan/Lease Coverage, 4.30
Automatic Termination, 4.25
Automobile Insurance for High-Risk Drivers, 2.13
Automobile Insurance Plans, **2.14**
Automobile Insurance Rate Regulation, 2.15
Avoidance, **1.22**

B

Bankruptcy of Insured, 4.21
Basic Characteristics of OASDHI, 10.22
Basic medical expense coverage, **11.16**
Beachfront and Windstorm Plans, 7.34
Beneficiary, **9.22**
Beneficiary Designations, 9.22
Benefit Periods, 11.7
Benefits Provided, 11.9
Benefits Required by No-Fault Laws, 2.12
Benefits Typically Excluded, 11.30
Benefits Typically Provided, 11.29
Binding authority, **6.21**
Blanket basis, **8.5**
Blended Families, 9.6
Boatowners and Yacht Policies, 8.12
Bodily injury, **6.3**
Bodily Injury From Nuclear Weapons or War, 3.33
Bodily Injury to an Employee of an Insured, 3.18
Broadened Home-Sharing Host Activities Coverage Endorsement, 6.39
Broadened Residence Premises Definition Endorsement, 6.38
Business, 6.13

C

Cancellation, **4.24**, 6.21
Case Analysis Tools, 3.24, 3.35, 3.52, 4.13, 4.37, 7.14, 8.22
Case Facts, 3.23, 3.35, 3.51, 4.12, 4.36, 5.29, 6.23, 6.43, 7.13, 8.20
Cause of Loss, **1.4**, 1.8, 1.9
Changes in the Policy, 4.21
Characteristics and Components, 8.3
Choice No-Fault Plans, **2.11**
Civil law, **1.9**
Claim Settlement That Prejudices Insurer's Right of Recovery, 3.44
Claims Expenses, 6.7
Coinsurance, **11.25**
Collapse, 7.7
Collision coverage, **3.14**, 4.3
Common Endorsements to the Personal Auto Policy, 4.26
Common Life Insurance Contractual Provisions, 9.22
Common Life Insurance Contractual Provisions and Riders, 9.21
Common Life Insurance Riders, 9.26

Common Policy Provisions, 1.32, 8.4
Commonly Used Endorsements that Modify the 2011 ISO Homeowners Policies, 6.34–6.35
Community Eligibility, 7.24
Compensation of Auto Accident Victims, 2.3
Compensatory damages, **3.15**
Competition, 2.19
Compulsory Auto Insurance Laws, **2.5**
Conditions, 1.37, 8.19
Conditions Applicable to Section II, 6.16
Conditions Applicable to Sections I and II, 6.20
Condominium, **6.32**
Consumer-Directed Health Plans, **11.19**
Contractual Liability, 1.11
Convertible, **9.14**
Cooperative corporation, **6.32**
Costs Associated With Premature Death, 9.3
Coverage A—Dwelling, 5.11, 7.4
Coverage A—Dwelling and Coverage B—Other Structures, 7.8
Coverage Basics, 11.28
Coverage B—Other Structures, 5.11, 7.4
Coverage C—Personal Property, 5.12, 7.5, 7.8
Coverage D—Fair Rental Value and Coverage E—Additional Living Expense, 7.5
Coverage D—Loss of Use, 5.14
Coverage E—Personal Liability, 6.3
Coverage E—Personal Liability and Coverage F—Medical Payments to Others, 6.12
Coverage F—Medical Payments to Others, 6.6
Coverage for Damage to Your Auto (Maximum Limit of Liability), 4.32
Coverage for Liability and Theft Losses, 7.9
Coverage Triggers, 11.29
Coverage Variations in ISO Homeowners Forms, 6.29
Coverages, 7.4, 7.34, 7.35, 8.5
Covered Occupations, 10.22
Credit Card, Electronic Fund Transfer Card or Access Device, Forgery and Counterfeit Money Coverage—Increased Limit, 6.37
Current Assumption Whole Life, 9.17
Customizing Equipment, 4.8

D

Damage to Property of Others, 6.8
Damages, **1.8**
Damages and Defense Costs Covered, 3.14
Death, 6.22
Debris Removal, 7.6
Debt Elimination Needs, 9.9
Declarations, 1.32, 3.3, 3.7, 5.8
Declarations page (declarations, or dec.), **1.32**
Deductibles, **4.3**, 4.6, 5.22
Deferred annuity, **10.19**
Defined Benefit 401(k) Plans, 10.17
Defined Benefit Plans, **10.16**
Defined Contribution Plans, **10.16**
Definition of Disability, 11.8
Definitions, **1.33**, 3.10
Description of Insured Autos, 3.7

Determination of Amounts Payable, 3.28, 3.41, 3.55–3.58, 4.16, 4.42, 5.34, 6.28, 6.48, 7.18, 8.27
Determination of Coverage, 3.25, 3.36, 3.52–3.55, 4.14, 4.40, 5.30, 6.25, 6.44, 7.16, 8.22
Determining the Amount of Life Insurance to Own, 9.7
Determining Whether Homeowners Section II—Liability Coverages Covers a Claim, 6.23
DICE Analysis Step 1: Declarations, 5.30, 6.25, 6.44
DICE Analysis Step 2: Insuring Agreement, 5.31, 6.26, 6.45
DICE Analysis Step 3: Conditions, 5.31, 6.27, 6.47
DICE Analysis Step 4: Exclusions, 5.32, 6.27, 6.47
Difference in conditions (DIC) policy, or DIC insurance, **7.34**
Disability, 10.26
Disability and Health-Related Personal Loss Exposures, 11.3
Disability Definition, 11.14
Disability Income Insurance, 11.6
Disability Loss Exposures, 11.4
Diversification, **1.24**
Dividend Options, 9.22
Duplication, **1.23**
Duties After "Occurrence", 6.17
Duties of an Injured Person—Coverage F—Medical Payments to Others, 6.19
Dwelling Coverage Case Study, 7.13
Dwelling Policies, 7.3
Dwelling Policy Conditions, 7.9
Dwelling Policy General Exclusions, 7.9

E

Earthquake, 6.36
Electronic Equipment, 4.7
Elements of Loss Exposures, 1.3–1.4
Eligibility Provisions, 11.34
Eligibility Requirements for Insured Status, 10.23
Eligible Property, 7.34, 7.35
Elimination period, **11.33**
Emergency program, **7.25**
Employer-Sponsored Retirement Plans, 10.16
Endorsements, **1.33**, 3.4
Environmental Issues, 2.20
ESOP, 10.15
Establishment of a Disability Period, 11.15
Excess Electronic Equipment Coverage, 4.31
Excluded Risks, 9.22
Exclusions, **1.37**, 3.17, 3.31, 3.44, 4.7, 8.19
Exclusions That Apply Only to Coverage E, 6.15
Exclusions That Apply Only to Coverage F, 6.16
Exclusive provider organization (EPO), **11.18**
Expected or Intended Injury, 6.13
Expense Needs, 9.28
Extended Non-Owned Coverage—Vehicles Furnished or Available for Regular Use, 4.29

F

Factors Considered in Rating, 5.9
Factors That Influence the Retirement Loss Exposure, 10.3

Fair Rental Value and Additional Living Expense, 7.6
FAIR and Beachfront and Windstorm Plans, 7.32–7.33
FAIR Plans, 7.33
Family Living Expense Needs, 9.9
Final Expenses Needs, 9.8
Financial Consequences of Loss, 1.4, 1.8, 1.11
Financial Responsibility, 3.22
Financial Responsibility Laws, **2.4**
Fire Department Service Charge, 7.7
First Aid Expenses, 6.7
First party, **2.6**
First-to-Die (Joint) Life Insurance, 9.17
Flood hazard boundary map, **7.25**
Flood Insurance Coverage, 7.27
Flood Insurance Rate Map (FIRM), **7.25**
Flood Insurance Reform, 7.30
Fraud, 4.22
Functional replacement cost, **5.6**

G

Garage Business Use, 3.18
Garage Location, 3.8
General damages, **1.9**
General Duties, 4.19
Glass or Safety Glazing Material, 7.7
Government Destruction or Confiscation, 4.8
Government-Provided Health Insurance Plans, 11.21–11.22
Grace period, **9.23**
Group Disability Income Insurance, 11.12
Guaranteed insurability rider (guaranteed purchase option), **9.26**
Guaranteed Renewability, 11.32

H

Health and Disability Loss Exposures, 1.14, 1.30
Health Insurance (Medicare), 10.27
Health Insurance Plans, 11.15–11.16
Health maintenance organization (HMO), **11.17**
Health reimbursement arrangement (HRA), **11.19**
Health-Related Loss Exposures, 11.5
HO-2 Broad Form Compared With HO-3, 6.29
HO-3 Coverage Case, 6.43–6.44
HO-3 Section I—Conditions, 5.22
HO-3 Section I—Perils Insured Against and Exclusions, 5.17
HO-3 Section I—Property Coverages, 5.10
HO-3 Section II—Conditions, 6.16–6.17
HO-3 Section II—Exclusions, 6.10
HO-3 Section II—Liability Coverages, 6.3
HO-3 Watercraft Coverage, 8.8
HO-4 Contents Broad Form Compared With HO-3, 6.31
HO-5 Comprehensive Form Compared With HO-3, 6.32
HO-6 Unit-Owners Form Compared With HO-3, 6.32
HO-8 Modified Coverage Form Compared With HO-3, 6.33
Home Business Insurance Coverage (HOMEBIZ), 6.37
Home-Sharing Host Activities Amendatory Endorsement, 6.38
HSA, **11.19**

Hull insurance, **8.12**
Human life value approach, **9.7**, 9.11

I

Immediate annuity, **10.19**
Improvements, Alterations, and Additions, 7.6
Incentives and Programs, 7.25
Incontestable clause, **9.23**
Indemnity plan, **11.16**
Individual Annuities, 10.18
Individual Disability Income Insurance, 11.10
Individual Retirement Accounts, 10.9
Inflation Guard, 6.36
Inflation Protection, 11.32
Inherent vice, **8.6**
Injury During the Course of Employment, 3.31
Inland Marine Floaters, 8.3
Inland marine insurance, **8.3**
Insurable Interest and Limit of Liability, 5.22
Insurance, **1.25**
Insurance as a Risk Financing Technique, 1.27
Insurance Treatment of Disability, Health-Related, and Long-Term Care Loss Exposures, 11.6
Insured Persons, 3.43
Insurer, 3.7
Insurer's Right to Recover Payment, 4.22
Insuring Agreements, **1.35**, 3.14, 3.30, 3.42, 4.3, 8.16–8.18
Intentional Injury, 3.17
Investing to Achieve Financial Goals, 10.5
ISO Homeowners Coverage, 5.3

J

Joint Underwriting Associations (JUAs), **2.15**

K

Keogh Plan, 10.14

L

Legal Action Against the Insurer, 4.22
Liability coverage, **4.33**
Liability Loss Exposures, **1.8**
Liberalization Clause, **4.22**, 6.20
Lienholder, 3.8
Life Insurance and Other Assets, 9.9
Life Insurance Case Study, 9.27
Life Insurance Contractual Provisions and Riders, 9.32
Limit of Liability, 3.21, 3.33, 3.46, 4.9, 6.17
Limited Mexico Coverage, 4.30
Limited Transportation Network Driver Coverage (No Passenger) Endorsement, 4.35
Limited Water Back-Up and Sump Discharge or Overflow Coverage, 6.38
Limits Trigger or Damages Trigger, 3.49–3.50
Long-Term Care Insurance, 11.27–11.28
Long-Term Care Loss Exposures, 11.5
Loss assessment, 6.8, **6.15**
Loss exposure, **1.3**

Loss Payable Clause, 5.28
Loss Payment, 5.27
Loss prevention, **1.23**
Loss reduction, **1.23**
Loss Settlement, 5.23
Loss to a Pair or Set, 5.25

M

Major medical insurance, **11.16**
Managed-Care Plans, **11.17**
Mandatory or Optional Coverage, 3.49
Matching Price to Exposure, 2.19
Media and Accessories, 4.8
Medicaid, **11.25**
Medical payments coverage, **4.33**
Medicare, **11.22**
Medicare Advantage (Part C), 11.22
Medicare Advantage plans, **11.19, 11.22**
Medicare Prescription Drug Coverage (Part D), 11.24
Medicare Supplement Insurance (Medigap), 11.24
Miscellaneous Provisions, 1.38
Miscellaneous Type Vehicle Endorsement, 4.26
Misstatement of Age or Sex, 9.23
Mobilehome Coverages, 7.19, 7.21
Mobilehome Exposures, 7.19
Modified No-Fault Plans, 2.10
Monetary threshold (dollar threshold), **2.10**
Monthly Cash Benefits, 11.15
Mortgage Clause, 5.27
Motor Vehicle and Other Motorized Craft—Exclusions, 6.10
Motor Vehicle Liability, 6.10
Motorized Vehicles With Fewer Than Four Wheels, 3.31

N

Named insured, **3.7**
Named Non-Owner Coverage, 4.29
Named perils coverage, **5.17**
National Flood Insurance Program, 7.24
Necessary Reference Materials, 5.30, 6.25, 6.44
Needs Analysis Steps, 9.28
Needs approach, **9.7**
Negligence, **1.10**
No Benefit to Bailee, 4.10, 5.28
No Benefit to Workers Compensation or Disability Benefits Insurer, 3.45
No-fault automobile insurance, **2.8**
No-fault laws, **2.9**
No-Fault Automobile Laws, 2.9
Nonforfeiture options, **9.24**, 11.32
Nonowned Autos, 4.5
Nonowned Auto Used in Garage Business, 4.9
Nonowned Auto Used Without Reasonable Belief of Being Entitled, 4.8
Nonrenewal, 4.24, 6.22
Nuclear Energy Liability Losses, 3.19
Nuclear Radiation, 3.33

O

Occurrence, **6.3**
Optional Limits Transportation Expenses Coverage, 4.32
Ordinance or Law, 7.8
Ordinance or Law—Increased Amount of Coverage, 6.37
Original Medicare, 11.22
Other Business Use, 3.19
Other Coverage E and Coverage F Exclusions, 6.14
Other Coverages, 7.5
Other Discounts and Credits, 2.18
Other Insurance, 3.22, 3.34, 3.47
Other Insurance and Service Agreement, 5.26
Other Programs, 2.15
Other Property Exposure Considerations, 7.21
Other Rating Factors, 2.17
Other Regulatory Issues, 2.19
Other Sources of Recovery, 4.10
Other Structures, 7.6
Other Termination Provisions, 4.25
Other Than Collision Coverage, **3.14**, 4.4
Other Types of Life Insurance, 9.16
Other Vehicles Owned by Insured or Available for Insured's Regular Use, 3.20, 3.32
Our Option, 5.26
Out of State Coverage, 3.22
Overview of Coverages, 3.4
Overview of Homeowners Form HO-3, 5.6
Overview of Steps, 5.30, 6.25
Overview of the Personal Auto Policy, 3.3
Owned But Not Insured Vehicle, 3.44
Owned Vehicle With Primary UM Coverage in Other Policy, 3.44

P

Part A—Liability Coverage, 3.14
Part A—Liability Coverage Case Study, 3.23
Part B—Medical Payments Coverage, 3.30
Part B—Medical Payments Coverage Case Study, 3.34–3.36
Part C—Uninsured Motorists Coverage, 3.42–3.43
Part C—Uninsured Motorists Coverage Case Study, 3.51
Part D—Coverage for Damage to Your Auto, 4.3
Part D—Coverage for Damage to Your Auto Case Study, 4.11–4.14
Part E—Duties After an Accident or Loss, 4.18
Part F—General Provisions, 4.21–4.22
Payment of Claim—Coverage F—Medical Payments to Others, 6.19
Payment of Loss, 4.10
Perils Insured Against, 7.8, 11.8
Perils Insured Against for Coverage C, 5.18
Perils Insured Against for Coverages A and B, 5.17
Perils of the sea, **8.9**
Permanent partial disability (PPD), **1.15**
Permanent total disability (PTD), **1.15**
Personal Articles Standard Loss Settlement Form, 8.6
Personal Auto Coverage Case Study, 4.36

Index 5

Personal Auto Endorsements for Transportation Network Exposures, 4.33
Personal Auto Policy Watercraft Coverage, 8.10
Personal effects, **8.7**
Personal Effects Form, 8.7
Personal financial planning loss exposures, **1.12**
Personal Injury Coverage, 6.39
Personal Injury for Aircraft Liability Excluded, 6.40–6.42
Personal injury protection (PIP) coverage, **2.12**
Personal Liability Supplement, 7.9–7.12
Personal property, **1.5**, 1.6
Personal Property Form, 8.6
Personal Property Replacement Cost Loss Settlement, 6.35
Personal Umbrella Coverages, 8.16
Personal Umbrella Liability Insurance, 8.15
Personal Vehicle Sharing, 3.21
Personal Vehicle Sharing Program, 3.33, 3.46, 4.9
Personal Watercraft Insurance, 8.7–8.8
Persons and Organizations Insured, 3.15
Physical damage coverages, **4.3**
Point-of-service (POS) plan, **11.18**
Policy Analysis, 1.38–1.39
Policy condition, **1.37**
Policy Loan Provisions, 9.24
Policy period, **3.7**
Policy Period and Territory, 4.23
Policy provision, **1.32**
Policy termination, **4.23**
Postjudgment interest, **3.17**
Post-Loss Policy Analysis, 1.39
Preferred provider organization (PPO), **11.18**
Prejudgment interest, **3.15**
Pre-Loss Policy Analysis, 1.39
Premature Death Loss Exposures, 1.13, 1.13–1.14, 1.29, 9.3
Primary Rating Factors, 2.16
Private fee-for-service (PFFS) plans, **11.24**
Profit-Sharing Plan, 10.13
Proof of loss, **4.20**
Property and Liability Loss Exposures, 1.27
Property damage, **6.3**
Property Loss Exposures, **1.5**–1.6
Property Not Covered, 5.13
Property Owned or Transported, 3.18
Property Removed, 7.7
Property Rented to, Used by, or in the Care of the Insured, 3.18
Protection and indemnity (P&I) insurance, **8.13**
Provisions of a Disability Income Policy, 11.7
Public or livery conveyance, **3.18**, 3.31, 3.45, 4.7
Public or Livery Conveyance Exclusion Endorsement, 4.34
Punitive Damages, **1.9**, 3.46
Purpose and Operation, 7.33, 7.35
Purpose of Coverage, 3.48–3.49
Purposes of Personal Umbrella Coverage, 8.16

R

Racing, 3.20, 3.33, 4.9
Radar and Laser Detection Equipment, 4.8

Radioactive Contamination or War, 4.7
Rating Factors, 2.16
Rating Information, 3.8
Real Property, **1.5**, 1.6
Reasonable Repairs, 7.6
Recommendations, 9.32
Regular program, **7.26**
Reinstatement Clause, 9.24
Reinsurance facility, **2.15**
Renewal or Continuance Provision, 11.10
Rental Vehicles, 4.9
Residence premises, **8.3**
Residential Theft Coverage, 7.12
Residual market, **2.13**
Residual Market Programs, 2.14
Retention, **1.24**
Retirement Income Needs, 9.9, 9.29
Retirement Loss Exposure and Achieving Financial Goals, 10.3
Retirement Loss Exposures, 1.12, 1.28
Retirement (Old Age) Benefits, 10.25
Rider, **9.26**
Rising Healthcare Costs, 2.19
Risk control, **1.19**
Risk Control Techniques, 1.22
Risk financing, **1.19**
Risk Financing Techniques, 1.24
Risk management process, **1.17**
Risk Management Techniques, 1.21
Role of Endorsements, 5.9
Roth IRA, **10.9**

S

Safe driver insurance plan (SDIP), **2.14**
"Sandwiched" Families, 9.6
Schedule of Coverages, 3.8
Scheduled coverage, **6.36**
Scheduled Personal Property, 6.36
Second-to-Die (Survivorship) Life Insurance, 9.17
Section I—Exclusions, 5.21
Section I—Property Coverages, 5.8
Section II—Additional Coverages, 6.7
Section II—Liability Coverages, 5.9
SEP Plan, 10.15
Separation, **1.23**
Settlement options, **9.25**
Severability of Insurance, 6.17
Severability of Insurance condition, **6.17**
Signature, 3.8
SIMPLE, 10.14
Single-limits basis, **3.15**
Single-Parent Families, 9.4
Singles Without Children, 9.4
Slander Lawsuit, 8.26
Small Boat Policies, 8.10
Snowmobile Endorsement, 4.28
Social Security Disability Income Program, 11.14
Social Security Program (OASDHI), 10.21, 10.21–10.22
Sources of Life Insurance, 9.18, 9.18–9.19
Special damages, **1.9**

Special flood hazard area (SFHA), **7.25**
Special form coverage, **5.17**
Special Limits of Liability, 5.12
Special Needs, 9.9, 9.29
Special needs plans (SNPs), **11.19**, **11.24**
Split-limits basis, **3.15**
Stacking, 3.50
State Variations, 3.49–3.50
Statutory Liability, 1.11
Step 1: Identifying Loss Exposures, 1.17
Step 2: Analyzing Loss Exposures, 1.18
Step 3: Examining the Feasibility of Risk Management Techniques, 1.19
Step 4: Selecting the Appropriate Risk Management Techniques, 1.20
Step 5: Implementing the Selected Risk Management Techniques, 1.20
Step 6: Monitoring Results and Revising the Risk Management Program, 1.21
Structure of Homeowners Form HO-3, 5.7–5.8
Structures Eligible for Dwelling Policies, 7.3
Subrogation, **2.13**, 6.22
Suicide clause, **9.25**
Suit Against Us, 6.20
Supplemental Loss Assessment Coverage, 6.38
Supplementary payments, **3.17**
Survivors (Death) Benefits, 10.26
Syndicate, **7.33**

T

Tax Treatment, 11.33
Temporary partial disability (TPD), **1.15**
Temporary total disability (TTD), **1.15**
Term insurance, **9.13**
Term Life, 9.13
Term life insurance, **9.18**
Termination, 4.23
Third party, **6.3**
Thrift Plan, 10.13
Tort, **1.9**
Tort Liability, 1.10
Tort Liability System, 2.3
Total Life Insurance Needs, 9.31
Total Needs, 9.30
Towing and Labor Costs Coverage, 4.33
"Traditional" Families, 9.5
Traditional Health Insurance Plans, 11.16
Traditional individual retirement account (IRA), **10.9**
Trailer, Camper Body, or Motor Home, 4.8
Trailer/Camper Body Coverage (Maximum Limit of Liability), 4.28
Transfer, **1.25**
Transfer of Insured's Interest in the Policy, 4.25
Transportation expenses, **4.6**
Transportation network company, **4.33**
Transportation Network Driver Coverage (No Passenger) Endorsement, 4.35
Trees, Shrubs, and Other Plants, 7.7
Two or More Auto Policies, 4.26
Two-Income Families With Children, 9.5
Two-Income Families Without Children, 9.5
Types and Sources of Life Insurance, 9.32

Types of Benefits Provided by Social Security, 10.24
Types of Life Insurance, 9.12–9.13
Types of No-Fault Laws, 2.10
Types of Tax-Deferred Retirement Plans, 10.12–10.13

U

Umbrella Coverage Case Study, 8.20
UM/UIM Endorsements and State Variations, 3.48–3.50
Underinsured Motorists Coverage, **2.7**
Unemployment, 1.16
Unemployment Loss Exposures, 1.31
Uninsured boaters coverage, **8.15**
Uninsured Motorists Coverage, **2.6**
Uninsured motor vehicle, **3.43**
Uninsured Motor Vehicles, 3.43
United States Longshore and Harbor Workers' Compensation Act (LHWCA), **8.15**
Universal Life, 9.14
Universal life insurance, **9.14**
Unsatisfied judgment fund, **2.6**

V

Variable Life, 9.15
Variable life insurance, **9.15**
Variable Universal Life, 9.16
Variable universal life insurance, **9.16**
Vehicle identification number (VIN), **3.7**
Vehicle Modifications, 2.20
Vehicle Occupied Without Reasonable Belief of Being Entitled, 3.32
Vehicle Used Without Reasonable Belief of Being Entitled, 3.19, 3.45
Vehicles Owned by or Available for Family Member's Regular Use, 3.20, 3.32
Vehicles Used as a Residence or Premises, 3.31
Vehicles Used in the Business of an Insured, 3.32
Vehicles With Fewer Than Four Wheels or Designed for Off-Road Use, 3.20
Verbal threshold, **2.10**
Voluntary Market Programs, 2.13
Vulnerability to Additional Exposures, 7.20

W

Waiting Period, 7.28, 11.8
Waiver, **6.21**
Waiver of Premium, 11.33
Waiver or Change of Policy Provisions, 6.21
Warranty, **8.12**
Watercraft Liability, 6.11
Wear and Tear, Freezing, Breakdown, and Road Damage to Tires, 4.7
Whole Life, 9.14
Whole life insurance, **9.14**
Workers compensation, **1.30**
Worldwide Coverage, 7.6
Write-your-own (WYO) program, 7.28

Y

Your Duties After Loss, 5.23